JOINDER

HOW, HOW MANY, AND WHEN CLAIMS AND PARTIES MAY BE AGGREGATED INTO A SINGLE LAWSUI

JOINDER OF CLAIMS

1. Joinder of claims is generally permissive.
2. Party asserting original claim, counterclaim, cross-claim, or third-party claim may join as many extant claims. (FRCP 18(a)). *M.K. v. Tenet*, 216 F.R.D. 133 (D.Cl. 2002).
   a. Counterclaims. *Plant v. Blazer Financial Services*, 598 F.2d 1357 (5th Cir. 1979).
      i. Compulsory. (FRCP 13(a))
         a. Must arise from same transaction/occurrence.
         b. If omitted, waived.
      ii. Permissive. (FRCP 13(b))
         a. Does not arise from same transaction/occurrence.
         b. Asserted at party's option.
   b. Cross-claims. (FRCP 13(g)). *Lasa per l'industria del Marmo Societa per Azioni v. Alexander*, 414 F. 2d 153 (1969).
      i. Asserted by co-parties.
      ii. Must arise from same transaction/occurrence as:
         a. Original claim;
         b. Counterclaim; or
         c. Property in issue.

JOINDER OF PARTIES – INTERPLEADER

Owner of property subject to multiple claims may invoke to require parties to litigate in single proceeding; *Cohen v. The Republic of the Philippines*, 146 F.R.D. 90 (S.D.N.Y. 1993).

1. Statutory interpleader. *State Farm Fire & Casualty Co. v. Tashire*, 386 U.S. 532 (1967).
   a. Minimal diversity.
   b. Jurisdictional amount minimum: $500.
2. Rule interpleader.
   a. Complete diversity or federal question.
   b. If diversity, jurisdictional amount: $75,000.

JOINDER OF PARTIES – INTERVENTION

Third party initiates joinder to action already in progress.

1. As of right (FRCP 24(a)(2)), requires:
   a. Risk of impairment of interest.
   b. Timely application.
   c. Lack of adequate representation.
   Natural Resources Defense Council v. United States Nuclear Regulatory Commission, 578 F.2d 1341 (10th Cir. 1978).
2. Permissive (FRCP 24(b)(1)-(2)) requires:
   a. Conditional right under federal statute.
   b. Claim or defense and main action have common question of law or fact.

JOINDER OF PARTIES – COMPULSORY

FRCP 19

Applies to a party needed for just adjudication. *Temple v. Synthes Corp.*, 498 U.S. 5 (1990); *Helzberg's Diamond Shops v. Valley West Des Moines Shopping Center*, 564 F.2d 816 (8th Cir. 1977).

1. Complete relief not available in its absence.
2. Absence of party would impair ability to protect interests. *Provident Trademens Bank & Trust Co. v. Patterson*, 390 U.S. 102 (1968).
3. Absence of party would expose other parties to substantial risk of inconsistent or multiple obligations.

JOINDER OF PARTIES – CLASS ACTI

Hansberry v. Lee, 311 U.S. 32 (1940); *Communi for Equity v. Michigan High School Athletic Assn.*, 1999 U.S. Dist. LEXIS 5780 (W.D. Mich. 1999).

1. Numerosity: too many class members to join individually.
2. Commonality: common question of law or fact.
3. Typicality: claims of named representatives must match those of the class.
4. Adequacy: named representatives must provide adequate representation.

JOINDER OF PARTIES – IMPLEADER

FRCP 18(a)

1. Joinder of additional party who may be liable to indemnify existing party.
2. Once joined, joinder of additional claims is also allowed.

JOINDER OF PARTIES – PERMISSIVE

Amchem Products v. Windsor, 521 U.S. 591 (1997).

1. Same transaction or occurrence.
2. Common question of law or fact.
3. Complete diversity and jurisdictional amount requirements apply.

PRECLUSION DOCTRINES

MUTUALITY DOCTRINE

Common law doctrine requiring the parties to the second action to be the same or in privity to the parties to the first action.

1. Preclusion cannot be used against person not a party to first action.
2. Exception: Collateral estoppel generally available by party not bound by first litigation. *Parklane Hosiery Co., Inc. v. Shore*, 439 U.S. 322 (1979).

COLLATERAL ESTOPPEL (ISSUE PRECLUSION)

1. Relitigating an issue of law or fact prohibited if issue was
   a. actually litigated and necessarily determined; and
   b. essential to a valid and final judgment.
2. Entered previously in litigation to which that person was a party, provided estopped party had incentive and opportunity to litigate issue conclusively. *Parklane Hosiery Co., Inc. v. Shore*, 439 U.S. 322 (1979).
3. Subject to additional fairness constraints when asserting party not party to prior litigation.
4. Subject to additional fairness constraints when issue was litigated in companion cases that reached inconsistent outcomes. *State Farm Fire & Casualty Co. v. Century Home Components*, 275 Or. 97 (1976).

RES JUDICATA (CLAIM PRECLUSION)

A valid, final judgment rendered on the merits constitutes an absolute bar to a subsequent action between the same parties or those in privity, upon same claim or demand. Requires:

1. State court judgments in state court: the Full Faith and Credit Clause (Art. IV, §1) requires states to give preclusive effect to valid judgments in other states. *Durfee v. Duke*, 375 U.S. 106 (1963).
2. State court judgments in federal court: the Full Faith and Credit Act (28 U.S.C.§1738) requires federal courts to give preclusive effect to valid judgments rendered by state courts. *Gargallo v. Merrill Lynch, Pierce, Fenner & Smith*, 918 F.2d 658 (6th Cir. 1990).

DISCOVERY

BASIC DEVICES

1. Oral and written depositions. (FRCP 30 & 31)
2. Interrogatories. (FRCP 33). *In re Convergent Technologies Securities Litigation*, 108 F.R.D. 328 (1985).
3. Request for production of documents and orders for inspection. (FRCP 34). *Kozlowski v. Sears, Roebuck & Co.*, 73 F.R.D. 73 (1976).
4. Physical and mental examinations. (FRCP 35)
5. Requests for admission (FRCP 36):
   a. admission of truthfulness of facts; or
   b. admission of genuineness of documents.

SCOPE OF DISCOVERY

1. Inclusive – discovery is available for any matter: *Davis v. Precoat Metals*, 2002 WL 1759828 (N.D. Ill. 2002).
   a. Relevant to subject matter of action (FRCP 26(b)(1)),
   b. which appears reasonably calculated to lead to admissible evidence.
2. Exceptions:
   a. Privileged matter (attorney-client, self-incrimination, spousal, physician-patient). *Upjohn Co. v. United States*, 449 U.S. 383 (1981); *Butler v. Rigsby*, 1998 U.S. Dist. LEXIS 4618 (E.D. La. 1998).
   b. Attorney work-product. (FRCP 26(b)(3))
3. Experts. (FRCP 26(b)(4)). *Thompson v. The Haskell Co.*, 65 F. Empl. Prac. Cas. (BNA) 1088 (M.D. Fla. 1994); *Chiquita International Ltd. v. M/V Bolero Reefer*, 1994 U.S. Dist. LEXIS 5820 (S.D.N.Y. 1994).
4. Abuse and sanctions. (FRCP 26 & 27) *Zubulake v. UBS Warburg LLP*, 220 F.R.D. 212 (S.D.N.Y. 2003).
   a. Unreasonable/excessive use of discovery.
   b. Unreasonable compliance or refusal.
5. Duty to supplement responses (FRCP 26(e)):
   a. General rule: no duty to supplement to include later-acquired information or for correction.
   b. Exceptions:
      i. Disclosure materially incomplete or incorrect, if not made known to other parties. (FRCP 26 (e)(1))
      ii. If obtaining information that response was incorrect or failure to correct would constitute concealment.
      iii. If required by agreement among court and parties.

PRE-TRIAL PROCEDURE/ DISPOSITIONS

VOLUNTARY AND INVOLUNTARY DISMISSALS

1. Voluntary dismissal. (FRCP 41(a)). *McCants v. Ford Motor Co.*, 781 F. 2d 855 (1986).
   a. Without prejudice: plaintiff may reinstate action, within limitations period.
   b. With prejudice:
      i. Court order required.
      ii. Second voluntary dismissal.
      iii. Court or parties do not specify otherwise.
2. Involuntary dismissal. (FRCP 41(b)). *Link v. Wabash R.R.*, 370 U.S. 626 (1962).
   a. Defendant may seek for action or any claim, alleging:
      i. Failure to prosecute.
      ii. Failure to comply with federal rules.
      iii. Failure to comply with court order.
   b. Presumptively, with prejudice:
      i. Constitutes adjudication on merits.
      ii. Bars plaintiff, triggers *res judicata.*
   c. Exceptions:
      i. Lack of jurisdiction.
      ii. Improper venue.
      iii. Failure to join party. (FRCP 19)

PRETRIAL CONFERENCES OR ORDERS

Judge brings parties together to do the following:

1. Resolve procedural and discovery matters.
2. Schedule pretrial matters and conferences.
3. Consider settlement or other early disposition.
4. Simplify legal and factual issues for trial. *Sanders v. Union Pacific RR. Co.*, 154 F. 3d 1037 (9th Cir. 1998); *McKey v. Fairbairn*, 345 F. 2d 739 (D.C. Cir. 1965).
   a. Pretrial conferences (FRCP 16) to:
      i. expedite litigation;
      ii. control the case;
      iii. streamline pretrial activities;
      iv. encourage preparation for trial; and
      v. encourage settlement
   b. Discovery planning meeting (FRCP 26(f)) must be held and discovery plan submitted. District court then issues scheduling order that limits time in which:
      i. pleadings may be amended;
      ii. parties may be joined;
      iii. motions may be filed; and
      iv. discovery may be completed.
   c. Scheduling order must be issued within 120 days of service of complaint upon defendant.
   d. Court enters pretrial order (FRCP 16(d)).
   e. Sanctions available on motion or *sua sponte*:
      i. failure to obey scheduling order;
      ii. failure to make an appearance;
      iii. substantial lack of preparedness; or
      iv. failure to participate in good faith.

SUMMARY JUDGMENT

FRCP 56

1. Absence of a genuine issue of material fact. *Anderson v. Liberty Lobby, Inc.*, 477 U.S. 242 (1986).
2. Moving party entitled to judgment as matter of law and establishes:
   a. Nonexistence of a critical fact.
   b. That nonmoving party lacks sufficient evidence to prove critial fact. *Celotex Corp. v. Catrett*, 477 U.S. 317 (1986).
   c. Burden then shifts to nonmoving party to show that there is a genuine issue of material fact. *Bias v. Advantage International Inc.*, 905 F.2d 1558 (1990).
3. Procedure:
   a. Plaintiff may move any time after 20 days from commencement of action. (FRCP 56(a))
   b. Defendant may move immediately. (FRCP 56(b))
   c. Motion must be served at least 10 days before hearing date. (FRCP 56(c))
4. Required evidence (*Adickes v. S. H. Kress & Co.*, 378 U.S. 144 (1970)):
   a. Affidavits:
      i. based on personal knowledge;
      ii. containing facts admissible in evidence;
      iii. demonstrating witness competency.
   b. All products of discovery.
5. Partial summary judgment also available. (FRCP 56 (d))

DEFAULT JUDGMENT

FRCP 55. *Peralta v. Heights Medical Center*, 485 U.S. 80 (1980).

1. Entry of party's default:
   a. Answering party fails to plead or defend.
   b. Default secured by filing affidavit with clerk.
2. Clerk of court enters judgment.

TRIAL/RIGHT TO TRIAL

STAGES OF TRIAL PROCESS

1. Pre-trial conference.
2. Motions in limine.
3. Voir dire.
4. Opening statement.
5. Plaintiff's case-in-chief.
6. Motion (JMOL).
7. Defendant's case-in-chief.
8. Rebuttal evidence.
9. Motions (JMOL).
10. Closing arguments.
11. Jury instructions.
12. Jury deliberations.

RIGHT TO TRIAL

1. Constitution-based (Seventh Amendment). *Teamsters Local No. 391 v. Terry*, 494 U.S. 558 (1990).
2. Applies to cases that mix law and equity. *Ross v. Bernhard*, 396 U.S. 531 (1970).
3. Exceptions:
   a. Bankruptcy cases. *Katchen v. Landy*, 383 U.S. 323 (1966).
   b. Section 1981 cases.

JURY INSTRUCTIONS

Three types:

1. General verdict: finding in favor of one party without explanation.
2. Special verdict: specific written findings on some/all factual issues.
3. Mixture of general/special: See FRCP 49(b).

TRIAL/POST-TRIAL MOTIONS

JUDGMENT AS A MATTER OF LAW (JMOL) (DIRECTED VERDICT)

Pennsylvania R.R. v. Chamberlain, 288 U.S. 333 (1933).

Judge may grant a JMOL or directed verdict if opposing party fails to produce evidence sufficient to support a finding in its favor. (FRCP 50)

1. Timing: generally at close of opposing party's evidence, but may be made at end of opening statements.
2. If renewed at conclusion of all evidence in case, party retains right to move later for post-verdict JMOL.

POST-VERDICT MOTIONS

1. Post-verdict or renewed JMOL (JNOV) requires:
   a. Evidence insufficient to make a case for the jury.
   b. Timeliness: motion must be made within 10 days after judgment or jury dismissal.
2. Motion for a new trial (FRCP 59) requires (*Lind v. Schenley Industries*, 278 F.2d 79 (3d Cir. 1960)):
   a. Verdict against great weight of the evidence. *Peterson v. Wilson*, 141 F.3d 573 (5th Cir. 1998).
   b. Timeliness: must be made within 10 days of entry of judgment.
3. Extraordinary Postjudgment Relief (FRCP 60):
   a. "clerical mistakes."
   b. "mistake, inadvertence or excusable neglect."
   c. "fraud, misrepresentation, misconduct."

APPEAL

REQUIREMENT OF FINALITY

1. Final judgment rule: No appeal may be taken until a final judgment has been issued. *Cohen v. Beneficial Industrial Loan Corp.*, 337 U.S. 541 (1949); *Liberty Mutual Insurance Co. v. Wetzel*, 424 U.S. 737 (1976).
2. Exception – the collateral order doctrine for orders that:
   a. conclusively determine the disputed question;
   b. resolve important issue not related to merits;
   c. are unreviewable by appeal.
3. Partial exception – right to appeal certain interlocutory orders. (28 U.S.C. §1292(a)). *Gulfstream Aerospace Corp. v. Mayacamas Corp.*, 485 U.S. 271 (1988).
4. Partial exception – extraordinary writs (Mandamus). *Kerr v. United States District Court*, 426 U.S. 394 (1976).

STANDARDS OF REVIEW

1. Errors of law ("abuse of discretion"). *Salve Regina College v. Russell*, 499 U.S. 225 (1999).
2. Errors of fact ("clearly erroneous"). *Anderson v. City of Bessemer*, 479 U.S. 564 (1985).
3. Harmless error. *Harnden v. Jayco, Inc.*, 496 F.3d 579 (6th Cir. 2007).

QUICK COURSE OUTLINE
CIVIL PROCEDURE

TERRITORIAL JURISDICTION

Territorial jurisdiction is the authority of the court to exercise jurisdiction over a defendant or property.

TYPES OF JURISDICTION

1. *In personam:* Whether the court has the power to adjudicate claims against a particular person depends on whether the person over whom jurisdiction is sought has a sufficient territorial connection to the forum state.
   - **a.** Defendant is present in state and process is physically served.
   - **b.** Domicile.
   - **c.** Consent. *Carnival Cruise Lines v. Shute*, 499 U.S. 585 (1991); *Hess v. Pawloski*, 274 U.S. 352 (1927).
   - **d.** State long-arm statute grants personal jurisdiction over defendant or property. *Gray v. American Radiator & Standard Sanitary Corp.*, 22 Ill.2d 432 (1961).
2. *In rem:* Jurisdiction over a particular item of property. *Shaffer v. Heitner*, 433 U.S. 186 (1977).
   - **a.** Determines who owns certain property in territorial control of the forum.
   - **b.** Adjudicates ownership interests of world at large to the property.
3. *Quasi in rem:* Rights of particular person to certain property. *McGee v. International Life Insurance Co.*, 355 U.S. 220 (1957).
   - **a.** Suit in which dispute arises out of parties' interests in the property.
   - **b.** Attachment jurisdiction.
     - **i.** Suit in which dispute between the parties has nothing to do with the presence of the property within the forum state.
     - **ii.** Property can be attached by court as "hostage" to a suit against the owner of the property.

DUE PROCESS REQUIREMENTS

Pennoyer v. Neff, 95 U.S. 714 (1877).

1. Fair and adequate notice. *Mullane v. Central Hanover Bank & Trust Co.*, 339 U.S. 306 (1950).
2. Minimum contacts with forum state. *International Shoe Co. v. Washington*, 326 U.S. 310 (1945).

MINIMUM CONTACTS ANALYSIS

International Shoe Co., v. Washington, 326 U.S. 310 (1945).

Defined – The minimal connection with the forum state necessary to justify general jurisdiction.

1. Does the defendant have any contacts within the forum state?
2. Are the contacts purposeful? *Burger King Corp. v. Rudzewicz*, 471 U.S. 462 (1985).
   - **a.** Forseeability of litigation? *World-Wide Volkswagen Corp. v. Woodson*, 444 U.S. 286 (1980).
   - **b.** "Stream of commerce." *Asahi Metal Industry Co. v. Superior Ct.*, 480 U.S. 102 (1987).
   - **c.** "Purposeful availment." *Hanson v. Deckla*, 357 U.S. 235 (1958).
3. Are the contacts continuous, systematic and substantial enough to justify general jurisdiction?
4. If there is no general jurisdiction, are the defendant's purposeful contacts with the forum sufficiently related to the litigation or do they constitute minimum contacts conferring the power to exercise specific jurisdiction?
5. Is the exercise of jurisdiction reasonable? *Burger King Corp. v. Rudzewicz*, 471 U.S. 462 (1985).

FEDERAL SUBJECT MATTER JURISDICTION

DIVERSITY JURISDICTION

28 U.S.C. §1332

1. Complete diversity of citizenship: No plaintiff may be a citizen of the same state as any defendant.
   - **a.** Refers to suits between:
     - **i.** Citizens of different states.
     - **ii.** Citizens of a state and citizens of a foreign state. *Redner v. Sanders*, 2000 WL 1161080 (S.D.N.Y. 2000).
     - **iii.** Citizens of different states and in which citizens of a foreign state are additional parties.
     - **iv.** Plaintiff in a foreign state and citizens of a state or different states.
   - **b.** An individual is a citizen of the state in which he is domiciled (place of fixed residence). *Saadeh v. Farouki*, 107 F.3d 52 (D.C. Cir. 1997).
   - **c.** A corporation is a citizen of any state in which it is incorporated or in which it has its principal place of business. (28 U.S.C. §1332(c)(1))
2. Jurisdictional amount requirement.
   - **a.** In excess of $75,000.
   - **b.** Good-faith allegations of the amount.
   - **c.** Exclusive of interest and costs.

THE ERIE DOCTRINE

Erie R.R. v. Tompkins, 304 U.S. 64 (1938).

In a diversity case, a federal court must apply state substantive law; however, even in diversity cases the federal courts may follow their own express procedural rules & statutes. *Hanna v. Plummer*, 380 U.S. 460 (1965).

1. Is the issue clearly substantive and not even arguably procedural?
2. If not, is federal law specified by federal legislation or an express federal rule?
3. If not, has the state conditioned the enjoyment of a state-created right in issue on enforcement of it according to state law?
4. If not, is the foreseeable impact on outcome of conforming to state law substantially likely to encourage forum shopping and the inequitable administration of the laws? *Byrd v. Blue Ridge Electrical Coop*, 356 U.S. 525 (1958).
5. If yes, are there countervailing considerations of federal policy that outweigh application of state law in diversity cases?

Note: In general *Guaranty Trust Co. v. York*, 326 U.S. 99 (1945), requires state law to apply if a different outcome would result under federal law. *Byrd* & *Hanna* are exceptions.

FEDERAL VENUE 28 U.S.C. §1391

1. District in which any defendant resides, if all reside in same state.
2. District in which substantial part of the events / omissions occurred or in which property is located.
3. "Fallback venue" applies only if otherwise there is no district in which venue is proper.
   - **a.** In diversity cases, where defendants are subject to personal jurisdiction when action commenced.
   - **b.** If no diversity, where any defendant is found. *"Forum non conveniens:"* State or federal court may refuse to exercise jurisdiction because forum has no interest, and controversy may be litigated more conveniently elsewhere. Transfer permitted between federal district courts. (28 U.S.C. §§1404 and 1406). *Piper Aircraft Co. v. Gaynell Reyno, et al.*, 454 U.S. 235 (1981).

SUPPLEMENTAL JURISDICTION

28 U.S.C. §1367. *In re Ameriquest Mortgage Co. Mortgage Lending Practices Litigation*, 2007 U.S. Dist. LEXIS 70805 (N.D. Ill. 2007); *Szendrey-Ramos v. First Bancorp*, 2007 U.S. Dist. LEXIS 74896 (D.P.R. 2007).

In any action in which the federal court has original jurisdiction, it also has supplemental jurisdiction over any other claims in the action that may form part of the same case or controversy. This includes claims involving the joinder or intervention of additional parties. Supplemental jurisdiction is limited in diversity cases. Courts may decline to exercise supplemental jurisdiction if:

1. novel or complex state-law issue;
2. the supplemental claim substantially predominates over the main claim(s);
3. the district court has dismissed all claims; or
4. there are other compelling reasons for declining.

FEDERAL QUESTION JURISDICTION

28 U.S.C. §1331. *Louisville & Nashville R.R. v. Mottley*, 211 U.S. 149 (1908).

1. Confers subject-matter jurisdiction over all suits to enforce federally created rights to relief.
2. In rare instances may also confer federal jurisdiction over suits to enforce state-created rights to relief that necessarily turn on substantial and disputed issues of federal law.

Federal Subject-Matter Judiction continues on page 2

REMOVAL JURISDICTION

28 U.S.C. §1441. *Caterpillar Inc. v. Lewis*, 519 U.S. 61 (1996).

Any civil action that was filed in state court may be removed to federal court for the district in which the case was pending, if the case is within the original jurisdiction of the federal court.

1. Original jurisdiction in federal court.
2. Only defendants may remove, all must agree.
3. Judicial district in which action was pending.

PLEADING

GENERAL TYPES OF PLEADINGS

1. Code-pleading – complaint requires a statement of fact that constitutes a cause of action. *Gillespie v. Goodyear Service Stores*, 258 N.C. 487 (1963).
2. Notice pleading – (FRCP 8) merges law and equity. Complaint merely requires (a) jurisdictional statement, (b) "short and plain" statement of the claim showing pleader is entitled to relief, and (c) demand for judgment. *Bell Atlantic v. Twombly*, 127 S. Ct. 1955 (2007).

ATTACKING THE PLEADINGS (OBJECTIONS)

1. Preliminary Objections. *Haddle v. Garrison*, no. 96-00029-CV-1 (S.D. 1996); *Haddle v. Garrison*, 525 U.S. 121 (1998).
   - **a.** May be raised by motion or in responsive pleading.
   - **b.** Objections to the manner in which action was initiated:
     - **i.** lack of subject-matter jurisdiction;
     - **ii.** lack of personal jurisdiction;
     - **iii.** improper venue;
     - **iv.** insufficient process;
     - **v.** insufficient service of process; and
     - **vi.** failure to join an indispensable party.
2. Formal pleading objections.
   - **a.** Procedural errors.
   - **b.** Motions to strike or motions for more definitive statement.
3. Substantive pleading objections.
   - **a.** Attack legal theory of claim.
4. Federal pleading objections: Pleadings may be attached by responsive pleadings or by motion.
5. Code pleading objections, e.g., demurrer.
6. Motions to dismiss.

THE ANSWER

1. Admissions and denials of allegations in complaint. (FRCP 8(b)). *Zielinski v. Philadelphia Piers, Inc.*, 139 F. Supp. 408 (E.D. Pa. 1956).
2. Affirmative defenses available.
3. Other defenses of a preliminary nature. (FRCP 12(b)). *Huddle v. Garrison*, 525 U.S. 121 (1958).
4. Counterclaim or cross-claim making allegations of liability owed the answering party (federal practice only).

SPECIAL PLEADING REQUIREMENTS

FRCP 9

1. Allegations of fraud or mistake.
2. Special damages.
3. Complex proceedings.
4. Alternative/inconsistent allegations are permitted.

TRUTHFULNESS IN PLEADING

Requires that all parties be candid and proceed in good faith.

1. Verification. Party who files pleading must:
   - **a.** do so under oath; and
   - **b.** sign her name attesting that matters therein are true to best information and belief.
2. Lawyers' certification. (FRCP 11)
3. Courts retain power to sanction bad-faith conduct. *Christian v. Mattel*, 286 F.3d 1118 (2003).

AMENDMENTS TO PLEADINGS

FRCP 15

1. Before trial. *Beeck v. The Aquaslide 'n' Dive Corp.*, 562 F.2d 537 (1977).
   - **a.** After any responsive pleading is served.
   - **b.** Within 20 days after served, if pleading itself does not permit responsive pleading, and action not yet on trial calendar. (FRCP 15)
2. Any time during/after trial with consent of all adverse parties.
3. Relatng back. *Bonerb v. Richard J. Caron Foundation*, 159 F.R.D. 16 (W.D.N.Y. 1994).
   - **a.** Amendments relate back automatically if permitted by applicable statute of limitations.
   - **b.** Amendments relate back to original pleading if claim or defense arose out of the same conduct, transactions, or occurrence.
4. Changing a party. *Moore v. Baker*, 989 F.2d 1129 (1993).
   - **a.** Relates back if:
     - **i.** Same conduct, transaction or occurrence.
     - **ii.** Party received sufficient notice.
     - **iii.** Party knew or should have known, but for a mistake, that the action would have been brought against him.
     - **iv.** Notice for (ii) and (iii) must be provided within 120 days after filing complaint.

VALIDITY AND ENFORCEMENT OF THE JUDGMENT

THE THREE ELEMENTS OF VALIDITY

1. Valid subject-matter jurisdiction. *See above*
2. Valid territorial jurisdiction. *See above*
3. Proper notice. *See **Due Process Requirements***.

THE SIX STEP APPROACH [DETERMINING VALIDITY]

1. Local law of trial court subject-matter jurisdiction.
2. Federal constitutional limits on subject-matter jurisdiction. *Kalb v. Feurstein*, 308 U.S. 433 (1940).
3. Local law of trial court territorial jurisdiction.
   - **a.** State courts:
     - **i.** *In personam* jurisdiction: against persons personally served within state.
     - **ii.** *In rem* jurisdiction: against property subject to attachment within state.
     - **iii.** State long-arm statutes authorize service on absent defendant. *Gibbons v. Brown*, 716 So. 2d 868 (Fla. Dist. Ct. App. 1998).
   - **b.** Federal courts:
     - **i.** Have jurisdiction over any served party (FRCP 4) while that person present in the state.
     - **ii.** *In rem* jursidction: may exercise only in accordance with local law.
     - **iii.** *In personam* jurisdiction: may generally exercise against person served outside state, as authorized by local state law.
     - **iv.** Nationwide service is specifically authorized by FRCP 4(k)(1)(C)–(D) under Federal Interpleader Act and other federal statutes.
4. Federal constitutional limits on territorial jurisdiction. *Baldwin v. Iowa State Traveling Men's Assoc.*, 283 U.S. 522 (1931).
5. Local law of proper notice.
   - **a.** State court service of process:
     - **i.** Careful compliance with technical details.
     - **ii.** Process includes summons and complaint.
     - **iii.** Service requirements.
       - *Personal:*
         - ***a.*** Delivery in hand to named defendant.
         - ***b.*** To entity: delivery to person appointed to accept.
       - *Substituted:*
         - ***a.*** Delivery to person of suitable age and discretion, who lives with defendant.
         - ***b.*** Service by mail may require acknowledgment.
       - *Constructive:*
         - ***a.*** Newspaper publication.
         - ***b.*** Posting at designated location.
     - **iv.** federal court service of process (FRCP 4).
6. Federal constitutional standards for proper notice. *Mullane v. Central Hanover Bank & Trust Co.*, 339 U.S. 306 (1950).

ENFORCEMENT OF JUDGMENTS (PROVISIONAL REMEDIES)

1. Attachment – holding asset when defendant not available. *Connecticut v. Doehr*, 501 U.S. 1 (1991).
2. Garnishment – attachment of wages or other income.
3. Preliminary injunctions / Temporary Restraining Orders (TROs) (FRCP 65) – available ex parte when defendant acting in way that would render the judgment ineffectual. *William Inglis & Sons Baking Co. v. ITT Continental Baking Co.*, 526 F.2d 86 (9th Cir. 1976).
4. Receivership – appointment of overseer to manage assets pendente lite, generally in cases of insolvency. (FRCP 66)
5. Civil arrest – functional equivalent of imprisonment for debt and severely restricted.
6. Notice of Pendency – not strictly a remedy, but notice to third parties concerning property in dispute, etc.

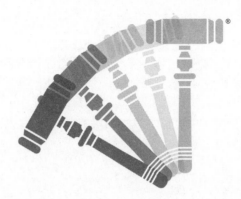

Casenote® Legal Briefs

CIVIL PROCEDURE

Keyed to Courses Using

**Friedenthal, Miller, Sexton, and Hershkoff's
Civil Procedure: Cases and Materials**

Eleventh Edition and Compact Eleventh Edition for Shorter Courses

Wolters Kluwer

Law & Business

This publication is designed to provide accurate and authoritative information in regard to the subject matter covered. It is sold with the understanding that the publisher is not engaged in rendering legal, accounting, or other professional services. If legal advice or other expert assistance is required, the services of a competent professional person should be sought.

— From a Declaration of Principles adopted jointly by a Committee of the American Bar Association and a Committee of Publishers and Associates

Printed in the United States of America.

1 2 3 4 5 6 7 8 9 0

ISBN 978-1-4548-4075-6

About Wolters Kluwer Law & Business

Wolters Kluwer Law & Business is a leading global provider of intelligent information and digital solutions for legal and business professionals in key specialty areas, and respected educational resources for professors and law students. Wolters Kluwer Law & Business connects legal and business professionals as well as those in the education market with timely, specialized authoritative content and information-enabled solutions to support success through productivity, accuracy and mobility.

Serving customers worldwide, Wolters Kluwer Law & Business products include those under the Aspen Publishers, CCH, Kluwer Law International, Loislaw, ftwilliam.com and MediRegs family of products.

CCH products have been a trusted resource since 1913, and are highly regarded resources for legal, securities, antitrust and trade regulation, government contracting, banking, pension, payroll, employment and labor, and healthcare reimbursement and compliance professionals.

Aspen Publishers products provide essential information to attorneys, business professionals and law students. Written by preeminent authorities, the product line offers analytical and practical information in a range of specialty practice areas from securities law and intellectual property to mergers and acquisitions and pension/benefits. Aspen's trusted legal education resources provide professors and students with high-quality, up-to-date and effective resources for successful instruction and study in all areas of the law.

Kluwer Law International products provide the global business community with reliable international legal information in English. Legal practitioners, corporate counsel and business executives around the world rely on Kluwer Law journals, looseleafs, books, and electronic products for comprehensive information in many areas of international legal practice.

Loislaw is a comprehensive online legal research product providing legal content to law firm practitioners of various specializations. Loislaw provides attorneys with the ability to quickly and efficiently find the necessary legal information they need, when and where they need it, by facilitating access to primary law as well as state-specific law, records, forms and treatises.

ftwilliam.com offers employee benefits professionals the highest quality plan documents (retirement, welfare and non-qualified) and government forms (5500/PBGC, 1099 and IRS) software at highly competitive prices.

MediRegs products provide integrated health care compliance content and software solutions for professionals in healthcare, higher education and life sciences, including professionals in accounting, law and consulting.

Wolters Kluwer Law & Business, a division of Wolters Kluwer, is headquartered in New York. Wolters Kluwer is a market-leading global information services company focused on professionals.

Format for the Casenote® Legal Brief

Nature of Case: This section identifies the form of action (e.g., breach of contract, negligence, battery), the type of proceeding (e.g., demurrer, appeal from trial court's jury instructions), or the relief sought (e.g., damages, injunction, criminal sanctions).

Fact Summary: This is included to refresh your memory and can be used as a quick reminder of the facts.

Rule of Law: Summarizes the general principle of law that the case illustrates. It may be used for instant recall of the court's holding and for classroom discussion or home review.

Facts: This section contains all relevant facts of the case, including the contentions of the parties and the lower court holdings. It is written in a logical order to give the student a clear understanding of the case. The plaintiff and defendant are identified by their proper names throughout and are always labeled with a (P) or (D).

Palsgraf v. Long Island R.R. Co.

Injured bystander (P) v. Railroad company (D)

N.Y. Ct. App., 248 N.Y. 339, 162 N.E. 99 (1928).

Party ID: Quick identification of the relationship between the parties.

NATURE OF CASE: Appeal from judgment affirming verdict for plaintiff seeking damages for personal injury.

FACT SUMMARY: Helen Palsgraf (P) was injured on R.R.'s (D) train platform when R.R.'s (D) guard helped a passenger aboard a moving train, causing his package to fall on the tracks. The package contained fireworks which exploded, creating a shock that tipped a scale onto Palsgraf (P).

🏛 RULE OF LAW
The risk reasonably to be perceived defines the duty to be obeyed.

FACTS: Helen Palsgraf (P) purchased a ticket to Rockaway Beach from R.R. (D) and was waiting on the train platform. As she waited, two men ran to catch a train that was pulling out from the platform. The first man jumped aboard, but the second man, who appeared as if he might fall, was helped aboard by the guard on the train who had kept the door open so they could jump aboard. A guard on the platform also helped by pushing him onto the train. The man was carrying a package wrapped in newspaper. In the process, the man dropped his package, which fell on the tracks. The package contained fireworks and exploded. The shock of the explosion was apparently of great enough strength to tip over some scales at the other end of the platform, which fell on Palsgraf (P) and injured her. A jury awarded her damages, and R.R. (D) appealed.

ISSUE: Does the risk reasonably to be perceived define the duty to be obeyed?

HOLDING AND DECISION: (Cardozo, C.J.) Yes. The risk reasonably to be perceived defines the duty to be obeyed. If there is no foreseeable hazard to the injured party as the result of a seemingly innocent act, the act does not become a tort because it happened to be a wrong as to another. If the wrong was not willful, the plaintiff must show that the act as to her had such great and apparent possibilities of danger as to entitle her to protection. Negligence in the abstract is not enough upon which to base liability. Negligence is a relative concept, evolving out of the common law doctrine of trespass on the case. To establish liability, the defendant must owe a legal duty of reasonable care to the injured party. A cause of action in tort will lie where harm, though unintended, could have been averted or avoided by observance of such a duty. The scope of the duty is limited by the range of danger that a reasonable person could foresee. In this case, there was nothing to suggest from the appearance of the parcel or otherwise that the parcel contained fireworks. The guard could not reasonably have had any warning of a threat to Palsgraf (P), and R.R. (D) therefore cannot be held liable. Judgment is reversed in favor of R.R. (D).

DISSENT: (Andrews, J.) The concept that there is no negligence unless R.R. (D) owes a legal duty to take care as to Palsgraf (P) herself is too narrow. Everyone owes to the world at large the duty of refraining from those acts that may unreasonably threaten the safety of others. If the guard's action was negligent as to those nearby, it was also negligent as to those outside what might be termed the "danger zone." For Palsgraf (P) to recover, R.R.'s (D) negligence must have been the proximate cause of her injury, a question of fact for the jury.

Concurrence/Dissent: All concurrences and dissents are briefed whenever they are included by the casebook editor.

▶ ANALYSIS

The majority defined the limit of the defendant's liability in terms of the danger that a reasonable person in defendant's situation would have perceived. The dissent argued that the limitation should not be placed on liability, but rather on damages. Judge Andrews suggested that only injuries that would not have happened but for R.R.'s (D) negligence should be compensable. Both the majority and dissent recognized the policy-driven need to limit liability for negligent acts, seeking, in the words of Judge Andrews, to define a framework "that will be practical and in keeping with the general understanding of mankind." The Restatement (Second) of Torts has accepted Judge Cardozo's view.

Analysis: This last paragraph gives you a broad understanding of where the case "fits in" with other cases in the section of the book and with the entire course. It is a hornbook-style discussion indicating whether the case is a majority or minority opinion and comparing the principal case with other cases in the casebook. It may also provide analysis from restatements, uniform codes, and law review articles. The analysis will prove to be invaluable to classroom discussion.

Quicknotes

FORESEEABILITY A reasonable expectation that change is the probable result of certain acts or omissions.

NEGLIGENCE Conduct falling below the standard of care that a reasonable person would demonstrate under similar conditions.

PROXIMATE CAUSE The natural sequence of events without which an injury would not have been sustained.

Issue: The issue is a concise question that brings out the essence of the opinion as it relates to the section of the casebook in which the case appears. Both substantive and procedural issues are included if relevant to the decision.

Holding and Decision: This section offers a clear and in-depth discussion of the rule of the case and the court's rationale. It is written in easy-to-understand language and answers the issue presented by applying the law to the facts of the case. When relevant, it includes a thorough discussion of the exceptions to the case as listed by the court, any major cites to the other cases on point, and the names of the judges who wrote the decisions.

Quicknotes: Conveniently defines legal terms found in the case and summarizes the nature of any statutes, codes, or rules referred to in the text.

Note to Students

Wolters Kluwer Law & Business is proud to offer *Casenote® Legal Briefs*—continuing thirty years of publishing America's best-selling legal briefs.

Casenote® Legal Briefs are designed to help you save time when briefing assigned cases. Organized under convenient headings, they show you how to abstract the basic facts and holdings from the text of the actual opinions handed down by the courts. Used as part of a rigorous study regimen, they can help you spend more time analyzing and critiquing points of law than on copying bits and pieces of judicial opinions into your notebook or outline.

Casenote® Legal Briefs should never be used as a substitute for assigned casebook readings. They work best when read as a follow-up to reviewing the underlying opinions themselves. Students who try to avoid reading and digesting the judicial opinions in their casebooks or online sources will end up shortchanging themselves in the long run. The ability to absorb, critique, and restate the dynamic and complex elements of case law decisions is crucial to your success in law school and beyond. It cannot be developed vicariously.

Casenote® Legal Briefs represents but one of the many offerings in Legal Education's Study Aid Timeline, which includes:

- *Casenote® Legal Briefs*
- *Emanuel® Law Outlines*
- Emanuel® *Law in a Flash* Flash Cards
- Emanuel® *CrunchTime®* Series
- *Siegel's Essay and Multiple-Choice Questions and Answers Series*

Each of these series is designed to provide you with easy-to-understand explanations of complex points of law. Each volume offers guidance on the principles of legal analysis and, consulted regularly, will hone your ability to spot relevant issues. We have titles that will help you prepare for class, prepare for your exams, and enhance your general comprehension of the law along the way.

To find out more about Wolters Kluwer Law & Business' study aid publications, visit us online at *www.wolterskluwerlb.com* or email us at *legaledu@wolterskluwer.com*. We'll be happy to assist you.

How to Brief a Case

A. Decide on a Format and Stick to It

Structure is essential to a good brief. It enables you to arrange systematically the related parts that are scattered throughout most cases, thus making manageable and understandable what might otherwise seem to be an endless and unfathomable sea of information. There are, of course, an unlimited number of formats that can be utilized. However, it is best to find one that suits your needs and stick to it. Consistency breeds both efficiency and the security that when called upon you will know where to look in your brief for the information you are asked to give.

Any format, as long as it presents the essential elements of a case in an organized fashion, can be used. Experience, however, has led *Casenote® Legal Briefs* to develop and utilize the following format because of its logical flow and universal applicability.

NATURE OF CASE: This is a brief statement of the legal character and procedural status of the case (e.g., "Appeal of a burglary conviction").

There are many different alternatives open to a litigant dissatisfied with a court ruling. The key to determining which one has been used is to discover *who is asking this court for what.*

This first entry in the brief should be kept as *short as possible*. Use the court's terminology if you understand it. But since jurisdictions vary as to the titles of pleadings, the best entry is the one that addresses who wants what in this proceeding, not the one that sounds most like the court's language.

RULE OF LAW: A statement of the general principle of law that the case illustrates (e.g., "An acceptance that varies any term of the offer is considered a rejection and counteroffer").

Determining the rule of law of a case is a procedure similar to determining the issue of the case. Avoid being fooled by red herrings; there may be a few rules of law mentioned in the case excerpt, but usually only one is *the* rule with which the casebook editor is concerned. The techniques used to locate the issue, described below, may also be utilized to find the rule of law. Generally, your best guide is simply the chapter heading. It is a clue to the point the casebook editor seeks to make and should be kept in mind when reading every case in the respective section.

FACTS: A synopsis of only the essential facts of the case, i.e., those bearing upon or leading up to the issue.

The facts entry should be a short statement of the events and transactions that led one party to initiate legal proceedings against another in the first place. While some cases conveniently state the salient facts at the beginning of the decision, in other instances they will have to be culled from hiding places throughout the text, even from concurring and dissenting opinions. Some of the "facts" will often be in dispute and should be so noted. Conflicting evidence may be briefly pointed up. "Hard" facts must be included. Both must be *relevant* in order to be listed in the facts entry. It is impossible to tell what is relevant until the entire case is read, as the ultimate determination of the rights and liabilities of the parties may turn on something buried deep in the opinion.

Generally, the facts entry should not be longer than three to five *short* sentences.

It is often helpful to identify the role played by a party in a given context. For example, in a construction contract case the identification of a party as the "contractor" or "builder" alleviates the need to tell that that party was the one who was supposed to have built the house.

It is always helpful, and a good general practice, to identify the "plaintiff" and the "defendant." This may seem elementary and uncomplicated, but, especially in view of the creative editing practiced by some casebook editors, it is sometimes a difficult or even impossible task. Bear in mind that the *party presently* seeking something from this court may not be the plaintiff, and that sometimes only the cross-claim of a defendant is treated in the excerpt. Confusing or misaligning the parties can ruin your analysis and understanding of the case.

ISSUE: A statement of the general legal question answered by or illustrated in the case. For clarity, the issue is best put in the form of a question capable of a "yes" or "no" answer. In reality, the issue is simply the Rule of Law put in the form of a question (e.g., "May an offer be accepted by performance?").

The major problem presented in discerning what is *the* issue in the case is that an opinion usually purports to raise and answer several questions. However, except for rare cases, only one such question is really the issue in the case. Collateral issues not necessary to the resolution of the matter in controversy are handled by the court by language known as *"obiter dictum"* or merely *"dictum."* While dicta may be included later in the brief, they have no place under the issue heading.

To find the issue, ask *who wants what* and then go on to ask *why did that party succeed or fail in getting it.* Once this is determined, the "why" should be turned into a question.

The complexity of the issues in the cases will vary, but in all cases a single-sentence question should sum up the issue. *In a few cases,* there will be two, or even more rarely, three issues of equal importance to the resolution of the case. Each should be expressed in a single-sentence question.

Since many issues are resolved by a court in coming to a final disposition of a case, the casebook editor will reproduce the portion of the opinion containing the issue or issues most relevant to the area of law under scrutiny. A noted law professor gave this advice: "Close the book; look at the title on the cover." Chances are, if it is Property, you need not concern yourself with whether, for example, the federal government's treatment of the plaintiff's land really raises a federal question sufficient to support jurisdiction on this ground in federal court.

The same rule applies to chapter headings designating sub-areas within the subjects. They tip you off as to what the text is designed to teach. The cases are arranged in a casebook to show a progression or development of the law, so that the preceding cases may also help.

It is also most important to remember to *read the notes and questions* at the end of a case to determine what the editors wanted you to have gleaned from it.

HOLDING AND DECISION: This section should succinctly explain the rationale of the court in arriving at its decision. In capsulizing the "reasoning" of the court, it should always include an application of the general rule or rules of law to the specific facts of the case. Hidden justifications come to light in this entry: the reasons for the state of the law, the public policies, the biases and prejudices, those considerations that influence the justices' thinking and, ultimately, the outcome of the case. At the end, there should be a short indication of the disposition or procedural resolution of the case (e.g., "Decision of the trial court for Mr. Smith (P) reversed").

The foregoing format is designed to help you "digest" the reams of case material with which you will be faced in your law school career. Once mastered by practice, it will place at your fingertips the information the authors of your casebooks have sought to impart to you in case-by-case illustration and analysis.

B. Be as Economical as Possible in Briefing Cases

Once armed with a format that encourages succinctness, it is as important to be economical with regard to the time spent on the actual reading of the case as it is to be economical in the writing of the brief itself. This does not mean "skimming" a case. Rather, it means reading the case with an "eye" trained to recognize into which "section" of your brief a particular passage or line fits and having a system for quickly and precisely marking the case so that the passages fitting any one particular part of

the brief can be easily identified and brought together in a concise and accurate manner when the brief is actually written.

It is of no use to simply repeat everything in the opinion of the court; record only enough information to trigger your recollection of what the court said. Nevertheless, an accurate statement of the "law of the case," i.e., the legal principle applied to the facts, is absolutely essential to class preparation and to learning the law under the case method.

To that end, it is important to develop a "shorthand" that you can use to make marginal notations. These notations will tell you at a glance in which section of the brief you will be placing that particular passage or portion of the opinion.

Some students prefer to underline all the salient portions of the opinion (with a pencil or colored underliner marker), making marginal notations as they go along. Others prefer the color-coded method of underlining, utilizing different colors of markers to underline the salient portions of the case, each separate color being used to represent a different section of the brief. For example, blue underlining could be used for passages relating to the rule of law, yellow for those relating to the issue, and green for those relating to the holding and decision, etc. While it has its advocates, the color-coded method can be confusing and time-consuming (all that time spent on changing colored markers). Furthermore, it can interfere with the continuity and concentration many students deem essential to the reading of a case for maximum comprehension. In the end, however, it is a matter of personal preference and style. Just remember, whatever method you use, underlining must be used sparingly or its value is lost.

If you take the marginal notation route, an efficient and easy method is to go along underlining the key portions of the case and placing in the margin alongside them the following "markers" to indicate where a particular passage or line "belongs" in the brief you will write:

N   (NATURE OF CASE)
RL (RULE OF LAW)
I   (ISSUE)
HL (HOLDING AND DECISION, relates to the RULE OF LAW behind the decision)
HR (HOLDING AND DECISION, gives the RATIONALE or reasoning behind the decision)
HA (HOLDING AND DECISION, applies the general principle(s) of law to the facts of the case to arrive at the decision)

Remember that a particular passage may well contain information necessary to more than one part of your brief, in which case you simply note that in the margin. If you are using the color-coded underlining method instead of marginal notation, simply make asterisks or checks in the margin next to the passage in question in the colors that indicate the additional sections of the brief where it might be utilized.

The economy of utilizing "shorthand" in marking cases for briefing can be maintained in the actual brief writing process itself by utilizing "law student shorthand" within the brief. There are many commonly used words and phrases for which abbreviations can be substituted in your briefs (and in your class notes also). You can develop abbreviations that are personal to you and which will save you a lot of time. A reference list of briefing abbreviations can be found on page x of this book.

C. Use Both the Briefing Process and the Brief as a Learning Tool

Now that you have a format and the tools for briefing cases efficiently, the most important thing is to make the time spent in briefing profitable to you and to make the most advantageous use of the briefs you create. Of course, the briefs are invaluable for classroom reference when you are called upon to explain or analyze a particular case. However, they are also useful in reviewing for exams. A quick glance at the fact summary should bring the case to mind, and a rereading of the rule of law should enable you to go over the underlying legal concept in your mind, how it was applied in that particular case, and how it might apply in other factual settings.

As to the value to be derived from engaging in the briefing process itself, there is an immediate benefit that arises from being forced to sift through the essential facts and reasoning from the court's opinion and to succinctly express them in your own words in your brief. The process ensures that you understand the case and the point that it illustrates, and that means you will be ready to absorb further analysis and information brought forth in class. It also ensures you will have something to say when called upon in class. The briefing process helps develop a mental agility for getting to the *gist* of a case and for identifying, expounding on, and applying the legal concepts and issues found there. The briefing process is the mental process on which you must rely in taking law school examinations; it is also the mental process upon which a lawyer relies in serving his clients and in making his living.

Abbreviations for Briefs

acceptance	acp	offer	O
affirmed	aff	offeree	OE
answer	ans	offeror	OR
assumption of risk	a/r	ordinance	ord
attorney	atty	pain and suffering	p/s
beyond a reasonable doubt	b/r/d	parol evidence	p/e
bona fide purchaser	BFP	plaintiff	P
breach of contract	br/k	prima facie	p/f
cause of action	c/a	probable cause	p/c
common law	c/l	proximate cause	px/c
Constitution	Con	real property	r/p
constitutional	con	reasonable doubt	r/d
contract	K	reasonable man	r/m
contributory negligence	c/n	rebuttable presumption	rb/p
cross	x	remanded	rem
cross-complaint	x/c	res ipsa loquitur	RIL
cross-examination	x/ex	respondeat superior	r/s
cruel and unusual punishment	c/u/p	Restatement	RS
defendant	D	reversed	rev
dismissed	dis	Rule Against Perpetuities	RAP
double jeopardy	d/j	search and seizure	s/s
due process	d/p	search warrant	s/w
equal protection	e/p	self-defense	s/d
equity	eq	specific performance	s/p
evidence	ev	statute	S
exclude	exc	statute of frauds	S/F
exclusionary rule	exc/r	statute of limitations	S/L
felony	f/n	summary judgment	s/j
freedom of speech	f/s	tenancy at will	t/w
good faith	g/f	tenancy in common	t/c
habeas corpus	h/c	tenant	t
hearsay	hr	third party	TP
husband	H	third party beneficiary	TPB
injunction	inj	transferred intent	TI
in loco parentis	ILP	unconscionable	uncon
inter vivos	I/v	unconstitutional	unconst
joint tenancy	j/t	undue influence	u/e
judgment	judgt	Uniform Commercial Code	UCC
jurisdiction	jur	unilateral	uni
last clear chance	LCC	vendee	VE
long-arm statute	LAS	vendor	VR
majority view	maj	versus	v
meeting of minds	MOM	void for vagueness	VFV
minority view	min	weight of authority	w/a
Miranda rule	Mir/r	weight of the evidence	w/e
Miranda warnings	Mir/w	wife	W
negligence	neg	with	w/
notice	ntc	within	w/i
nuisance	nus	without	w/o
obligation	ob	without prejudice	w/o/p
obscene	obs	wrongful death	wr/d

Table of Cases I

If you are using the Eleventh Edition of the casebook, use this Table of Cases. If you are using the Compact Eleventh Edition for a Shorter Course, use the Table of Cases on page 13. Note: Briefs are organized according to the chapters in the Eleventh Edition.

Table of Cases II

If you are using the Compact Eleventh Edition for a Shorter Course of the casebook, use this Table of Cases. If you are using the Eleventh Edition, use the Table of Cases on page 11. Note: Briefs are organized according to the chapters in the Eleventh Edition.

CHAPTER 1

A Survey of the Civil Action

Quick Reference Rules of Law

Capron v. Van Noorden

Complainant (P) v. Alleged trespasser (D)

6 U.S. (2 Cranch) 126 (1804).

NATURE OF CASE: Appeal from defense verdict in action of trespass on the case.

FACT SUMMARY: Capron (P) argued that his failure to allege his residence deprived the federal court of diversity jurisdiction.

🏛 RULE OF LAW
Even where the parties to a suit brought in federal court appear and consent to the court's diversity jurisdiction, if no actual diversity of citizenship exists between the parties, the court has no power to hear the case.

FACTS: Capron (P) sued Van Noorden (D) in federal court. Capron's (P) complaint did not allege that he himself was an alien or a citizen of any place, nor did it indicate his residence. The circuit court heard the case and decided against Capron (P). On appeal, Capron (P) argued that the circuit court lacked jurisdiction since no basis for claiming diversity citizenship was presented in his complaint.

ISSUE: Where the parties to a suit brought in federal court appear and consent to the court's diversity jurisdiction, if no actual diversity of citizenship exists between the parties, does the court have the power to hear the case?

HOLDING AND DECISION: [Judge not stated in casebook excerpt.] No. The judgment of the circuit court is reversed because it lacked diversity of citizenship jurisdiction over the original matter. [There is no further discussion.] Reversed.

▶ ANALYSIS

Although based on the citizenship of the respective parties involved, diversity jurisdiction is actually a type of subject matter jurisdiction which federal courts are authorized to accept. Since the primary reason for its existence is to provide an impartial forum for the out-of-state visitor, where no diversity is apparent, the court lacks the power, or the reason, to hear the case. Parties appearing before the court cannot give the court a power it does not have.

■=■

Quicknotes

DIVERSITY OF CITIZENSHIP Parties are citizens of different states, or one party is an alien; a factor, along with a statutorily set dollar value of the matter in controversy, that allows a federal district court to exercise its authority to hear a lawsuit based on diversity jurisdiction.

DIVERSITY JURISDICTION The authority of a federal court to hear and determine cases involving parties who are of different states and an amount in controversy greater than a statutorily set amount.

TRESPASS ON THE CASE Action at common law in early England granting a remedy to a person who sustains injury to his person or property as a result of the defendant's conduct.

■=■

Tickle v. Barton

Car accident victim (P) v. Driver's agent (D)

W. Va. Sup. Ct. App., 142 W.Va. 188, 95 S.E.2d 427 (1956).

NATURE OF CASE: Action of trespass on the case; plea in abatement.

FACT SUMMARY: Attorney for Tickle (P) lured Barton (D) into proper jurisdiction for service by inviting him to a football banquet without disclosing his real purpose (service of summons).

🏛 RULE OF LAW
Where service of process is procured by fraud, the court will refuse to exercise jurisdiction and such process will be deemed invalid.

FACTS: Tickle (P) sued Barton (D) for injuries received from an auto accident in McDowell County, West Virginia, in which an agent of Barton (D) was involved. Because Barton (D) was a citizen of Virginia, process could not be served on him there. In order to lure Barton (D) into West Virginia, Tickle's (P) lawyer invited Barton (D) to a football banquet in McDowell County, without either identifying himself as Tickle's (P) lawyer or otherwise disclosing his purpose. Barton (D) was served, and then filed a plea in abatement (a form of pleading in which a party may challenge service without challenging the merits of the underlying claim) challenging the service. The trial court overruled Tickle's (P) demurrer to the plea of abatement. Tickle (P) appealed.

ISSUE: Is service of process valid where the party served is brought within the jurisdiction of the court by fraud?

HOLDING AND DECISION: (Haymond, J.) No. Where service of process is procured by fraud, the court will refuse to exercise jurisdiction and such process will be deemed invalid. If a person residing outside the jurisdiction of a particular court is inveigled, enticed, or induced by any false representation, deceitful contrivance, or wrongful device of the adverse party, to come within the jurisdiction of the court to be served with process, such process will be invalid. The law will not lend its sanction to any act, whether or not lawful in itself, which is accomplished by unlawful means. Here, the factual allegations in Barton's (D) plea clearly establish a basis for finding that the unauthorized (by the banquet committee) invitation extended by Tickle's (P) attorney to Barton (D) was a deceitful contrivance sufficient to invalidate service. The existence of the allegations is enough to sustain the overruling of the demurrer. Judgment is affirmed.

DISSENT: (Given, J.) Tickle's (P) attorney's actions merely exploited an opportunity. The absence of any active misrepresentation took this case out of the definition of fraud.

▶ ANALYSIS

This case shows the general rule that fraudulently served process may be quashed upon motion by the aggrieved party. (Note, however, that this does not automatically mean that any judgment obtained under fraudulent service is necessarily subject to collateral attack because of such service.) The rule applies not only to personal jurisdiction cases, as above, but also to cases where quasi-in-rem jurisdiction is achieved by fraudulently inducing a party to bring his property into a jurisdiction where it may be subjected to garnishment or attachment.

Quicknotes

DEMURRER The assertion that the opposing party's pleadings are insufficient and that the demurring party should not be made to answer.

PLEA IN ABATEMENT A plea brought by a defendant contesting the plaintiff's place, mode or time of asserting his claim without challenge to its merits.

TRESPASS ON THE CASE Action at common law in early England granting a remedy to a person who sustains injury to his person or property as a result of the defendant's conduct.

Case v. State Farm Mutual Automobile Insurance Co.

Insurance agent (P) v. Insurance companies (D)

294 F.2d 676 (5th Cir. 1961).

NATURE OF CASE: Appeal from dismissal of complaint for failure to state cause of action.

FACT SUMMARY: Case (P) sued State Farm Mutual Automobile Insurance Co. (D), alleging in his complaint that his agency contract had been wrongfully terminated.

🏛 RULE OF LAW
It is not the duty of the court to create a claim upon which relief may be granted if such does not appear in the complaint.

FACT: Case (P) had an agency contract with three State Farm Insurance Companies (State Farm) (D). The contract gave each of the parties the right to terminate without cause. State Farm (D) canceled the contract, and Case (P) sued, contending the cancellation was wrongful. The trial court granted State Farm's (D) motion to dismiss for failure to state a cause of action. Case (P) appealed, contending the complaint alleged sufficient facts which could have given rise to a claim for relief.

ISSUE: Is it the duty of a court to create a claim upon which relief may be granted if such is not included in the complaint?

HOLDING AND DECISION: (Cameron, J.) No. It is not the duty of the court to create a claim upon which relief may be granted if such does not appear in the complaint. It is clear that no cause of action was stated in the complaint. Had Case (P) alleged that his business had been wrongfully interfered with, he could easily have stated a cause of action. His failure to do so subjected his complaint to dismissal. Affirmed.

▶ ANALYSIS

This case illustrates the scope of a court's duty to allow a case to be proved based on an evaluation of the pleadings. Had this case been brought in state court, the proper opposition pleading should have been a demurrer, which has the same practical effect as the federal motion to dismiss.

■=■

Quicknotes

DEMURRER The assertion that the opposing party's pleadings are insufficient and that the demurring party should not be made to answer.

■=■

Temple v. Synthes Corp.

Patient (P) v. Medical device manufacturer (D)

498 U.S. 5 (1990).

NATURE OF CASE: Appeal of dismissal with prejudice of action for damages for products liability, medical malpractice, and negligence.

FACT SUMMARY: Temple's (P) federal suit against Synthes Corp. (D), the manufacturer of a plate implanted in Temple's (P) back, was dismissed when Temple (P) failed to join the doctor and the hospital responsible for installing the plate.

🏛 RULE OF LAW
Joint tortfeasors are not necessary parties under Fed. R. Civ. P. 19.

FACTS: A plate and screw device implanted in Temple's (P) back malfunctioned. Temple (P) filed a federal court products liability action against Synthes Corp. (D), the manufacturer of the device. Temple (P) also filed a state court medical malpractice and negligence action against the doctor who implanted the device and the hospital where the operation was performed. Synthes (D) filed a motion to dismiss the federal lawsuit under Fed. R. Civ. P. 19 for Temple's (P) failure to join necessary parties. The district court agreed that the doctor and the hospital were necessary parties and gave Temple (P) twenty days to join them. When Temple (P) did not, the court dismissed the suit with prejudice. The court of appeals affirmed, finding that Rule 19 allowed the district court to order joinder in the interest of complete, consistent, and efficient settlement of controversies. It further found that overlapping, separate lawsuits would have prejudiced Synthes (D) because Synthes (D) might claim the device was not defective but that the doctor and the hospital were negligent, and the doctor and the hospital might claim the opposite. Temple (P) appealed, arguing that joint tortfeasors are not necessary parties under Rule 19.

ISSUE: Are joint tortfeasors necessary parties under Fed. R. Civ. P. 19?

HOLDING AND DECISION: (Per curiam) No. Joint tortfeasors are not necessary parties under Fed. R. Civ. P. 19. It has long been the rule that joint tortfeasors need not be named as defendants in a single lawsuit. Rule 19 does not change that principle. The Advisory Committee Notes to Rule 19(a) state that a tortfeasor with the usual joint and several liability is merely a permissive party. There is a public interest in avoiding multiple lawsuits. However, since the threshold requirements of Rule 19(a) have not been met, the district court had no authority to order dismissal. Reversed and remanded.

▶ ANALYSIS

The function of compulsory joinder as codified in Fed. R. Civ. P. 19 is to bring all affected parties into the same lawsuit. Joinder is often required where the suit involves jointly held rights or liabilities, where more than one party claims the same property, or where granting relief necessarily would affect the rights of parties not in the lawsuit. Though there is a strong interest in "complete, consistent, and efficient settlement of controversies," compulsory joinder is limited. There is a strong tradition of allowing the parties themselves to determine who shall be a party, what claims shall be litigated, and what litigation strategies shall be followed.

Quicknotes

INDISPENSABLE PARTY Parties whose joining in a lawsuit is essential for the adequate disposition of the action and without whom the action cannot proceed.

JOINT TORTFEASORS Two or more parties that either act in concert, or whose individual acts combine to cause a single injury, rendering them jointly and severally liable for damages incurred.

DiMichel v. South Buffalo Railway Co.

Injured employee (P) v. Employer (D)

N.Y. Ct. App., 80 N.Y.2d 184, 590 N.Y.S.2d 1, 604 N.E.2d 63 (1992).

NATURE OF CASE: Review of order compelling discovery in action for damages for personal injury.

FACT SUMMARY: DiMichel (P) contended that he was entitled to obtain, via discovery, any surveillance films taken of him by South Buffalo Railway Co. (D).

🏛 RULE OF LAW
A plaintiff is entitled to obtain, by discovery, any surveillance films taken of him that a defendant intends to use at trial.

FACTS: DiMichel (P) sued South Buffalo Railway Co. (South Buffalo) (D) for personal injury. During the course of pretrial discovery, he demanded production of any surveillance films taken of him. South Buffalo (D) refused, claiming work product. DiMichel (P) moved for an order to compel. The appellate division ruled that only those films South Buffalo (D) intended to introduce at trial were discoverable. The court of appeals granted review.

ISSUE: Is a plaintiff entitled to obtain, by discovery, any surveillance films taken of him that a defendant intends to use at trial?

HOLDING AND DECISION: (Wachtler, C.J.) Yes. A plaintiff is entitled to obtain, by discovery, any surveillance films taken of him that a defendant intends to use at trial. As an initial matter, it must be remembered that New York's stated policy is to encourage full and open discovery. The competing considerations in the issue at hand are the defendant's right to confidentiality in its materials prepared in anticipation of litigation, and the plaintiff's interest in viewing potentially devastating surveillance footage. It is well known that stratagems such as slow motion, fast motion, and creative editing can alter a film's depiction of reality, and a plaintiff has an interest in having the opportunity to ascertain whether this has happened. The best compromise appears to be the position taken by the appellate division that a plaintiff can view any film that a defendant plans to show at trial, but only after he has been deposed, so he cannot tailor his testimony to explain what is going on in the film. Affirmed.

▌ ANALYSIS

At common law, discovery was unknown. Parties would go to trial not knowing much about the other side's file, which resulted in frequent surprise. Modern discovery rules represent a complete about-face in this situation; almost complete discovery is allowed; surprise is now the exception.

Quicknotes

PRETRIAL DISCOVERY Pretrial procedure during which one party makes certain information available to the other.

■▬■

Alderman v. Baltimore & Ohio R. Co.

Train passenger (P) v. Railroad (D)

113 F. Supp. 881 (S.D. W.Va. 1953).

NATURE OF CASE: Action to recover for personal injuries.

FACT SUMMARY: Baltimore & Ohio R. Co. (D) moved for summary judgment claiming that Alderman's (P) complaint failed to state sufficient facts to substantiate a charge of willfulness, a necessary element of Alderman's (P) case.

🏛 RULE OF LAW
A motion for summary judgment will be granted where the facts are undisputed, or undisputable, and where the other party's complaint or defense fails to establish a legal premise, based upon the facts, for which relief could be granted.

FACTS: Alderman (P) sued Baltimore & Ohio R. Co. (the Railroad) (D) to recover for injuries sustained by her as a result of a train derailment. Alderman (P), who had paid no fare, had traveled on a free pass. On the pass was a printed disclaimer on the Railroad's (D) part from all liability arising from injury to non-fare-paying passengers. Alderman (P) originally charged the Railroad (D) with negligence. After a pretrial motion in which the effect of the release from liability was discussed, however, Alderman (P) amended her complaint to charge the Railroad (D) with wanton or willful conduct. On the basis of the amended complaint, the Railroad (D) moved for summary judgment under Rule 56. Alderman (P) did not dispute the fact that the defect which caused the derailment was not visible upon inspection.

ISSUE: Will a motion for summary judgment be granted even when it is apparent to the court that the burden of proof on the plaintiff to substantiate allegations necessary to his cause of action is heavy because of lack of access to evidence?

HOLDING AND DECISION: (Moore, C.J.) Yes. Because there is no relevant West Virginia law that governs both the effect to be given the release and the degree of care owed the plaintiff, it is proper to examine similar federal statutes. For reasons of public policy, a railroad cannot relieve itself of liability for willful or wanton acts. However, this is the sole duty imposed upon the Baltimore & Ohio R. Co. (D). Because the statement of facts, which is not disputed by either party, does not indicate that the Railroad (D) knew of any defect in the rail, and because consciousness is an element that must be proved to establish a cause of action, the motion for summary judgment must be granted. The undenied affidavits of the Railroad (D) show clearly that Alderman (P) cannot establish facts showing willful and wanton conduct. Summary judgment sustained.

▶ ANALYSIS

A motion for summary judgment seeks the same end as a motion for judgment on the pleadings—termination of litigation without going to trial. However, whereas a motion for judgment on the pleadings goes to the legal sufficiency of the opponent's pleadings, a motion for summary judgment, on the other hand, attacks the basic merits of the case regardless of what the opponent's pleadings state. As a result, so long as there is any material fact which can be tried, the motion for summary judgment cannot succeed.

■━■

Quicknotes

SUMMARY JUDGMENT Judgment rendered by a court in response to a motion by one of the parties, claiming that the lack of a question of material fact in respect to an issue warrants disposition of the issue without consideration by the jury.

■━■

Alexander v. Kramer Bros. Freight Lines, Inc.

Truck driver (P) and owner (P) v. Truck owner (D)

273 F.2d 373 (2d Cir. 1959).

NATURE OF CASE: Action to recover damages arising out of negligence, and a defense of contributory negligence.

FACT SUMMARY: Kramer Bros. Freight Lines, Inc. (D) failed to request a charge on the issue of contributory negligence or to take exception to the charge given, which was clearly in error, except to take exception in conference (colloquy) with the court at the close of Alexander's (P) case.

🏛 RULE OF LAW
Since Fed. R. Civ. P. 51 requires that objections must be made to matters in the jury charge in order to raise them on appeal, a party who fails to properly and timely make his objection, cannot challenge the jury charge on appeal.

FACTS: Alexander (P) sued Kramer Bros. Freight Lines, Inc. (Kramer Bros.) (D) for injuries suffered when Alexander's (P) truck collided with a Kramer Bros. (D) truck. Kramer Bros. (D) denied any negligence on its part and raised the defense of contributory negligence. At the trial, the drivers' stories were contradictory and raised issues as to the exact location of the accident and the manner in which it occurred. In conference (colloquy) with the judge near the close of Alexander's (P) case, Kramer Bros. (D) said, "I take an exception" to the court's statement that "the burden of proof of contributory negligence is on the defendant." Kramer Bros. (D) failed to request a jury charge on that subject, and did not object to the charge that was actually given. The jury found a verdict for Alexander (P), and Kramer Bros. (D) appealed on the ground that the court's jury charge was in error.

ISSUE: Since Fed. R. Civ. P. 51 requires that objections must be made to matters in the jury charge in order to raise them on appeal, can a party who fails to properly and timely make his objection challenge the jury charge on appeal?

HOLDING AND DECISION: (Swan, J.) No. Although the court's jury charge was in error, the cases relied upon by Kramer Bros. (D) to prove the charge wrong were never brought to the trial court's attention. Had they been, the judge probably would have changed his jury charge. The obvious purpose of Rule 51 (a party may not appeal an instruction unless objection is made before the jury retires) is to permit the trial judge to evaluate the objection and correct his charge. This purpose is not served by taking an exception to the charge several days in advance when nothing was before the judge requiring a ruling. What is

involved here is different from those situations where the question is whether the exception was sufficiently explicit or in evidentiary rulings. Nor is the present case of the exceptional character in which the appellate court overlooks the failure to properly object to an erroneous charge. Affirmed.

▶ ANALYSIS

State practice will often reach a contrary result where a party has failed to properly object to a jury charge at trial and later attempts to raise the issue on appeal. Most state courts, on the theory that the trial judge is obligated to correctly instruct the jury, will not find a waiver. However, where the party has himself proposed the jury instruction or has proposed one similar to it, he is barred from appealing it, since the incorrect instruction is "invited error."

Quicknotes

COLLOQUY The connection between the libelous statements of the defendant and the plaintiff in a defamation action.

CONTRIBUTORY NEGLIGENCE Behavior on the part of an injured plaintiff falling below the standard of ordinary care that contributes to the defendant's negligence, resulting in the plaintiff's injury.

Diniero v. United States Lines Co.

Ship engineer (P) v. Employer (D)

288 F.2d 595 (2d Cir.), *cert. denied*, 368 U.S. 831 (1961).

NATURE OF CASE: Action to recover damages for personal injury allegedly incurred in the performance of duties.

FACT SUMMARY: After submitting the case to the jury, along with some factual questions to be signed and returned as the jury's verdict, the trial judge withdrew all the questions and asked the jury for a general verdict when it was unable to answer an ambiguous question.

🏛 RULE OF LAW
Withdrawal by a trial court judge of Fed. R. Civ. P. 49 interrogatories from a jury which indicates that one such question is too ambiguous in form and content to be resolved is not an abuse of that judge's discretion, even though Rule 49(b) does not expressly authorize such conduct.

FACTS: Diniero (P), a ship engineer, sued United States Lines Co. (D) to recover damages for injuries alleged to have been suffered when Diniero (P), in the performance of his duties, operated a valve. The issues at trial were whether Diniero's (P) back problems were long continuing or were the result of his operating the valve and whether he was obligated to turn the valve in a certain way. At the close of the evidence, the trial judge submitted the case to the jury along with eight questions (interrogatories) to be signed and returned as the jury's verdict. The jury indicated it had trouble with the first question which read, "Did the plaintiff injure himself aboard (the ship) because in operating the blow-down valve he had to remove the floor plates, then crouch and exert physical effort with a wrench and not his hand to stop it from leaking?" The judge attempted to resolve the ambiguity inherent in the word "had," but after further deliberations, the jury indicated it was unable to agree on the first question. Thereupon, the trial judge, over United States Lines Co.'s (D) objections, withdrew all the questions from the consideration of the jury and asked the jury for a general verdict instead. After further deliberations, the jury returned a verdict in favor of Diniero (P). United States Lines Co. (D) appealed on two grounds: (1) Rule 49(b) of the Federal Rules of Civil Procedure authorizes the submission of written interrogatories but does not authorize their withdrawal once they have been submitted and the jury has commenced its deliberations; (2) withdrawal smoothes the way for a reluctant jury, unable to agree on the facts basic to recovery, to do "popular justice" through a general recovery.

ISSUE: Did the trial judge abuse his discretion in withdrawing all the interrogatories when a particular question was confusing and unclear?

HOLDING AND DECISION: (Medina, J.) No. Withdrawing all the questions was done for the purpose of eliminating the confusion caused by the formulation of the improper question. A confusing interrogatory cannot be fairly considered a "material" question or one the answer to which "is necessary to a verdict." Here, the jury had continued to deliberate for some four hours after the withdrawal, thereby suggesting that it was not looking for an easy "out" to deciding the case. If the question had not been ambiguous or unclear, the withdrawal would have been grounds for reversal, since this would probably be prejudicial to the defendant. Affirmed.

▶ ANALYSIS

This case points out the nature of Fed. R. Civ. P. 49(a), which authorizes the use of special verdicts in federal trials. A special verdict consists of the jury's specific answers to specific factual questions put to it by the judge, and upon which one will render judgment. The rule has the advantages of relieving the judge of the responsibility of instructing and the jury of the problem of understanding the appropriate law. A problem arises, however, whenever a jury returns inconsistent findings on different questions. In such cases, the judge must disregard one finding, return the matter to the jury, or order a new trial. If a jury fails to answer an interrogatory, the court must base its judgment on other answers, or, as above, upon a general verdict returned by the jury. Where an issue is omitted in the interrogatories, it is decided by the judge with jury trial rights deemed waived as to it.

▬▬

Quicknotes

GENERAL VERDICT A verdict stating the prevailing party without specific factual findings.

INTERROGATORIES A method of pretrial discovery in which written questions are provided by one party to another who must respond in writing under oath.

SPECIAL VERDICT Determination by a jury of specific findings of fact in an action in which, application of the law is left to the court.

▬▬

Texas Employers' Ins. Assn. v. Price

Insurer (D) v. Injured employee (P)

Texas Ct. Civ. App., 336 S.W.2d 304 (1960).

NATURE OF CASE: Appeal of verdict for the plaintiff in action to set aside award of a workman's compensation board.

FACT SUMMARY: In a trial where the issue was whether a worker, Price (P), had suffered total or partial disability from an on-the-job accident, the jury chose to ignore all expert testimony; one juror, during deliberations, even offered his own experience as original evidence.

🏛 RULE OF LAW
(1) It is the province of the jury to determine the weight to be given evidence and to reconcile conflicts or inconsistencies.
(2) It is misconduct—inviting reversible error—for a juror to relate to the other jurors his own personal experience as original evidence of material facts to be considered in their deliberations.

FACTS: Price (P) received an accidental on-the-job injury. Dissatisfied with the award given him by the Industrial Accident Board, he brought suit to have the award set aside and a larger one given him because he claimed total disability. At trial, he testified he could not work without pain, that he had to wear a brace, and that his condition was worsening. However, his own doctor testified that Price (P) was not totally disabled. The jury returned with a verdict and large award for Price (P). It was later revealed that, during deliberations, a juror had related his own personal experience to the effect that he knew companies would not hire applicants who had suffered any type of back injury.

ISSUE:
(1) Is it within the province of the jury, when confronted with conflicting testimony, to ignore the expert testimony and give more weight to the words of one of the parties?
(2) Is it reversible error for a juror to submit his own personal experience as original evidence to be considered during deliberations?

HOLDING AND DECISION: (Collings, J.)
(1) Yes. It is within the province of the jury, when confronted with conflicting testimony, to ignore the expert testimony and give more weight to the words of one of the parties. The matter under consideration was not one for experts and skilled witnesses alone. A jury is allowed to assign weight to the evidence presented when there is conflicting or inconsistent testimony.

(2) Yes. It is misconduct—inviting reversible error—for a juror to relate to the other jurors his own personal experience as original evidence to be considered in their deliberation. This is reversible error since the offered statements were offered to persuade the jury on a material issue at trial. Reversed and remanded.

▶ ANALYSIS

Although, generally, misconduct on the part of jurors in their deliberations may be shown only by impeaching testimony of affidavits by nonjurors (this to protect the secrecy of jury deliberation), a few exceptions are recognized. Among these factors which would permit a juror himself to testify concerning jury misconduct are included: (1) gross misconduct (drunkenness, accepting bribes, unauthorized visitations to the scene of the crime); (2) concealing of grounds which would have disqualified a juror on voir dire; (3) verdicts arrived at by chance; and (4) agreements to abide by a majority vote.

Quicknotes

VOIR DIRE Examination of potential jurors on a case.

Lavender v. Kurn

Estate administrator (P) v. Railroad company trustees (D)

327 U.S. 645 (1946).

NATURE OF CASE: Review of appellate judgment reversing award of damages in action under Federal Employer's Liability Act.

FACT SUMMARY: Haney was killed while working for the St. Louis-San Francisco Railway Co. (D) and the Illinois Central Railroad (D) due to head injuries suffered on the job.

🏛 RULE OF LAW
An appellate court's function in reviewing a jury verdict is exhausted as soon as it determines that there is an evidentiary basis for the jury's verdict, and only when it finds a complete absence of probative facts to support a verdict may the court reverse it as clearly erroneous.

FACTS: Lavender (P), as administrator of the estate of Haney, sued Kurn (D) and other trustees (D) of the St. Louis-San Francisco Railway Co. and the Illinois Central Railroad (Railroad) (D) under the Federal Employer's Liability Act. Haney died from head injuries suffered on his job while working as a switch-tender for the Illinois Central Railroad (D). At trial, Lavender (P) attempted to prove that Haney had been killed by a mail hook protruding from a moving train (i.e., negligence). This theory depended upon the jury finding that Haney was standing exactly at one certain spot on a mound near the tracks so that the hook would have hit him at exactly 63½ inches above the ground. The Railroad's (D) defense was that Lavender (P) was murdered. The jury entered judgment for Haney. On appeal, the Missouri Supreme Court reversed the jury, stating, "it would be mere speculation and conjecture to say that Haney was struck by the mail hook," and such was not sufficient to sustain a verdict. Lavender (P) appealed.

ISSUE: May an appellate court reverse a jury verdict as erroneous merely because the jury may have engaged in "speculation and conjecture" in reaching their verdict?

HOLDING AND DECISION: (Murphy, J.) No. An appellate court's function in reviewing a jury verdict is exhausted as soon as it determines that there is an evidentiary basis for the jury's verdict, and only when it finds a complete absence of probative facts to support a verdict may the court reverse it as clearly erroneous. The jury is free to discard or disbelieve whatever facts are inconsistent with its conclusion. Whenever facts are in dispute or evidence is such that fair-minded men might draw different inferences, a measure of speculation and conjecture is required on the part of the jury whose duty it is to choose the most reasonable inference. The appellate court was unjus-

tified in reversing on such grounds. The judgment of the Supreme Court of Missouri is reversed and the case remanded.

▶ ANALYSIS

The standard is that the court will not interfere with the judgment of the trier of fact unless it is "clearly erroneous." The jury is to be controlled only where its actions are so clearly out of line ("clearly erroneous") that justice cannot be served in any manner other than reversal. Compare this to the procedure "judgment n.o.v."

━━━

Quicknotes

JUDGMENT N.O.V. A judgment entered by the trial judge reversing a jury verdict if the jury's determination has no basis in law or fact.

RES GESTAE RULE A doctrine whereby words spoken contemporaneously with, or immediately following, an event are deemed to be part of the event and thus are admissible in evidence.

━━━

Hicks v. United States

Estate administrator (P) v. Federal government (D)

368 F.2d 626 (4th Cir. 1966).

NATURE OF CASE: Appeal from dismissal of action under Federal Tort Claims Act.

FACT SUMMARY: Carol Greitens died of an obstruction in her intestine after being sent home by a Navy doctor who improperly diagnosed her condition as a "bug."

🏛 RULE OF LAW

Fed. R. Civ. P. 52(a) states that a trial judge's findings of fact are not to be disturbed unless "clearly erroneous," but, where the facts of a case are undisputed and the judge makes a determination of liability (negligence), this conclusion is freely reviewable on appeal as a question of law, not fact.

FACTS: Hicks (P) sued as administrator of the estate of Carol Greitens, who died of an obstruction in her small intestine after being sent home by a Navy doctor who improperly diagnosed her condition as a "bug." Two doctors in the area testified at trial that the doctor's conduct was contra the prevailing practice in their community of inquiring about diarrhea and making a rectal examination in cases where patients had symptoms like those of Carol Greitens. Since such steps would have led to a proper diagnosis and could have saved Greitens's life, Hicks (P) contended that the doctor had failed to exercise "ordinary care" and should be held liable for negligently causing her death. The trial court dismissed the complaint for insufficient evidence. Hicks (P) appealed. The Government (D) cited Fed. R. Civ. P. 52(a) and denied jurisdiction to review.

ISSUE: Does Fed. R. Civ. P. 52(a) preclude review of a trial judge's determination of facts where those facts are undisputed?

HOLDING AND DECISION: (Sobeloff, J.) No. Fed. R. Civ. P. 52(a) states that a trial judge's findings of fact are not to be disturbed unless "clearly erroneous," but, where the facts of a case are undisputed and the judge makes a determination of liability (negligence), this conclusion is freely reviewable on appeal as a matter of law, not fact. The determination of negligence depends upon both a formulation of a legal standard by the trial judge and its application to the evidentiary facts of the case. Since the latter here are uncontested, the question of law prevails and the clearly erroneous rule is inapplicable. Although the absence of a factual dispute does not always mean that the conclusion of the judge is a question of law, it becomes so here since the ultimate conclusion to be drawn from the basic facts (i.e., negligence) is a question of law. The judgment must be reversed and the cause remanded.

▶ ANALYSIS

This case points up the general rule for one application of the fact/law dichotomy in appellate review. The "clearly erroneous" standard applies to questions of fact. Where questions of fact and law merge (as in negligence) the factual determinations may, nevertheless, be routinely reviewable so far as they interrelate with questions of law. Note that "clearly erroneous" is the appellate standard in the federal rules. Rule 52(a) [renumbered as 52(a)(6) in 2007] has codified the previous majority rule for review. Note, finally, that negligence cases lend themselves particularly well to this problem. Negligence is a finding both of fact and law (cause in fact and proximate cause, for example) and often leads to the formulation of fine distinctions.

━■■

Quicknotes

FED. R. CIV. P. 52(a) Renumbered as 52(a)(6) in 2007; requires that findings of fact not be set aside unless clearly erroneous.

NEGLIGENCE Conduct falling below the standard of care that a reasonable person would demonstrate under similar conditions.

━■■

Des Moines Navigation & Railroad Co. v. Iowa Homestead Co.

Railroad company (D) v. Iowa corporation (P)

123 U.S. 552 (1887).

NATURE OF CASE: Action to recover taxes on land mutually claimed.

FACT SUMMARY: After other defendants caused an action to be removed from state to federal court, the Iowa Homestead Co. (P) contested the matters in dispute in the circuit court, and in the United States Supreme Court on appeal, without taking any objection to the jurisdiction, and then sought to bring a new action in state court claiming that the prior judgment was void for lack of jurisdiction.

🏛 RULE OF LAW
A party who fails to challenge federal court jurisdiction over the subject matter of an action, either in the trial court or on appeal, is bound by the res judicata effect of the first action in subsequent suits based upon it.

FACTS: The Iowa Homestead Company (Homestead Company) (P), an Iowa corporation, brought an action against the Des Moines Navigation & Railroad Co. (Des Moines) (D), an Iowa corporation, and other defendants, citizens of New York, in state court. The New York defendants, by common consent, apparently caused the entire suit to be transferred to federal court, which accepted jurisdiction based on diversity of citizenship. It may have been an error for the entire case, and all the parties, to be transferred since both the Homestead Company (P) and Des Moines (D) were citizens of the same state. Nevertheless, the Homestead Company (P) contested the matters in dispute with Des Moines (D), and in the United States Supreme Court on appeal, without taking any objection to federal court jurisdiction. The Homestead Company (P) lost, but refiled the same action in state court, claiming that federal court jurisdiction was improper and, therefore, it was not bound by any earlier judgment, since the federal court decree was null and void. The trial court agreed, and Des Moines (D) appealed.

ISSUE: Is a party who fails to challenge federal court jurisdiction over the subject matter of an action, either in the trial court or on appeal, bound by the res judicata effect of the first action in subsequent suits based upon it?

HOLDING AND DECISION: (Waite, C.J.) Yes. A party who fails to challenge federal court jurisdiction over the subject matter of an action, either in the trial court or on appeal, is bound by the res judicata effect of the first action in subsequent suits based upon it. The point is not whether it was error in the circuit court to take jurisdiction of the suit, but as to the binding effect of the

decree of the United States Supreme Court when appeal was taken. If jurisdiction is not alleged in lower federal court proceedings, their judgments and decrees may be reversed for that cause on a writ of error or appeal; but until reversed they are conclusive between the parties. They are not "nullities." It was within the power of the circuit court to assume jurisdiction over the entire matter. Whether it reached the right decision on the matter was to be challenged on appeal. Since the Homestead Company (P), at the time of appeal in the United States Supreme Court, had failed to do so, it was barred from raising the issue of jurisdiction in a second action; the state court must now give full faith and credit to the judgment of the federal court in the first action. Reversed.

▶ ANALYSIS

The res judicata doctrine states that a final judgment in a civil action must be accepted as finally settling the rights and liabilities of the involved parties pertinent to those issues actually in litigation; no renewed litigation will be permitted to overturn, or modify, the first court's judgment or decree. When the term "bar" is employed, what is meant is that the original judgment defeats the plaintiff's claim, and precludes any new action by the plaintiff or his privies against the defendant and his privies on the same cause of action or claim. So long as the new claims arise out of the same cause of action, the "bar" will take effect regardless of whether they were raised in the initial action.

◼◼◼

Quicknotes

RES JUDICATA The rule of law a final judgment by a court precludes subsequent litigation between the parties regarding the same cause of action.

◼◼◼

CHAPTER 2

Jurisdiction Over the Parties or Their Property

Quick Reference Rules of Law

Pennoyer v. Neff

Land purchaser (D) v. Landowner (P)

95 U.S. (5 Otto) 714 (1877).

NATURE OF CASE: Review of judgment for plaintiff in action to recover possession of land.

FACT SUMMARY: Neff (P) alleged that Pennoyer's (D) deed from a sheriff's sale was invalid because the court ordering the sale had never obtained personal jurisdiction over Neff (P).

🏛 RULE OF LAW
Where the object of the action is to determine the personal rights and obligations of the parties, service by publication against nonresidents is ineffective to confer jurisdiction on the court.

FACTS: Neff (P) owned real property in Oregon. Mitchell brought suit in Oregon to recover legal fees allegedly owed him by Neff (P). Neff (P), a nonresident, was served by publication and Mitchell obtained a default judgment. The court ordered Neff's (P) land sold at a sheriff's sale to satisfy the judgment. Pennoyer (D) purchased the property. Neff (P) subsequently learned of the sale and brought suit in Oregon to recover possession of his property. Neff (P) alleged that the court ordering the sale had never acquired in personam jurisdiction over him. Therefore, the court could not adjudicate the personal rights and obligations between Neff (P) and Mitchell and the default judgment had been improperly entered. The lower court agreed, and Pennoyer (D) appealed.

ISSUE: Where an action involves the adjudication of personal rights and obligations of the parties, is service by publication against a nonresident sufficient to confer jurisdiction?

HOLDING AND DECISION: (Field, J.) No. Every state possesses exclusive jurisdiction and sovereignty over persons and property within its territory. Following from this, no state can exercise direct jurisdiction and authority over persons or property outside of its territory. These are two well-established principles of public law respecting the jurisdiction of an independent state over persons and property. However, the exercise of jurisdiction which every state possesses over persons and property within it will often affect persons and property outside it. A state may compel persons domiciled within it to execute, in pursuance of their contracts respecting property situated elsewhere, instruments transferring title. Likewise, a state may subject property situated within it which is owned by nonresidents to the payment of the demands of its own citizens. Substituted service by publication or by other authorized means may be sufficient to inform the parties of the proceedings where the property is brought under the control of the court or where the judg-ment is sought as a means of reaching such property or effectuating some interest therein. That is, such service is effectual in proceedings in rem. The law assumes that property is always in the possession of its owner or an agent. It proceeds upon the theory that a seizure of the property will inform the owner that he must look to any proceedings upon such seizure for the property's condemnation or sale. But where the entire object of the action is to determine personal rights and obligations, the action is in personam and service by publication is ineffectual to confer jurisdiction over the nonresident defendant upon the court. Process sent out of state to a nonresident is equally ineffective to confer personal jurisdiction. In an action to determine a defendant's personal liability, he must be brought within the court's jurisdiction by service of process within the state or by his voluntary appearance. Without jurisdiction, due process requirements are not satisfied. In the case herein, Neff (P) was not personally served and he never appeared. Hence, the personal judgment obtained against Neff (P) was not valid and the property could not be sold. Affirmed.

▌ ANALYSIS

This is the leading case on the extent of the court's power to compel a defendant's attendance. At common law, the presence of the defendant within the jurisdiction, plus service while there, were the indispensable ingredients for the acquisition of jurisdiction of the person of the defendant. It still remains the basic method of acquiring jurisdiction over the defendant. It does not matter how transient the defendant's presence is if he is served within the jurisdiction. One case held that service on a defendant while he was in an airplane passing over a state is sufficient. Of course, a voluntary appearance by a defendant also gives the court jurisdiction over him, unless he enters a special appearance to contest jurisdiction only.

■=■

Quicknotes

IN PERSONAM An action against a person seeking to impose personal liability.

IN REM An action against property.

SERVICE BY PUBLICATION A means of serving process pursuant to statute upon a defendant, upon whom service of process cannot be accomplished personally by publication of a summons as an advertisement in a newspaper specified by the court.

■=■

Hess v. Pawloski

Nonresident driver (D) v. Accident victim (P)

274 U.S. 352 (1927).

NATURE OF CASE: Review of verdict in plaintiff's favor in action to recover damages for personal injuries.

FACT SUMMARY: A Massachusetts statute provided that nonresident motorists were deemed to have appointed a state official as their agent for service of process in cases growing out of accidents or collisions involving them. Pawloski (P) sued Hess (D), a nonresident, for damages due to an auto accident in Massachusetts.

🏛 RULE OF LAW
In advance of a nonresident's use of its highways, a state may require the nonresident to appoint one of the state's officials as his agent on whom process may be served in proceedings growing out of such highway use.

FACTS: Pawloski (P) alleged that Hess (D) negligently drove a car on a Massachusetts highway, thereby injuring Pawloski (P). Hess (D) was a nonresident of Massachusetts. No personal service was made on him, and no property belonging to him was attached. A Massachusetts statute provided that nonresident motorists were deemed to have appointed the registrar of motor vehicles as their agent for service of process in cases arising out of accidents or collisions in which nonresidents were involved. The statute also required that notice of such service and a copy of the process be sent by registered mail to the defendant. Hess (D) moved to dismiss on due process grounds, but the lower courts held the statute to be a valid exercise of the police power. The United States Supreme Court granted review.

ISSUE: Does a state statute by which nonresident motorists are deemed to have appointed a state official as their agent for service of process in cases arising out of accidents involving them, violate due process?

HOLDING AND DECISION: (Butler, J.) No. Motor vehicles are dangerous vehicles. In the public interest, the state may make and enforce regulations reasonably calculated to promote care on the part of all who use its highways. The statute involved in this case limits the nonresident's implied consent to proceedings growing out of accidents or collisions on a highway involving the nonresident. It requires that he receive notice of the service and a copy of the process. It makes no hostile discrimination against nonresidents. The state's power to regulate the use of its highways extends to its use by nonresidents as well as residents. In advance of the operation of a motor vehicle on its highway by a nonresident, the state may require him to appoint one of its officials as his agent on whom process may be served in proceedings growing out of such use. Affirmed.

▶ ANALYSIS

Other states were quick to pass similar nonresident motorist statutes, and thus provide their citizens with local forums for injuries caused by nonresident motorists. Some passed statutes subjecting nonresident boat and airplane owners to local forums also. Under the reasoning of *Hess*, it was thought that in order to subject the nonresident to local jurisdiction the activity engaged in must be one subject to state regulations under its police power. Consequently, the first extensions of *Hess* were to such situations as the sale of securities, an industry subject to a high degree of regulation, and the ownership of local real estate.

Quicknotes

PLAINTIFF IN ERROR Appellant; a party that appeals from a lower court judgment.

International Shoe Co. v. Washington

Nonresident corporation (D) v. State (P)

326 U.S. 310 (1945).

NATURE OF CASE: Review of judgment permitting state to recover unemployment contributions.

FACT SUMMARY: A state statute authorized the mailing of notice of assessment of delinquent contributions for unemployment compensation to nonresident employers. International Shoe Co. (International) (D) was a nonresident corporation. Notice of assessment was served on one of its salespersons within the State of Washington and was mailed to International's (D) office in Missouri.

🏛 RULE OF LAW
For a state to subject a nonresident defendant to in personam jurisdiction, due process requires that he have certain minimum contacts with it such that the maintenance of the suit does not offend traditional notions of fair play and substantial justice.

FACTS: A Washington statute set up a scheme of unemployment compensation, requiring contributions by employers. The statute authorized the commissioner, Washington (P), to issue an order and notice of assessment of delinquent contributions by mailing the notice to nonresident employers. International Shoe Co. (International) (D), a Delaware corporation having its principal place of business in Missouri, employed 11 to 13 salespersons under the supervision of managers in Missouri. These salespeople resided in Washington and did most of their work there. They had no authority to enter into contracts or make collections. International (D) did not have any office in Washington and made no contracts there. Notice of assessment was served upon one of International's (D) Washington salespersons and a copy of the notice was sent by registered mail to International's (D) Missouri address. International (D) claimed that service was improper, but the lower courts ruled that Washington (P) was entitled to recover the unpaid contributions. The United States Supreme Court granted review.

ISSUE: For a state to subject a nonresident defendant to in personam jurisdiction, does due process require only that he have certain minimum contacts with it, such that the maintenance of the suit does not offend notions of fair play and substantial justice?

HOLDING AND DECISION: (Stone, C.J.) Yes. Historically the jurisdiction of courts to render judgment in personam is grounded on their power over the defendant's person, and his presence within the territorial jurisdiction of a court was necessary to a valid judgment. But now, due process requires only that in order to subject a defendant to a judgment in personam, if he is not present

within the territorial jurisdiction, he has certain minimum contacts with the territory such that the maintenance of the suit does not offend traditional notions of fair play and substantial justice. The contacts must be such as to make it reasonable, in the context of our federal system, to require a defendant corporation to defend the suit brought there. An estimate of the inconveniences which would result to the corporation from a trial away from its "home" is relevant. To require a corporation to defend a suit away from home where its contact has been casual or isolated activities has been thought to lay too unreasonable a burden on it. However, even single or occasional acts may, because of their nature, quality and circumstances, be deemed sufficient to render a corporation liable to suit. Hence, the criteria to determine whether jurisdiction is justified is not simply mechanical or quantitative. Satisfaction of due process depends on the quality and nature of the activity in relation to the fair and orderly administration of the laws. In this case, International's (D) activities were neither irregular nor casual. Rather, they were systematic and continuous. The obligation sued upon here arose out of these activities. They were sufficient to establish sufficient contacts or ties to make it reasonable to permit Washington (P) to enforce the obligations International (D) incurred there. Affirmed.

DISSENT: (Black, J.) The U.S. Constitution leaves to each state the power to tax and to open the doors of its courts for its citizens to sue corporations who do business in the state. It is a judicial deprivation to condition the exercise of this power on this Court's notion of "fair play."

▶ ANALYSIS

Before this decision, three theories had evolved to provide for suits by and against foreign corporations. The first was the consent theory. It rested on the proposition that since a foreign corporation could not carry on its business within a state without the permission of that state, the state could require a corporation to appoint an agent to receive service of process within the state. However, it soon became established law that a foreign corporation could not be prevented by a state from carrying on interstate commerce within its borders. The presence doctrine required that the corporation was "doing business" and "present" in the state. The third theory used either the present or consent doctrine, and it was necessary to determine whether the corporation was doing business within the state either to

Continued on next page.

decide whether its consent could properly be implied or to discover whether the corporation was present.

■■■■

Quicknotes

IN PERSONAM JURISDICTION The power of a court over a person, as opposed to a court's power over a person's interest in property.

MINIMUM CONTACTS The minimum degree of contact necessary in order to sustain a cause of action within a particular forum, consistent with the requirements of due process.

■■■■

Gray v. American Radiator & Standard Sanitary Corp.

Exploding heater victim (P) v. Valve manufacturer (D) and Radiator manufacturer (D)

Ill. Sup. Ct., 22 Ill. 2d 432, 176 N.E.2d 761 (1961).

NATURE OF CASE: Direct appeal from dismissal of action to recover damages for personal injury.

FACT SUMMARY: Gray (P) alleged that Titan's (D), an Ohio corporation, negligent construction of a valve sold to American Radiator & Standard Sanitary Corp. (D), which incorporated the valve into a water heater, caused an explosion in Illinois, injuring her.

> 🏛 **RULE OF LAW**
> Whether a nonresident activity within a state is adequate to subject it to jurisdiction of that state depends upon the facts of each case, and the relevant inquiry is whether the defendant engaged in some act or conduct by which he invoked the benefits and protections of the forum.

FACTS: Gray (P) alleged that Titan (D), an Ohio corporation, negligently constructed a valve which it sold to American Radiator & Standard Sanitary Corp. (D), which incorporated it into a water heater. Titan's (D) negligence, Gray (P) alleged, caused the heater to explode, thereby injuring her. The explosion occurred in Illinois. Titan (D) did no business in Illinois and had no agent physically present there.

ISSUE: Where a nonresident's only contact with a state is an injury, is that contact adequate to subject the nonresident to jurisdiction of the state without violating due process?

HOLDING AND DECISION: (Klingbiel, J.) Yes. A tortious act is committed where the resulting damage occurs. Since the *Pennoyer* decision, 95 U.S. (5 Otto) 714 (1877), the power of a state to exert jurisdiction over nonresidents has been greatly expanded, particularly with respect to foreign corporations. Since the *International Shoe* decision, 326 U.S. 310 (1945), the requirements for jurisdiction have further relaxed. Now it is sufficient if the act or transaction itself has a substantial connection with the state. It is no longer necessary that the business done by the foreign corporation be of a substantial volume. Hence, it has been held sufficient for due process requirements where the action was based on a contract which had a substantial connection with the state. Continuous activity is not required, and the commission of a single tort within the state has been held sufficient to sustain jurisdiction. Whether the activity conducted within the state is adequate to satisfy due process depends upon the facts in the particular case. In application of this flexible test, the relevant question is whether the defendant engaged in some act or conduct by which he invoked the benefits and protections of the law of the state. In this case, Titan (D) does not claim that the present use of its product in Illinois is an isolated instance. It is a reasonable inference that its commercial transactions, like those of other manufacturers, result in substantial use and consumption in Illinois. To the extent that its businesses may be directly affected by transactions occurring in Illinois, it enjoys benefits from the laws of this state. The fact that the benefit Titan (D) derives from Illinois's law is an indirect one does not make it any less essential to the conduct of its business. It is not unreasonable, where a cause of action arises from alleged defects in a nonresident's product, to say that the use of such product in the ordinary course of commerce is sufficient contact with the state to justify that the nonresident defend there. Further, witnesses on the issues of injury, damages, etc., will be most likely found where the accident occurred. Titan's (D) contact with Illinois is sufficient to support the exercise of jurisdiction. Reversed and remanded.

▌ *ANALYSIS*

After the *International Shoe* decision, states began to enact "long arm" statutes. The Illinois statute (which was involved in this case) was the first to be passed. The primary purpose of these statutes is to provide local forums for local plaintiffs on locally generated causes of action. The chief barrier to an undue extension of long-arm jurisdiction is the Fourteenth Amendment. It is reinforced by the First Amendment in libel suits where free speech and free press are involved. In those cases greater contact with the state must be shown.

■▬■

Quicknotes

CIVIL PRACTICE ACT § 16 Provides that summons may be personally served upon any party outside the state.

CIVIL PRACTICE ACT § 17(b) A nonresident who commits a tortious act within the state of Illinois submits to jurisdiction.

■▬■

World-Wide Volkswagen Corp. v. Woodson

Vehicle distributor (P) v. District judge (D)

444 U.S. 286 (1980).

NATURE OF CASE: Appeal from denial of writ of prohibition restraining exercise of in personam jurisdiction.

FACT SUMMARY: The Robinsons bought a new Audi in New York from Seaway and while traveling in Oklahoma were involved in a fiery crash allegedly aggravated by Audi's negligent placement of the gas tank, and the district court asserted personal jurisdiction over Seaway and World-Wide Volkswagen Corp. (P), another dealer.

RULE OF LAW
The sale of an automobile by a corporate defendant is not a sufficient purposeful availment of the benefits and protection of the laws of a state where the automobile is fortuitously driven so as to constitute the requisite "minimum contacts" with that state for personal jurisdiction purposes.

FACTS: The Robinsons purchased a new Audi from Seaway, a dealer, in New York. Then they left New York for a new home in Arizona, but en route were involved in a fiery crash in Oklahoma. Alleging that the injuries sustained were aggravated by Audi's negligent placement of the gas tank and other fuel system design defects, the Robinsons brought an action in federal court in Oklahoma against Seaway and another dealer, World-Wide Volkswagen Corp. (World-Wide) (P). Both were located in New York and neither had an office in Oklahoma nor conducted any business in that state. No evidence was adduced that any of the cars sold by either had ever entered the state of Oklahoma on any prior occasion, until the Robinsons' mishap. The district court rejected World-Wide's (P) constitutional objections to any assertion of personal jurisdiction over it and Seaway. World-Wide (P) then applied to the Supreme Court of Oklahoma for a writ of prohibition against District Judge Woodson (D), restraining him from exercising personal jurisdiction over it. The court denied the writ and the United States Supreme Court granted certiorari.

ISSUE: Is the sale of an automobile by a corporate defendant a sufficient purposeful availment of the benefits and protections of the laws of a state where the automobile is fortuitously driven so as to constitute the requisite "minimum contacts" with that state for purposes of personal jurisdiction?

HOLDING AND DECISION: (White, J.) No. The Due Process Clause limits the power of a state court to render a valid personal judgment against a nonresident defendant. It has long been held that for such a judgment to be rendered, the nonresident defendant must have "minimum contacts" with the forum state. There is a total absence in this case of any affiliating circumstances with Oklahoma. No sales were closed there nor services provided. While it is argued that the "minimum contacts" test is satisfied by the foreseeability that the car would enter other states, the mere unilateral activity of a purchaser in moving the automobile from New York to Oklahoma cannot satisfy the requirement. The defendant must "purposely avail" itself of the benefits and protections of the laws of the forum state, and this neither Seaway nor World-Wide (P) did. The sale of an automobile by a corporate defendant is not a sufficiently purposeful availment of the benefits and protections of the laws of a state where the automobile is fortuitously driven so as to constitute the requisite "minimum contacts" with that state for personal jurisdiction purposes. Reversed.

DISSENT: (Brennan, J.) The "minimum contacts" doctrine is merely a vehicle for ascertaining fairness. The amount of contacts necessary for jurisdiction to exist varies from situation to situation. Here, where a dealer of highly mobile articles is involved, it is hardly unfair to require him to defend in the state where the auto was taken.

ANALYSIS

The "purposeful availment of the benefits and protections of the laws of the forum state" involves some action designed to benefit the actor through an effect in the state asserting jurisdiction. In this case, the court found that the car was "fortuitously" in Oklahoma, negating the inference that the sale of the car brought revenue to World-Wide (P) in anticipation that the car would be driven there.

Quicknotes

DUE PROCESS CLAUSE Clauses, found in the Fifth and Fourteenth Amendments to the United States Constitution, providing that no person shall be deprived of "life, liberty, or property, without due process of law."

IN PERSONAM An action against a person seeking to impose personal liability.

MINIMUM CONTACTS The minimum degree of contact necessary in order to sustain a cause of action within a

Continued on next page.

particular forum, consistent with the requirements of due process.

WRIT OF PROHIBITION A writ issued by a superior court prohibiting a lower court from exceeding its jurisdiction or from usurping jurisdiction beyond that authorized by law.

■=■

Asahi Metal Industry Co. v. Superior Court

Tire valve manufacturer (P) v. Court (D)

480 U.S. 102 (1987).

NATURE OF CASE: Appeal from discharge of writ quashing service of summons.

FACT SUMMARY: Asahi Metal Industry Co. (Asahi) (P) appealed from a decision of the California Supreme Court discharging a peremptory writ issued by the appeals court quashing service of summons in Cheng Shin's indemnity action, contending that there did not exist minimum contacts between California and Asahi (P) sufficient to sustain jurisdiction.

RULE OF LAW
Minimum contacts sufficient to sustain jurisdiction are not satisfied simply by the placement of a product into the stream of commerce coupled with the awareness that this product would reach the forum state.

FACTS: Asahi Metal Industry Co. (Asahi) (P), a Japanese corporation, manufactured tire valve assemblies in Japan, selling some of them to Cheng Shin, a Taiwanese company which incorporated them into the motorcycles it manufactured. Zurcher was seriously injured in a motorcycle accident, and a companion was killed. He sued Cheng Shin, alleging the motorcycle tire, manufactured by Cheng Shin, was defective. Cheng Shin sought indemnity from Asahi (P), and the main action settled. Asahi (P) moved to quash service of summons, contending that jurisdiction could not be maintained by California, the state in which Zurcher filed his action, consistent with the Due Process Clause of the Fourteenth Amendment. The evidence indicated that Asahi's (P) sales to Cheng Shin took place in Taiwan, and shipments went from Japan to Taiwan. Cheng Shin purchased valve assemblies from other manufacturers. Sales to Cheng Shin never amounted to more than 1.5 percent of Asahi's (P) income. Approximately 20 percent of Cheng Shin's sales in the United States are in California. In declaration, an attorney for Cheng Shin stated he made an informal examination of tires in a bike shop in Solano County, where Zurcher was injured, finding approximately 20 percent of the tires with Asahi's (P) trademark (25 percent of the tires manufactured by Cheng Shin). The Superior Court (D) denied the motion to quash, finding it reasonable that Asahi (P) defend its claim of defect in their product. The court of appeals issued a peremptory writ commanding the Superior Court (D) to quash service of summons. The California Supreme Court reversed and discharged the writ, finding that Asahi's (P) awareness that some of its product would reach California by placing it into the stream of commerce satisfied minimum contacts

sufficient to sustain jurisdiction. From this decision, Asahi (P) appealed.

ISSUE: Are minimum contacts sufficient to sustain jurisdiction satisfied by the placement of a product into the stream of commerce, coupled with the awareness that this product would reach the forum state?

HOLDING AND DECISION: (O'Connor, J.) No. Minimum contacts sufficient to sustain jurisdiction are not satisfied by the placement of a product into the stream of commerce, coupled with the awareness that this product would reach the forum state. To satisfy minimum contacts, there must be some act by which the defendant purposefully avails itself of the privilege of conducting activities within the forum state. Although the courts that have squarely addressed this issue have been divided, the better view is that the defendant must do more than place a product in the stream of commerce. The unilateral act of a consumer bringing the product to the forum state is not sufficient. Asahi (P) has not purposefully availed itself of the California market. It does not do business in the state, conduct activities, maintain offices or agents, or advertise. Nor did it have anything to do with Cheng Shin's distribution system, which brought the tire valve assembly to California. Assertion of jurisdiction based on these facts exceeds the limits of due process. [The Court went on to consider the burden of defense on Asahi (P) and the slight interests of the state and Zurcher, finding the assertion of jurisdiction unreasonable and unfair.] Reversed and remanded.

CONCURRENCE: (Brennan, J.) The state supreme court correctly concluded that the stream of commerce theory, without more, has satisfied minimum contacts in most courts which have addressed the issue, and it has been preserved in the decision of this Court.

CONCURRENCE: (Stevens, J.) The minimum contacts analysis is unnecessary; the Court has found by weighing the appropriate factors that jurisdiction under these facts is unreasonable and unfair.

ANALYSIS

The Brennan concurrence is quite on point in criticizing the plurality for its characterization that this case involves the act of a consumer in bringing the product within the forum state. The argument presented in *World-Wide Volkswagen Corp. v. Woodson*, 444 U.S. 286 (1980), cited by the

Continued on next page.

plurality, seems more applicable to distributors and retailers, than to manufacturers of component parts.

■══■

Quicknotes

MINIMUM CONTACTS The minimum degree of contact necessary in order to sustain a cause of action within a particular forum, consistent with the requirements of due process.

■══■

J. McIntyre Machinery, Ltd. v. Nicastro

Product manufacturer (D) v. Injured worker (P)

131 S. Ct. 2780 (2011).

NATURE OF CASE: Appeal of judgment by a state's highest court asserting jurisdiction over a foreign manufacturer in a products liability action.

FACT SUMMARY: Nicastro (P) was injured when he used a piece of heavy machinery and sued the foreign manufacturer in New Jersey state court. The company disputed the state's jurisdiction.

🏛 RULE OF LAW
In products liability cases, the "stream-of-commerce" doctrine cannot displace the general rule that the exercise of judicial power is not lawful unless the defendant purposefully avails itself of the privilege of conducting activities within the forum state, thus invoking the benefits and protections of its laws.

FACTS: Nicastro (P) injured his hand while using a metal-shearing machine that was manufactured by J. McIntyre Machinery, Ltd. (J. McIntyre) (D). The machine was manufactured in England, where J. McIntyre (D) is incorporated and operates, and the injury occurred in New Jersey. Nicastro (P) filed suit in New Jersey state court. The New Jersey Supreme Court, applying a "stream-of-commerce" doctrine, found that it had jurisdiction over J. McIntyre (D) on the theory that so long as a manufacturer knows or reasonably should know that its products are distributed through a nationwide distribution system that might lead to its products being sold in any of the 50 states, it is subject to the jurisdiction of a state's courts. The New Jersey Supreme Court determined it had jurisdiction because: J. McIntyre (D) machines were sold in the United States, albeit only through a distributor that was not controlled by J. McIntyre (D); the company attended annual conventions in the United States (but not in New Jersey) for the scrap recycling industry to advertise alongside the distributor; no more than four machines, including the one that injured Nicastro (P), were identified as being in New Jersey; and J. McIntyre (D) guided advertising and sales efforts for the U.S. distributor. However, J. McIntyre (D) neither marketed goods in New Jersey, nor shipped goods there. J. McIntyre (D) did not, in any sense, target New Jersey. It also did not consent to the court's jurisdiction. J. McIntyre (D) appealed, and the United States Supreme Court granted certiorari.

ISSUE: In products liability cases, can the "stream-of-commerce" doctrine displace the general rule that the exercise of judicial power is not lawful unless the defendant purposefully avails itself of the privilege of conducting activities within the forum state, thus invoking the benefits and protections of its laws?

HOLDING AND DECISION: (Kennedy, J.) No. In products liability cases, the "stream-of-commerce" doctrine cannot displace the general rule that the exercise of judicial power is not lawful unless the defendant purposefully avails itself of the privilege of conducting activities within the forum state, thus invoking the benefits and protections of its laws. The Supreme Court of New Jersey held that New Jersey's courts can exercise jurisdiction over a foreign manufacturer of a product as long as the manufacturer knows or reasonably should know that its products are distributed through a nationwide distribution system that might lead to those products being sold in any of the 50 states. That "stream-of-commerce" rule is taken from *Asahi Metal Industry Co. v. Superior Court of Cal., Solano County*, 480 U.S. 102 (1987), but the New Jersey Supreme Court misapplied that rule, which was imprecise to begin with and has caused confusion. Based on that test, the court concluded that J. McIntyre (D) was subject to New Jersey jurisdiction, even though the company had at no time advertised in, sent goods to, or in any way targeted the state. A court may subject a defendant to judgment only when the defendant has sufficient contacts with the sovereign such that the maintenance of the suit does not offend traditional notions of fair play and substantial justice. Free-form fundamental fairness notions divorced from traditional practice cannot transform a judgment rendered without authority into law. As a general rule, the sovereign's exercise of power requires some act by which the defendant purposefully avails itself of the privilege of conducting activities within the forum state, thus invoking the benefits and protections of its laws. In cases like this one, it is the defendant's purposeful availment that makes jurisdiction consistent with "fair play and substantial justice" notions. No "stream-of-commerce" doctrine can displace that general rule for products-liability cases. Where the individual or corporation explicitly consents to jurisdiction, is present in a state at the time a suit starts, is a citizen or has a domicile within the state, or is incorporated in the state, jurisdiction is proper, because all of those situations indicate an intent to submit to the laws of the state. Jurisdiction may also be proper where a defendant purposefully avails itself of the privilege of conducting activities within the forum state, thus invoking the benefits and protections of its laws. The stream-of-commerce exception to the general rule refers to the movement of goods from manufacturers through distributors to consumers, and advocates of the exception argue that the placement of goods into the stream of commerce with the expectation

Continued on next page.

that they will be purchased by consumers indicates purposeful availment. But the exception only holds where the activities manifest an intention to submit to the power of the sovereign. As a general rule, it is not enough that the defendant might have predicted that its goods would end up in the forum state. Although some of the justices in the *Asahi* case made foreseeability the touchstone of jurisdiction, this approach was rejected by other justices and did not muster a majority. Instead, *Asahi* required an act of the defendant purposefully directed at the forum state. It is the defendant's actions, not its expectations, which confer jurisdiction, since jurisdiction is in the first instance a question of authority rather than fairness or foreseeability. Moreover, personal jurisdiction requires a forum-by-forum, or sovereign-by-sovereign, analysis. The question is whether a defendant has followed a course of conduct directed at the society or economy existing within the jurisdiction of a given sovereign, so that the sovereign has the power to subject the defendant to judgment concerning that conduct. Applying these principles to the case at bar, J. McIntyre (D) directed marketing and sales efforts at the United States, but not directly to New Jersey, and because of that, a federal court might have jurisdiction, but a New Jersey state court does not. It is J. McIntyre's (D) purposeful contacts with New Jersey, not with the United States, that are relevant. Because J. McIntyre has not engaged in conduct purposefully directed at New Jersey, New Jersey state courts did not have jurisdiction to hear the case. Reversed.

CONCURRENCE: (Breyer, J.) The judgment is correct, but the outcome is determined by precedent, rather than by the plurality's strict no-jurisdiction rule. There is no reason to construct new general rules that limit jurisdiction, since the case can be decided on the basis of existing precedent. No precedent finds that a single isolated sale, even if accompanied by sales similar to the ones that occurred here, is sufficient. Nicastro (P) failed to meet his burden of showing that it was constitutionally proper to exercise jurisdiction over J. McIntyre (D), so there is no need to go beyond established precedent. Because the incident at issue does not implicate modern concerns, such as sales directed at the world via the internet, and because the factual record leaves many open questions, this is an unsuitable vehicle for making broad pronouncements that refashion basic jurisdictional rules. At a minimum, such a change to the law, in the way either the plurality or the New Jersey Supreme Court suggests, should not be made without a better understanding of the relevant contemporary commercial circumstances. Insofar as such considerations are relevant to any change in present law, they might be presented in a case (unlike the present one) in which the Solicitor General participates.

DISSENT: (Ginsburg, J.) J. McIntyre (D) wanted to establish a market for its product in the United States and took steps to do so. Where in the United States buyers of the product lived or where its machinery was operated was irrelevant; it simply wanted to sell its product in the United States. However, it also wanted to avoid products liability litigation, so it hired a distributor to ship its machines to the United States. Under longstanding precedent in *International Shoe Co. v. Washington*, 326 U.S. 310 (1945), personal jurisdiction would be established; the manufacturer would not be able to avoid being hauled into court simply by hiring an intermediary to make its sales for it. Thus, the plurality's decision turns the clock back to the days before long-arm statutes prevented such a liability-limiting scenario. Because J. McIntyre (D) targeted the entire United States, and because injury occurred in one of the states as a result of the alleged defect in its product, the state where the injury occurred is a forum entirely appropriate for adjudication of Nicastro's (P) claim. The relationship among the defendant, the forum, and the litigation determines whether due process permits the exercise of personal jurisdiction over a defendant, and "fictions of implied consent" or "corporate presence" do not advance the proper inquiry. Thus, the plurality's notion that consent is the animating concept draws no support from controlling precedent. Quite the contrary, precedent holds that a forum can exercise jurisdiction when its contacts with the controversy are sufficient; invocation of a fictitious consent, the Court has repeatedly said, is unnecessary and unhelpful. The marketing arrangement between J. McIntyre (D) and its distributor is representative of such arrangements for sales in the United States that are common in today's commercial world. The modern approach to jurisdiction covers such arrangements by emphasizing reason and fairness—it seems completely fair and reasonable, given the mode of trading involved, to require the international seller to defend at the place its products cause injury. Also litigational-convenience and choice-of-law considerations point in that direction. Due process would not be offended by requiring J. McIntyre (D) to defend in New Jersey as an incident of its efforts to develop a market for its industrial machines anywhere and everywhere in the United States, and the burden on it to defend in New Jersey would be fair, i.e., it would be a reasonable cost of transacting business internationally, in comparison to the burden on Nicastro (P) to have to go to England to gain recompense for an injury he sustained using J. McIntyre's (D) product at his workplace in New Jersey. J. McIntyre (D) purposefully availed itself of the U.S. market nationwide through its distributor, and thus purposefully availed itself of the market in each state in which its distributor sold its products. It would undermine principles of fundamental fairness to insulate the foreign manufacturer from accountability in court at the place within the United States where the manufacturer's products caused injury. Further, no precedent weighs against the judgment made by the New Jersey Supreme Court, and, as a practical matter, the plurality's judgment puts U.S.

Continued on next page.

plaintiffs at a disadvantage in comparison to similarly situated complainants elsewhere in the world. Finally, as those commentators who have articulated the concept of specific jurisdiction have advocated, it is appropriate to have considerations of litigational convenience and the respective situations of the parties determine when it is appropriate to subject a defendant to trial in the plaintiff's community.

▶ ANALYSIS

The absence of a majority opinion makes it difficult to identify a reliable rule. Three justices voted to reverse on the basis of a new rule that limits jurisdiction more severely than precedent; three others voted to reverse on the basis of precedent, with making a new rule; and three others voted to affirm on the basis of precedent. In addition, some of the litigational considerations referenced by the dissent, which are some of the considerations to be made in specific jurisdiction cases, include the convenience of witnesses and the ease of ascertaining the governing law. As to the parties, courts would differently appraise two situations: (1) cases involving a substantially local plaintiff, like Nicastro (P), injured by the activity of a defendant engaged in interstate or international trade; and (2) cases in which the defendant is a natural or legal person whose economic activities and legal involvements are largely home-based, i.e., entities without designs to gain substantial revenue from sales in distant markets. Courts presented with the first scenario, such as the one at bar—a local plaintiff injured by the activity of a manufacturer seeking to exploit a multistate or global market— have repeatedly confirmed that jurisdiction is appropriately exercised by courts of the place where the product was sold and caused injury.

Quicknotes

FORUM STATE The state in which a court, or other location in which a legal remedy may be sought, is located.

PURPOSEFUL AVAILMENT An element in determining whether a defendant had the required minimum contacts in a forum necessary in order for a court to exercise jurisdiction over the party, whereby the court determines whether the defendant intentionally conducted activities in the forum and thus knows, or could reasonably expect, that such conduct could give rise to litigation in that forum.

Goodyear Dunlop Tires Operations, S.A. v. Brown

Foreign subsidiaries of U.S. corporation (D) v. Decedents' parents (P)

131 S. Ct. 2846 (2011).

NATURE OF CASE: Appeal from state court's assertion of personal jurisdiction over foreign companies.

FACTS SUMMARY: The parents (P) of two American boys killed in a bus accident in France brought suit in North Carolina, where the boys had lived, against foreign tire companies (D) that were indirect subsidiaries of The Goodyear Tire and Rubber Company (D), a United States company. The foreign tire companies (D) moved to dismiss for lack of personal jurisdiction.

🏛 RULE OF LAW
A state may not exercise general personal jurisdiction over a foreign subsidiary of a U.S. corporation where the subsidiary lacks continuous and systematic business contacts with the state.

FACTS: The parents (P) of two American boys who were killed in a bus accident in France brought suit in North Carolina state court against Goodyear Tire and Rubber Company (Goodyear USA) (D) and three Goodyear subsidiaries (D) operating in Turkey, France, and Luxembourg. The parents (P) claimed that the accident resulted from a defective tire manufactured at the Turkish subsidiary's plant. Although Goodyear USA (D) operates in North Carolina, the three foreign subsidiaries (D) have no place of business, employees, or bank accounts in the state and neither solicit nor do business in the state. A small percentage of the subsidiaries' (D) tires were distributed in North Carolina by other Goodyear USA (D) affiliates, however. The subsidiaries (D) moved to dismiss the claims against them for lack of personal jurisdiction. The trial court denied the motion, and the North Carolina Court of Appeals affirmed, holding that the court had general jurisdiction over the subsidiaries (D) because their tires had reached the state through "the stream of commerce." The state's highest court denied review, and the United States Supreme Court granted certiorari.

ISSUE: May a state exercise general personal jurisdiction over a foreign subsidiary of a U.S. corporation where the subsidiary lacks continuous and systematic business contacts with the state?

HOLDING AND DECISION: (Ginsburg, J.) No. A state may not exercise general personal jurisdiction over a foreign subsidiary of a U.S. corporation where the subsidiary lacks continuous and systematic business contacts with the state. As stated in *International Shoe Co.* v. *Washington*, 326 U.S. 310, 316 (1945), and its progeny, a distinction exists between general and specific personal jurisdiction. General personal jurisdiction arises from a defendant's "continuous and systematic" affiliation with a state and permits a state to exercise personal jurisdiction over the defendant for any claim, regardless of whether the claim itself has any connection to the defendant's activities in the state. Specific personal jurisdiction arises from a connection between the state and the underlying claim, and permits a state to exercise jurisdiction only with respect to that claim. In this case, the North Carolina courts conflated the two types of jurisdiction, improperly using the isolated presence of the subsidiaries' products in the state as a result of others' actions to justify jurisdiction over the subsidiaries for claims having nothing to do with those products. The North Carolina court's stream-of-commerce analysis elided the essential difference between case-specific and general jurisdiction. Flow of a manufacturer's products into the forum may bolster an affiliation germane to specific jurisdiction, but ties serving to bolster the exercise of specific jurisdiction do not warrant a determination that based on those ties, the forum has general jurisdiction over a defendant. A corporation's "continuous activity of some sorts within a state," *International Shoe* instructed, "is not enough to support the demand that the corporation be amenable to suits unrelated to that activity." Reversed.

▶ ANALYSIS

Key to this case is the distinction between two types of personal jurisdiction: general and specific. General jurisdiction is all-purpose, in the sense that it allows any claim to be brought against a defendant as long as the defendant has "systematic and continuous" contacts with that forum. Specific jurisdiction exists where there is a connection between a forum and a particular controversy, and it is limited to that controversy. In this case, only general jurisdiction was in issue: The site of the accident and the factory where the tires were made were both outside of North Carolina, so there was no connection between the state and the controversy, and specific jurisdiction was therefore not properly at issue. As to whether general jurisdiction existed, the Court focused on "stream-of-commerce," and reached the conclusion that jurisdiction did not exist.

Quicknotes

GENERAL JURISDICTION Refers to the authority of a court to hear and determine all cases of a particular type.

PERSONAL JURISDICTION The court's authority over a person or parties to a lawsuit.

Community Trust Bancorp., Inc. v. Community Trust Financial Corp.

Kentucky corporation (P) v. Texas corporation (D)

2011 WL 673751 (U.S. District Ky. 2011).

NATURE OF CASE: Federal trial court's consideration of defendants' motion to dismiss on the grounds the court lacked personal jurisdiction over the corporate defendants.

FACT SUMMARY: In a Kentucky federal court, Community Trust Bancorp. (P) of Kentucky sued Community Trust Financial (D) of Texas on the grounds its use of the "Community Trust" designation was a trademark violation. Community Trust Financial (D) moved to dismiss the case for lack of personal jurisdiction.

🏛 RULE OF LAW
A company purposely avails itself of the privilege of conducting business in a state if the company's website is interactive enough to conclude that the company intended to interact with the residents of that state.

FACTS: In a Kentucky federal court, Community Trust Bancorp. (P) of Kentucky sued Community Trust Financial (D) of Texas on the grounds its use of the "Community Trust" designation was a trademark violation. Community Trust Financial (D) was also incorporated in Louisiana. Community Trust Financial (D) has offices only in Texas, Louisiana and Mississippi. The company promotes its business only in those states and does not promote in Kentucky. However, four residents of Kentucky accessed the website of Community Trust Financial (D) and submitted applications for new bank accounts. Community Trust Financial (D) approved the applications and sent the four customers passwords to access their new accounts. Of Community Trust Financial's (D) 69,000 accounts, these were the only four created by Kentucky residents. Community Trust Financial (D) moved to dismiss on the grounds the court lacked personal jurisdiction over it.

ISSUE: Does a company purposely avail itself of the privilege of conducting business in a state if the company's website is interactive enough to conclude that the company intended to interact with the residents of that state?

HOLDING AND DECISION: (Caldwell, J.) Yes. A company purposely avails itself of the privilege of conducting business in a state if the company's website is interactive enough to conclude that the company intended to interact with the residents of that state. When determining whether a court has specific personal jurisdiction over a defendant, the following factors are relevant. First, the defendant must purposefully avail himself of the privilege of acting in the forum state. Second, the cause of action must arise from the defendant's activities in the state.

Third, the acts of the defendant must have a substantial enough connection with the state to allow the exercise of jurisdiction to be reasonable. When the connection is a website, courts have developed a sliding scale to determine if a website can subject a company to personal jurisdiction in a particular state. At one end of the scale, a company purposely avails itself of the privilege of conducting business in a state if the company's website is interactive enough to conclude that the company intended to interact with the residents of that state. Typically, such a website allows residents of a state to enter into contracts with the company for a service or a product provided by the company. At the other end of the scale are passive, information-only websites that do not allow residents to purchases the company's products or services directly from the website. Here, it is true that only four of Community Trust Financial's (D) 69,000 accounts are in Kentucky. It is also true that Community Trust Financial (D) does not market itself in Kentucky. However, the significant fact is that when those four Kentucky residents applied for accounts via the website, Community Trust Financial (D) approved the accounts and sent those residents passwords to initialize the accounts. Accordingly, Community Trust Financial (D) intentionally sought to do business in the state of Kentucky. It is the nature and quality of the contact and not the quantity which is paramount. In addition, Community Trust Bancorp.'s (P) claim of trademark infringement has a substantial to Community Trust Financial's (D) activities in Kentucky. Lastly, jurisdiction in Kentucky is reasonable because Kentucky has an interest in protecting the interests of its citizens. The motion to dismiss is denied.

▌ ANALYSIS

As the text notes, the federal Sixth Circuit Court of Appeals found the court did not have personal jurisdiction over Community Trust Financial (D) and reversed this decision. It reversed on the ground that Community Trust Bancorp.'s (P) claim of trademark infringement did not arise from Community Trust Financial's (D) contacts with the state of Kentucky. The court found there was no substantial connection between the fact that four residents of Kentucky had accounts with Community Trust Financial (D) and Community Trust Bancorp.'s (P) general claim of trademark infringement.

■▬■

Continued on next page.

Quicknotes

MOTION TO DISMISS   Motion to terminate an action based on the adequacy of the pleadings, improper service or venue, etc.

PERSONAL JURISDICTION   The court's authority over a person or parties to a lawsuit.

Shaffer v. Heitner

Corporation (D) and corporate officers (D) v. Nonresident shareholder (P)

433 U.S. 186 (1977).

NATURE OF CASE: Appeal from a finding of state jurisdiction.

FACT SUMMARY: Heitner (P) brought a derivative suit against Greyhound (D) directors for antitrust losses it had sustained in Oregon. The suit was brought in Delaware, Greyhound's (D) state of incorporation.

RULE OF LAW
Jurisdiction cannot be founded on property within a state unless there are sufficient contacts within the meaning of the test developed in *International Shoe.*

FACTS: Heitner (P) owned one share of Greyhound (D) stock. Greyhound (D) had been subjected to a large antitrust judgment in Oregon. Heitner (P), a nonresident of Delaware, brought a derivative suit in Delaware, the state of Greyhound's (D) incorporation. Jurisdiction was based on sequestration of Greyhound (D) stock which was deemed to be located within the state of incorporation. The Delaware sequestration statute allowed property within the state to be seized ex parte to compel the owner to submit to the in personam jurisdiction of the court. None of the stock was actually in Delaware, but a freeze order was placed on the corporate books. Greyhound (D) made a special appearance to challenge the court's jurisdiction to hear the matter. Greyhound (D) argued that the sequestration statute was unconstitutional under the line of cases beginning with *Snidatch,* 395 U.S. 337 (1969). Greyhound (D) also argued that there were insufficient contacts with Delaware to justify an exercise of jurisdiction. The Delaware courts found that the sequestration statute was valid since it was not a per se seizure of the property and was merely invoked to compel out-of-state residents to defend actions within the state. Little or no consideration was given to the "contact" argument based on a finding that the presence of the stock within the state conferred quasi-in-rem jurisdiction.

ISSUE: May a state assume jurisdiction over an issue merely because defendant's property happens to be within the state?

HOLDING AND DECISION: (Marshall, J.) No. Mere presence of property within a state is insufficient to confer jurisdiction on a court absent independent contacts within the meaning of *International Shoe,* 326 U.S. 310 (1945), which would make acceptance constitutional. We expressly disapprove that line of cases represented by *Harris v. Balk,* 198 U.S. 215 (1905), which permits jurisdiction merely because the property happens to be within the state.

If sufficient contacts do not exist to assume jurisdiction absent the presence of property within the state, it cannot be invoked on the basis of property within the court's jurisdiction. We base this decision on the fundamental concepts of justice and fair play required under the Due Process and Equal Protection Clauses of the Fourteenth Amendment. Here, the stock is not the subject of the controversy. There is no claim to ownership of it or injury caused by it. The defendants do not reside in Delaware or have any contacts there. The injury occurred in Oregon. No activities complained of were done within the forum. Finally, Heitner (P) is not even a Delaware resident. Jurisdiction was improperly granted. Reversed.

CONCURRENCE: (Powell, J.) Property permanently within the state, e.g., real property, should confer jurisdiction.

CONCURRENCE: (Stevens, J.) Purchase of stock in the market place should not confer in rem jurisdiction in the state of incorporation.

CONCURRENCE AND DISSENT: (Brennan, J.) The Delaware sequestration statute's sole purpose is to force in personam jurisdiction through a quasi-in-rem seizure. The opinion is purely advisory in that if the court finds the statute invalid, the rest of the opinion is not required. Delaware never argued that it was attempting to obtain in rem jurisdiction. Further, a derivative suit may be brought in the state of incorporation. Greyhound's (D) choice of incorporation in Delaware is a prima facie showing of submission to its jurisdiction.

ANALYSIS

While the corporation could be sued in its state of incorporation under the dissent's theory, the suit is against the directors and neither the site of the wrong nor the residence of a defendant is in Delaware. The decision will only have a major impact in cases such as herein where the state really has no reason to want to adjudicate the issue. Of course, real property would still be treated as an exception.

■=■

Quicknotes

EX PARTE A proceeding commenced by one party without providing any opposing parties with notice or which is uncontested by an adverse party.

IN REM An action against property.

Continued on next page.

JURISDICTION The authority of a court to hear and declare judgment in respect to a particular matter.

Burnham v. Superior Court

Husband (P) v. Court (D)

495 U.S. 604 (1990).

NATURE OF CASE: Review of order denying motion to quash service of summons.

FACT SUMMARY: Burnham (P) was personally served with process while temporarily in California on business, while visiting his children.

🏛 RULE OF LAW
The Fourteenth Amendment does not deny a state jurisdiction over a person personally served with process while temporarily in a state, in a suit unrelated to his activities in the state.

FACTS: The Burnhams lived in New Jersey. After they separated, the wife moved to California. Mrs. Burnham filed a divorce action in California. At one point, Mr. Burnham (P) came to California on business. He had no other contacts with California. On this trip, he was served with the divorce action papers. He moved to quash, contending that his contacts with California were insufficient to confer jurisdiction. The trial court denied the motion, and the state court of appeal denied his petition for mandamus. The United States Supreme Court granted review.

ISSUE: Does the Fourteenth Amendment deny a state jurisdiction over a person personally served with process while temporarily in a state, in a suit unrelated to his activities in the state?

HOLDING AND DECISION: (Scalia, J.) No. The Fourteenth Amendment does not deny a state jurisdiction over a person personally served with process while temporarily in a state, in a suit unrelated to his activities in the state. It is a firmly established principle of personal jurisdiction that courts of a state have jurisdiction over persons physically present in a state. The case decided by this court which raise fourteenth amendment due process considerations are those where state attempts to exercise jurisdiction over a nonresident who is not physically present. In a situation where the nonresident is served while physically present, no due process implication is made by service of process, no matter what the reason for his presence may be. Affirmed.

CONCURRENCE: (White, J.) The rule here is so well established that no facial or as-applied challenge can be made.

CONCURRENCE: (Brennan, J.) The plurality incorrectly emphasizes the historical acceptance of the rule. This is an incorrect approach, as this Court may strike down a well-established rule it finds unconstitutional. Rather, in any fairness analysis, it does not offend notions of fair play and justice to subject a physically present nonresident to jurisdiction.

CONCURRENCE: (Stevens, J.) The various opinions give excessive analysis to a very easy case whose result was self-evident.

▶ ANALYSIS

United States Supreme Court jurisprudence in this area goes back to 1877 with *Penneyer v. Neff*, 95 U.S. 714. Since that case, the court has fashioned a rule that out-of-state service may only be had on defendants having certain contacts with the state. The present case represents a total rejection of the notion of applying the same test to a physically-in-state defendant.

■══■

Quicknotes

DUE PROCESS The constitutional mandate requiring the courts to protect and enforce individuals' rights and liberties consistent with prevailing principles of fairness and justice and prohibiting the federal and state governments from such activities that deprive its citizens of life, liberty, or property interest.

QUASH To vacate, annul, void.

■══■

Providing Notice and an Opportunity to Be Heard

Quick Reference Rules of Law

Mullane v. Central Hanover Bank & Trust Co.

Special guardian (D) v. Corporate trustee (P)

339 U.S. 306 (1950).

NATURE OF CASE: Review of judgment over-ruling objections to the sufficiency of the notice provision of the New York Banking Law.

FACT SUMMARY: Central Hanover Bank & Trust Co. (P) pooled a number of small trust funds, and beneficiaries (some of whom lived out of state) were notified by publication in a local newspaper.

🏛 RULE OF LAW
In order to satisfy due process challenges, notice must be by means calculated to inform the desired parties, and, where they reside outside the state and their names and addresses are available, notice by publication is insufficient.

FACTS: A New York statute allowed corporate trustees to pool the assets of numerous small trusts administered by them. This allowed more efficient and economical administration of the funds. Each participating trust shared ratably in the common fund, but the trustees held complete control of all assets. A periodic accounting of profits, losses, and assets were to be submitted to the courts for approval. Beneficiaries were to be notified of the accounting so that they might object to any irregularities in the administration of the common fund. Once approved by the court, their claims would be barred. A guardian was appointed to protect the interests of principal and income beneficiaries. Central Hanover Bank & Trust Co. (P) established a common fund by consolidating the corpus of 113 separate trusts under their control. Notice of the common fund was sent to all interested parties along with the relevant portions of the statute. Notice of accountings was by publication in a local New York newspaper. Mullane (D) was the appointed guardian for all parties known and unknown who had an interest in the trust's income. He objected to the sufficiency of the statutory notice provisions claiming that they violated the Due Process Clause of the Fourteenth Amendment. Notice by publication was not a reasonable method of informing interested parties that their rights were being affected, especially with regard to out-of-state beneficiaries. Mullane's (D) objections were overruled in state courts and the present federal appeal was brought by him.

ISSUE: Is notice by publication sufficient to satisfy due process challenges where the parties to be informed reside outside the state and an alternative means, better calculated to give actual notice, is available?

HOLDING AND DECISION: (Jackson, J.) No. The purpose of a notice requirement is to inform parties that their rights are being affected. Therefore, the method chosen should, if at all possible, be reasonably designed to accomplish this end. Notice in a New York legal paper is not reasonably calculated to provide out-of-state residents with the desired information. While the state has a right to discharge trustees of their liabilities through the acceptance of their accounting, it must also provide beneficiaries with adequate notice so that their rights to contest the accounting are not lost. In cases where the identity or whereabouts of beneficiaries or future interest holders are unknown, then publication is the most viable alternate means available for giving notice. Publication is only a supplemental method of giving notice. However, the court will approve its use where alternative methods are not reasonably possible or practical. Where alternative methods, better calculated to give actual notice, are available, publication is an impermissible means of providing notice. Notice to known beneficiaries via publication is inadequate, not because it, in fact, fails to inform everyone, but, because under the circumstances, it is not readily calculated to reach those who could easily be informed by other means at hand. Since publication to known beneficiaries is ineffective, the statutory requirement violates the Due Process Clause of the Fourteenth Amendment. These parties have, at least potentially, been deprived of property without due process of law. With respect to remote future interest holders and unknown parties, publication is permissible. Reversed.

▶ ANALYSIS

Ineffective notice provisions violate procedural due process rights. As in all due process challenges, there must be a legitimate state interest and the means selected must be reasonably adapted to accomplish the state's purpose. While in *Mullane* the state's ends were permissible, the method of giving notice was unreasonable as it pertained to known parties. As has been previously stated, publication is only a supplementary method for giving notice. It is normally used in conjunction with other means when personal service by hand is unavailable or impractical. *Mullane* has been applied to condemnation cases where a known owner of property was never personally served. See *Schroeder v. City of New York*, 371 U.S. 208 (1962). Factors considered by the Court involve the nature of the action, whether the party's whereabouts or identity is known or unknown, whether he is a resident, and whether or not he has attempted to avoid personal service. If an attempt to avoid service is made, then constructive service by

Continued on next page.

publication in conjunction with substitute service by mail is permitted. Finally, foreign corporations are generally required to appoint resident agents authorized to accept service of process.

∎═∎

Quicknotes

DUE PROCESS CLAUSE Clauses found in the Fifth and Fourteenth Amendments to the United States Constitution providing that no person shall be deprived of "life, liberty, or property, without due process of law."

NOTICE BY PUBLICATION A means of providing notice pursuant to statute to parties having an interest in a suit by publication in a newspaper of general circulation.

∎═∎

National Equipment Rental, Ltd. v. Szukhent

Farm equipment supplier (P) v. Defaulting lessee (D)

375 U.S. 311 (1964).

NATURE OF CASE: Appeal from dismissal of action to recover on a lease.

FACT SUMMARY: Szukhent (D) leased farm equipment from National Equipment Rental, Ltd. (National) (P). The printed lease provided that Szukhent (D) designated Weinberg as agent to accept service of process in New York. When National (P) commenced this action on the lease, Weinberg was served, and she mailed the summons to Szukhent (D).

🏛 RULE OF LAW
A party to a private contract may appoint an agent to receive service of process where the agent is not personally known to the party and is not expressly required to transmit notice to the party but does promptly accept and transmit notice.

FACTS: Szukhent (D), a Michigan resident, leased farm equipment from National Equipment Rental, Ltd. (National) (P), a New York corporation. The lease was a printed one. It provided that Szukhent (D), a lessee, designated Weinberg, a New York resident, as agent for the purpose of accepting service of any process within New York. Szukhent (D) did not know Weinberg, and the lease did not expressly require Weinberg to transmit notice to Szukhent (D). National (P) brought this action, alleging that Szukhent (D) had failed to make any payments as required by the lease. The marshall delivered copies of the summons and complaint to Weinberg who, the same day, mailed them to Szukhent (D) with a letter stating that the documents had been served on her as Szukhent's (D) agent. National (P) also notified Szukhent (D) of the service of process on Weinberg. The district court granted Szukhent's (D) motion to quash service because the lease agreement had not explicitly required Weinberg to notify Szukhent (D) of the service of process. The court of appeals affirmed and National (P) petitioned for certiorari.

ISSUE: Is a person, who is designated by a party to a private contract to act as agent to receive service of process, who is unknown to the party and is not expressly required to transmit notice to the party but does promptly accept and transmit notice, an agent authorized by appointment?

HOLDING AND DECISION: (Stewart, J.) Yes. This case does not involve a due process problem since Szukhent (D) did, in fact, receive timely and complete notice. Here, the purpose underlying the provision designating Weinberg was to assure that any litigation under the lease would be conducted in New York. Parties to a contract may agree in advance to submit to the jurisdiction of a given court, to permit notice to be served by the opposing

party, or to waive notice altogether. Further, Weinberg's prompt acceptance and transmittal to Szukhent (D) of the summons and complaint was sufficient to validate the agency even though there was no explicit requirement that she do so. Weinberg was appointed Szukhent's (D) agent for the single purpose of receiving service of process. An agent with such limited authority can in no meaningful sense be deemed to have an interest antagonistic to Szukhent (D). Hence, the fact that Szukhent (D) did not know her is irrelevant. Here, prompt notice to Szukhent (D) having been given, Weinberg was his agent authorized by appointment to receive process within the meaning of Fed. R. Civ. P. 4(e)(2). Reversed and remanded.

DISSENT: (Black, J.) This decision will encourage large companies to write their contracts so that any persons whom they want to sue will have to come to the company's state to defend. The very threat of such a suit may force payment of alleged claims, even where they're without merit. Further, since National (P) prepared the printed lease, Szukhent (D) should not be bound by the appointment without proof that he understandingly consented to be sued in a state that is not his residence.

DISSENT: (Brennan, J.): Who is "an agent authorized by appointment" should be determined by federal standards, not state law. The rule should be interpreted as denying validity to the appointment of a purported agent whose interest conflict with those of his supposed principal. In addition, the appointment should include an explicit condition the agent transmit process to the principal. Finally, the individual purchaser should not be bound by the appointment without proof, in addition to his signature, that the individual consented to being sued in a state that is not his residence, because the corporate plaintiff prepared the printed form contract.

▶ ANALYSIS

When a person files a general appearance he consents to the jurisdiction of the court. In cases involving contracts, it has been held that a party may consent in advance to the jurisdiction of a court in the event that a lawsuit arises. However, as expressed by the dissent, all courts are not agreed upon the validity of such clauses. There is a growing tendency to find no true consent existed if the agreement was an adhesion contract. [Note: In 2007, Fed. R. Civ. P. 4(e)(2) was renumbered as 4(e)(2)(A)-(C).]

Continued on next page.

Quicknotes

LAW OF AGENCY A fiduciary relationship whereby authority is granted to an agent to act on behalf of the principal in order to effectuate the principal's objective.

QUASH To vacate, annul, void.

State ex rel. Sivnksty v. Duffield

Reckless driver (P) v. Trial court judge (D)

W. Va. Sup. Ct. App., 137 W.Va. 112, 71 S.E.2d 113 (1952).

NATURE OF CASE: Petition for a writ of prohibition in an action to recover damages for personal injury.

FACT SUMMARY: While he was vacationing, Sivnksty's (P), a nonresident, automobile struck and injured two children. While he was in jail awaiting trial for reckless driving, he was served with service of process in a civil suit brought by one of the children.

🏛 RULE OF LAW
A person confined in jail on a criminal charge or imprisoned on conviction for such charge is subject to service of civil process, irrespective of the question of residence, if he was voluntarily in the jurisdiction at the time of the arrest and confinement.

FACTS: While he was vacationing, Sivnksty's (P) car struck and injured two children. Sivnksty (P) was a nonresident. He was arrested for reckless driving and, being unable to post bond, was incarcerated in the county jail until his trial three days later. While he was in jail, he was served with process in a tort action brought by one of the children. He appeared in the civil action and filed a plea in abatement alleging that the court was without jurisdiction because at the time of service he was a nonresident and a prisoner in the jail. When the court sustained a demurrer to the plea, Sivnksty (P) petitioned for a writ of prohibition.

ISSUE: May a nonresident defendant who came into the jurisdiction for only a few days and is confined in jail on a criminal charge be served with process commencing a civil action based on the same facts as those involved in the criminal prosecution?

HOLDING AND DECISION: (Riley, J.) Yes. A person confined in jail on a criminal charge or imprisoned on conviction for such charge is subject to service of civil process, irrespective of the question of residence, if he was voluntarily in the jurisdiction at the time of the arrest and confinement. The purpose for the privilege of immunity from civil process on nonresidents of a county or state charged with a crime there was the protection of the court from interference with judicial processes. Later, the rule was enlarged for the protection of suitors, witnesses, jurors, and court officials from process in both civil and criminal cases. The immunity has underlying it the public policy that a person, charged with a crime in a state or county where he is not a resident, will not be deterred from appearing before the courts there. The immunity will, hopefully, encourage the appearance of a person so charged. The rule is generally stated that a nonresident

who voluntarily submits to the jurisdiction of a state court in answer to an indictment, and who is not at the time a fugitive from justice, is privileged while attending court from service of process in a civil suit. In this case, Sivnksty (P) did not enter the county in response to a criminal process. At the time he entered, he had committed no crime. Since he did not come into the county under criminal process, the reason for the application of the immunity rule is not present, and he is not entitled to the writ. Writ denied.

DISSENT: (Lovins, J.) Whether Sivnksty (P) entered the county voluntarily or not is irrelevant. The immunity is applicable to him here.

▶ ANALYSIS

The general rule is that the immunity extends to witnesses, parties, and perhaps attorneys during the necessary time required to attend the court proceeding. As demonstrated here, the controlling purpose of the trip must be attendance at court. Another public policy purpose for the immunity is to encourage the attendance of witnesses and thus develop the full facts of the case. One court has held that none of the historical reasons for the immunity exist today, and that the problem is best solved by the application of the doctrine of forum non conveniens. Under that doctrine, the court may dismiss an action if it determines that it would not be a fair and appropriate place for trial, and that another and more appropriate forum is available.

Quicknotes

DEMURRER The assertion that the opposing party's pleadings are insufficient and that the demurring party should not be made to answer.

FORUM NON CONVENIENS An equitable doctrine permitting a court to refrain from hearing and determining a case when the matter may be more properly and fairly heard in another forum.

PLEA IN ABATEMENT A plea brought by a defendant contesting the plaintiff's place, mode or time of asserting his claim without challenge to its merits.

WRIT OF PROHIBITION A writ issued by a superior court prohibiting a lower court from exceeding its jurisdiction or from usurping jurisdiction beyond that authorized by law.

Wyman v. Newhouse

Florida resident (P) v. Former lover (D)

93 F.2d 313 (2d Cir. 1937), *cert. denied*, 303 U.S. 664 (1938).

NATURE OF CASE: Appeal from dismissal of action following a judgment entered by default in a Florida state court. The recovery there was for money loaned, money advanced, and for seduction under promise of marriage.

FACT SUMMARY: Wyman (P), a Florida resident, wrote Newhouse (D), a New York resident and her lover, she was leaving the United States and wanted to see him one more time. When he arrived in Florida, he was served with process.

🏛 RULE OF LAW
A judgment recovered in a sister state, through the fraud of the party procuring the appearance of another, is not binding on the latter when an attempt is made to enforce such judgment in another state.

FACTS: Wyman (P) and Newhouse (D) were both married, but before this suit Wyman's (P) husband died. They had known each other for many years and had engaged in meretricious relations. Wyman (P), a Florida resident, sent Newhouse (D), a New York resident, a telegram and letter saying that her mother was dying in Ireland and that she was leaving the United States for good and wanted to see Newhouse (D) and discuss her affairs with him before she left. She repeated this in a phone conversation and wrote another letter expressing her love and affection for him. When Newhouse (D) got off the plane in Florida, he was met by a sheriff's deputy who served him with process. Newhouse (D) returned to New York and consulted his lawyer who advised him to ignore the summons. He did so, and judgment was entered by default. The judgment was overturned and, before trial, the complaint was dismissed. Wyman (P) appealed.

ISSUE: Does a judgment which was procured fraudulently lack jurisdiction?

HOLDING AND DECISION: (Manton, J.) Yes. A judgment procured fraudulently lacks jurisdiction and is null and void. A fraud affecting the jurisdiction is equivalent to a lack of jurisdiction. A judgment recovered in a sister state, through the fraud of the party procuring the appearance of another, is not binding on the latter when an attempt is made to enforce such judgment in another state. In this case, Newhouse (D) was not required to proceed against the judgment in Florida. He was not required to make out a defense to the merits of that suit. His equitable defense in answer to a suit on the judgment is sufficient. The judgment dismissing the complaint is affirmed.

▶ ANALYSIS

A court will decline to exercise jurisdiction over a defendant even though he has been properly served with process, where he was induced to come into the state by the plaintiff's fraud or trickery, as this case demonstrates. Actually, if the defendant was personally served within the territorial boundaries of the court, and if the fraud was not called to the court's attention, the court could proceed with the case. The more accurate statement of the rule is that upon proof of the fraud, the court will decline to exercise jurisdiction.

Quicknotes

FRAUD A false representation of facts with the intent that another will rely on the misrepresentation to his detriment.

MERETRICIOUS RELATIONSHIP A stable, marital-like relationship where both parties cohabit with knowledge that a lawful marriage between them does not exist.

Connecticut v. Doehr

State (D) and Tort claimant (D) v. Tortfeasor (P)

501 U.S. 1 (1991).

NATURE OF CASE: Review of order quashing attachment levied on real estate.

FACT SUMMARY: Connecticut (D) law permitted ex parte prejudgment attachment of real estate without a showing of exigent circumstances.

🏛 RULE OF LAW
A state may not allow ex parte prejudgment attachment of property without a showing of exigent circumstances.

FACTS: DiGiovanni (D), a tort claimant against Doehr (P), utilized Connecticut's (D) prejudgment attachment procedure. Ex parte, he filed a declaration setting forth the nature of his claim against Doehr (P). State law required no showing of exigent circumstances necessitating prejudgment attachment. The court issued an attachment order. Doehr (P) responded with a federal suit challenging the constitutionality of the procedure. The district court upheld the procedure's validity, but the Second Circuit reversed. The United States Supreme Court granted review.

ISSUE: May a state allow an ex parte prejudgment attachment of real estate without a showing of exigent circumstances?

HOLDING AND DECISION: (White, J.) No. A state may not allow ex parte prejudgment attachment of property without a showing of exigent circumstances. In the context of suits between private parties, the analysis for the validity of prejudgment remedies involves (1) consideration of the private interest involved, (2) the risk of erroneous deprivation of that interest, and (3) the interest of the party seeking the prejudgment remedy. Here, Connecticut's (D) statutory attachment procedure clearly fails under this analysis. First, the owner of the attached property has an obvious interest in his property, and attachment places a severe restriction on the property's alienability and encumberability. The ex parte nature of the proceeding presents serious risk of erroneous deprivation, as a self-serving declaration will suffice to allow the attachment. Finally, if the party seeking attachment has no reason to fear the property may be secreted, his interest is not all that compelling. For these reasons, absent exigent circumstances, an ex parte application is insufficient to warrant attachment of real estate. Affirmed and remanded.

CONCURRENCE: (Rehnquist, C.J.) Unlike attachment of personalty, attachment of realty should not require a bond.

▶ ANALYSIS

The analysis used by the Court was devised in *Mathews v. Eldridge*, 424 U.S. 319 (1976). That case involved deprivation by government as opposed to a private litigant. The Court, in adopting the analysis, believed the basic considerations to be the same without regard to the public or private status of the litigant.

Quicknotes

ATTACHMENT The seizing of the property of one party in anticipation of, or in order to satisfy, a favorable judgment obtained by another party.

EX PARTE A proceeding commenced by one party.

EXIGENT CIRCUMSTANCES Circumstances requiring an extraordinary or immediate response; an exception to the prohibition on a warrantless arrest or search when police officers believe probable cause to exist and there is no time for obtaining a warrant.

CHAPTER 4

Jurisdiction Over the Subject Matter of the Action—The Court's Competency

Quick Reference Rules of Law

Lacks v. Lacks

Divorcing husband (P) v. Wife (D)

N.Y. Ct. App., 41 N.Y.2d 71, 359 N.E.2d 384 (1976).

NATURE OF CASE: Appeal from order vacating final judgment of divorce.

FACT SUMMARY: Mrs. Lacks (D) moved to vacate her husband's (P) divorce judgment contending the court lacked subject matter jurisdiction.

🏛 **RULE OF LAW**
A final judgment is not void for lack of subject matter jurisdiction if the defect alleged concerns a judicial error as to the existence of a necessary element of the cause of action.

FACTS: Mrs. Lacks (D) contended that because her husband (P) failed to meet the residency requirements of a New York statute under which he had obtained a final divorce judgment, the rendering court lacked subject matter jurisdiction. Thus she argued that judgment was void. The appellate courts held the judgment valid, and Mrs. Lacks (D) appealed.

ISSUE: Is a final judgment void for lack of subject matter jurisdiction if the rendering court erroneously found present all the requisite elements of the cause of action?

HOLDING AND DECISION: (Breitel, C.J.) No. A final judgment is not void for lack of subject matter jurisdiction merely because the rendering court erroneously found the existence of a necessary element of the cause of action. The absence of a necessary element of the cause of action presents a different question than that concerning the existence of subject matter jurisdiction. The court's subject matter jurisdiction is statutory and is unquestionable in this case. There is no jurisdictional question present. Affirmed.

▌ *ANALYSIS*

There are two necessary issues which must be resolved before a particular action may be entertained by a particular tribunal. The more important issue is whether the particular court has jurisdiction over the subject matter of the action. If it does not, it has no power to act. Subject matter jurisdiction is purely statutory and cannot be stipulated to. Personal jurisdiction, on the other hand, can be agreed to by the parties. A court must have both subject matter jurisdiction and jurisdiction over the parties in order to act.

Quicknotes

SUBJECT MATTER JURISDICTION The authority of the court to hear and decide actions involving a particular type of issue or subject.

Mas v. Perry

Apartment renters (P) v. Voyeuristic owner (D)

489 F.2d 1396 (5th Cir.), *cert. denied*, 419 U.S. 842 (1974).

NATURE OF CASE: Appeal from award of damages for invasion of privacy.

FACT SUMMARY: Perry (D) appealed a damages award, contending it had been entered in the absence of diversity of citizenship, and thus the federal court lacked subject matter jurisdiction.

🏛 RULE OF LAW
Mere residence in a state does not establish domicile for purposes of diversity jurisdiction.

FACTS: The Mases (P) returned to Louisiana to complete Mr. Mas's (P) education. Formerly, Mr. Mas (P) was a French citizen, and Mrs. Mas (P) was a citizen of Mississippi. After Mas (P) finished his education, they were unsure of where they would live. While in Louisiana, they rented an apartment from Perry (D) and subsequently discovered he had used two-way mirrors to invade their privacy. They sued in federal court on the basis of diversity and obtained a $20,000 judgment. Perry (D) appealed, contending they were citizens of Louisiana, and, therefore, a lack of diversity existed.

ISSUE: Does residence in a state create domicile for purposes of federal diversity jurisdiction?

HOLDING AND DECISION: (Ainsworth, J.) No. Mere residence in a state does not establish domicile for purposes for diversity jurisdiction. Domicile is the true, fixed, permanent home and principal establishment of home base. In this case, the Mases (P) had no fixed intent to remain in Louisiana. Thus, Mrs. Mas (P) remained a Mississippi domiciliary and Mr. Mas (P) remained a France domiciliary. As a result, complete diversity existed. Affirmed.

▌*ANALYSIS*

Citizenship refers to a person's domicile for purposes of diversity jurisdiction. As can be seen from this case, domicile is a more permanent statement of abode than mere residency. The proper time to determine whether diversity exists is at the time suit is commenced. Subsequent changes in domicile are irrelevant.

■=■

Quicknotes

DIVERSITY OF CITIZENSHIP Parties are citizens of different states, or one party is an alien; a factor, along with a statutorily set dollar value of the matter in controversy, that allows a federal district court to exercise its authority to hear a lawsuit based on diversity jurisdiction.

DIVERSITY JURISDICTION The authority of a federal court to hear and determine cases involving parties who are of different states and an amount in controversy greater than a statutorily set amount.

DOMICILE A person's permanent home or principal establishment to which he has an intention of returning when he is absent therefrom.

■=■

H.K. Huilin International Trade Co., Ltd. v. Kevin Multiline Polymer Inc.

Nonresident alien corporation (P) v. U.S. citizen and nonresident alien (D)

___ F. Supp.2d ___, 2012 WL 5386103, U.S. Dist. Ct., (E.D.N.Y. 2012).

NATURE OF CASE: Federal trial court's consideration of whether it had subject matter jurisdiction over a case involving a nonresident alien corporation on one side and a United States citizen and an alien resident on the other.

FACT SUMMARY: H.K. Huilin International Trade Co. (P) was a non-resident alien corporation. It brought suit in federal court against a New York corporation and an alien residing in New York.

🏛 RULE OF LAW
28 U.S.C. § 1332(a)(2) and (3), the diversity jurisdiction statute, does not provide jurisdiction over a case involving a nonresident alien on one side and resident aliens and United States citizens on the other.

FACTS: H.K. Huilin International Trade Co. (H.K. Huilin) (P), a Chinese corporation, was a nonresident alien corporation with its principle place of business in Hong Kong. It brought suit against three companies with their principle place of business in New York, one of which was Kevin Multiline Polymer Inc. (D). A fourth defendant was an individual, Chao Ming Zhen (D). Zhen (D) was a Chinese citizen living in New York. Several defendants moved to dismiss the action on the grounds the federal trial court did not have subject matter jurisdiction because Zhen (D) was not a United States citizen.

ISSUE: Does 28 U.S.C. § 1332(a)(2) and (3), the diversity jurisdiction statute, provide jurisdiction over a case involving a nonresident alien on one side and resident aliens and United States citizens on the other?

HOLDING AND DECISION: (Garaufis, J.) No. 28 U.S.C. § 1332(a)(2) and (3), the diversity jurisdiction statute, does not provide jurisdiction over a case involving a nonresident alien on one side and resident aliens and United States citizens on the other. A prior version of the statute held that aliens living within a state should be viewed as residing in that state for purposes of the diversity analysis. A minority of courts viewed this statute as providing for subject matter jurisdiction when the case was between a foreign subject and an alien residing in a particular state. Congress passed an amendment in 2011 to confirm that aliens are viewed as living in a particular state only when the other party to the suit is a U.S. citizen. If those two parties reside in the same state, diversity jurisdiction does not arise. However, when one party is an alien and the other party is an alien, that fact that the second party resides in a state does not give rise to diversity jurisdiction. Diversity jurisdiction involving an alien is possible between an alien and a citizen of a state. Diversity jurisdiction is not possible where the suit is between an alien on one side and an alien and a United States citizen on the other. In this case, diversity jurisdiction may arise if H.K. Huilin (P), the alien plaintiff, decided to drop Zhen (D), the resident alien, from the case.

▶ ANALYSIS

As the case provides, diversity jurisdiction typically arises between citizens of different states. It may also arise when a foreign subject or alien sues a United States citizen. It does not arise when aliens sue each other in federal court, even if one of the parties is a United States citizen. An alien or foreign subject can be a party to a lawsuit via diversity jurisdiction only if United States citizens are both plaintiffs and defendants. In each case, the amount in question must exceed $75,000.

Quicknotes

DIVERSITY JURISDICTION The authority of a federal court to hear and determine cases involving a statutory sum and in which the parties are citizens of different states, or in which one party is an alien.

SUBJECT MATTER JURISDICTION The authority of the court to hear and decide actions involving a particular type of issue or subject.

A.F.A. Tours, Inc. v. Whitchurch

Travel agency (P) v. Competing ex-employee (D)

937 F.2d 82 (2d Cir. 1991).

NATURE OF CASE: Appeal from dismissal of action for damages for misappropriation of trade secrets.

FACT SUMMARY: A.F.A. Tours, Inc.'s (P) diversity action was dismissed on the grounds that the amount-in-controversy requirement had not been satisfied, even though the issue had not been briefed.

🏛 RULE OF LAW
A court may not dismiss a diversity action for failure to meet the amount-in-controversy requirement without allowing a plaintiff to brief the issue.

FACTS: A.F.A. Tours, Inc. (A.F.A.) (P) was in the business of providing guided tours. Whitchurch (D), a former A.F.A. (P) employee, formed a competing company. A.F.A. (P) filed an action in federal court, alleging misappropriation of trade secrets, namely customer lists. Jurisdiction was based on diversity. At a hearing, the court raised sua sponte the issue of whether A.F.A.'s (P) damages could meet the $50,000 jurisdictional requirement. Concluding it could not, the court dismissed. A.F.A. (P) appealed.

ISSUE: May a court dismiss a diversity action for failure to meet the amount-in-controversy requirement without allowing a plaintiff to brief the issue?

HOLDING AND DECISION: (Kearse, J.) No. A court may not dismiss a diversity action for failure to meet the amount-in-controversy requirement without allowing a plaintiff to brief the issue. The law requires that a court cannot dismiss for failure to meet the jurisdictional requirement in diversity cases unless appears to a legal certainty that such is the case. In all but the most extreme situations, the record before a court which raises the issue sua sponte without briefing will be insufficient for a court to meet this requirement. Here, whether A.F.A. (P) has in fact suffered losses of at least $50,000 requires a somewhat detailed factual analysis, which the court could not have done on the record before it. Reversed.

▶ ANALYSIS

Diversity jurisdiction was created to protect defendants from unduly parochial local judges and juries. With the advent of modern travel and communications, such concerns have lessened. Some have called for consequent abolition of diversity jurisdiction. Congress's response in 1988 was to increase the amount in controversy requirement from $10,000 to $50,000.

Quicknotes

AMOUNT IN CONTROVERSY The value of a claim sought by a party to a lawsuit.

DIVERSITY ACTION An action commenced by a citizen of one state against a citizen of another state or against an alien, involving an amount in controversy of $10,000 or more, over which the federal court has jurisdiction.

SUA SPONTE An action taken by the court by its own motion and without the suggestion of one of the parties.

Freeland v. Liberty Mut. Fire Ins. Co.

Insured owner of vehicle (P) v. Insurance company (D)

632 F.3d 250 (6th Cir. 2011).

NATURE OF CASE: Federal appeals court's consideration as to whether district court had subject matter jurisdiction over the case.

FACT SUMMARY: The Freelands' (P) son and daughter-in-law were killed in a car crash. The Freelands' (P) insurance company, Liberty Mutual Fire Ins. Co. (D), only offered them $25,000. The Freelands (P) brought suit seeking $100,000 under the insurance policy.

🏛 RULE OF LAW
When a plaintiff seeks a declaratory judgment in federal court alleging subject matter jurisdiction via diversity of the parties, the amount in controversy is not the amount of money sought by the plaintiff, but rather the value of the monetary consequences to the defendant that may result from the litigation.

FACTS: The Freelands (P) loaned their car to their son and daughter-in-law. Both were later killed in a car crash. At the time of the accident, their son was an uninsured motorist. Liberty Mutual Fire Ins. Co. (Liberty Mutual)(D) accordingly offered the Freelands (P) $25,000 pursuant to the policy's section regarding coverage for uninsured motorists. The Freelands (P) argued they were due $100,000 under the policy's bodily injury section. The parties litigated the case in federal district court. On appeal, the Sixth Circuit took up the issue of whether the case satisfied the federal amount in controversy requirement.

ISSUE: When a plaintiff seeks a declaratory judgment in federal court alleging subject matter jurisdiction via diversity of the parties, is the amount in controversy not the amount of money sought by the plaintiff, but rather the value of the monetary consequences to the defendant that may result from the litigation?

HOLDING AND DECISION: (Thapar, J.) Yes. When a plaintiff seeks a declaratory judgment in federal court alleging subject matter jurisdiction via diversity of the parties, the amount in controversy is not the amount of money sought by the plaintiff, but rather the value of the monetary consequences to the defendant that may result from the litigation. In this case, Liberty Mutual (D) has offered the Freelands (P) $25,000. If the Freelands (P) prevail in this action, the value of the consequence of that victory to Liberty Mutual (D) would be the difference between the $25,000 Liberty Mutual (D) had offered and the $100,000 sought by the Freelands (P). The amount of that difference is exactly $75,000. Under the statute regarding diversity jurisdiction, the amount in controversy must exceed $75,000. Accordingly, the district court did not have subject matter jurisdiction over this case. Reversed and remanded.

▶ ANALYSIS

The amount in controversy is exclusive of any additional costs or interest sought by the plaintiff. Most courts use the majority rule that the amount in controversy is determined simply by the amount sought by the plaintiff in the complaint. Federal district courts have the discretion to hold hearings or request further evidence from the plaintiff if there is some indication the complaint does not meet the threshold.

Quicknotes

AMOUNT IN CONTROVERSY The value of a claim sought by a party to a lawsuit.

DECLARATORY JUDGMENT A judgment of the court establishing the rights of the parties.

DIVERSITY JURISDICTION The authority of a federal court to hear and determine cases involving parties who are of different states and an amount in controversy greater than a statutorily set amount.

Louisville & Nashville R. Co. v. Mottley

Railroad (D) v. Pass holders (P)

211 U.S. 149 (1908).

NATURE OF CASE: Appeal of a decision overruling a demurrer in an action for specific performance of a contract.

FACT SUMMARY: Mottley (P) was injured on a train owned by Louisville & Nashville R. Co. (D), which granted Mottley (P) a lifetime free pass which he now sought to enforce.

🏛 RULE OF LAW
Alleging an anticipated constitutional defense in the complaint does not give a federal court jurisdiction if there is no diversity of citizenship between the litigants.

FACTS: In 1871, Mottley (P) and his wife (P) were injured while riding on the Louisville & Nashville R. Co. (D) train. The Mottleys (P) released their claims for damages against the Louisville & Nashville R. Co. (D) upon receiving a contract granting free transportation during the remainder of their lives. In 1907, the Louisville & Nashville R. Co. (D) refused to renew the Mottleys' (P) passes relying upon an act of Congress which forbade the giving of free passes or free transportation. The Mottleys (P) filed an action in a Circuit Court of the United States for the Western District of Kentucky. The Mottleys (P) and the Louisville & Nashville R. Co. (D) were both citizens of Kentucky. Therefore, the Mottleys (P) attempted to establish federal jurisdiction by claiming that the Louisville & Nashville R. Co. (D) would raise a constitutional defense in their answer, thus raising a federal question. The Louisville & Nashville R. Co. (D) filed a demurrer to the complaint for failing to state a cause of action. The demurrer was denied. On appeal, the United States Supreme Court did not look at the issue raised by the litigants, but on its own motion raised the issue of whether the federal courts had jurisdiction to hear the case.

ISSUE: Does an allegation in the complaint that a constitutional defense will be raised in the answer raise a federal question which would give a federal court jurisdiction if no diversity of citizenship is alleged?

HOLDING AND DECISION: (Moody, J.) No. Neither party to the litigation alleged that the federal court had jurisdiction in this case, and neither party challenged the jurisdiction of the federal court to hear the case. Because the jurisdiction of the circuit court is defined and limited by statute, it is their duty to see that such jurisdiction is not exceeded. Both parties to the litigation were citizens of Kentucky and so there was no diversity of citizenship. The only way that the federal court could have jurisdiction in this case would be if there was a federal question involved. Mottley (P) did allege in his complaint

that the Louisville & Nashville R. Co. (D) based their refusal to renew the free pass on a federal statute. Mottley (P) then attempted to allege information that would defeat the defense of the Louisville & Nashville R. Co. (D). This is not sufficient. The plaintiff's complaint must be based upon the federal laws of the U.S. Constitution to confer jurisdiction on the federal courts. Mottley's (P) cause of action was not based on any federal laws or constitutional privileges; it was based on a contract. Even though it is evident that a federal question will be brought up at the trial, plaintiff's cause of action must be based on a federal statute or the Constitution in order to have a federal question that would grant jurisdiction to the federal courts. Reversed and remanded to dismiss the suit.

▶ ANALYSIS

If the Mottleys (P) could have alleged they were basing their action on a federal right, it would have been enough to have given the federal court jurisdiction. The federal court would have had to exercise jurisdiction at least long enough to determine whether there actually was such a right. If the federal court ultimately concludes that the claimed federal right does not exist, the complaint would be dismissed for failure to state a claim upon which relief can be granted rather than for lack of jurisdiction. The court has the power to determine the issue of subject matter jurisdiction on its own motion as it did in this case. Subject matter jurisdiction can be challenged at any stage of the proceeding.

Quicknotes

DIVERSITY OF CITIZENSHIP Parties are citizens of different states, or one party is an alien; a factor, along with a statutorily set dollar value of the matter in controversy, that allows a federal district court to exercise its authority to hear a lawsuit based on diversity jurisdiction.

DEMURRER The assertion that the opposing party's pleadings are insufficient and that the demurring party should not be made to answer.

FEDERAL COURT JURISDICTION The authority of the federal courts to hear and determine in the first instance matters pertaining to the federal Constitution, federal law, or treaties of the United States.

SUBJECT MATTER JURISDICTION The authority of the court to hear and decide actions involving a particular type of issue or subject.

T.B. Harms Co. v. Eliscu

Copyrights assignee (P) v. Songwriter (D)

339 F.2d 823 (2d Cir. 1964), *cert. denied*, 381 U.S. 915 (1965).

NATURE OF CASE: Appeal from dismissal of action to determine ownership of copyrights.

FACT SUMMARY: T.B. Harms Co. (P) brought an action in federal court to determine the ownership of copyrights after Eliscu's (D) contract rights had expired.

🏛 RULE OF LAW

The proper forum to hear a case is the one having control over the laws that created the cause of action.

FACTS: Eliscu (D) contracted to use T.B. Harms Co.'s (Harms) (P) copyright. A controversy arose at the time the contract came up for renewal. Eliscu (D) brought an action in state court seeking a declaration of its rights. Harms (P) brought an action in district court to determine ownership rights. A motion to dismiss was granted; the court finding title to the copyright was a matter of state rather than federal law and it was therefore without jurisdiction. Harms (P) appealed.

ISSUE: May a federal court hear an action, absent diversity, where state law creates the cause of action?

HOLDING AND DECISION: (Friendly, J.) No. Copyrights are subject to federal law. If infringement had been alleged, a federal action would have been created since it would have involved an application of the Copyright Act. Where the matter involves contract or title questions, it is a matter of state law. The proper forum to hear a case is the one having control over the laws that created the cause of action—here, state court. No federal question is present and the copyright is only incidentally involved in a question concerning title to property. No explicit cause of action over title questions was created by the Act and federal courts should therefore refrain from entering into a province left to the state. Affirmed.

▶ ANALYSIS

See also *Arvin Industries, Inc. v. Berns Air King Corp.*, 510 F.2d 1070 (7th Cir. 1975), wherein the court denied federal jurisdiction in a dispute between a licensee and a patent owner over royalties. In *American Well Works Co. v. Layne and Bowler Co.*, 241 U.S. 257 (1916), relied on by the court in *Harms*, federal jurisdiction was deemed present if the statute gives an express remedy for the ill complained of or covers the issues involved in the suit.

Quicknotes

CASE SUB JUDICE A matter that is before the court for determination.

Grable & Sons Metal Products, Inc. v. Darue Engineering & Manufacturing

Former owner of seized property (P) v. New owner (D)

545 U.S. 308 (2005).

NATURE OF CASE: Review of federal appeals court decision.

FACT SUMMARY: Property owned by a company that was delinquent in paying its federal taxes was seized and sold. The company sued the new owner, claiming that the Internal Revenue Service should have provided notice by personal service, according to federal tax law. The new owner removed the case to federal court.

🏛 RULE OF LAW
A case involving the interpretation of federal tax law may be removed to federal court from state court.

FACTS: In 1994, the Internal Revenue Service (IRS) seized property owned by Grable & Sons Metal Products, Inc. (Grable) (P) to satisfy Grable's (P) tax debt, and gave Grable (P) notice by certified mail before selling the property to Darue Engineering & Manufacturing (Darue) (D). Grable (P) received the notice. Grable (P) later sued in state court, claiming Darue's (D) title was invalid because federal law required the IRS to give Grable (P) notice of the sale by personal service, not certified mail. Darue (D) removed the case to federal district court, arguing that the case presented a federal question because Grable's (P) claim depended on an interpretation of federal tax law. The district court agreed and ruled for Darue (D). The Sixth Circuit affirmed.

ISSUE: May a case involving the interpretation of federal tax law be removed to federal court from state court?

HOLDING AND DECISION: (Souter, J.) Yes. A case involving the interpretation of federal tax law may be removed to federal court from state court. The case involved a federal question and could thus be removed to federal court. The case implicated serious federal issues. The national interest in providing a federal forum for federal tax litigation warranted removing the case to federal court. Affirmed.

CONCURRENCE: (Thomas, J.) In an appropriate case, limiting § 1331 to cases in which federal law creates the cause of action pleaded by a plaintiff should be considered.

▷ ANALYSIS

The United States Supreme Court was unanimous in affirming the Third Circuit's decision by holding that the national interest in providing a federal forum for federal tax

litigation is sufficiently substantial to support the exercise of federal question jurisdiction. The interests of the United States are affected by the case, via the federal tax law. Otherwise, the case would have been a state cause of action.

■=■

Gunn v. Minton

Attorney (D) v. Client (P)

___ U.S. ___, 133 S.Ct. 1059, 185 L.Ed.2d 72 (2013).

NATURE OF CASE: Appeal from a state supreme court decision finding a state law attorney malpractice case involving a question of federal patent law belonged in federal court as opposed to state court.

FACT SUMMARY: Minton (P) sued Gunn (D) in state court alleging Gunn (D) committed attorney malpractice while representing Minton (P) in a prior patent lawsuit.

▥ RULE OF LAW

A state law claim may be adjudicated in federal court if the state claim raises a federal issue that is actually disputed and substantial and the federal court's hearing of the case does not disturb the congressionally-mandated balance of federal and state judicial responsibilities.

FACTS: Minton (P) sued Gunn (D) in state court alleging Gunn (D) committed legal malpractice while representing Minton (P) in a prior patent lawsuit in federal court. The specific claim was that Gunn (D) failed to raise an "experimental use" exception under federal patent law. In that prior case, Minton's (P) patent was found invalid. In the legal malpractice action, the state trial court and an intermediate state appellate court found the case involved only a state law issue. The Texas Supreme Court reversed on the ground the case belonged in federal court because it involved a determination of a federal patent law issue. The United States Supreme Court granted Gunn's (D) petition for review.

ISSUE: May a state law claim be adjudicated in federal court if the state claim raises a federal issue that is actually disputed and substantial and the federal court's hearing of the case does not disturb the congressionally-mandated balance of federal and state judicial responsibilities.

HOLDING AND DECISION: (Roberts, C.J.) Yes. A state law claim may be adjudicated in federal court if the state claim raises a federal issue that is actually disputed and substantial and the federal court's hearing of the case does not disturb the congressionally-mandated balance of federal and state judicial responsibilities. Typically, cases arise under federal law when federal law creates the cause of action that is being adjudicated. However, a federal court may entertain purely state law issues when the state claim involves a substantial and actually disputed federal issue. The court agrees that an issue of federal law, whether Gunn (D) could have argued the experimental use exception, is an actually disputed in this case. That particular determination will resolve the state law legal malpractice claim.

However, the federal issue presented is not substantial in the relevant sense. The issue must not just be substantial to the parties involved in the case, but to the federal system as a whole. Here, because of the hypothetical nature of the legal malpractice case, the outcome of that state law claim will not change the real world result that Minton's (P) patent was found invalid. In addition, a state court's determination of the case within a case, i.e. the federal patent law question, will carry little precedential value in federal forum. Moreover, state courts have a special interest in maintaining the professional levels of their licensed professional attorneys. Accordingly, because there is no substantial federal issue involved, the state court should retain subject matter jurisdiction over this case. Reversed and remanded.

▌ *ANALYSIS*

Any time a federal court is presented with a case involving only a state law claim, the judge will review the case carefully to determine if subject matter jurisdiction is appropriate. In this case, there was no dispute the legal malpractice case turned on the determination of the federal patent law issue. The United States Supreme Court found the federal issue was not substantial because the outcome of the case would not overturn the prior federal court's decision regarding Minton's (P) patent. Federal courts are also not bound by state court decisions arising from attorney malpractice cases involving federal patents.

■▬■

Quicknotes

CAUSE OF ACTION A fact or set of facts the occurrence of which entitles a party to seek judicial relief.

FEDERAL COURT JURISDICTION The authority of the federal courts to hear and determine in the first instance matters pertaining to the federal Constitution, federal law, or treaties of the United States.

■▬■

United Mine Workers of America v. Gibbs

International union (D) v. Threatened superintendent (P)

383 U.S. 715 (1966).

NATURE OF CASE: Review of award of damages for violation of § 303 of the Labor Management Relations Act and for interference with a business interest.

FACT SUMMARY: Gibbs (P) lost his job as superintendent of a coal mining company because of alleged unlawful influence of United Mine Workers of America (D).

🏛 RULE OF LAW
Under pendent jurisdiction, federal courts may decide state issues which are closely related to the federal issues being litigated.

FACTS: There was a dispute between United Mine Workers of America (United Mine Workers) (D) and the Southern Labor Union over who should represent the coal miners in the southern Appalachian area. Tennessee Consolidated Coal Company closed down a mine in southern Tennessee where over 100 men belonging to United Mine Workers (D) were employed. Later, Grundy Company, a wholly owned subsidiary of Tennessee Consolidated Coal Company, hired Gibbs (P) to open a new mine using members of the Southern Labor Union. Gibbs (P) was also given a contract to haul the mine's coal to the nearest railroad loading point. Members of Local 5881 of the United Mine Workers (D) forcibly prevented the opening of the mine. Gibbs (P) lost his job and never entered into performance of his haulage contract. He soon began to lose other trucking contracts and mine leases he held in the area. Gibbs (P) claimed this was a result of a concerted union plan against him. He filed suit in the United States District Court for the Eastern District of Tennessee for violation of § 303 of the Labor Management Relations Act and a state law claim, based on the doctrine of pendent jurisdiction, that there was an unlawful conspiracy and boycott aimed at him to interfere with his contract of employment and with his contract of haulage. The jury's verdict was that the United Mine Workers (D) had violated both § 303 and the state law. On motion, the trial court set aside the award of damages for the haulage contracts and entered a verdict for United Mine Workers (D) on the issue of violation of § 303, which was the federal claim. The award as to the state claim was sustained. The court of appeals affirmed.

ISSUE: Can federal courts decide state issues that are closely related to the federal issues being litigated?

HOLDING AND DECISION: (Brennan, J.) Yes. When there are both state and federal claims involved in the same set of facts and the claims are such that the

plaintiff would ordinarily be expected to try them all in one judicial proceeding, the federal court has the power to hear both the state and the federal claims. The federal claims must have substance sufficient to confer subject matter jurisdiction on the court. This is the doctrine of pendent jurisdiction. The court isn't required to exercise this power in every case. It has consistently been recognized that pendent jurisdiction is a doctrine of discretion, not of plaintiff's right. The court should look at judicial economy, convenience, and fairness to litigants in deciding whether to exercise jurisdiction over the state claims. If the factual relationship between the state and federal claims is so close that they ought to be litigated at the same trial, the court ought to grant pendent jurisdiction in order to save an extra trial. If the issues are so complicated that they are confusing to the jury then the court probably should dismiss the state claims. The issue of whether pendent jurisdiction has been properly assumed is one which remains open throughout the litigation. If, before the trial, the federal claim is dismissed, then the state claim should also be dismissed. The court went on to hold that the plaintiff could not recover damages for conspiracy under the state claim. Reversed.

▌ *ANALYSIS*

This case helped clarify the law that had been established by the case of *Hurn v. Oursler*, 289 U.S. 238 (1933). That case set the rule for determining if a federal court could hear the state claim. If a case had two distinct grounds in support of a single cause of action, one of which presents a federal question, then the court could hear the state claim. But if a case had two separate and distinct causes of action and only one was a federal question, then the court could not hear the state claim. Now, the state and federal claims can state separate causes of action so long as they are factually closely related.

■▬■

Quicknotes

LABOR MANAGEMENT RELATIONS ACT Federal law prohibiting secondary boycotts.

PENDENT JURISDICTION A doctrine granting authority to a federal court to hear a claim that does not invoke diversity jurisdiction if it arises from the same transaction or occurrence as the primary action.

■▬■

Exxon Mobil Corp. v. Allapattah Services, Inc.

Class members (P) v. Corporations (D)

545 U.S. 546 (2005).

NATURE OF CASE: Appeal of judgment regarding supplemental jurisdiction.

FACT SUMMARY: [Only some members of a class met the amount-in-controversy to establish diversity jurisdiction, and the circuit courts were split as to whether each member's claim must meet the requirement in order for their claims to go forward, if the claims of other members of the class meet the requirement.]

🏛 RULE OF LAW
Where one plaintiff's claim satisfies the minimum amount-in-controversy requirement for federal diversity jurisdiction and another plaintiff's related claim does not, 28 U.S.C. § 1367 allows federal courts to exercise supplemental jurisdiction over the claim that is less than the required amount.

FACTS: These cases were consolidated and the United States Supreme Court granted certiorari to resolve a circuit split over the federal supplemental jurisdiction statute, 28 U.S.C. § 1367. The plaintiffs in the *Exxon* case are a class of approximately 10,000 gas dealers (P) who claimed that Exxon (D) over-charged them for fuel purchases. The court of appeals affirmed the district court's verdict for the dealers (P), and held that the federal supplemental jurisdiction statute allows a district court in a class-action lawsuit to exercise supplemental jurisdiction over class members whose claims do not meet the jurisdictional minimum amount. In *Ortega v. Star-Kist Foods, Inc.*, 370 F.3d 124 (1st Cir. 2004), a nine-year-old girl injured her finger on a can of Star-Kist tuna. The girl (P) and her family (P) sued in federal court, on the basis of diversity jurisdiction. The district court dismissed the claims for lack of jurisdiction, holding that the girl's (P) and family members' (P) claims did not meet the minimum amount for jurisdiction. The First Circuit Court of Appeals reversed as to the girl (P), but upheld the district court's conclusion that none of the family members (P) satisfied the amount-in-controversy requirement.

ISSUE: Where one plaintiff's claim satisfies the minimum amount-in-controversy requirement for federal diversity jurisdiction and another plaintiff's related claim does not, does 28 U.S.C. § 1367 allow federal courts to exercise supplemental jurisdiction over the claim that is less than the required amount?

HOLDING AND DECISION: (Kennedy, J.) Yes. Where one plaintiff's claim satisfies the minimum amount-in-controversy requirement for federal diversity jurisdic-

tion and another plaintiff's related claim does not, 28 U.S.C. § 1367 allows federal courts to exercise supplemental jurisdiction over the claim that is less than the required amount. Courts only need to determine whether they have original jurisdiction over one of the claims in a case. If they do, courts can then decide to extend supplemental jurisdiction to the other related claims. The indivisibility and contamination theories are easily dismissed. The indivisibility theory is inconsistent with the whole notion of supplemental jurisdiction, and the contamination theory is inconsistent with the amount-in-controversy requirement. The unambiguous text of the statute indicates that jurisdiction should extend to the other plaintiffs, regardless of legislative history or other extrinsic material. Judgment of the court of appeals for the Eleventh Circuit affirmed and judgment of the court of appeals for the First Circuit reversed.

DISSENT: (Stevens, J.) The Court's rationale for ignoring clear congressional intent is unpersuasive. The House Report specifically rejected a broad reading of the statute. Typically, such committee reports are considered authoritative when determining congressional intent. It is clear that Congress's limited task was to undo this Court's 5-4 ruling in *Finley v. United States*, 490 U.S. 545. 109 S. Ct. 2003 (1989).

DISSENT: (Ginsburg, J.) The majority's reading of the statute is plausible, but broad. It should be read as instructing that the district court have original jurisdiction over the action first, before supplemental jurisdiction can attach. This would be a less disruptive reading of the statute.

▶ ANALYSIS

The Court's holding greatly expands the limits of diversity jurisdiction. This case overrules *Zahn v. International Paper*, 414 U.S. 291 (1973), which held that in order for a federal court to exercise diversity jurisdiction, all plaintiffs in the case had to satisfy 28 U.S.C. § 1332's amount-in-controversy requirement. The courts of appeal had divided on the question and the United States Supreme Court had previously failed to resolve the issue in the 2000 case *Free v. Abbott Laboratories, Inc.*, 529 U.S. 333 (2000).

Quicknotes

AMOUNT IN CONTROVERSY The value of a claim sought by a party to a lawsuit.

Continued on next page.

CLASS ACTION A suit commenced by a representative on behalf of an ascertainable group that is too large to appear in court, who share a commonality of interests and who will benefit from a successful result.

DIVERSITY JURISDICTION The authority of a federal court to hear and determine cases involving parties who are of different states and an amount in controversy greater than a statutorily set amount.

ORIGINAL JURISDICTION The power of a court to hear an action upon its commencement.

SUPPLEMENTAL JURISDICTION A doctrine granting authority to a federal court to hear a claim that does not invoke diversity jurisdiction if it arises from the same transaction or occurrence as the primary action.

Executive Software North America, Inc. v. United States District Court for the Central District of California

Defendant in discrimination suit (P) v. Federal court (D)

24 F.3d 1545 (9th Cir. 1994).

NATURE OF CASE: Petition for a writ of mandamus in an employment discrimination suit.

FACT SUMMARY: Page filed a complaint in state court against her former employer, Executive Software North America, Inc. (P), alleging federal and state claims of religious and racial discrimination.

🏛 RULE OF LAW
Absent extraordinary circumstances, 28 U.S.C. § 1367(c)(1)-(c)(3) sets forth the exclusive circumstances under which a federal court may appropriately decline pendent jurisdiction.

FACTS: Page, a black woman, asserted that Executive Software North America, Inc. (Executive Software) (P) required all of its employees to study the teachings of the Church of Scientology. When she refused to comply, she was charged with a number of errors in her work and was subsequently fired when she attempted to contest the charges. Page filed a complaint in state court alleging a federal claim under Title VII, a federal claim under 42 U.S.C. § 1983, and three state law causes of action for racial and religious discrimination, wrongful termination, and negligent supervision. Based on the two federal claims, Executive Software (P) removed the action to federal court. Shortly thereafter, the district court (D) issued an order sua sponte to show cause why the three state-law claims should not be remanded to state court, stating that its jurisdiction over the claims depended upon whether it exercised its discretion to retain them. The district court (D) later remanded the three state law claims, but provided no reasons. Executive Software (P) petitioned the court of appeals for a writ of mandamus to compel the district court (D) to retain jurisdiction over the pendent state-law claims.

ISSUE: Absent extraordinary circumstances, does 28 U.S.C. § 1367(c)(1)-(c)(3) set forth the exclusive circumstances under which a federal court may appropriately decline pendent jurisdiction?

HOLDING AND DECISION: (Nelson, J.) Yes. Absent extraordinary circumstances, 28 U.S.C. § 1367(c)(1)-(c)(3) sets forth the exclusive circumstances under which a federal court may appropriately decline pendent jurisdiction. Generally, federal courts may assert jurisdiction over state law claims when the state and federal claims derive from a common nucleus of operative fact and the claims are such that they would ordinarily be expected to be tried in one judicial proceeding. Federal statute 28 U.S.C. § 1367(c)(1)-(c)(3) sets out three specific instances under which a federal court may

decline pendent jurisdiction. U.S.C. § 1367(c)(4) permits a discretionary remand of pendent claims only in exceptional circumstances when there exist other compelling reasons for declining jurisdiction. Congress intended that subsection (c)(4) be narrowly applied, and that "exceptional circumstances" be strictly interpreted. Nonetheless, this subsection does require an additional inquiry by a court to determine whether in its judgment a declination of jurisdiction should be compelled. The district court (D) clearly erred in failing to apply the appropriate statutory analysis. A narrow writ of mandamus is granted, and the case remanded to vacate the order entered by the district court (D).

DISSENT: (Leavy, J.) It is unclear precisely upon which ground the district court (D) relied in declining jurisdiction. The majority has concluded that the district court did not rely on an enumerated section in 28 U.S.C. § 1367(c), and therefore committed a clear error. The district court (D) can be said to have committed an error only if it relied on an unauthorized ground in exercising its discretion to remand, and the record does not support such a conclusion.

▶ ANALYSIS

The history of 28 U.S.C. § 1367 is a complicated one. Prior to its enactment in 1988, courts were forced to rely on case law in making determinations of whether pendent, ancillary, or pendent-party jurisdiction was required. Nonetheless, the statute has not made such determinations as easy as was hoped, because the case law was only partly encapsulated in the statute.

Quicknotes

28 U.S.C. § 1367 Codifies supplemental jurisdiction and those factors that warrant declining jurisdiction.

SUA SPONTE An action taken by the court by its own motion and without the suggestion of one of the parties.

SUPPLEMENTAL JURISDICTION A doctrine granting authority to a federal court to hear a claim that does not invoke diversity jurisdiction if it arises from the same transaction or occurrence as the primary action.

WRIT OF MANDAMUS A court order issued commanding a public or private entity, or an official thereof, to perform a duty required by law.

Davis v. City of Shreveport Police Dept.

Individual (P) v. Local police department (D)

2012 WL 4189511 (W.D. La. 2012).

NATURE OF CASE: Federal district court's consideration of one defendant's motion to remand the case back to state court.

FACT SUMMARY: After his arrest, Davis (P) brought state and federal law claims against the Shreveport Police Department (D) and KSLA (D), a local news channel, for defamation, libel and violations of his federal due process rights in state court. The Shreveport Police (D) removed the case to federal court without KSLA's (D) consent.

RULE OF LAW
Pursuant to the removal statute, 28 U.S.C. Section 1446(b), all defendants must join in a notice of removal to federal court or consent to such removal within the applicable thirty day time period.

FACTS: The Shreveport Police (D) arrested Davis (P) for allegedly contributing to the delinquency of a minor. KSLA (D) then ran a news story about the arrest. After his arrest, Davis (P) brought state and federal law claims against the Shreveport Police (D) and KSLA (D) for defamation, libel and violations of his federal due process rights in state court. The Shreveport Police (D) removed the case to federal court without KSLA's (D) consent. In federal court, KSLA (D) filed a motion to remand the case to state court on the grounds it did not consent to the removal. Davis (P), joined by the Shreveport Police (D), opposed the motion.

ISSUE: Pursuant to the removal statute, 28 U.S.C. Section 1446(b), must all defendants join in a notice of removal to federal court or consent to such removal within the applicable thirty day time period?

HOLDING AND DECISION: (Hayes, J.) Yes. Pursuant to the removal statute, 28 U.S.C. Section 1446(b), all defendants must join in a notice of removal to federal court or consent to such removal within the applicable thirty day time period. Failure of all defendants to consent to removal typically renders the removal defective. Davis (P) properly served KSLA (D) with the complaint prior to the removal of this case. Accordingly, KSLA (D) was required to join in the notice of removal or consent to such action. It did neither. KSLA (D) has also timely filed this motion to remand. The case is remanded to state court.

ANALYSIS

As with any case filed in federal court first, a case removed from state to federal court must include federal causes of action. Defendants often remove police misconduct cases to federal court on the theory the federal forum is less sympathetic to the plaintiffs. Conversely, plaintiffs typically seek to keep such matters in state court because of the local nature of such courts. Plaintiffs will often craft their complaints to prevent the removal of their cases to federal court.

Quicknotes

REMOVAL Petition by a defendant to move the case to federal court.

CHAPTER 5

Venue, Transfer, and Forum Non Conveniens

Quick Reference Rules of Law

Reasor-Hill Corp. v. Harrison

Pesticide manufacturer (P) v. Circuit court judge (D)

Ark. Sup. Ct., 220 Ark. 521, 249 S.W.2d 994 (1952).

NATURE OF CASE: Action to dismiss a cross-complaint for injury to real property.

FACT SUMMARY: Barton sought damages in an Arkansas court from Reasor-Hill Corp. (P) for selling an insecticide which damaged Barton's cotton crop in Missouri.

🏛 RULE OF LAW
If a local action cannot be brought at the situs of the property because of lack of jurisdiction of the defendant, the action may be brought in the state where the defendant resides.

FACTS: The Planters Flying Service sought to collect an account for having sprayed insecticide on Barton's cotton crop in Missouri. Barton charged in his answer that Planters Flying Service had used an adulterated insecticide. Barton also filed a cross-complaint against Reasor-Hill Corp. (P) for putting on the market a chemical unsuited for spraying cotton. Reasor-Hill (P) moved to dismiss the cross-complaint on the grounds that the injury to the cotton crop occurred in Missouri and, therefore, only the Missouri court had jurisdiction to hear the cross-complaint. Reasor-Hill (P) was an Arkansas corporation and the Missouri courts could not obtain jurisdiction over Reasor-Hill (P) if Reasor-Hill (P) did not enter the state of Missouri. The lower court (D) overruled the motion to dismiss the cross-complaint. Reasor-Hill (P) then applied for a writ of prohibition.

ISSUE: In an action to recover damages for injury to real property, must the action be brought in the state where the property is located?

HOLDING AND DECISION: (Smith, J.) No. Barton was injured and if he is required to bring his action in Missouri where the damaged property was situated, he would not be able to obtain jurisdiction over the parties responsible for the damage. The majority rule is that local actions must be brought where the property is located. The leading case is *Livingston v. Jefferson*, Fed. Case No. 8411, 1 Brock 203, decided in the early 1800s. American courts have given at least three reasons to justify the rule. The first reason was that courts are not in a position to pass upon the title to land outside their jurisdiction. This was probably true as between nations, but because of the excellent law libraries, each state has access to the statutes and cases of all the other states and, therefore, there is no problem in determining the law of some other state. State courts are willing to apply the law of some other state in transitory actions. If the state courts can determine the law of some other state well enough to apply it to transitory actions, they can determine it well enough to apply it to local actions. The second reason given is that since the tort must take place where the land is situated, the plaintiff must pursue his remedy before the defendant leaves the jurisdiction. Again, this particular reason has merit only for nations because nations can stop a party from leaving the country, but states cannot restrict the travel of the parties involved in order to maintain jurisdiction over them. The third reason used is that a state is reluctant to subject their own citizens to suits by residents of other states when, if the situation is reversed, the courts of the other states would not allow the nonresident to bring an action against the state resident in the state court protect one of their citizens who had destroyed property in another state and then sought refuge in their state. Since the local rule doctrine was established by English courts in the thirteenth century for reasons no longer applicable, Barton should be allowed to have his day in court. Even though the damaged property is situated in Missouri, the Arkansas court (D) has jurisdiction to hear the case. Writ denied.

DISSENT: (McFaddin, J.) More is needed to apply the law of another state than a good law library. Most trial courts are not equipped to determine the law of other states. Each state is sovereign except as to those areas of federal control and, therefore, one state should not be able to decide issues pertaining to property situated in another state. Also, it is not for the court to decide that Arkansas won't afford an Arkansas citizen's sanctuary from damages actions by citizens of other states. That is a question for the legislature to decide.

▶ ANALYSIS

The rule in this case is a minority rule. The only other state to so hold is Minnesota. Actions that involve real property must be tried in the state where the property is located. In most states, the action must be brought in the court located in the county or district where the property is located. Other courts in the state do not have the proper venue to hear the case. Because venue is regarded more as a matter of procedure, a court having jurisdiction can render a valid judgment even without proper venue. If the defendant fails to object to improper venue, the defect is usually considered waived. In some states, the local action rule is adhered to so strongly as to become almost a jurisdictional requirement.

Continued on next page.

Quicknotes

SITUS Location; in community property, the location of an asset.

■▬■

Bates v. C & S Adjusters, Inc.

Debtor (P) v. Collection agency (D)

980 F.2d 865 (2d Cir. 1992).

NATURE OF CASE: Appeal from order dismissing for improper venue a Fair Debt Collection Practices Act action.

FACT SUMMARY: Bates (P) contended that venue was proper in his action under the Fair Debt Collection Practices Act in the district where he received an allegedly offending letter from C & S Adjusters, Inc. (D), a collection agency.

🏛 RULE OF LAW
Venue is proper under the Fair Debt Collection Practices Act in the district where an allegedly offending letter is received.

FACTS: Bates (P) received a collection letter from C & S Adjusters, Inc. (C & S) (D), a collection agency. Contending that the letter violated the Fair Debt Collection Practices Act, Bates (P) filed an action in the Western District of New York, where he resided and received the letter. C & S (D), which was not located in that district and had not mailed the letter there, moved to dismiss for improper venue. The court granted the motion, and Bates (P) appealed.

ISSUE: Is venue proper under the Fair Debt Collection Practices Act in the district where an allegedly offending letter is received?

HOLDING AND DECISION: (Newman, J.) Yes. Venue is proper under the Fair Debt Collection Practices Act in the district where an allegedly offending letter is received. In 1990, Congress amended the general federal-question venue statute, 28 U.S.C. § 1391, from placing venue "in the judicial district ... in which the claim arose" to "a judicial district in which a substantial part of the events or omissions giving rise to the claim occurred." The purpose of this change was to clarify the rather vague language of the pre-1990 statute and to overrule Supreme Court precedent tending to limit venue under this section to only one possible district. In the case of an action under the FDCPA, receipt of an offending letter is a substantial part of the events giving rise to the cause of action. Consequently, venue in such a district—here, the Western District of New York—is proper. Reversed and remanded.

▶ ANALYSIS

Prior to 1966, venue in federal-question cases was limited to the district in which a defendant resided. This led to the splitting of cases in which multiple defendants residing in different districts were present. Congress's response was the addition of the language later amended in 1990.

■══■

Quicknotes

28 U.S.C. § 1391 Permits venue to be placed where a substantial part of the events giving rise to the claim occurred.

VENUE The specific geographic location over which a court has jurisdiction to hear a suit.

■══■

Hoffman v. Blaski

Federal judge (D) v. Patent holder (P)

363 U.S. 335 (1960).

NATURE OF CASE: Appeal of an order remanding this case from an Illinois district court to the Texas district court in an action for patent infringement.

FACT SUMMARY: Hoffman (D), a federal district court judge in Illinois, denied Blaski's (P) motion to re-transfer a patent infringement action which Blaski (P) brought against Howell in federal district court in Texas back to that Texas court.

RULE OF LAW
Under 28 U.S.C. § 1404(a), a federal court can only transfer a case to a court where the plaintiff could have originally brought the case.

FACTS: Blaski (P) filed a patent infringement action against one Howell in a Texas federal district court. Howell moved under 28 U.S.C. § 1404(a) (change of venue) to transfer the action to federal district court in Illinois. Blaski (P) objected to this transfer on the ground that, as Howell could not have been served in Illinois, the action could not have been transferred there because it could not have been brought there originally. The Texas court granted the motion, reasoning that Howell had waived any objection to the Illinois court's lack of venue and that the transfer was convenient to the parties and witnesses and within the interests of justice. Blaski (P) then moved in the Illinois court, of which Hoffman (D) was a district judge, to retransfer the case back to Texas. After Judge Hoffman (D) denied the motion with misgivings, Blaski (P) petitioned for a writ of mandamus directing Judge Hoffman (D) to reverse his order. The Seventh Circuit Court of Appeals issued the writ, and Judge Hoffman (D) appealed.

ISSUE: Can a federal court transfer a case to another court in which the plaintiff could not have originally brought the case?

HOLDING AND DECISION: (Whittaker, J.) No. 28 U.S.C. § 1404(a) is to be strictly construed. The statute states that the court can only transfer a case to a court in which the plaintiff could have originally brought the case. It is not sufficient that the plaintiff could bring the case in the court at the time of the transfer. In this case, Hoffman (D) agreed to waive its objections to the Illinois court's lack of venue in the case and to submit to the personal jurisdiction of the court. This would permit Blaski (P) to bring the action in the Illinois court. It is enough that the transfer would be in the interest of convenience and justice; it must also qualify under the requirement that the transfer be to a court in which Blaski (P) could have originally filed his case. Affirmed.

DISSENT: (Frankfurter, J.) The intent of § 1404(a) was to enable courts to transfer cases to the court which would be most convenient to the parties and would best serve the ends of justice. If a case could be better handled by another court and the case could have been brought there at the time of transfer, the case should be transferred.

ANALYSIS

There are several exceptions to the above rule. 11 U.S.C. § 55(c), applicable to bankruptcy proceedings, and 46 U.S.C. § 742, applicable to admiralty suits against the United States, may be transferred for the convenience of the parties regardless of whether venue would have been proper when the suit was instigated. Both the plaintiff and the defendant may make a motion for a transfer for convenience under § 1404(a). The moving party must file and serve a written notice of the motion along with affidavits showing that the transfer would better serve the interests of justice and the convenience of the parties or witnesses. The motion must be made within a reasonable time after the institution of the suit. The court has the power to dismiss the action for forum non conveniens in addition to its power to transfer the action to another court.

Quicknotes

28 U.S.C. § 1404(a) Permits either plaintiff or defendant to make a motion for a transfer for convenience.

WRIT OF MANDAMUS A court order issued commanding a public or private entity, or an official thereof, to perform a duty required by law.

Piper Aircraft Co. v. Reyno

Airplane manufacturer (D) v. Decedents' representative (P)

454 U.S. 235 (1981).

NATURE OF CASE: Appeal from dismissal of wrongful death action.

FACT SUMMARY: Reyno (P), the representative of five victims of an air crash, brought suit in California even though the location of the crash and the homes of the victims were in Scotland.

🏛 RULE OF LAW
A plaintiff may not defeat a motion to dismiss for forum non conveniens merely by showing that the substantive law that would be applied in the alternative forum is less favorable to him than that of the present forum.

FACTS: Reyno (P) was the representative of five air crash victims' estates and brought suit for wrongful death in United States, district court in California, even though the accident occurred and all the victims resided in Scotland. Piper Aircraft Co. (D) moved to dismiss for forum non conveniens, contending that Scotland was the proper forum. Reyno (P) opposed the motion on the basis that the Scottish laws were less advantageous to her than American laws. The district court granted the motion, while the court of appeals reversed. The United States Supreme Court granted certiorari.

ISSUE: May a plaintiff defeat a motion to dismiss for forum non conveniens merely on the basis that the laws of the alternative forum are less advantageous?

HOLDING AND DECISION: (Marshall, J.) No. A plaintiff may not defeat a motion to dismiss for forum non conveniens merely by showing that the substantive law of the alternative forum is less advantageous than that of the present forum. In this case, all the evidence, witnesses, and interests were in Scotland. Thus, the most convenient forum was there. As a result, the motion was properly granted. Reversed.

▌ ANALYSIS

The Court in this case specifically noted that under some circumstances, the fact that the chosen state's laws are less attractive to the defendant could be used to defeat a motion to dismiss for forum non conveniens. If the state chosen by the plaintiff has the only adequate remedy for the wrong alleged, then the motion may be denied.

Quicknotes

FORUM NON CONVENIENS An equitable doctrine permitting a court to refrain from hearing and determining a case when the matter may be more properly and fairly heard in another forum.

Ascertaining the Applicable Law

Quick Reference Rules of Law

Erie R. Co. v. Tompkins

Railroad (D) v. Injured pedestrian (P)

304 U.S. 64 (1938).

NATURE OF CASE: Action to recover damages for personal injury allegedly caused by negligent conduct.

FACT SUMMARY: In a personal injury suit, the federal district court trial judge refused to apply applicable state law because such law was "general" (judge-made) and not embodied in any statute.

🏛 RULE OF LAW
Although the 1789 Rules of Decision Act left federal courts unfettered to apply their own rules of procedure in common law actions brought in federal court, state law governs substantive issues. State law includes not only statutory law, but case law as well.

FACTS: Tompkins (P) was walking in a right of way parallel to some railroad tracks when an Erie Railroad (Erie) (D) train came by. Tompkins (P) was struck and injured by what he would, at trial, claim to be an open door extending from one of the rail cars. Under Pennsylvania case law (the applicable law since the accident occurred there), state courts would have treated Tompkins (P) as a trespasser in denying him recovery for other than wanton or willful misconduct on Erie's (D) part. Under "general" law, recognized in federal courts, Tompkins (P) would have been regarded as a licensee and would only have been obligated to show ordinary negligence. Because Erie (D) was a New York corporation, Tompkins (P) brought suit in a federal district court in New York, where he won a judgment for $30,000. Upon appeal to a federal circuit court, the decision was affirmed.

ISSUE: Was the trial court in error in refusing to recognize state case law as the proper rule of decision in deciding the substantive issue of liability?

HOLDING AND DECISION: (Brandeis, J.) Yes. The Court's opinion is in four parts: (1) *Swift v. Tyson*, 41 U.S. (16 Pet.) 1 (1842), which held that federal courts exercising jurisdiction on the ground of diversity of citizenship need not, in matters of general jurisprudence, apply the unwritten law of the state as declared by its highest court, is overruled. Section 34 of the Federal Judiciary Act of 1789, c. 20, 28 U.S. § 725 requires that federal courts in all matters except those where some federal law is controlling apply as their rules of decision the law of the state, unwritten as well as written. Up to this time, federal courts had assumed the power to make "general law" decisions even though Congress was powerless to enact "general law" statutes. (2) *Swift* had numerous political and social defects. The hoped-for uniformity among state courts had not occurred; there was no satisfactory way to distinguish between local and general law. On the other hand, *Swift* introduced grave discrimination by non-

citizens against citizens. The privilege of selecting the court for resolving disputes rested with the noncitizen who could pick the more favorable forum. The resulting far-reaching discrimination was due to the broad province accorded "general law" in which many matters of seemingly local concern were included. Furthermore, local citizens could move out of the state and bring suit in federal court if they were disposed to do so; corporations, similarly, could simply reincorporate in another state. More than statutory relief is involved here; the unconstitutionality of *Swift* is clear. (3) Except in matters governed by the Federal Constitution or by acts of Congress, the law to be applied in any case is the law of the state. There is no federal common law. The federal courts have no power derived from the Constitution or by Congress to declare substantive rules of common law applicable in a state whether they are "local" or "general" in nature. (4) The federal district court was bound to follow the Pennsylvania case law which would have denied recovery to Tompkins (P). Reversed.

DISSENT: (Butler, J.) Since no constitutional question was presented or argued in the lower court, and a 1937 statute which required notice to the Attorney General whenever a constitutionality of an act of Congress was raised was not followed, the court's conduct was improper.

CONCURRENCE IN PART: (Reed, J.) It is unnecessary to go beyond interpreting the meaning of "laws" in the Rule of Decision Act. Article III, and the necessary and proper clause of Article I of the Constitution, might provide Congress with the power to declare rules of substantive law for federal courts to follow.

▶ ANALYSIS

Erie can fairly be characterized as the most significant and sweeping decision on civil procedure ever handed down by the United States Supreme Court. As interpreted in subsequent decisions, *Erie* held that while federal courts may apply their own rules of procedure, issues of substantive law must be decided in accord with the applicable state law—usually the state in which the federal court sits. Note, however, how later Supreme Court decisions have made inroads into the broad doctrine enunciated here.

■=■

Quicknotes

SUBSTANTIVE LAW Law that pertains to the rights and interests of the parties and upon which a cause of action may be based.

■=■

Guaranty Trust Co. v. York

Trustee (D) v. Note holder (P)

326 U.S. 99 (1945).

NATURE OF CASE: Review of reinstatement of federal diversity action alleging fraud and misrepresentation.

FACT SUMMARY: York (P), barred from filing suit in state court because of the state statute of limitations, brought an equity action in federal court based upon diversity of citizenship jurisdiction.

🏛 RULE OF LAW
Where a state statute that would completely bar recovery in state court has significant effect on the outcome-determination of the action, even though the suit is brought in equity, the federal court is bound by the state law.

FACTS: Van Swerigen Corporation, in 1930, issued notes and named Guaranty Trust Co. (Guaranty) (D) as trustee with power and obligations to enforce the rights of the note holders in the assets of the corporation, and the Van Swerigens. In 1931, when it was apparent that the corporation could not meet its obligations, Guaranty (D) cooperated in a plan for the purchase of the outstanding notes for 50 percent of the notes' face value and an exchange of 20 shares of the corporation's stock for each $1,000 note. In 1934, York (P) received some cash, her donor not having accepted the rate of exchange. In 1940, three accepting note holders sued Guaranty (D), charging fraud and misrepresentation, in state court. York (P) was not allowed to intervene. Summary judgment in favor of Guaranty (D) was affirmed. In 1942, York (P) brought a suit in federal court based on diversity of citizenship and charged Guaranty (D) with breach of trust. Guaranty (D) moved for and was granted summary judgment on the basis of the earlier state decision. The court of appeals reversed on the basis that the earlier state decision did not foreclose this federal court action, and held that, even though the state statute of limitations had run, the fact that the action was brought in equity released the federal court from following the state rule.

ISSUE: Does a state statute of limitations, which would bar a suit in state court, also act as a bar to the same action if the suit is brought in equity in federal court, with jurisdiction being based on diversity of citizenship?

HOLDING AND DECISION: (Frankfurter, J.) Yes. *Erie R. Co. v. Tompkins*, 304 U.S. 64 (1938), overruled a particular way of looking at law after its inadequacies had been laid bare. Federal courts have traditionally given state-created rights in equity greater respect than rights in law, since the former are more frequently defined by legislative enactment. Even though federal equity may be thought of as a separate legal system, the substantive right is created by the state, and federal courts must respect state law which governs that right. While state law cannot define the remedies which a federal court must give simply because a federal court in diversity jurisdiction is available as an alternative, a federal court may afford an equitable remedy for a substantive right recognized by a state even though a state court cannot give it. Federal courts enforce state-created substantive rights if the mode of proceeding and remedy were consonant with the traditional body of equitable remedies, practice, and procedure. Matters of "substance" and of "procedure" turn on different considerations. Here, since the federal court is adjudicating a state-created right solely because of diversity of citizenship of the parties it is, in effect, only another court of the state; it cannot afford recovery if the right to recovery is made unavailable by the state. The question is not whether a statute of limitations is "procedural," but whether the statute so affects the result of litigation as to be controlling in state law. It is, therefore, immaterial to make a "substantive-procedure" dichotomy—*Erie R. Co. v. Tompkins* was not an endeavor to formulate scientific legal terminology, but rather an expression of a policy that touches the distribution of judicial power between state and federal courts. *Erie* ensures that insofar as legal rules determine the outcome of litigation, the result should not be any different in a federal court extending jurisdiction solely on the basis of diversity of citizenship. Through diversity jurisdiction, Congress meant to afford out-of-state litigants another tribunal, and not another body of law. Reversed and remanded.

DISSENT: (Rutledge, J.) Whether an action will be barred by a statute of limitations depends on the law of the forum state where the action may be brought, rather than on the law of the state that creates the substantive rights for which enforcement is sought. This follows from the principle that the forum state may apply its own period of limitations, regardless of whether the state creating the substantive right would bar suit on it.

▶ ANALYSIS

Guaranty Trust, which clarified *Erie*, may itself be in the process of being slowly eroded by modern courts. *Hanna v. Plumer*, 380 U.S. 460 (1965), held that where state law conflicts with the Federal Rules of Civil Procedure, the latter prevails regardless of the effect on outcome of the litigation. And in *Byrd v. Blue Ridge Elec. Cooperative*, 356

Continued on next page.

U.S. 525 (1958), the Court suggested that some constitutional doctrines (here, the right to a jury trial in federal court) are so important as to be controlling over state law—once again, the outcome notwithstanding.

■=■

Quicknotes

DIVERSITY OF CITIZENSHIP Parties are citizens of different states, or one party is an alien; a factor, along with a statutorily set dollar value of the matter in controversy, that allows a federal district court to exercise its authority to hear a lawsuit based on diversity jurisdiction.

EQUITABLE REMEDY A remedy that is based upon principles of fairness as opposed to rules of law.

STATUTE OF LIMITATIONS A law prescribing the period in which a legal action may be commenced.

■=■

Byrd v. Blue Ridge Rural Electric Cooperative, Inc.

Injured lineman (P) v. Power supply company (D)

356 U.S. 525 (1958).

NATURE OF CASE: Review of reversal of jury verdict for plaintiff in negligence action for damages.

FACT SUMMARY: Byrd (P) was injured while connecting power lines for a subcontractor of Blue Ridge Rural Electric Cooperative, Inc. (D).

🏛 RULE OF LAW
The *Erie* doctrine requires that federal courts in diversity cases respect definitions of rights and obligations created by state courts, but state laws cannot alter the essential characteristics and functions of the federal courts, and the jury function is such an essential function (provided for in the Seventh Amendment).

FACTS: Byrd (P) was injured while connecting power lines as an employee of a subcontractor of Blue Ridge Rural Electric Cooperative, Inc. (Blue Ridge) (D). Byrd (P) sued Blue Ridge (D) in federal court on a negligence theory. Because Byrd (P) was a citizen of North Carolina and Blue Ridge (D) was a South Carolina corporation, jurisdiction was grounded in diversity of citizenship. At trial, Blue Ridge (D) offered an affirmative defense based on a South Carolina law which would limit Byrd (P) to workmen's compensation benefits by defining him as a statutory employee of Blue Ridge (D) as well as the subcontractor (thereby precluding any collateral negligence action). The jury returned a verdict for Byrd (P). However, the court of appeals reversed and directed a verdict for Blue Ridge (D). Byrd (P) appealed to the United States Supreme Court. Blue Ridge (D) argued that the issue of immunity should be decided by the judge, pursuant to state law. Byrd (P), however, claimed that despite the *Erie* doctrine, *Erie R. Co. v. Tompkins*, 304 U.S. 64 (1938), South Carolina law cannot be allowed to preclude his right to a jury.

ISSUE: Do *Erie* doctrine considerations require that all state determinations of rights be upheld regardless of their intrusions into federal determinations?

HOLDING AND DECISION: (Brennan, J.) No. The *Erie* doctrine requires that federal courts in diversity cases respect the definitions of rights and obligations created by state courts, but state laws cannot alter the essential function (provided for in the Seventh Amendment). The South Carolina determination here that immunity is a question of law to be tried by a judge is merely a determination of the form and mode of enforcing immunity. It does not involve any essential relationship or determination of right created by the state. Of course, the *Erie* doctrine will reach even such form and mode determinations where no affir-

mative countervailing considerations can be found. Here, however, the Seventh Amendment makes the jury function an essential factor in the federal process protected by the Constitution. Reversed and remanded.

▶ ANALYSIS

This case is a major retreat by the court in its interpretation of the *Erie* doctrine. The *Guaranty Trust* case, 326 U.S. 99 (1945), had stated that the *Erie* doctrine required that federal courts not tamper with state remedies for violations of state-created rights. In *Byrd*, the Court retreats, stating that questions of mere "form and mode" of remedy (i.e., trial by jury or judge) are not necessarily the province of the states where essential federal rights (i.e., Seventh Amendment) are involved. Note that the Court does not abandon the *Guaranty Trust* rationale, however (that the outcome of a case should not be affected by the choice of court in which it is filed). The Court expresses doubt that the permitting of trial by jury here will make any difference in the final determination of the case. Note the inconsistency of argument here, since the Court first states that trial by jury is an essential right, and then states that it is really insignificant after all.

Quicknotes

DIVERSITY OF CITIZENSHIP Parties are citizens of different states, or one party is an alien; a factor, along with a statutorily set dollar value of the matter in controversy, that allows a federal district court to exercise its authority to hear a lawsuit based on diversity jurisdiction.

ERIE DOCTRINE Federal courts must apply state substantive law and federal procedural law.

SEVENTH AMENDMENT Provides that no fact tried by a jury shall be otherwise re-examined in any court of the United States, other than according to the rules of the common law.

Hanna v. Plumer

Car accident victim (P) v. Decedent's executor (D)

380 U.S. 460 (1965).

NATURE OF CASE: Appeal of summary judgment for the defense in federal diversity tort action.

FACT SUMMARY: Hanna (P) filed a tort action in federal court in Massachusetts, where Plumer (D) resided, for an auto accident that occurred in South Carolina.

🏛 RULE OF LAW
The *Erie* doctrine mandates that federal courts are to apply state substantive law and federal procedural law, but, where matters fall roughly between the two and are rationally capable of classification as either, the Constitution grants the federal court system the power to regulate their practice and pleading (procedure).

FACTS: Hanna (P), a citizen of Ohio, filed a tort action in federal court in Massachusetts against Plumer (D), the executor of the estate of Louise Plumer Osgood, a Massachusetts citizen. It was alleged that Mrs. Osgood caused injuries to Hanna (P) in an auto accident in South Carolina. Service on Plumer (D) was accomplished pursuant to Fed. R. Civ. P. 4(d)(1) by leaving copies of the summons with Plumer's (D) wife. At trial, motion for summary judgment by Plumer (D) was granted on the grounds that service should have been accomplished pursuant to Massachusetts law (by the *Erie* doctrine) [*Erie R. Co. v. Tompkins*, 304 U.S. 64 (1938)], which requires service by hand to the party personally. On appeal, Hanna (P) contended that *Erie* should not affect the application of the Federal Rules of Civil Procedure to this case. Plumer (D), however, contended that (1) a substantive law question under *Erie* was any question in which permitting application of federal law would alter the outcome of the case (the so-called "outcome determination" test); (2) the application of federal law here (i.e., 4[d][1]) would necessarily affect the outcome of the case (from a necessary dismissal to litigation); and so, therefore, (3) *Erie* required that the state substantive law requirement of service by hand be upheld along with the trial court's summary judgment.

ISSUE: Does the *Erie* doctrine classification of "substantive law questions" extend to embrace questions involving both substantive and procedural considerations merely because such a question might have an effect on the determination of the substantive outcome of the case?

HOLDING AND DECISION: (Warren, C.J.) No. The *Erie* doctrine mandates that federal courts are to apply state substantive law and federal procedural law, and, where matters fall roughly between the two and are rationally capable of classification as either, the Constitution grants

the federal court system the power to regulate their practice and pleading (procedure). It is well settled that the Enabling Act for the Federal Rules of Civil Procedure requires that a procedural effect of any rule on the outcome of a case be shown to actually "abridge, enlarge, or modify" the substantive law in a case for the *Erie* doctrine to come into play. Since, here, the question only goes to procedural requirements (i.e., service of summons), a dismissal for improper service would not alter the substantive right of Hanna (P) to serve Plumer (D) personally and re-file or affect the substantive law of negligence in the case. Article III and the Necessary and Proper Clause provide that the Congress has a right to provide rules for the Federal Court system such as Fed. R. Civ. P. 4(d)(1). Outcome determination analysis was never intended to serve as a talisman for the *Erie* doctrine. The judgment of the trial court must be reversed.

CONCURRENCE: (Harlan, J.) The Court was wrong in stating that anything arguably procedural is constitutionally placed within the province of the federal government to regulate. The test for "substantive" would be whether "the choice of rule would substantially affect those primary decisions respecting human conduct which our constitutional system leaves to state regulation."

▶ ANALYSIS

This case returns to the basic rationales of *Erie R. Co. v. Tompkins*, 304 U.S. 64 (1938). First, the Court asserts that one important consideration in determining how a particular question should be classified (substantive or procedural) is the avoidance of "forum shopping" (the practice of choosing one forum, such as federal, to file in, in order to gain the advantages of one), which permits jurisdictions to infringe on the substantive law defining powers of each other. Second, the Court seeks to avoid inequitable administration of the laws which would result from allowing jurisdictional considerations to determine substantive rights. Justice Warren here, in rejecting the "outcome determination" test, asserts that any rule must be measured ultimately against the Federal Rules Enabling Act and the Constitution. [Note: Rule 4(d)(1) was renumbered as 4(e)(2) in 2007.]

▬▬▬

Quicknotes

ERIE DOCTRINE Federal courts must apply state substantive law and federal procedural law.

▬▬▬

Walker v. Armco Steel Corp.

Injured carpenter (P) v. Nail manufacturer (D)

446 U.S. 740 (1980).

NATURE OF CASE: Appeal from dismissal of complaint for personal injuries.

FACT SUMMARY: Walker (P) contended that Rule 3 of the Federal Rules of Civil Procedure governed the manner in which an action is commenced in federal court for all purposes, including the tolling of the state statute of limitations.

🏛 RULE OF LAW
In diversity actions, Fed. R. Civ. P. 3 governs the date from which timing requirements of the federal rules begin to run but does not affect state statutes of limitations.

FACTS: Walker (P), a carpenter, was injured on August 22, 1975, while pounding a Sheffield nail manufactured by Armco Steel Corp. (Armco) (D) into a cement wall. Since there was diversity of citizenship, suit was brought in the U.S. District Court for the Western District of Oklahoma. The complaint was filed on August 19, 1977, but service of process was not made until December 1, 1977. On January 5, 1978, Armco (D) filed a motion to dismiss the complaint on the ground that the action was barred by the Oklahoma statute of limitations, which stated that an action is not commenced for purposes of the statute of limitations until service of the summons on the defendant. In his reply brief, Walker (P) admitted that his case would be foreclosed in state court but argued that Fed. R. Civ. P. 3 governs the manner in which an action is commenced in federal court for all purposes, including the tolling of the state statute of limitations. Fed. R. Civ. P. 3 states that an action is commenced by filing a complaint with the court. After the court of appeals affirmed the district court's dismissal of the action as barred by the Oklahoma two-year statute of limitations, Walker (P) appealed.

ISSUE: In diversity actions does Fed. R. Civ. P. 3 affect state statutes of limitations?

HOLDING AND DECISION: (Marshall, J.) No. In diversity actions, Fed. R. Civ. P. 3 governs the date from which various timing requirements of the federal rules begin to run but does not affect state statutes of limitations. Rule 3 simply states that a civil action is commenced by filing a complaint with the court. There is no indication that the Rule was intended to toll a state statute of limitations, much less that it purported to displace state tolling rules for purposes of state statutes of limitations. In contrast to Rule 3, the Oklahoma statute is a statement of a substantive decision by that state that actual service on and actual notice on the defendant are integral parts of the several policies served by the statute of limitations. Affirmed.

ANALYSIS

The Court in this case applied the rules enunciated in *Erie R. Co. v. Tompkins*, 304 U.S. 64 (1938), regarding the application of state law in federal diversity actions. In the *Erie* case, the court held that "except in matters governed by the Federal Constitution or by Acts of Congress, the law to be applied in any (diversity) case is the law of the State." Id. at 78.

Quicknotes

DIVERSITY OF CITIZENSHIP Parties are citizens of different states, or one party is an alien; a factor, along with a statutorily set dollar value of the matter in controversy, that allows a federal district court to exercise its authority to hear a lawsuit based on diversity jurisdiction.

ERIE DOCTRINE Federal courts must apply state substantive law and federal procedural law.

STATUTE OF LIMITATIONS A law prescribing the period in which a legal action may be commenced.

Stewart Organization, Inc. v. Ricoh Corp.

Marketing company (P) v. Copier products manufacturer (D)

487 U.S. 22 (1988).

NATURE OF CASE: Review of ruling in motion to change venue.

FACT SUMMARY: Ricoh Corp. (D) contended that federal, not state, rules should apply in a motion for change of venue.

🏛 RULE OF LAW
In a federal diversity suit, federal rules, not state rules, should govern questions of venue.

FACTS: Stewart Organization, Inc. (P) sued Ricoh Corp. (D) in District Court for the Northern District of Alabama, alleging breach of dealership contract. The contract contained a venue clause mandating venue only in Manhattan. Ricoh (D) brought a motion for change of venue under 28 U.S.C. § 1404(a). Stewart Organization (P) contended that Alabama law disfavored venue clauses, and that Alabama law should be applied. The district court agreed and denied the motion. The court of appeals reversed. The United States Supreme Court granted certiorari.

ISSUE: In a federal diversity suit, should federal rules, not state rules, govern questions of venue?

HOLDING AND DECISION: (Marshall, J.) Yes. In a federal diversity suit, federal rules, not state rules, should govern questions of venue. When a federal rule to be applied is a statute and the statute applies to the issue before the court, the statute will be applied if it was enacted within the limits of constitutional authority. Here, § 1404(a) mandates a flexible, factor-based, case-by-case analysis for change of venue in federal cases. This undoubtedly covers the issue at hand. It is equally without doubt that the statute was within the power of Congress, as the Constitution gives Congress the power to create pleading rules for courts created by it, as are district courts. This being so, the approach of the district court was erroneous, and it was properly reversed. Remanded to the district court for determination of the appropriate effect under federal law of the parties' forum-selection clause on respondent's § 1404(a) motion.

CONCURRENCE: (Kennedy, J.) The majority is correct, but it is worth noting that negotiated forum-selection clauses benefit the entire judicial system. Courts should actively encourage the use of such clauses. In a § 1404(a) analysis, a valid, negotiated forum-selection clause should almost always be the controlling factor.

DISSENT: (Scalia, J.) The Court correctly starts by asking whether 28 U.S.C. § 1404(a) covers the forum-selection clause at issue here. Section 1404(a), however, does not cover that clause. Moreover, *Erie*'s twin-aims test, 304 U.S. 64 (1938), precludes federal courts from formulating a common-law rule for this case's issue of contract validity. Although § 1404(a) does not explicitly resolve this case, it does offer guidance by requiring consideration of present and future facts, facts that do exist or will exist. Today's ruling grafts a retrospective aspect onto § 1404(a) by requiring courts to examine past facts surrounding the contract's formation. Further, *Erie* means that state law governs whether the forum-selection clause here is valid. Using federal law to determine the clause's validity encourages forum-shopping. The holding today also fails the second prong of *Erie*'s twin-aims analysis by causing laws to be applied inequitably.

▶ ANALYSIS

As the Court states, § 1404(a) provides a flexible basis for venue rulings. The intent of the parties drafting a forum-selection clause is a factor properly considered. However, it is not the sole factor. A district court would be under no categorical duty to give effect to such a clause.

━■━

Quicknotes

28 U.S.C. § 1404(a) Authorizes transfer for the convenience of parties and witnesses, in the interest of justice.

━■━

Gasperini v. Center for Humanities, Inc.

Photographer (P) v. Educational organization (D)

518 U.S. 415 (1996).

NATURE OF CASE: Review of reversal of award for damages for lost transparencies.

FACT SUMMARY: Gasperini (P) filed suit against The Center for Humanities, Inc. (the Center) (D) after it lost several hundred slides that he had loaned the Center (D) for use in an educational film.

🏛 RULE OF LAW
The Seventh Amendment does not preclude appellate review of a trial judge's denial of a motion to set aside a jury verdict as excessive.

FACTS: Gasperini (P), a California resident, was a journalist for CBS News and the Christian Science Monitor who spent seven years reporting in Central America. In 1990, Gasperini (P) agreed to supply The Center for Humanities, Inc. (the Center) (D) with 300 original color transparencies for use in an educational videotape. The Center (D) used 110 of the slides in the video, and agreed to return all of the originals to Gasperini (P). Upon completion of the project, the Center (D) could not find the slides. Gasperini (P) filed suit in a New York federal district court, invoking diversity jurisdiction pursuant to 28 U.S.C. § 1332. The Center (D) conceded liability for the lost transparencies, and the jury awarded the photographic community's "industry standard" of $1,500 per slide to Gasperini (P) for a total of $450,000. The Center (D) appealed on the grounds that the award was excessive, and the court of appeals vacated the judgment, citing New York statutory law. The court of appeals concluded "industry standard" was not the only factor to consider in determining damages, and that the slides' uniqueness and the photographer's earning level should also be considered. The court ordered a new trial unless Gasperini (P) agreed to accept an award of $100,000. Gasperini (P) appealed, arguing that the Seventh Amendment precluded review of such federal court proceedings.

ISSUE: Does the Seventh Amendment preclude appellate review of a trial judge's denial of a motion to set aside a jury verdict as excessive?

HOLDING AND DECISION: (Ginsburg, J.) No. The Seventh Amendment does not preclude appellate review of a trial judge's denial of a motion to set aside a jury verdict as excessive. New York statutory law requires that when appellate review of a money judgment is granted, the court shall determine if the award is excessive or inadequate based upon whether it "materially deviates" from what would be reasonable compensation. A damages award in federal court cannot be significantly larger than the recovery that would be tolerated in state court. Therefore, if a federal court in New

York were permitted to ignore the prescribed New York standard and instead apply the federal "shock the conscience" test, substantial variations between state and federal judgments would result. The Seventh Amendment governs proceedings in federal courts and controls the allocation of trial functions between judge and jury and the allocation of authority to review verdicts. However, the appropriate court to apply New York statutory law as it pertains to a factual determination such as a damages award is the district court, and not the court of appeals, which will have the opportunity on appeal to review for abuse of discretion. Therefore, the court of appeals judgment shall be vacated, and the case shall be remanded to the district court so that the trial judge can apply the "deviates materially" standard.

DISSENT: (Stevens, J.) The majority was correct in most of its reasoning, but not in the disposition of the case. There is no reason that the district court should be required to repeat a task that has already been well performed by the reviewing appellate court. The judgment of the court of appeals should be affirmed.

DISSENT: (Scalia, J.) The Court has overruled a longstanding and well-reasoned precedent that prohibited federal appellate courts from reviewing refusals by district courts to set aside civil jury awards as contrary to the weight of the evidence. Additionally, the Court's holding that a state practice that relates to division of duties between state judges and juries must be followed by federal courts in diversity cases is directly contrary to prior Supreme Court decisions.

▶ ANALYSIS

The federal court system relies on a premise of fairly strict finality prior to appeal. Judges and jurors traditionally have been granted a high degree of autonomy within the federal system. In fact, the Seventh Amendment's mandate that findings by juries be allowed to stand subject only to certain exceptions, dates back to eighteenth-century common law.

■══■

Quicknotes

28 U.S.C. § 1332 Governs the requirements for diversity jurisdiction.

SEVENTH AMENDMENT Provides that no fact tried by a jury shall be otherwise reexamined in any court of the United States, other than according to the rules of the common law.

■══■

Shady Grove Orthopedic Associates v. Allstate Insurance Co.

Medical association (P) v. Insurance company (D)

559 U.S. 393 (2010).

NATURE OF CASE: Grant of a writ of certiorari.

FACT SUMMARY: Shady Grove Orthopedic Associates, P.A. (P) sued Allstate Insurance Co. (D) for the insurance company's (D) alleged failure to pay interest on overdue insurance payments, on behalf of itself and a class of plaintiffs. The district court dismissed the case on the grounds that New York law prevented a class action lawsuit to recover "penalties," and the Second Circuit affirmed.

RULE OF LAW
Federal Rule of Civil Procedure 23 preempts state law as to when a class action lawsuit may be filed in federal court.

FACTS: Shady Grove Orthopedic Associates, P.A. (Shady Grove) (P) provided medical care to Galvez for her injuries resulting from a car accident. Galvez had an automobile insurance policy from Allstate Insurance Co. (Allstate) (D). Shady Grove (P) submitted a claim to Allstate (D) for Galvez's treatment. Allstate's (D) payment to Shady Grove (P) was late, and Allstate (D) refused to pay interest, a charge for which is allowable under New York law. Shady Grove (P) then filed a class action lawsuit in federal court, arguing that Allstate (D) violated New York law by failing to pay interest to policyholders. Allstate (D) moved to dismiss, arguing that under Section 901(b) of the New York Civil Practice Law and Rules, Shady Grove (P) and Galvez could not use a class action lawsuit to collect a statutory penalty unless specifically authorized under the statute, and that such a lawsuit was not specifically authorized by statute. Shady Grove (P) and Galvez argued that § 901(b) did not apply in federal courts because it was a procedural rule and it conflicted with Federal Rule of Civil Procedure 23, which governs class action lawsuits in federal court. The district court held that Shady Grove's (P) class action claim was not authorized, and, because the amount in dispute fell far short of the amount-in-controversy requirement for individual suits in federal court, it dismissed the action. The court of appeals affirmed, and the United States Supreme Court granted certiorari.

ISSUE: Does Federal Rule of Civil Procedure 23 preempt state law as to when a class action lawsuit may be filed in federal court?

HOLDING AND DECISION: (Scalia, J.) Yes. Federal Rule of Civil Procedure 23 preempts state law as to when a class action lawsuit may be filed in federal court. Section 901(b) of the New York Rules of Civil Procedure does not preclude a federal court sitting in diversity from

hearing a class action under Rule 23 of the Federal Rules of Civil Procedure. If Rule 23 answers the question in dispute, it governs, unless it exceeds its statutory authorization or Congress's rulemaking power. Here, Rule 23 answers the question in dispute—the question being whether Shady Grove's (P) suit may proceed as a class action—and is therefore controlling. Rule 23 states that "[a] class action may be maintained" if certain conditions are met. Since § 901(b) attempts to answer the same question, stating that Shady Grove's (P) suit "may not be maintained as a class action" because of the relief it seeks, that provision cannot apply in diversity suits unless Rule 23 is ultra vires. The view of the court of appeals that § 901(b) and Rule 23 address different issues is rejected. It concluded that Rule 23 concerns only the criteria for determining whether a given class can and should be certified, whereas § 901(b) addresses an antecedent question: whether the particular type of claim is eligible for class treatment in the first place—a question on which Rule 23 is silent. The line between eligibility and certifiability is entirely artificial because they are both preconditions for maintaining a class action, and, in any event, Rule 23 explicitly empowers a federal court to certify a class in every case meeting its criteria. Allstate's (D) arguments based on the exclusion of some federal claims from Rule 23's reach pursuant to federal statutes and on § 901's structure are unpersuasive, since Congress can create exceptions to an individual rule as it sees fit without rendering the Rule generally inapplicable. The Dissent's claim that § 901(b) can coexist with Rule 23 because it addresses only the remedy available to class plaintiffs is foreclosed by § 901(b)'s text, notwithstanding the statute's perceived purpose of restricting remedies. Such purpose cannot override the statute's clear text, which achieves the statute's goal by limiting a plaintiff's power to maintain a class action. In other words, the outcome cannot depend on the state legislature's subjective intentions. Further, regardless of the policies underpinning § 901(b), that statute flatly contradicts Rule 23. The principle that courts should read ambiguous Federal Rules to avoid overstepping the authorizing statute, 28 U.S.C. § 2072(b), does not apply because Rule 23 is clear. The Dissent's approach does not avoid a conflict between § 901(b) and Rule 23 but instead would render Rule 23 partially invalid. The Rules Enabling Act, not *Erie* [*Erie Railroad Co. v. Tompkins*, 304 U.S. 64 (1938)], controls the validity of a federal rule of civil procedure, even if that results in opening the federal courts to class actions that cannot proceed in state court. It has been long held that the

Continued on next page.

limitation in the Enabling Act that the rules of procedure "shall not abridge, enlarge or modify any substantive rights" means that a given rule of procedure must really regulate procedure. If the rule governs the manner and the means by which the litigants' rights are enforced, it is valid; if it alters the rules of decision by which the court will adjudicate those rights, it is not. Applying this criterion to Rule 23, insofar as it allows willing plaintiffs to join their separate claims against the same plaintiff in a class action—falls within § 2072(b)'s authorization. Contrary to Allstate's (D) argument, Rule 23 is substantively neutral. The mere likelihood that some (even many) plaintiffs will be induced to sue by the availability of a class action is just the sort of incidental effect that has long been held to not violate § 2072(b). Further, the substantive nature of New York's law, or its substantive purpose, makes no difference. A Federal Rule of Procedure is not valid in some jurisdictions and invalid in others—or valid in some cases and invalid in others—depending upon whether its effect is to frustrate a state substantive law (or a state procedural law enacted for substantive purposes). The Rule itself is looked to, and it is not the substantive or procedural nature or purpose of the affected state law that matters, but the substantive or procedural nature of the Federal Rule. The Concurrence's analysis conflicts with the Court's precedent in *Sibbach v. Wilson & Co.*, 312 U.S. 1 (1941)—that the single test is whether the federal rules "really regulate procedure." According to the Concurrence, a state procedural rule is not preempted so long as it is so bound up with, or sufficiently intertwined with, a substantive state-law right or remedy that it defines the scope of that substantive right or remedy. The rule announced by *Sibbach* leaves no room for special exemptions based on the function or purpose of a particular state rule. Thus, the Concurrence's approach in reality does not seek to apply *Sibbach*, but to overrule it—and there is no good justification for doing so. Finally, it must be acknowledged keeping the federal court doors open to class actions that cannot proceed in state court will produce forum shopping. That, however, is the inevitable, and even intended, result of a uniform system of federal procedure. Reversed.

CONCURRENCE: (Stevens, J.) Rule 23 applies in this case, but it also must be recognized that in some cases federal courts should apply state procedural rules in diversity cases, because they function as part of the state's definition of substantive rights and remedies. Federal rules must be interpreted with some degree of sensitivity to important state interests and regulatory policies, and applied to diversity cases against the background of Congress's command that such rules not alter substantive rights. The balance Congress has struck turns, in part, on the nature of the state law that is being displaced by a federal rule, and, the application of that balance does not necessarily turn on whether the state law at issue takes the form of what is traditionally described as substantive or procedural. Instead, it turns on whether the state law actu-

ally is part of a state's framework of substantive rights or remedies. When a state chooses to use a traditionally procedural vehicle as a means of defining the scope of substantive rights or remedies, federal courts must recognize and respect that choice so as not to limit the ways that sovereign states define their rights and remedies. An application of a federal rule that effectively abridges, enlarges, or modifies a state-created right or remedy violates Congress's mandate in § 2072(b), regardless of the form that right or remedy takes. Therefore, when a federal rule appears to abridge, enlarge, or modify a substantive right, federal courts must consider whether the rule can reasonably be interpreted to avoid that impermissible result, and if the rule cannot be so construed, the rule violates the Enabling Act, and federal courts cannot apply it. Contrary to Justice Scalia's belief, the sole Enabling Act question is not just whether the federal rule "really regulates procedure," because such an interpretation ignores the limitation that such rule not abridge, enlarge or modify any substantive right. Also, the plurality misreads *Sibbach*, in which the question of the obligation of federal courts to apply the substantive law of a state did not arise. The dissent seems to find that Rule 23 covers only those cases in which its application would create no *Erie* problem, and would apply the Rules of Decision Act inquiry under *Erie* even to cases in which there is a governing federal rule, and thus the Act, by its own terms, does not apply. Such an approach has the potential for working an end run around Congress's system of uniform federal rules, since in cases where there is a governing federal rule the question is only whether the Enabling Act is satisfied. In the case at bar, § 901 is facially procedural in nature, and Rule 23 governs the particular question at issue, i.e., it governs class certification. Therefore, in this case, the only decision is whether certifying a class in this diversity case would "abridge, enlarge or modify" New York's substantive rights or remedies. Although one can argue that class certification would enlarge New York's "limited" damages remedy, such arguments rest on extensive speculation about what the New York Legislature had in mind when it created § 901(b). Such speculation is obviated by the statute's plain text, which appears in the state's procedural code; to displace Rule 23 there must be more than just a possibility that § 901 is different than it appears.

DISSENT: (Ginsburg, J.) The majority opinion used Rule 23 to override New York's statutory restriction on the availability of damages and consequently turned a $500 case into a $5,000,000 one. It is important to interpret the Federal Rules with sensitivity to state regulatory policies. There was no need to find conflict between Rule 23 and New York's legitimate interest in keeping certain monetary awards reasonably bounded, and in prior decisions, the Court has avoided immoderate interpretations of the

Continued on next page.

Federal Rules that would trench on state prerogatives without serving any countervailing federal interest. And, where there is no controlling Federal Rule, the Rules of Decision Act controls and directs federal courts to apply state law when failure to do so would invite forum-shopping and yield markedly disparate litigation outcomes. Here, New York's decision to block class-action proceedings for statutory damages is clearly a means to the substantive end of limiting a defendant's liability in a single lawsuit to prevent the exorbitant inflation of penalties. Section 901 was not designed with the fair conduct or efficiency of litigation in mind. Thus, Rule 23 does not collide with it. Rule 23 prescribes the considerations relevant to class certification and postcertification proceedings, but, unlike § 901(b), it does not command that a particular remedy be available when a party sues in a representative capacity. In other words, Rule 23 describes a method of enforcing a claim for relief, while § 901(b) defines the dimensions of the claim itself. Looking at the reasons for the statutes, it is clear that Rule 23 authorizes class treatment for suits satisfying its prerequisites because the class mechanism generally affords a fair and efficient way to aggregate claims for adjudication. The reason for Section 901(b) is completely different. It does not allow class members to recover statutory damages because the state legislature considered the result of adjudicating such claims en masse to be exorbitant. The fair and efficient conduct of class litigation is the legitimate concern of Rule 23; the remedy for an infraction of state law, however, is the legitimate concern of the State's lawmakers and not of the federal rulemakers. Additionally, because federal courts sitting in diversity can accord respect for both federal and state rules, plaintiffs seeking to vindicate claims for which the state has provided a statutory penalty may pursue relief through a class action if they forgo statutory damages and instead seek actual damages or injunctive or declaratory relief; any putative class member who objects can opt out and pursue actual damages, if available, and the statutory penalty in an individual action. Moreover, *Erie* and its progeny—and the federalism principles underlying them—do not provide precedent for finding that Rule 23 authorizes a claim for relief when the state that created the remedy disallows its pursuit in class actions. Given that the two statutes at issue do not conflict, and because giving effect to Rule 23 will inevitably encourage forum shopping in favor of federal courts, as well as greatly augmented potential liability for defendants, the Rules of Decision Act commands application of the state's law. It has long been recognized to displace, in a diversity action, state-law limitations on state-created remedies. To hold otherwise erodes the federalism principles underpinning *Erie*.

▶ ANALYSIS

Forum shopping is a likely and important consequence of *Shady Grove.* If the federal rules preempt state statutes limiting class actions, as in this case, litigants will likely try to file in federal court. *Shady Grove* may therefore increase the number of class actions brought in federal court, and also might raise strategic considerations about removal for defendants sued in state courts. The plurality recognized this risk, acknowledging "the reality that keeping the federal-court door open to class actions that cannot proceed in state court will produce forum shopping." Justice Ginsburg, in her dissent, points out an irony she sees in this regard as a result of the majority's decision. Shady Grove (P) was able to pursue its claim in federal court only by virtue of the enactment of the Class Action Fairness Act of 2005 (CAFA), 28 U.S.C. § 1332(d). In CAFA, Congress opened federal-court doors to state-law-based class actions so long as there is minimal diversity, at least 100 class members, and at least $5,000,000 in controversy. By providing a federal forum, Congress sought to check what it considered to be the overreadiness of some state courts to certify class actions. In other words, Congress envisioned fewer class actions overall. According to Justice Ginsburg, Congress never anticipated that CAFA would make federal courts a mecca for suits of the kind *Shady Grove* launched: class actions seeking state-created penalties for claims arising under state law—claims that would be barred from class treatment in the state's own courts.

◼▬◼

Quicknotes

CLASS ACTION A suit commenced by a representative on behalf of an ascertainable group that is too large to appear in court, who shares a commonality of interests and who will benefit from a successful result.

FORUM SHOPPING Refers to a situation in which one party to an action seeks to have the matter heard and determined by a court or in a jurisdiction that will provide it with the most favorable result.

◼▬◼

Mason v. American Emery Wheel Works

Injured consumer (P) v. Manufacturer (D)

241 F.2d 906 (1st Cir. 1957).

NATURE OF CASE: Appeal of dismissal of action for damages for personal injury.

FACT SUMMARY: A federal court sitting in diversity held itself obligated to follow an old Mississippi Supreme Court decision regarding standing to sue in a products liability case.

⚖ RULE OF LAW
A state supreme court ruling on an issue need not be followed by a federal court sitting in diversity if that ruling has lost its vitality.

FACTS: Mason (P) was injured by an emery wheel manufactured by American Emery Wheel Works (American) (D). Mason (P) sued in federal court, jurisdiction being based on diversity. Mason (P) had not obtained the wheel directly from American (D). The district court, following a 1928 Mississippi Supreme Court decision holding that privity of contract was necessary to sue a product manufacturer for injuries, granted summary judgment in favor of American (D). Mason (P) appealed.

ISSUE: Must a state supreme court ruling on an issue be followed by a federal court sitting in diversity, even if that ruling has lost its vitality?

HOLDING AND DECISION: (Magruder, C.J.) No. A state supreme court ruling on an issue need not be followed by a federal court sitting in diversity if that ruling has lost its vitality. There is no question but that a federal court sitting in diversity must follow state law. Generally speaking, a pronouncement of a state supreme court will be final on a given issue. Where, however, the decision appears to have lost its vitality, it is up to the district court to try to decide how the state court would rule on that issue today. Here, there has been a major shift in products liability law since 1928, and it is unlikely that the Mississippi Supreme Court would follow its own precedent. This is borne out by dicta in at least one case indicating dissatisfaction with the 1928 precedent. In light of this, it seems relatively clear that the true state of the law in Mississippi is not to require contractual privity. The order of the district court is vacated and the case is remanded to the district court for further proceedings.

CONCURRENCE: (Hartigan, J.) The decision today was made much easier by the dicta to which reference was made in the opinion. It is much less clear how far a federal court in diversity can go in rejecting state supreme court precedent which has not been undercut in subsequent decisions.

▶ ANALYSIS

Obviously, not every issue that comes before a federal court sitting in diversity will have been ruled upon by a state supreme court. When this occurs, the role of a federal court becomes much like a state trial court. It must search through other state precedents to rule on an issue.

Quicknotes

PRIVITY OF CONTRACT A relationship between the parties to a contract that is required in order to bring an action for breach.

Clearfield Trust Co. v. United States

Check guarantor (D) v. Federal government (P)

318 U.S. 363 (1943).

NATURE OF CASE: Review of reversal of order dismissing action based on a guaranty.

FACT SUMMARY: A district court held that state law applied in an action by the Government (P) concerning commercial paper issued by it.

RULE OF LAW
In an action by the federal government concerning commercial paper issued by it, federal law shall apply.

FACTS: A check issued by the Government (P) was mailed, but was intercepted before it reached its intended recipient. The interceptor forged the endorsement, and cashed it at J.C. Penney Co., which in turn endorsed it to Clearfield Trust Co. (Clearfield) (D), which endorsed it with a guaranty of all prior endorsements and collected the amount from the Federal Reserve. Upon discovering the forgery, federal officials delayed eight months before demanding payment from Clearfield (D) on the guaranty. When Clearfield (D) refused, the Government (P) sued. The district court, applying Pennsylvania law, held the delay fatal to the Government's (P) claim. The court of appeals reversed.

ISSUE: In an action by the federal government concerning commercial paper issued by it, shall federal law apply?

HOLDING AND DECISION: (Douglas, J.) Yes. In an action by the federal government concerning commercial paper issued by it, federal law shall apply. When the federal government disburses funds or pays its debts, it is exercising power given it by the Constitution. The powers and duties of the federal government with respect to commercial paper issued by it thus find their roots in federal sources. In the absence of an applicable act by Congress, it is for the federal courts to fashion the governing rule of law according to their own standards. The desirability of a uniform rule is plain, and adopting the state standards is antithetical to this. [The Court held the eight-month delay not fatal to the Government's (P) case.] Affirmed.

▶ ANALYSIS

The key to the decision here appeared to be the need for uniformity. An inherent problem exists with this as a rationale in adopting federal standards in many cases. The United States Supreme Court cannot possibly announce standards in all areas in which uniformity might be desirable, as it can handle only so many cases. This leaves much decision-making up to the circuits, which can and often do contradict one another.

■━■

Quicknotes

COMMERCIAL PAPER A negotiable instrument; a written promise, signed by the promisee, to pay a specified sum of money to the promisor either on demand or on a specified date.

■━■

Boyle v. United Technologies Corp.

Father of accident victim (P) v. Federal military contractor (D)

487 U.S. 500 (1988).

NATURE OF CASE: Appeal from a jury verdict holding a federal military contractor liable under state tort law.

FACT SUMMARY: Boyle (P), the father of a U.S. military helicopter pilot, filed a diversity suit against the Sikorsky Division of United Technologies Corp. (Sikorsky) (D), the company that made the helicopter in which Boyle's (P) son died. A jury returned a verdict against Sikorsky (D) under either of two theories of Virginia state tort law, and the trial court denied Sikorsky's (D) motion to enter judgment for Sikorsky (D) notwithstanding the verdict. On appeal, the federal court of appeals reversed the judgment, in part because Sikorsky (D), as a federal military contractor, was immune from liability under state tort law.

🏛 RULE OF LAW
A federal military contractor is immune from liability for design defects under state tort law.

FACTS: A U.S. Marine helicopter pilot, the son of Boyle (P), died in a training exercise after his helicopter crashed into the sea off the coast of Virginia. The crash itself did not kill Boyle's (P) son: He died because under water, the helicopter's doors could not open, and Boyle's (P) son thus was trapped inside the helicopter, where he drowned. Boyle (P) sued the Sikorsky Division of United Technologies Corp. (Sikorsky) (D) in a federal diversity action, alleging, and presenting to the jury, two theories of liability under Virginia state tort law. Boyle (P) alleged that Sikorsky (D) had defectively repaired the part of the helicopter's control system that malfunctioned (the "servo") and caused the helicopter to crash. Boyle (P) also alleged that Sikorsky (D) had defectively designed the helicopter's emergency escape system by designing the door to open out instead of in, and by designing the handle of the escape hatch so that other equipment obstructed it. The jury awarded Boyle (P) $725,000 on a general judgment, and the trial judge denied Sikorsky's (D) motion for judgment notwithstanding the verdict. On appeal, the federal court of appeals reversed, reasoning in part that Boyle's (P) evidence did not support a verdict under his defective-repair theory in accordance with Virginia state law. On Boyle's (P) defective-design theory of liability, the appeals court ruled that, under federal law, Sikorsky (D) was immune from liability as a federal military contractor. Boyle (P) petitioned the United States Supreme Court for further review on the immunity issue.

ISSUE: Is a federal military contractor immune from liability for design defects under state tort law?

HOLDING AND DECISION: (Scalia, J.) Yes. A federal military contractor is immune from liability for design defects under state tort law. This Court's precedents have established that areas implicating "uniquely federal interests" are so governed by federal law that the federal interest preempts state law in those areas. This case presents two such federal interests: (1) the contract rights and liabilities of the United States and (2) the civil liability of federal employees for actions taken within the scope of their employment. This latter federal interest also applies to Sikorsky (D), whose fulfillment of the federal government's military procurement contract with the company obviously promotes the federal government's interest. Displacement of state law is appropriate, however, only when a "significant conflict" exists between the state law and the federal interest. This case presents just such a conflict because, unlike the government contract at issue in *Miree v. DeKalb County*, 433 U.S. 25 (1977), the contract here imposes a duty that directly opposes the state-imposed duty of care required by Boyle's (P) defective-design theory. This holding is consistent with federal statute. Although the Federal Tort Claims Act authorizes damages against the federal government for negligent or wrongful conduct by federal officials, the Act also exempts claims based on discretionary decisions. Selecting an effective design for military equipment is unquestionably a discretionary function within the meaning of the Act. Thus, in cases such as this one, federal policy "significantly conflicts" with state tort law, and the state law therefore must yield. Vacated and remanded.

DISSENT: (Brennan, J.) According to the majority, Sikorsky's (D) immunity derives solely from its contractual affiliation with the federal government: If Sikorsky (D) had designed the same product for a private company, Boyle (P) could have sued Sikorsky (D) under Virginia tort law and recovered damages for his son's death. The injustice in this decision is this Court's own willingness to legislate in an area in which Congress has remained conspicuously silent. Compounding the injustice of the new government contractor defense is that the sweep of the ruling seems limitless, apparently applying to any gadget made for the federal government after a federal official has previewed the product's planned design. This Court has no power to create such a rule, as the Court recognized in *Erie R. Co. v. Tompkins*, 304 U.S. 64 (1938). After *Erie*, our cases have limited the imposition of federal common law to "few and restricted" situations: The rights and duties of the federal government, disputes involving conflicting rights of states

Continued on next page.

or the federal government's relations with foreign countries, and cases sounding in admiralty. Generally, it is the role of elected legislators to create law in other areas. The legal system assumes that tort liability encourages companies to design safe products. Even if that liability is an inefficient way to achieve the system's goals, Congress, not this unelected Court, is the proper body to limit the civil liability of government contractors.

DISSENT: (Stevens, J.) This Court should defer the creation of entirely new federal law to Congress.

▶ *ANALYSIS*

After *Erie,* it is axiomatic that "there is no federal common law." Cases such as *Boyle,* though, demonstrate the flexibility of *Erie*'s pronouncement. The interplay between the majority and the dissenters in *Boyle* further clarifies that flexibility. The majority obviously based its holding on precedent, or at least a reading of precedent, which contradicts Justice Stevens's assumption that the majority has "create[d] [an] entirely new [federal] doctrine." Also, Justice Brennan's dissent seems to undercut itself by explicitly acknowledging that cases involving "the rights and obligations of the United States"—i.e., cases presumably like *Boyle* itself—are properly resolved by allowing judicially created federal law to displace state law. But though the majority seem to have the stronger argument on the question of federal common law, Justice Scalia's opinion goes further. Perhaps because the dissenters so strongly advocated letting Congress decide whether to exempt federal government contractors from state tort liability, Justice Scalia also observed that the application of judicially created law in *Boyle* does coincide with congressional intent as expressed in the "discretionary decisions" exemptions permitted by the Federal Tort Claims Act.

■══■

Quicknotes

DEFECTIVE DESIGN A product that is manufactured in accordance with a particular design; however, such design is inherently flawed so that it presents an unreasonable risk of injury.

JUDGMENT N.O.V. A judgment entered by the trial judge reversing a jury verdict if the jury's determination has no basis in law or fact.

■══■

Dice v. Akron, Canton & Youngstown R. Co.

Injured railroad fireman (P) v. Employer (D)

342 U.S. 359 (1952).

NATURE OF CASE: Review of judgment n.o.v. for the defense in negligence action under Federal Employers' Liability Act.

FACT SUMMARY: Dice (P), a railroad fireman, was injured in an accident involving a train of the Akron, Canton & Youngstown R. Co. (D).

🏛 RULE OF LAW
Though federal claims may be adjudicated by state courts, state laws are never controlling on the question of what the incidents of any federal right may be.

FACTS: Dice (P), a railroad fireman, was injured when an engine of the Akron, Canton & Youngstown R. Co. (Railroad) (D) jumped the track. He sued in an Ohio state court under the Federal Employers' Liability Act, charging negligence. At trial, the Railroad (D) offered in defense a document signed by Dice (P) which purported to release the Railroad (D) of all liability over and above $924.63 which Dice (P) had already received. Dice (P) contended that he had not read the statement before signing it, relying on fraudulent representations of the Railroad (D) that the document was merely a receipt for the $924.63. The jury found for Dice (P), but the trial court entered "judgment notwithstanding the verdict" for the Railroad (D) on the grounds that under Ohio state law Dice (P) could not escape responsibility for signing the release. Under Ohio law, he was under a duty to read the document before signing it. The Ohio Court of Appeals reversed the trial judge on the grounds that federal law (that a finding of fraud will preclude the use of a release such as the one in this case) should have been applied. The Ohio Supreme Court reversed again and this appeal followed.

ISSUE: In adjudicating a claim arising out of federal law, may a state court properly apply state law?

HOLDING AND DECISION: (Black, J.) No. Though federal claims may be adjudicated by state courts, state laws are never controlling on the question of what the incidents of any federal right may be. Federal rights according relief to injured railroad employees could be defeated if states were permitted to have the final say as to what defenses could and could not be interposed here. It is true that Ohio normally allows the judge in an action to resolve all issues of fraud in a negligence action, and that, in itself, is a perfectly acceptable procedure. But it is well settled that the federal right to a jury trial is an essential one, which Ohio may not infringe upon. Reversed and remanded.

CONCURRENCE AND DISSENT: (Frankfurter, J.) Requiring federal standards for the determination of fraud unconstitutionally invades the state's reserved power to maintain the common law division between law (i.e., negligence determined by a jury) and equity (fraud relieved by a judge).

▶ ANALYSIS

This case points up the general rule for the treatment of federal rights in state courts. In short, they are always governed by federal law. The Seventh Amendment right to a civil jury trial is an exclusively federal right. It is not a fundamental right incorporated in the Fourteenth Amendment and extended to the states. As such, states may properly provide that certain issues are to be determined by judges. When a federal right is involved, however, such discretion ceases. The federal standard of the Seventh Amendment must prevail.

■=■

Quicknotes

FEDERAL EMPLOYERS' LIABILITY ACT Permits federal employees to file suit for injuries sustained as a result of their employer's negligent conduct.

JUDGMENT N.O.V. A judgment entered by the trial judge reversing a jury verdict if the jury's determination has no basis in law or fact.

SEVENTH AMENDMENT Provides that no fact tried by a jury shall be otherwise re-examined in any court of the United States, other than according to the rules of the common law.

■=■

The Development of Modern Procedure

Quick Reference Rules of Law

Veale v. Warner

Creditor (P) v. Debtor (D)

K.B., 1 Wms. Saund. 323, 326, 85 Eng. Rep. 463, 468 (1670).

NATURE OF CASE: Action to collect a debt.

FACT SUMMARY: Veale (P) alleged that Warner (D) owed him £2,000.

RULE OF LAW
On a demurrer, the court must look to the whole record and give judgment to the party who, on the whole, appears to be entitled to it.

FACTS: Veale (P) brought this action against Warner (D) to collect a £2,000 debt. Veale (P) followed the required forms of pleading in alleging that Warner (D) was in the custody of the marshal and that there were pledges of prosecution, namely John Doe and Richard Roe. Veale (P) went on to allege that he lent Warner (D) £2,000, which he was to repay on request by Veale (P). Veale (P) alleged that he had made request of Warner (D), but that he refused to repay the money, and so Veale (p) instigated this action. Warner (D) claimed that the writing containing the obligation was submitted to arbitrators who ruled that Warner (D) owed Veale (P) £3,169, and that he had paid the full amount. Warner (D) claimed that Veale (P) shouldn't be allowed to bring this action against him because he had already discharged the debt. Veale (P) claimed that he hadn't been paid and should be allowed to bring the action. Warner (D) responded that he had a writing where Veale (P) had acknowledged that Warner (D) had paid him. Both parties demurred to the pleadings of the other party.

ISSUE: On a demurrer, must the court look to the whole record and give judgment for the party who, on the whole, appears to be entitled to it?

HOLDING AND DECISION: [Judge not stated in casebook excerpt.] Yes. Warner (D) argued that the award of the arbitrators was not valid because Veale (P) didn't have to perform anything and Warner (D) was the only one required to perform under the award. Since the award was not valid, Warner (D) claimed it was not material whether he had performed or not, even though he had pleaded performance. Veale (P) had only presented part of the award of the arbitrators at the trial and Warner (D) had presented the other part of it. Because a court must look to the whole record when ruling on a demurrer, Warner (D) tricked Veale (P) into demurring to his rejoinder, so that the case could be decided before trial. To do this, Warner (D) pleaded a response in his rejoinder which was not allowed by the pleading rules, and so Veale (P) demurred to Warner's (D) rejoinder. When the court had the full record before them, they agreed with Warner (D) about the award being invalid. Since Warner (D) had used a trick in pleading in order to get the full record before the court, they would not give judgment to Warner (D), but they allowed Veale (P) to discontinue his action. Warner (D) was able to show in another court that Veale (P) was actually in his debt and that he did not owe Veale (P) anything. Demurrer and joinder in demurrer.

ANALYSIS

In the complaint, Veale (P) alleged that Warner (D) was in the custody of the marshal. This was necessary, because if an action was not commenced by a writ, the court would not have jurisdiction unless the person was in the custody of the court. At first, the person actually had to be in the custody of the marshal, but this eventually became wholly fictitious. If the case wasn't commenced by a writ, then custody of the defendant had to be pleaded; the defendant wasn't allowed to challenge the allegation of custody, even though it hadn't occurred. Originally, the plaintiff also had to furnish sureties who would be liable to pay a fine that was imposed upon unsuccessful claimants. In this case, the pledges of prosecution, as they were called, were John Doe and Richard Roe, which indicates that it was not only a matter of pleading. The rejoinder mentioned in the case refers to a responsible pleading by the defendant to the replication made by the plaintiff which was a response to the answer of the defendant.

Quicknotes

DEMURRER The assertion that the opposing party's pleadings are insufficient and that the demurring party should not be made to answer.

REJOINDER A pleading by a defendant during trial in answer to a plaintiff's rebuttal.

Scott, an Infant, by His Next Friend v. Shepherd, an Infant, by Guardian

Injured child (P) v. Squib thrower (D)

Ct. C.P., 2 Wm. Bl. 892, 96 Eng. Rep. 525 (1773).

NATURE OF CASE: Action in trespass vi et armis.

FACT SUMMARY: Scott (P) was injured when a squib (similar to a firecracker) lit by Shepherd (D) exploded after it had been tossed around a market-house.

🏛 RULE OF LAW
An injury caused as the result of a wrongful act is maintainable as an action in trespass, though arguably it should have been brought on the case.

FACTS: Shepherd (D) threw a lighted gunpowder-filled squib from the street into a market-house, where many people were assembled. The squib was quickly tossed around the house, in an effort by each tosser to remove it from his area, until it finally exploded, putting out Scott's (P) eye. Scott (P) sued Shepherd (D) in a trespass action for his injury. Shepherd (D) pleaded that the action should have been dismissed since it properly should have been brought on the case, not trespass.

ISSUE: Can an action in trespass be brought for an injury which occurred as the result of a wrongful act?

HOLDING AND DECISION: (Nares, J.) Yes. The question was whether the action should have been brought on the case rather than in trespass. Three of the four judges agreed that the action in trespass was proper, though arriving at that conclusion in different ways. Nares decided that any injury resulting from an unlawful act, be it immediate or consequential, was a trespass action. The "wrongfulness" of Shepherd's (D) act remained with the squib until it finally exploded. Verdict for Scott (P).

(Blackstone, J.) A trespass action only lay when the injury was immediate and direct; that when injury was consequential, the action must be on the case. The lawful/unlawful distinction is not determinative. The injury in this case was the result of the new motion of the merchants in the market-house, i.e., their picking up the squib and tossing it. The squib was "at rest" and, therefore, Shepherd's (D) illegality stopped until it was picked up and given new life by an intervener. The merchants' actions of tossing the squib were "unnecessary and incautious," and relieved Shepherd (D) from direct liability.

(Gould, J.) The consequences of an unlawful act are attributable to the original wrongdoer, and an action in trespass is maintainable. But Shepherd (D) is the direct cause of the injury.

(De Grey, C.J.) I agree with Blackstone's principles, but disagree with his application. He found the injury to be the direct and immediate act of Shepherd (D), who had intentionally introduced a dangerous squib indiscriminately and wantonly. All subsequent tossing of the squib was a continuation of the first act.

▶ ANALYSIS

The question of where "direct" injury ends and "consequential" injury begins is not at all clear and obvious. Even Blackstone and De Grey, who agreed in principle on the question to be determined (i.e., was it a continuation of the original throwing?), did not agree on the application of the principle in this particular case.

Quicknotes

PER QUOD Whereby.

POSTEA A formal statement documenting trial court proceedings.

SQUIB A firecracker.

TRESPASS Unlawful interference with, or damage to, the real or personal property of another.

Bushel v. Miller

Porter (P) v. Trespassing porter (D)

K.B., 1 Strange 128, 93 Eng. Rep. 428 (1718).

NATURE OF CASE: Action in trover to recover the value of converted property.

FACT SUMMARY: Bushel (P) attempted to recover the value of goods that he held as bailee for Miller (D).

🏛 RULE OF LAW
Trover does not lie against a party who has a right to handle the goods.

FACTS: On the custom-house wharf there was a small building where the porters put small parcels of goods if the ship was not ready to receive them when they were brought on the wharf. The porters, who had a right in this building, each had a designated space to put the items for which they were responsible. Both Bushel (P) and Miller (D) were porters, each having his own designated space in this building. Bushel (P) put goods belonging to him in the building in such a way that Miller (D) could not get to his space without moving Bushel's (P) goods. Miller (D) moved them about a yard toward the door and, without returning them to their place, went away. The goods were subsequently lost. Bushel (P) paid the value of the goods and brought this action in trover against Miller (D).

ISSUE: For an action in trover to be proper, must the goods in question have been converted?

HOLDING AND DECISION: [Judge not stated in casebook excerpt.] Yes. Miller (D) had a right to move the goods so that he could get to his designated area in the building. But in not returning the goods to the place where he found them, Miller (D) may have been guilty of trespass, but what he did, did not amount to conversion. Miller (D) made no attempt to exercise any dominion or control over the goods other than to move them, and something more is needed for conversion. Since there was no conversion, the action of trover was not proper. The court did hold that Bushel (P) had acquired a sufficient property interest in the goods by having paid A for this building.

▶ ANALYSIS

According to Prosser, the modern law of conversion is confined to those major interferences with the chattel or with the plaintiff's rights which are so serious that the defendant is required to pay the plaintiff the entire value of the goods. Today, trespass remains the remedy for minor interferences which result in some damage, but which are not serious enough to amount to conversion. The relevant factors to be considered in determining whether there has been a conversion is the extent and duration of the defendant's exercise of control over the chattel, the defendant's good or bad intentions, the harm done to the chattel, and the expense and inconvenience caused to the plaintiff.

Quicknotes

BAILEE Person holding property in trust for another party.

CHATTEL An item of personal property.

CONVERSION The act of depriving an owner of his property without permission or justification.

TRESPASS Unlawful interference with, or damage to, the real or personal property of another.

TROVER An action for damages resulting from the unlawful conversion of, or to recover possession of, personal property.

Gordon v. Harper

Lessor (P) v. Sheriff (D)

K.B., 7 T.R. 9, 101 Eng. Rep. 828 (1796).

NATURE OF CASE: Action for trover of household furniture.

FACT SUMMARY: Gordon (P) attempted to recover goods which Harper (D), the sheriff, seized in execution of a judgment.

RULE OF LAW
To maintain an action in trover, the plaintiff must: (1) have a right to the possession of the goods taken, and (2) be in actual possession of them.

FACTS: Gordon (P) leased a furnished house to A. Gordon (P) had purchased the furniture in the house from B some time before he leased the house to A. While A was in possession under the lease, Harper (D), the sheriff, seized the furniture in execution of a judgment against B. After Harper (D) had seized the furniture, he had it sold. At the time of trial, A was still in possession of the house as the lease had not yet expired. Gordon (P) brought this action in trover to recover the value of the furniture.

ISSUE: Can a party who does not have actual possession of goods nor a right to possession of the goods bring an action of trover to recover the value of the goods?

HOLDING AND DECISION: (Lord Kenyon, C.J.) No. In order to bring an action in trover, the party must have a right to the possession of the goods and must be actually in possession of them. Gordon (P) had leased the house and the furniture to A, and at the time of the trial, the lease had still not terminated. Therefore, Gordon (P) did not have a right to the possession of the furniture because he had leased it to A, and it was A who actually had possession of the furniture. Gordon (P) would have been a trespasser himself had he taken the goods from the tenant. The tenant, A, could have brought the action of trover because he had the right to possession of the furniture and was in actual possession of it. Gordon (P) would be able to maintain this action after he regained the possession of the house when the lease expired. Decision for the defendant.

(Ashurst, J.) A plaintiff must have the right of property and right of possession in order to have the right of trover.

(Grose, J.) Because he did not have actual possession or a right to possession, Gordon (P) had no right to recover them from any other person during the term.

(Lawrence, J.) If the sheriff's taking determined the tenant's interests, and then re-vested the interest in the landlord, the landlord might maintain trover. But the sheriff's taking did not determine the tenant's interest, so the tenant might maintain a trespass action.

ANALYSIS

The action of trover was an outgrowth of the writ of detinue. The writ of detinue allowed the plaintiff to recover his personal property from the defendant, who had possession and refused to relinquish it. Although the gist of the action was wrongful detention rather than wrongful taking, detinue would lie against a thief. The main problem with detinue was that the defendant could give back the property instead of paying damages even if the property was damaged. Under trover, the plaintiff could refuse the property and demand the value of the goods instead. The action of trover is still basically the same today as set forth in this case. The party must have a right to possession of the goods and the goods must be specific enough to be identified.

Quicknotes

TROVER An action for damages resulting from the unlawful conversion of, or to recover possession of, personal property.

WRIT OF DETINUE A writ to recover personal property wrongfully taken by another.

Slade's Case

Farmer (P) v. Buyer (D)

Ex. Ch., 4 Co. Rep. 92b, 76 Eng. Rep. 1074 (1602).

NATURE OF CASE: Action on the case for non-payment.

FACT SUMMARY: Slade (P) sold Morley (D) some wheat and rye for which the latter promised to pay Slade (P) £16 but had not done so.

🏛 RULE OF LAW
When one sells goods to another and agrees to deliver them, and the other agrees to pay upon delivery, both parties may have an action of debt or an action on the case on assumpsit at their election.

FACTS: Slade (P) alleged that he had sold some wheat and rye to Morley (D) for £16. Slade (P) brought this action on the case for nonpayment. Morley (D) pleaded non assumpsit modo et forma. Non assumpsit means that the defendant did not undertake or promise, as alleged. Modo et forma means that the defendant denies the other party's allegation, not only in its general effect, but in the exact manner and form in which it is made.

ISSUE: Will an action on the case lie for the nonpayment of money?

HOLDING AND DECISION: [Judge not stated in casebook excerpt.] Yes. Every executory contract imports in itself an assumpsit, for when one agrees to pay money or to deliver anything, he thereby assumes or promises to pay or deliver. Therefore, when one sells goods to another and agrees to deliver them, and the other agrees to pay upon delivery, both parties may have an action of debt or an action on the case on assumpsit. Also, although an action of debt lies upon the contract, the bargainor may have an action on the case or an action of debt at his election. In this action on the case on assumpsit, Slade (P) should not only recover damages for the special loss (if there are any) but also for the whole debt, so that a recovery or a bar in this action would be a good bar in an action of debt brought upon the same contract.

▶ ANALYSIS

This case recognizes general assumpsit or indebitatus assumpsit, which means "being indebted, he promised." The contract-like sanction it imposed upon an obligation that did not really arise out of a promise provided structure for whole new developments. When A has delivered goods to B or has performed services for B, it may be presumed that A expects payment and B expects to pay. However, the common law had furnished no remedy in the absence of an actual agreement. Now, a new action developed based upon an implied promise to pay, not unlike the imputed promise to pay the debt that furnished the basis of *Slade's Case.*

◼▬◼

Quicknotes

ASSUMPSIT An oral or written promise by one party to perform or pay another.

MODO ET FORMA The denial of an allegation of another party, pleading by way of traverse, to both its overall effect and to the manner and form in which it is pled.

NON ASSUMPSIT A manner of pleading whereby the defendant claims that he did not promise to fulfill an obligation as set forth by the plaintiff.

◼▬◼

Lamine v. Dorrell

Estate administrator (P) v. Former administrator (D)

Q.B., 2 Ld. Raym. 1216, 92 Eng. Rep. 303 (1705).

NATURE OF CASE: Action on indebitatus assumpsit.

FACT SUMMARY: Lamine (P) brought this action against Dorrell (D) for money he received for some Irish debentures which he obtained and disposed of while pretending to be administrator of the estate of J.S.

🏛 RULE OF LAW
An action on indebitatus assumpsit will lie for the recovery of an indebtedness, even though such recovery could be had in an action of trover or detinue.

FACTS: Lamine (P) brought this action on indebitatus assumpsit for money received by Dorrell (D) for the use of Lamine (P) as administrator of the estate of J.S. J.S. died intestate, possessed of certain Irish debentures. Dorrell (D), pretending to be administrator, obtained the debentures and disposed of them. Then Dorrell's (D) administration was repealed, and administration was granted to Lamine (P). Lamine (P) brought this action against Dorrell (D) for the money he sold the debentures for. Dorrell (D) objected that this action would not have foundation, because he sold the debentures as one that claimed a title and interest in them, and therefore could not be said to have received the money for the use of Lamine (P), and Lamine (P) should have brought an action of trover or detinue.

ISSUE: Will an action on indebitatus assumpsit lie where the defendant did not actually receive the money in question for the use of the plaintiff?

HOLDING AND DECISION: (Powell, J.) Yes. It is clear in this case that Lamine (P) might have maintained trover or detinue for the debentures. But he may also dispense with the wrong done by Dorrell (D), suppose that the sale of the debentures was by his own consent, and bring an action for the money they were sold for, as money received for his use.

(Holt, C.J.) A recovery in this action may be used by Dorrell (D) as evidence of his innocence in an action of trover, because by this action Lamine (P) makes and affirms Dorrell's (D) sale of the debentures to be lawful, and, consequently, the sale of them is no conversion.

▶ ANALYSIS

Actions on indebitatus assumpsit or general assumpsit demonstrate the extent of vagueness permissible in common law pleadings. If a plaintiff pleaded a simple formula of liability, he might recover, even though he proved differ-

ent facts, as demonstrated by this case, so long as the facts had the same legal effect as the facts within the formula. In *Lamine*, the "formula facts" were that defendant had received money for the use of the plaintiff. A plaintiff who declared this received-to-plaintiff's-use formula might prove that the defendant had stolen or converted plaintiff's goods, fraudulently induced plaintiff to buy some worthless article and that plaintiff thereafter rescinded the sale, or that plaintiff had paid or overpaid money to defendant by mistake, as well as the example provided by *Lamine*.

Quicknotes

DEBENTURES Long-term unsecured debt securities issued by a corporation.

DETINUE A writ to recover personal property wrongfully taken by another.

INDEBITATUS ASSUMPSIT An action alleging that the defendant contracted to perform an obligation or to pay a debt, which he failed to perform or pay.

INTESTATE To die without leaving a valid testamentary instrument.

TROVER An action for damages resulting from the unlawful conversion of, or to recover possession of, personal property.

Jones v. Winsor

Investors (P) v. Attorney (D)

S.D. Sup. Ct., 22 S.D. 480, 118 N.W. 716 (1908).

NATURE OF CASE: Appeal from an order overruling a demurrer to a complaint alleging conversion.

FACT SUMMARY: Jones (P) and others (P) alleged that of moneys they gave to Winsor (D) as their attorney for their use and benefit, he refused to return $1,000 that he wrongfully and fraudulently converted to his own use.

RULE OF LAW

While the state code has abolished forms of pleading, the distinctions between actions is still essential, and two theories of recovery cannot be combined in one action.

FACTS: Jones's (P) complaint alleged that they had employed Winsor (D) as their attorney, and that he gave them a statement charging $1,250 for his services and showing that he had received $1,000 from Jones (P). It further alleged that Winsor's (D) services were not worth more than $250, and that of money received by Winsor (D) for the benefit and use of Jones (P), $1,000 still remained in his hands. The complaint alleged that Jones (P) had asked Winsor (D) to return the money and he refused to do so, and he had wrongfully and fraudulently converted the $1,000 to his own use. Jones (P) demanded judgment against Winsor (D) for the sum of $1,000 for the wrongful conversion of said property. Winsor (D) demurred on the ground that the complaint does not state facts sufficient to constitute a cause of action in trover or conversion because it does not allege Jones's (P) ownership of the $1,000. The court states that it is difficult to determine from the complaint whether Jones (P) intended their action should be for money had and received or for conversion.

ISSUE: Are distinctions between actions not as essential under the state code so that two theories of recovery may be combined in one action?

HOLDING AND DECISION: (Corson, J.) No. A complaint framed with a double aspect or to unite distinct and separate causes of actions cannot be maintained. While the state code has abolished forms of pleading, and only requires that the facts be stated in a plain and concise manner without unnecessary repetition, still the distinctions between actions as they formerly existed cannot be entirely ignored. Here, Jones (P) contends that the allegations for conversion may be treated as surplusage and the complaint may be held good as an action in assumpsit for money had and received. However, to so hold would introduce into the law too much uncertainty and ambiguity in pleading which would have a tendency to mislead courts

and the opposing party. Jones's (P) complaint should have been framed on the theory that it was either a complaint in tort or one in ex contractu. The two theories cannot be combined in one action. The order overruling the demurrer is reversed.

ANALYSIS

The framers of the original codes sought to do away with the rigidity and resulting injustice of the common law pleadings. As *Jones* demonstrates, not all courts followed the code ideal of requiring the complaint to state the facts, not the law.

Quicknotes

ACTION IN ASSUMPSIT Action to recover damages for breach of an oral or written promise to perform or pay pursuant to a contract.

COMPLAINT EX CONTRACTU Action arising from the breach of a contractual promise.

CONVERSION The act of depriving an owner of his property without permission or justification.

DEMURRER The assertion that the opposing party's pleadings are insufficient and that the demurring party should not be made to answer.

TROVER An action for damages resulting from the unlawful conversion of, or to recover possession of, personal property.

Garrity v. State Board of Administration

Farmer (P) v. University regents (D)

Kan. Sup. Ct., 99 Kan. 695, 162 P. 1167 (1917).

NATURE OF CASE: Appeal of a decision granting a demurrer in an action to enforce an implied promise.

FACT SUMMARY: Garrity (P) sought to recover the value of a fossil that the board of regents of the state university had taken from his land.

RULE OF LAW

If a complaint can be brought under two different theories of law, the court, in its discretion, may view the complaint under the theory that it chooses.

FACTS: Garrity (P) alleged in his complaint that in July 1911 the assistant curator of mammals of the University of Kansas entered his farm and removed a large and valuable fossil and wrongfully converted it. Garrity (P) further alleged that the assistant curator was an agent of the Board of Regents. The Board of Regents was a corporate body created by the legislature to manage and control the state university. In 1913, the legislature replaced the Board of Regents with the State Board of Administration of Educational Institutions (State Board) (D) which was not made a corporate body. Garrity (P) filed this action in 1914, and named the State Board of Administration (D) as the defendant. Garrity (P) also alleged that the fossil was worth $2,500 and that he was not paid anything for it. Garrity (P) claimed that the Board of Administration (D), as successor to the Board of Regents, was subrogated to the rights, duties and responsibilities of the Board of Regents, and subject to its obligations and liable for its debts and contracts. The court sustained a demurrer to the complaint. The State Board (D) claimed that the complaint did not state a cause of action and if it did state a cause of action it was barred by the statute of limitations because the action was in tort and the two-year statute had run. Garrity (P) asserted that he waived the tort and sought to recover upon an implied promise to pay what the fossil is worth, which had a longer statute of limitations.

ISSUE: If a complaint can be brought under two different theories of law, may the court, in its discretion, view the complaint under the theory that it chooses?

HOLDING AND DECISION: (Porter, J.) Yes. Garrity (P) did state a valid cause of action. There were sufficient facts stated to authorize Garrity (P) to waive the tort and rely upon an implied promise to pay the value of the property. Because the statute of limitations for an action in contract was three years instead of the two-year statute in tort actions, the claim was filed within the allowable time limit. However, even though the State Board (D) was given the power to execute trusts or other obligations of any of the institutions, such power cannot be construed to make either the State Board (D) or its members liable for a tort committed by the Board of Regents. Furthermore, since the State Board (D) isn't liable in tort, Garrity (P) cannot, by waiving the tort, make either the State Board (D) or its members liable upon the theory of an implied promise. Affirmed.

ANALYSIS

The court in this case has gotten away from the strictness of the common law pleadings. Even though Garrity's (P) complaint sounded in tort, the court was willing to accept his theory of an implied promise in determining whether he had stated a cause of action and determining whether the statute of limitations had run. After the court had determined that the action was proper under a theory of implied promise, they held the action to be in tort in determining whether the State Board (D) was liable. The court gave no reason for doing so, and it appears that they may be relying on the common law notion that the pleadings should be construed against the party who filed the pleadings. Under that approach, even though Garrity (P) stated a cause of action for an implied promise, since the complaint also sounded in tort, the court could determine liability on either theory and since there would be no liability in tort, the complaint would be construed that way, which was most strongly against Garrity (P).

■=■

Quicknotes

DEMURRER The assertion that the opposing party's pleadings are insufficient and that the demurring party should not be made to answer.

STATUTE OF LIMITATIONS A law prescribing the period in which a legal action may be commenced.

■=■

Modern Pleading

Quick Reference Rules of Law

Dioguardi v. Durning

Disgruntled importer (P) v. Custom official (D)

139 F.2d 774 (2d Cir. 1944).

NATURE OF CASE: Action to recover damages for conversion and violation of 19 U.S.C. § 1491.

FACT SUMMARY: Dioguardi (P) filed a complaint against the Collector of Customs for conversion and violation of 19 U.S.C. § 1491.

RULE OF LAW
The Federal Rules of Civil Procedure only require that a complaint contain a short and plain statement of the claim showing a right to relief.

FACTS: Dioguardi (P) was not an attorney, but because of his distrust for attorneys he drew up his own complaint and filed it. Dioguardi (P) stated in a very ambiguous manner that the Collector of Customs at the Port of New York (D) had converted two cases of bottles belonging to Dioguardi (P). He also alleged that a public auction which Durning (D) held to sell items which had not been claimed at the Port of New York was illegal, as it did not comply with 19 U.S.C.A. § 1491. Dioguardi (P) alleged that he was the first bidder at $110 but that Durning (D) sold the goods to another party at the same price. The district court granted Durning's (D) motion to dismiss for failing to state facts sufficient to constitute a cause of action. Dioguardi (P) was allowed to amend his complaint, but again the district court, on Durning's (D) motion, made a final judgment dismissing the complaint. Dioguardi (P) appealed that judgment.

ISSUE: Is it sufficient if the complaint in federal court contains enough information to put the other party on notice of the action against him?

HOLDING AND DECISION: (Clark, J.) Yes. Under the Federal Rules of Civil Procedure, the complaint is only required to contain enough information to put the other party on notice of the complaint against him. Dioguardi (P) did state in his complaint facts sufficient to put Durning (D) on notice of what Dioguardi's (P) claims were and the grounds on which they rested. The facts were not well presented but the complaint should not be judged on the quality of the pleading, but on the required notice being given. The complaint does not have to contain facts sufficient to state a cause of action as required under code pleading. The Federal Rules are an attempt to get away from the rigid, formal requirements of code pleading. Under the Federal Rules, all that is required is the complaint contain a statement showing that the person making the complaint is entitled to relief. Since the challenge to the complaint went only to the face of the complaint and not to any of the evidence, the court should be careful not to deny a person his day in court because of the form of his complaint. Fed. R. Civ. P. 8(e) requires that all pleadings should be so construed as to do substantial justice. Reversed and remanded.

ANALYSIS

Many states have adopted this approach to pleading. Under the federal rules, less detail is required and less importance is attached to the pleadings. They have ended the problem of distinguishing between an ultimate fact and evidentiary fact and conclusions of law as required in code pleading. The federal rules rely on discovery procedures and other pretrial devices to develop the facts. There is some criticism that by requiring less detail in the pleading, many claims without merit will be filed, thus creating more work for the overcrowded courts. As yet, this appears to be an unfounded fear. There is an exception when the federal rules do require detailed pleadings of specific matters. Complaints dealing with fraud and mistake must be pled with particularity as required by Fed. R. Civ. P. 9(b).

Quicknotes

CONVERSION The act of depriving an owner of his property without permission or justification.

Bell Atlantic Corporation v. Twombly

Telephone subscribers (P) v. Telephone companies (D)

550 U.S. 544 (2007).

NATURE OF CASE: Appeal of judgment on the pleadings.

FACT SUMMARY: [Telephone and Internet subscribers alleged in a complaint that local telephone companies were violating antitrust laws. The district court dismissed the complaint for failure to state a claim, and the Second Circuit Court of Appeals reversed.]

🏛 RULE OF LAW

In order for a complaint to survive dismissal on the pleadings, the complaint must include enough facts to state a claim to relief that is plausible on its face.

FACTS: [Telephone and Internet subscribers alleged in a complaint that local telephone companies were violating antitrust laws by agreeing not to compete with each other and by agreeing to exclude other potential competitors, which allowed monopoly power in the market. The district court dismissed the complaint for failure to state a claim, and the Second Circuit Court of Appeals reversed.]

ISSUE: In order for a complaint to survive dismissal on the pleadings, must the complaint include enough facts to state a claim to relief that is plausible on its face?

HOLDING AND DECISION: (Souter, J.) Yes. In order for a complaint to survive dismissal on the pleadings, the complaint must include enough facts to state a claim to relief that is plausible on its face. In this case, in order to state an antitrust claim under the Sherman Act, the complaint must state enough factual matter to suggest that an agreement between the alleged conspirators was made. The complaint fails to show a plausible claim. The holding in *Conley v. Gibson*, 355 U.S. 41 (1957), which stated that a "complaint should not be dismissed for failure to state a claim unless it appears beyond doubt that the plaintiff can prove no set of facts in support of his claim that would entitle him to relief" must have been read by the court of appeals to say that any statement showing the theory of a claim will suffice, unless its factual impossibility may be shown from the face of the pleadings. But the standard interpreted by the *Conley* case should now be set aside, insofar as it has been held up as a minimum standard of adequate pleading for a complaint to survive dismissal. Because antitrust conspiracy was not suggested by the facts in the complaint, the complaint failed to state a claim and must be dismissed. Enough facts to state a claim to relief that is plausible on its face is required for a complaint to survive. That the claim is conceivable is not enough. It must be plausible. Reversed and remanded.

DISSENT: (Stevens, J.) This case alleges that the telephone companies acted in concert to cheat customers. Plaintiffs alleged the conspiracy, and because the complaint was dismissed in advance of the answer, the allegation has not even been denied. The case should therefore proceed. The departure from settled procedural law seems to stem from the enormous expense of private antitrust litigation, and the risk that jurors may mistakenly conclude that evidence of parallel conduct proves that the parties acted in accordance with agreement when they in fact merely made similar independent decisions. These concerns do not justify the dismissal of an adequately pleaded complaint. The court seems to have appraised the plausibility of the ultimate factual allegation, rather than its legal sufficiency.

▶ ANALYSIS

The court was careful to say, in the text of the opinion and in footnotes, that it did not apply a heightened pleading standard or broaden the scope of Rule 9. The risk of abusive litigation in certain subjects, like antitrust, require the plaintiff to state factual allegations with greater particularity than Rule 8 requires, and the court's concern in this case was not that the allegations in the complaint were insufficiently particularized, but that the complaint failed to show a plausible claim to relief. It is the totality of the claim in the complaint that the court says must indicate a plausible claim, which is beyond merely conceivable.

━■

Quicknotes

PLEADING A statement setting forth the plaintiff's cause of action or the defendant's defenses to the plaintiff's claims.

SHERMAN ACT Prohibits unreasonable restraint of trade.

━■

Ashcroft v. Iqbal

U.S. Attorney General (D) v. Pakistani citizen (P)

556 U.S. 662 (2009).

NATURE OF CASE: Certiorari to determine complaint sufficiency in constitutional claim.

FACT SUMMARY: Javaid Iqbal (P), a Pakistani citizen, was arrested in the United States on criminal charges and detained by federal officials soon after the 9/11 terrorist attacks. He claimed his confinement conditions violated his constitutional rights. The federal official defendants moved to dismiss Iqbal's (P) complaint as facially insufficient.

🏛 RULE OF LAW

A well-pleaded complaint requires nonconclusory, plausible, factual pleadings.

FACTS: United States officials arrested Javaid Iqbal (P), a Pakistani citizen and Muslim, on criminal charges and detained him after the 9/11 terrorist attacks. Iqbal (P) filed a federal complaint alleging he was deprived of certain constitutional rights while confined. He alleged the deprivations occurred because of his race, religion, or national origin. He named former U.S. Attorney General John Ashcroft (D) and FBI Director Robert Mueller (D) in addition to several others. Ashcroft (D) and Mueller (D) moved to dismiss the complaint as facially insufficient and raised the defense of qualified immunity based on their official status at the time of the confinement. The district court denied the motion and Ashcroft (D) and Mueller (D) took an interlocutory appeal to the Second Circuit Court of Appeals. The Second Circuit affirmed, and the United States Supreme Court granted certiorari.

ISSUE: Does a well-pleaded complaint require nonconclusory, plausible, factual pleadings?

HOLDING AND DECISION: (Kennedy, J.) Yes. A well-pleaded complaint requires nonconclusory, plausible, factual pleadings. Iqbal's (P) complaint alleges the federal government had a policy of detaining Arab Muslims after the 9/11 attacks until the individuals were "cleared" by the FBI. Iqbal (P) claimed Ashcroft (D) was the "architect" of this policy and Mueller (D) was instrumental in its "adoption, promulgation, and implementation." This Court held in *Bell Atlantic Corp. v. Twombly*, 550 U.S. 544 (2007), that pleadings required factual content that allows the court to draw the reasonable inference the defendant is liable for the alleged misconduct. The plausibility standard did not rise to a probability but requires more than conclusions of misconduct. *Twombly* supported the principles that a court accepts factual allegations as true but need not accept conclusory allegations as true. Fed. R. Civ. P. 8 may now permit more flexibility but it does not permit mere conclusions. Further, only a complaint that states a plausible claim survives a motion to dismiss. The courts may begin their analysis with determining which pleadings include factual allegations that will be entitled to a presumption of truth. Here, Iqbal (P) states only conclusory allegations that Ashcroft (D) was the principal architect and Mueller (D) was the principal implementer of the policies. These conclusory allegations are not entitled to a presumption of truth. Iqbal (P) fails to include factual allegations supporting his conclusions that Ashcroft (D) and Mueller (D) knew of the federal officials' behavior regarding his confinement. The consideration then becomes whether the complaint suggests an entitlement to relief. It does not. Iqbal (P) was plausibly held for reasons other than race, religion, or national origin. Detaining such suspects until cleared does not violate constitutional protections. Iqbal (P) argues *Twombly* should be limited to antitrust pleadings, but nothing supports this theory. *Twomby* is the pleading standard for all civil actions. Iqbal (P) finally argues Fed. R. Civ. P. 9(b) permits him "general" rather than "specific" pleading for an alleged constitutional violation. Rule 9(b) does not override the factual pleading requirements of Rule 8 but merely requires even greater specificity for the enumerated claims. Reversed and remanded.

DISSENT: (Souter, J.) Consistent with *Twombly*, nonconclusory allegations should be taken as true unless they are "sufficiently fantastic to defy reality." The key allegations here are not conclusory and the complaint was facially sufficient.

DISSENT: (Breyer, J.) The lower court expressly rejected minimally intrusive discovery in favor of dismissal. That would have been appropriate because the discovery could have been in anticipation of a summary judgment motion.

▶ ANALYSIS

Pleading requirements have become stricter so general notice is no longer sufficient. The defendant is not merely put on notice of the plaintiff's claim but is entitled to factual allegations informing it of the support for the claim. Some analysts were concerned about the future of litigation because of a fear that pleadings would have to be so specific that most plaintiffs would not be able to proceed. Most courts, however, have required factual pleading for a long time and did not become more stringent after

Continued on next page.

Iqbal. The rule stated in *Iqbal* is "plausibility" not "probability" so the allegations do not have to be proven on the face of the complaint but the facts alleged must be plausible and permit a reasonable inference of defendant's misconduct.

■■■■■

Quicknotes

INTERLOCUTORY APPEAL The appeal of an issue that does not resolve the disposition of the case but is essential to a determination of the parties' legal rights.

■■■■■

Garcia v. Hilton Hotels International, Inc.

Former employee (P) v. Employer (D)

97 F. Supp. 5 (D.P.R. 1951).

NATURE OF CASE: Action for damages for defamation. Motion to dismiss, motion to strike, and motion for a more definite statement.

FACT SUMMARY: Garcia (P) was discharged from Hilton Hotels International, Inc. (D) for allegedly procuring women for use as prostitutes in the hotel, and claimed that he was defamed by such allegations.

RULE OF LAW

A complaint viewed in its most favorable light should not be dismissed if the plaintiff at trial could make out a case entitling him to relief from the allegations of the complaint. A conditional privilege is not grounds for a dismissal, while an absolute privilege is. When material allegations are insufficient, a motion for a more definite statement is proper.

FACTS: Hilton Hotels International, Inc. (Hilton Hotels) (D) discharged Garcia (P), alleging that he had brought women into the hotel to be used as prostitutes. Garcia (P) filed suit, claiming that he was defamed. In Paragraph 4 of his complaint, he alleged that he was discharged for the above-stated reasons, but he didn't specifically allege publication of the libel. Hilton Hotels (D) moved to dismiss this cause of action on those grounds. In Paragraphs 5, 6, 7, and 8 of the complaint, Garcia (P) alleged that he was defamed at a hearing before the Labor Department, where Hilton Hotels (D) gave the above-mentioned reason for discharging Garcia (P). Hilton Hotels (D) moved to strike those paragraphs because they claimed an absolute privilege to make such statements at the hearing. Hilton Hotels (D) also asked for a more definite statement as to Paragraph 4.

ISSUE: Is a complaint that does not contain a material allegation necessarily subject to dismissal if the plaintiff could make out a case at trial entitling him to relief?

HOLDING AND DECISION: (Roberts, J.) No. When a party seeks to have a complaint dismissed, the complaint is to be construed in the light most favorable to the plaintiff with all doubts resolved in his favor. Garcia (P) did fail to allege that there was a publication of the defamatory remark, which is certainly a material element in stating a cause of action in defamation. The allegation is clear enough to put Hilton Hotels (D) on notice of the charges against them. However, since failure to plead publication resulted in the omission of a material allegation, Hilton Hotels' (D) motion for a more definite statement is granted. Hilton Hotels (D) has a right to all necessary allegations so that they may prepare a proper answer to the complaint. Hilton Hotels (D) claimed that they also had a conditional privilege to make the statements that they did. While this may be true, it is an issue of fact to be proven at the time of trial. Garcia (P) has the opportunity at trial to refute that conditional privilege, and so the fact that a conditional privilege may exist is not grounds to grant a motion to dismiss. Hilton Hotels (D) claimed an absolute privilege as to the statements made at the labor hearing. Section 4 of the Code of Civil Procedure of Puerto Rico does grant absolute privilege to statements made at a proceedings authorized by law, and the Labor Department hearing was such a meeting. Therefore, Garcia (P) did not state a cause action as to those statements made at that hearing and so Paragraphs 5–8 will be stricken from the complaint.

ANALYSIS

Garcia (P) could have saved himself a lot of trouble if he had framed his complaint better. In most jurisdictions it is well known that in stating a cause of action in areas such as defamation, certain facts must be pleaded. It was simply a case of poor draftsmanship to fail to plead that there had been a publication of the defamatory statement. Also, if Garcia (P) had left out the fact of an employee-employer relationship, there would have been no grounds for Hilton Hotels (D) to move for a dismissal on a conditional privilege theory. Hilton Hotels (D) could then only plead the conditional privilege as an affirmative defense to be proven at trial.

Quicknotes

CONDITIONAL PRIVILEGE Immunity from liability for libelous or slanderous statements communicated in the execution of a political, judicial, social or personal obligation, unless it is demonstrated that the statement was made with actual malice and knowledge of its falsity.

DEFAMATION An intentional false publication, communicated publicly in either oral or written form, subjecting a person to scorn, hatred or ridicule, or injuring him in relation to his occupation or business.

Denny v. Carey

Securities purchaser (P) v. Offeror (D)

72 F.R.D. 574 (E.D. Pa. 1976).

NATURE OF CASE: Motion to dismiss class action alleging violations of federal and state securities laws.

FACT SUMMARY: Carey (D) argued that the allegations Denny (P) made in a class action suit charging him and others with violating federal and state securities laws were not specific enough.

🏛 RULE OF LAW
The requirement of Federal Rule of Civil Procedure 9(b) is met when there is sufficient identification of the circumstances constituting the alleged fraud so that the defendant can prepare an adequate answer to the allegations.

FACTS: Denny (P) brought a class action suit on behalf of himself and other purchasers of First Pennsylvania Corp. He charged that Carey (D) and others had violated federal and state securities laws by acting fraudulently in conspiring to conceal the true picture of First Penn's financial condition by issuing false statements which unreasonably avoided recognition and accrual of losses and inadequately provided for loan losses and total reserves, thereby inflating First Penn's equity and net income. Carey (D) claimed these allegations failed to state the circumstances constituting fraud with sufficient particularity to comply with Federal Rule of Civil Procedure 9(b), and moved to dismiss.

ISSUE: So long as there is sufficient identification of the circumstances constituting the alleged fraud for the defendant to prepare an adequate answer to the allegations, has the requirement of Federal Rule of Civil Procedure 9(b) been met?

HOLDING AND DECISION: (Lord, C.J.) Yes. Federal Rule of Civil Procedure 9(b)'s requirement is met where there is sufficient identification of the circumstances constituting the alleged fraud so that the defendant can prepare an adequate answer to the allegations. A strict application of Rule 9(b) in class action securities fraud cases like this one could result in substantial unfairness to persons who are the victims of fraudulent conduct. In this type of case, the matters alleged are particularly within the knowledge of the defendants. Thus, once the plaintiff has satisfied the aforementioned minimum burden of Rule 9(b), as has Denny (P), he can then flesh out the allegations in his complaint through discovery. Motion denied.

▶ ANALYSIS
This same plaintiff instituted an almost identical suit in relation to fraud involving concealment of the true financial picture of Chase Manhattan Bank. In it, the court noted that the court in *Denny v. Carey* had sustained a complaint no more specific than the one it had before it, but went on to find it nonetheless inadequate under Rule 9(b). *Denny v. Barber*, 576 F.2d 465 (2d Cir. 1978).

Quicknotes

FED. R. CIV. P. 9(b) States that in all averments of fraud or mistake, the circumstances constituting fraud or mistake shall be stated with particularity.

Tellabs, Inc. v. Makor Issues & Rights, Ltd.

Defrauded stockholders (P) v. Corporation (D)

551 U.S. 308 (2007).

NATURE OF CASE: Review of circuit split on interpretation of federal law.

FACT SUMMARY: [Facts not stated in casebook excerpt.]

🏛 RULE OF LAW

In deciding whether a securities fraud complaint alleges facts sufficient to establish a "strong inference" that the defendant acted with intent to deceive under the Private Securities Litigation Reform Act of 1995, a court must consider competing inferences of an innocent mental state that might be drawn from the same facts.

FACTS: [Facts not stated in casebook excerpt.]

ISSUE: In deciding whether a securities fraud complaint alleges facts sufficient to establish a "strong inference" that the defendant acted with intent to deceive under the Private Securities Litigation Reform Act of 1995, must a court consider competing inferences of an innocent mental state that might be drawn from the same facts?

HOLDING AND DECISION: (Ginsburg, J.) Yes. In deciding whether a securities fraud complaint alleges facts sufficient to establish a "strong inference" that the defendant acted with intent to deceive under the Private Securities Litigation Reform Act of 1995, a court must consider competing inferences of an innocent mental state that might be drawn from the same facts. A court must consider each plausible inference of intent, both fraudulent and non-fraudulent, and then decide whether a reasonable person would consider the guilty inference at least as strong as any opposing inference. Vacated and remanded.

CONCURRENCE: (Scalia, J. I fail to see how an inference that is merely "at least as compelling as any opposing inference," . . . , can conceivably be called what the statute here at issue requires: a strong inference. The test should be whether the inference of scienter (if any) I more plausible than the inference of innocence.

CONCURRENCE: (Alito, J.) I agree with the Court that the Seventh Circuit used an erroneously low standard for determining whether the plaintiffs in this case satisfied their burden of pleading. I disagree with the Court in two respects. First, the best interpretation of the statute is that only those facts that are alleged "with particularity" may properly be considered in determining whether the allegations of scienter are sufficient Second, a "strong inference" of science, in the present context, means an inference that is more likely than not correct.

▶ ANALYSIS

Because this case made it more difficult to show scienter, it makes it more difficult for civil litigants to recover damages for securities fraud. Scienter can longer be "reasonably" inferred from the facts of a case; instead, a plaintiff must show that fraud is a more likely explanation than any other more innocent explanation. Allegations regarding scienter must be specifically stated in the complaint.

Quicknotes

SCIENTER Knowledge of certain facts; often refers to "guilty knowledge," which implicates liability.

Ziervogel v. Royal Packing Co.

Car crash victim (P) v. Other driver's employer (D)

Mo. Ct. App., 225 S.W.2d 798 (1949).

NATURE OF CASE: Appeal from award in action in negligence to recover damages for personal injuries.

FACT SUMMARY: Ziervogel (P) was awarded $2,000 in damages and Royal Packing Co. (D) sought a reversal on the grounds that certain items of special damage were not alleged in the complaint.

🏛 RULE OF LAW
When items of special damage are claimed, they must be specifically pleaded in the complaint.

FACTS: Ziervogel (P) was injured in an automobile collision with an employee of Royal Packing Co. (D). In the complaint, Ziervogel (P) alleged that she sustained injuries to her neck, back, spine, and nervous system. At the trial, Ziervogel (P) presented evidence that as a result of the accident her blood pressure was higher and that she injured her shoulder. Royal Packing Co. (D) objected to the evidence because those injuries had not been alleged in the complaint. The court overruled the objection and the jury awarded Ziervogel (P) $2,000. Royal Packing Co. (D) appealed the decision, asserting that since the high blood pressure and shoulder injury were not alleged in the complaint, the court should not have allowed evidence to be presented to the jury on those issues. Ziervogel (P) claimed that through discovery procedures Royal Packing Co. (D) had notice of Ziervogel's (P) claim as to those injuries. She also claimed that Form 10 of the Appendix of Illustrative Forms to the Federal Rules of Civil Procedure was controlling and it allowed the presentation of evidence at trial without specifically pleading it.

ISSUE: When items of special damage are claimed, must they be specifically pleaded?

HOLDING AND DECISION: (McCullen, J.) Yes. There is a specific Missouri statute which requires that items of special damage must be specifically pleaded. The Supreme Court of Missouri has held that a specific personal injury which is not the necessary or inevitable result of an injury alleged in the petition constitutes an element of special damage and must be specifically pleaded before evidence on that issue is admissible. There was no evidence that the high blood pressure and shoulder injury were an inevitable result of any injuries alleged in the complaint. Because this is a state court with a specific statute governing this situation, the forms in the Federal Rules are not controlling. The fact that Royal Packing Co. (D) had notice of the alleged injuries prior to trial has no effect because of the statute. Ziervogel (P) should have amended her complaint at the time of trial, but she refused to. Reversed.

HOLDING AND DECISION ON MOTION FOR REHEARING: (McCullen, J.) Ziervogel (P) has moved for a new trial or to transfer the case to the state supreme court. She claims that the Missouri statute was copied verbatim from Fed. R. Civ. P. 9(g) and her complaint would be sufficient under that Rule. However, there are no cases supporting her interpretation of Rule 9(g) and the Missouri statute is clear and controlling. Motion denied.

▶ ANALYSIS

Special damages are those which flow naturally, but not necessarily, from the defendant's wrongful act and they are not implied at law. In both code pleading and notice pleading jurisdictions they must be specifically pleaded or they cannot be recovered. General damages are those which so necessarily flow from the defendant's wrongful act that they will be implied by the law. These injuries do not have to be specifically pleaded. In a personal injury case, the pain and suffering are considered general damages, but the medical expenses and loss of earnings are considered special damages.

■=■

Quicknotes

MISSOURI RULE OF CIVIL PROCEDURE 55.19 Provides that when items of special damage are claimed, they shall be specifically stated.

■=■

American Nurses' Association v. Illinois

Female employees (P) v. State employer (D)

783 F.2d 716 (7th Cir. 1986).

NATURE OF CASE: Appeal from summary judgment for the defense in sex discrimination suit.

FACT SUMMARY: American Nurses' Association (P) contended that its class action complaint presented a cause of action for discrimination rather than comparable worth and thus should have been upheld.

🏛 RULE OF LAW
A federal complaint should not be dismissed for failure to state a claim unless it appears that the plaintiff can prove no set of facts in support of his claim which would entitle him to relief.

FACTS: American Nurses' Association (American) (P) sued the State of Illinois (D), filing an extensive complaint over the wages and working conditions of its members, registered nurses. The complaint indicated that wage rates in predominantly male categories were significantly higher than in predominantly female categories. The State (D) successfully moved for summary judgment on the basis that the complaint sounded in comparable worth and thus failed as a matter of law to state a claim upon which relief could be granted. American (P) appealed, contending the complaint, taken as a whole, could be interpreted as stating claims for equal protection and other valid bases and should not have been dismissed.

ISSUE: Should a federal complaint be summarily dismissed for failure to state a claim if it appears that the plaintiff can prove a set of facts in support of his claim based on the allegations therein?

HOLDING AND DECISION: (Posner, J.) No. A federal complaint should not be dismissed for failure to state a claim unless it appears that the plaintiff can prove no set of facts in support of his claim which would entitle him to relief. In this case, relative worth could be interpreted as a method by which American (P) could prove actionable discrimination and equal protection violations. The complaint is not drafted so as to require an interpretation that the sole basis for relief was comparable worth. As a result, the recognized rule requires an interpretation which would allow the action to go forward because an interpretation is available upon which relief could be granted. Reversed and remanded.

▶ ANALYSIS

The Federal Rules of Civil Procedure, as interpreted in case law such as *Conley v. Gibson*, 355 U.S. 41 (1957), have a much wider view of proper pleading than presented in this case. The Rules advise, but do not require, brevity in charging allegations, while allowing a claim to proceed "unless it appears beyond doubt that the plaintiff can prove no set of facts upon which relief is available." The opinion in this case indicates a literal reading of this rule is too expansive.

■■■

Ingraham v. United States

Patients (P) v. Federal government (D)

808 F.2d 1075 (5th Cir. 1987).

NATURE OF CASE: Appeal of award of damages for medical malpractice.

FACT SUMMARY: The Government (D), sued in a malpractice action, attempted to raise on appeal a state cap on general damages in malpractice actions.

> 🏛 **RULE OF LAW**
> A statutory cap on damages is an affirmative defense that is waived if not raised in the pleadings.

FACTS: Several individuals (P) brought suit against the Government (D) for negligent treatment by military physicians. At trial, damages in excess of $4 million were awarded. On appeal, the Government (D) attempted to raise for the first time a state limitation on general damages in malpractice awards.

ISSUE: Is a statutory cap on damages an affirmative defense that is waived if not raised in the pleadings?

HOLDING AND DECISION: (Politz, J.) Yes. A statutory cap on damages is an affirmative defense that is waived if not raised in the pleadings. Fed. R. Civ. P. 8(c) requires that any matter constituting an affirmative defense be raised in the pleadings. Several factors are relevant in determining whether a matter is in fact such a defense. These include whether a matter is intrinsic or extrinsic to a plaintiff's case, which party has better access to evidence, and whether fairness mandates disclosure of the defense early in the proceedings. Here, the cap on damages would appear extrinsic to the cause of action of the plaintiffs. Also, had the plaintiffs been apprised of this defense early in the proceedings, they might have tried to maximize special damages and minimize general damages. For these reasons, it appears that the statutory cap is an affirmative defense, and was waived when not raised in the pleadings. Affirmed.

▶ *ANALYSIS*

Fed. R. Civ. P. 8(c)(1) covers affirmative defenses. Nineteen specific defenses are listed as affirmative, requiring pleadings and proof by a defendant. The Rule also has a residuary clause mandating pleading of "any other matter constituting an affirmative defense." What constitutes these other matters is left to the discretion of the courts.

■=■

Quicknotes

FED. R. CIV. P. 8(c) Renumbered as 8(c)(1) in 2007, requires an affirmative defense to be raised in the pleadings.

GENERAL DAMAGES Measure of damages necessary to compensate victim for actual injuries suffered and which are the direct result of the wrongful act.

■=■

Beeck v. Aquaslide 'N' Dive Corp.

Injured water slider (P) v. Manufacturer (D)

562 F.2d 537 (8th Cir. 1977).

NATURE OF CASE: Appeal from trial court order allowing filing of amended answer in personal injury action.

FACT SUMMARY: In a personal injury action, Aquaslide 'N' Dive Corp. (D) was allowed to amend its answer to deny manufacture of a slide that had allegedly injured Beeck (P).

🏛 RULE OF LAW
A motion to amend an answer should be granted unless the opposing party can show prejudice.

FACTS: Beeck (P) filed suit against Aquaslide 'N' Dive Corp. (Aquaslide) (D) for injuries allegedly sustained from a slide. Relying on advice of insurers, Aquaslide (D) admitted in its answer that it manufactured the slide. Later evidence demonstrated that it had not. Aquaslide (D) moved to amend its answer to deny manufacture. The motion was granted, and Beeck (P) appealed from an adverse result.

ISSUE: Should a motion to amend an answer be granted unless the opposing party can show prejudice?

HOLDING AND DECISION: (Benson, J.) Yes. A motion to amend an answer should be granted unless the opposing party can show prejudice. Prejudice can be shown in various ways: delay, bad faith by the moving party, or dilatory motive by the moving party. However, prejudice must actually be shown, not merely suggested. Here, the trial court found that the motion to amend was made in good faith and that at the time the motion was granted, manufacture was a legitimate issue that could be fairly litigated. The fact that Aquaslide (D) later won does not mean that Beeck (P) was prejudiced at the time of the ruling on the motion. Affirmed.

▶ ANALYSIS

Fed. R. Civ. P. 15(b)(1) allows for the amendment of pleadings to conform to the evidence. The Rule states that leave to do so will be granted freely when the presentation of the merits of the action will be served thereby and the opposing party cannot show that such amendments will not prejudice him as to maintaining or defending his case on the merits. This was the standard applied by the court here. While the result definitely prejudiced Beeck (P) (he lost his case), it did not prejudice him on the merits.

Quicknotes

FED. R. CIV. P. 15(a) Renumbered 15(a)(2) in 2007; declares that leave to amend shall be freely given when justice so requires.

Krupski v. Costa Crociere S.p.A.

Cruise ship passenger (P) v. Cruise owner (D)

130 S. Ct. 2485 (2010).

NATURE OF CASE: Appeal of circuit court judgment.

FACT SUMMARY: Wanda Krupski (P) injured herself while on a cruise. She brought suit against the wrong party, and sought to amend a complaint to name the proper defendant after the limitations period lapsed. The Court of Appeals for the Eleventh Circuit held that the amended complaint did not relate back because she should have known the identity of the proper defendant.

🏛 RULE OF LAW
Federal Rule of Civil Procedure 15(c) permits an amended complaint to relate back to a previously filed complaint if the proper defendant knew or should have known within the time of service that but for a mistake in identity, the plaintiff would have asserted the claims against the proper defendant.

FACTS: Wanda Krupski (P) was injured while a passenger on the cruise ship Costa Magica. She sued Costa Cruise S.p.A. (D), the business through which she had booked her cruise and which had sent her travel documents. In its answer to the complaint, Costa Cruise (D) stated that it was only the North American sales and booking agent for the ship operator, Costa Crociere (D), which was the proper defendant. Krupski (P) amended her complaint to add Costa Crociere (D) as a party. But Costa Crociere (D), which was represented by the same attorney as Costa Cruise (D), argued that the expiration of the contractual one-year limitations period had expired. The Court of Appeals for the Eleventh Circuit held that Federal Rule of Civil Procedure 15(c) was not satisfied because Krupski (P) knew or should have known the identity of the proper defendant before the expiration of the limitations period, and that because she chose not to sue Costa Crociere (D), she didn't make the type of mistake about the identity of the defendant that Rule 15(c) contemplated. The court also held that relation back was not appropriate because the plaintiff had unduly delayed in seeking to amend.

ISSUE: Does Federal Rule of Civil Procedure 15(c) permit an amended complaint to relate back to a previously filed complaint if the proper defendant knew or should have known within the time of service that but for a mistake in identity, the plaintiff would have asserted the claims against the proper defendant.

HOLDING AND DECISION: (Sotomayor, J.) Yes. Federal Rule of Civil Procedure 15(c) permits an amended complaint to relate back to a previously filed complaint if the proper defendant knew or should have known within the time of service that but for a mistake in identity, the plaintiff would have asserted the claims against the proper defendant. Whether an amendment relates back under Rule 15(c)(1)(C) depends on what the party to be added knew or should have known, not on the amending party's knowledge or timeliness in seeking to amend the pleading. Rule 15 asks what the prospective defendant "knew or should have known," not what the plaintiff "knew or should have known," as was understood by the Eleventh Circuit. Costa Crociere (D) should have known that Krupski's (P) failure to name it as a defendant was due to a mistake concerning the proper party's identity. Reversed and remanded.

CONCURRENCE: (Scalia, J.) The Court reached the correct decision, but its use of the Notes of the Advisory Committee to the Federal Rules of Civil Procedure in reaching its decision was inappropriate.

▶ ANALYSIS

This decision illustrates a very basic fact about being human: People can make mistakes even when they know all of the facts. The Eleventh Circuit found that because Krupski (P) knew about the existence of Costa Crociere (D), and that the company was the owner of the ship, she could not have made a mistake when she chose to sue Costa Cruise (D). But Rule 15(c) does not require that the mistake of the plaintiff be reasonable. It requires only that a mistake was made.

━■━■■

Quicknotes

FED. R. CIV. P. 15(c) Provides that a claim or defense arising out of the conduct or occurrence set forth in the original pleading will relate back to the date of the original pleading.

━■━■■

Surowitz v. Hilton Hotels Corp.

Shareholder (P) v. Corporate officers (D)

383 U.S. 363 (1966).

NATURE OF CASE: Review of dismissal of a derivative action to recover damages for the corporation.

FACT SUMMARY: Surowitz (P) brought a derivative suit to recover money which the officers and directors of Hilton Hotels Corp. (D) had fraudulently taken.

🏛 RULE OF LAW
The party verifying a complaint as required by Federal Rule of Civil Procedure 23(b) [renumbered as 23.1 in 2007] is not required to verify the complaint on the basis of her own personal knowledge if she has been advised by a competent individual that the allegations in the complaint are true.

FACTS: Surowitz (P) had invested over $2,000 in Hilton Hotels Corp. (D). In December of 1962, Mrs. Surowitz (P) received a notice from Hilton Hotels (D) announcing a plan to purchase a large amount of its own stock. Surowitz (P) asked her son to explain what it meant as he was a graduate of the Harvard Law School and had a master's degree in economics and worked as a professional investment advisor. He and a friend decided to investigate the proposed plan and, by August 1963, decided that the directors and officers of Hilton Hotels (D) were engaged in a fraudulent scheme. Surowitz (P) agreed to file suit in her name. Her son's friend drew up a 60-page complaint, and then Surowitz's (P) son explained it to her and she verified it. Surowitz (P) had a limited education and understood only ordinary English. The attorney who drew up the complaint also verified it as required by Fed. R. Civ. P. 11. On Hilton Hotels' (D) motion, Surowitz (P) was required to submit to an oral examination by Hilton Hotels' (D) attorneys and it was shown that Surowitz (P) did not understand the complaint. Surowitz's (P) attorney filed affidavits showing the extensive investigation that had been made, but the district judge held that Surowitz (P) did not understand the complaint and so her verification was not valid. The court of appeals affirmed the district court's dismissal of the complaint as a sham pleading.

ISSUE: Is a party verifying a complaint in a derivative action as required by Federal Rule of Civil Procedure 23(b) [now 23.1] required to totally understand the complaint?

HOLDING AND DECISION: (Black, J.) No. The district court erred in requiring that Surowitz (P) be required to totally understand the pleadings. Her attorney had also verified the complaint and, as the complaint had been explained to her by her son, she did believe the allegations in the complaint to be true. Rule 23(b) requires verification of the complaint to discourage people from filing strike suits where a complaint that is without merit is filed in hopes the corporation would settle out of court in order to save the expense of litigating the case. From the affidavits that were filed, it was evident that Surowitz (P) intended no harm to Hilton Hotels (D) and any award that the court would have granted would have gone to the corporation, and not to her. Surowitz (P) had competent advice from a source she could trust and so her verification should have been held proper. Courts should use the rules of procedure to see that justice is done and to get away from rigid formalities that plagued the common law pleaders. The court should look past the face of the complaint. The court was supplied with affidavits showing the extensive investigation that had been made. Since there had been a wrong committed against the shareholders of the corporation, justice requires that the motion to dismiss be overruled and that Hilton Hotels (D) be required to answer the complaint. Reversed and remanded.

CONCURRENCE: (Harlan, J.) Rule 23(b) [now 23.1] directs that in a derivative suit "the complaint shall be verified by oath," but nothing dictates that the verification be that of the plaintiff shareholder.

▶ *ANALYSIS*

In federal courts the attorney is required to sign all pleadings and he is held to a good faith obligation in pleading. There have even been cases where the attorney has been disbarred for a gross violation of this good faith pleading requirement. Instead of dismissing a complaint for failing to have a proper verification, which in many cases means an end to the litigation because the statute of limitations will have run, the better approach would be to prosecute the party for perjury and let the defect in the complaint be corrected with an amendment. Note: In 2007, Rule 23(b) was renumbered as 23.1.

Quicknotes

SHAREHOLDER'S DERIVATIVE ACTION Action asserted by a shareholder in order to enforce a cause of action on behalf of the corporation.

STRIKE SUIT A derivative suit brought by a shareholder with the intent of receiving a settlement.

Hadges v. Yonkers Racing Corp.

Racehorse owner and driver (P) v. Racing association (D)

48 F.3d 1320 (2d Cir. 1995).

NATURE OF CASE: Appeal from imposition of sanctions against plaintiff and plaintiff's attorney in an employment blackballing case.

FACT SUMMARY: After Hadges (P) and his attorney made incorrect statements in a Rule 60(b) motion to the court, they received sanctions with little notice and scant time to respond.

🏛 RULE OF LAW
Pursuant to Rule 11, those facing sanctions must receive adequate notice and the opportunity to respond.

FACTS: Hadges (P), a harness racehorse driver, filed a Rule 60(b) motion asking a federal court to reconsider the dismissal of a due process claim he had filed against Yonkers Racing Corp. (YRC) (D) after YRC (D) had barred him from working at Yonkers Raceway. In the Rule 60(b) motion, Hadges (P) and his attorney (Kunstler) signed affidavits containing false information regarding Hadges's (P) opportunities to work and failed to inform the court of an ongoing state action. The court denied the Rule 60(b) motion and granted YRC's (D) request for sanctions against Hadges (P) and Kunstler. Hadges (P) and Kunstler appealed.

ISSUE: Pursuant to Rule 11, must those facing sanctions receive adequate notice and the opportunity to respond?

HOLDING AND DECISION: [Judge not stated in casebook excerpt.] Yes. Pursuant to Rule 11, those facing sanctions must receive adequate notice and the opportunity to respond. Here, neither Hadges (P) nor Kunstler were given adequate notice of the sanctions or the proper opportunity to respond. Rule 11 requires that the party requesting sanctions submit the request separately from all other requests and serve the offending party twenty-one days before presenting it to the court. YRC (D) did not submit separately, nor did it give Hadges (P) adequate time to retract his misstatements and thereby avoid sanctions altogether. Additionally, Kunstler was entitled to rely on his client's representations as to the facts of the case and therefore did not violate any duty to the court. Kunstler did not deserve sanctions for the failure to inform the court of the state action because the withholding of that information was not an intentional act done for any tactical advantage. Therefore, the imposition of sanctions is reversed.

▶ ANALYSIS

In 1983, Rule 11 was amended to require attorneys to inquire into the facts prior to filing a case and to permit judges to exercise discretion in their choice of sanctions. As a result, a specialized practice in Rule 11 litigation emerged. The amendments forced attorneys and courts to take Rule 11 sanctions seriously and greatly impacted the conduct of lawyers. After the amendments, attorneys paid greater attention to pre-filing rules and were often guided into taking special care with their cases because of the fear of sanctions.

■═■

Quicknotes

FED. R. CIV. P. 60(b) Authorizes relief from judgment based on certain specified grounds.

SANCTIONS A penalty imposed in order to ensure compliance with a statute or regulation.

■═■

Joinder of Claims and Parties: Expanding the Scope of the Civil Action

Quick Reference Rules of Law

Harris v. Avery

Slanderer (D) v. Accused horse thief (P)

Kan. Sup. Ct., 5 Kan. 146 (1869).

NATURE OF CASE: Action to recover damages for false imprisonment and slander.

FACT SUMMARY: Avery (P) alleged that Harris (D) called him a thief, said he had stolen a horse, took the horse from him and kept it for four or five days, and had him arrested.

🏛 RULE OF LAW
A plaintiff may unite causes of action where they have arisen from the same transaction or transactions connected with the same subject matter.

FACTS: Avery (P) alleged that Harris (D) called him a thief in the presence of several other persons. Harris (D) said Avery (P) had stolen a horse, and he took the horse from Avery (P) and kept it for four or five days. He also arrested Avery (P) and confined him in the county jail with felons for four or five days. Harris (D) demurred to Avery's (P) petition on the ground that several causes of action were improperly joined. The court decided that the facts constituted a single transaction. Harris (D) appealed.

ISSUE: Can the two causes of action, false imprisonment and slander, be united in the same petition when both arose out of the same transaction?

HOLDING AND DECISION: (Valentine, J.) Yes. The code provides that a plaintiff may unite several causes of action in the same petition where they have arisen from the same transaction or transactions connected with the same subject matter. This differs in many respects from the common law rule. At common law, a plaintiff could unite as many causes of actions as he might have, so long as they could all be sued in an action on the case. This was so even though the causes of actions had arisen out of different transactions, and at different times, and in different places. But a plaintiff could not join a cause of action which would have to be sued in an action in trespass and one which would have to be sued in an action on the case, and it would make no difference whether they both arose out of the same transaction or not. The code has abolished all common law forms of action and has established a system for the joinder of actions which follows the rules of equity more closely. Its purpose is to avoid the multiplicity of suits and to settle in one action, as equity did, as far as practicable, the whole subject matter of a controversy. Looking to the facts of this case, it is probably true that under the code the two causes of action for false imprisonment and slander cannot be united unless both arise out of the same transaction. This is because one is an injury to the person and the other is an injury to the character. However-er, here, both of Avery's (P) causes of action did arise out of one transaction, and so they may be united. Affirmed.

▶ ANALYSIS

Fed. R. Civ. P. 18 removes all obstacles to joinder of claims and permits the joinder of both legal and equitable actions. The only restriction on the claims that may be joined is imposed by subject matter jurisdiction requirements. The philosophy behind such a liberal rule is that when the time comes that parties cannot settle their differences and one of them brings the matter to court, they should settle all of their controversies in the same suit. If the joined claims are of a widely disparate nature, it is possible that the jury might be confused. To curb any extra expense, delay, confusion to the jury, or prejudice to any party which might result from the joinder of actions, the court is given authority to order separate trials for the various claims joined.

Quicknotes

DEMURRER The assertion that the opposing party's pleadings are insufficient and that the demurring party should not be made to answer.

FALSE IMPRISONMENT Intentional tort whereby the victim is unlawfully restrained.

JOINDER OF CLAIMS The joining of claims in a single suit by a party; the party seeking relief may join as many claims as he has against the opposing party.

SLANDER Defamatory statement communicated orally.

M.K. v. Tenet

Former CIA employees (P) v. CIA director et al. (D)

216 F.R.D. 133 (D.D.C. 2002).

NATURE OF CASE: Motion under Federal Rule 21 to sever the claims of some plaintiffs from those of other plaintiffs that were alleged in a proposed amended complaint.

FACT SUMMARY: Former Central Intelligence Agency (CIA) employees (P) sought to amend their complaint against the CIA (D) by adding new plaintiffs, adding new defendants, and clarifying the original plaintiffs' claims. The CIA (D) moved to sever the original plaintiffs' claims from those of the new plaintiffs.

RULE OF LAW
Federal Rule 18 permits joinder of all claims a party has against an opposing party.

FACTS: Six former Central Intelligence Agency (CIA) employees (P) submitted a proposed second amended complaint that named nine new plaintiffs, named thirty new defendants, and clarified the claims of the six original plaintiffs. The original complaint alleged that the CIA (D) had violated the CIA employees' (P) statutory privacy rights, as well as their constitutional rights involving alleged obstruction of access to counsel. The CIA (D) moved to sever the six original plaintiffs' obstruction-of-counsel claims, arguing that each claim would present unique questions of fact and law for each of the six plaintiffs.

ISSUE: Does Federal Rule 18 permit joinder of all claims a party has against an opposing party?

HOLDING AND DECISION: (Urbina, J.) Yes. Federal Rule 18 permits joinder of all claims a party has against an opposing party. The original plaintiffs' new claims thus should be joined in the proposed amended complaint against the CIA (D) here. Motion denied.

ANALYSIS

Especially in trial courts, sometimes a decision is as simple as applying the plain text of a court rule. Judge Urbina illustrates that point here.

Quicknotes

JOINDER OF CLAIMS The joining of claims in a single suit by a party; the party seeking relief may join as many claims as he has against the opposing party.

United States v. Heyward-Robinson Co.

Federal government (D) v. Prime contractor (P)

430 F.2d 1077 (2d Cir. 1970).

NATURE OF CASE: Appeal of award of damages for breach of contract.

FACT SUMMARY: D'Agostino Excavators (D) counterclaimed against Heyward-Robinson Co. (P) in federal court on two contracts, only one of which was subject to federal jurisdiction.

🏛 RULE OF LAW
When a counterclaim is asserted on a contract in federal court, a claim based on another contract may be joined, if there is a logical relationship between the claims.

FACTS: Heyward-Robinson Co. (P), general contractor on a construction project commenced by the Navy, hired D'Agostino Excavators (D'Agostino) (D). Heyward-Robinson (P), which was also the general contractor on another development, hired D'Agostino (D) on that job as well. Heyward-Robinson (P) reserved the right to terminate either contract in the event of breach of one, and both contracts were covered by the same insurance bond. Heyward-Robinson (P) brought a breach of contract action in federal court on the Navy contract. D'Agostino (D) counterclaimed and added a claim based on the other contract as well. A jury awarded damages to D'Agostino (D). Heyward-Robinson (P) appealed, contending that the second contractual claim was not properly joined.

ISSUE: When a counterclaim is asserted on a contract in federal court, may a claim based on another contract be joined if there is a logical relationship between the claims?

HOLDING AND DECISION: (Van Pelt Bryan, J.) Yes. When a counterclaim is asserted on a contract in federal court, a claim based on another contract may be joined, if there is a logical relationship between the claims. If the second claim can be characterized as a compulsory counterclaim to the original claim, it may be added to any counterclaim made against the original claim. Under Fed. R. Civ. P. 13(a), a counterclaim will be compulsory if it has a logical relationship to the original claim. Absolute factual identity is not required. Here, the two contracts in question involved the same parties, made reference to each other, and concerned the same sort of work. This court believes that this is sufficient to establish the right to join the claims under Fed. R. Civ. P. 13(a). Affirmed.

CONCURRENCE: (Friendly, J.) The two contracts in question were wholly separate and the overlap between them was of little legal significance. The only reason for combining these suits was that the funds from each were so commingled as to be untraceable.

▶ ANALYSIS

Fed. R. Civ. P. 13(a)(1) uses the words "transaction" and "occurrence" when describing the requisites of a compulsory counterclaim. The language appears to imply a single set of circumstances. Nonetheless, courts have held that the overlapping subject matter can be a series of occurrences, not merely a single incident.

■=■

Quicknotes

COUNTERCLAIM An independent cause of action brought by a defendant to a lawsuit in order to oppose or deduct from the plaintiff's claim.

■=■

LASA per L'Industria del Marmo Societa per Azioni v. Alexander

Marble supplier (P) v. Subcontractor (D)

414 F.2d 143 (6th Cir. 1969).

NATURE OF CASE: Appeal of a dismissal of two cross-claims and a third-party complaint filed in response to action for breach of contract.

FACT SUMMARY: LASA per L'Industria del Marmo Societa per Azioni (LASA) (P) filed suit against Alexander Marble and Tile Co. (Alexander) (D), alleging that it was owed a balance on its contract to supply marble to Alexander (D), and after LASA (P) filed suit, Alexander (D) filed a cross-claim and a third-party complaint, both of which were dismissed by the trial court as not arising from the same transaction or occurrence.

🏛 **RULE OF LAW**
Cross-claims, counterclaims, and third-party complaints arising from the same transaction or occurrence as the subject matter of the original complaint may be joined with the original complaint.

FACTS: Alexander Marble and Tile Co. (Alexander) (D) was hired as a subcontractor by Southern Builders, the principal contractor for construction of the Memphis, Tennessee City Hall. Alexander (D) then contracted with LASA per L'Industria del Marmo Societa per Azioni (LASA) (P) to supply it with marble. LASA (P) filed suit, alleging it had fully performed its contract with Alexander (D) and was still owed a balance on the contract price. Alexander (D) filed a counterclaim against LASA (P) for breach of contract, a cross-claim against the prime contractor, its surety, and the City of Memphis, and a third-party complaint against the architect. The prime contractor also filed a counterclaim against Alexander (D). The district court dismissed Alexander's (D) cross-claim and third-party complaint, along with the counterclaim of the prime contractor on the grounds that they did not arise out of the same transaction or occurrence that was the subject matter of the original action or of a counterclaim therein. This appeal followed.

ISSUE: May cross-claims, counterclaims, and third-party complaints arising out of the same transaction or occurrence as the original complaint be joined with the original complaint?

HOLDING AND DECISION: (Phillips, J.) Yes. Cross-claims, counterclaims, and third-party complaints arising out of the same transaction or occurrence as the original complaint may be joined with the original complaint. Under the Federal Rules of Civil Procedure, the rights of all parties generally should be adjudicated in one action. The words "transaction or occurrence" are given a broad and liberal interpretation in order to avoid a multiplicity of suits. Here, although different subcontracts are involved, they, along with

the prime contract and specifications, all relate to the same project and to problems arising out of the marble used in the erection of the Memphis City Hall. Many of the same or closely related factual and legal issues and some of the same evidence will necessarily be presented under the complaint, counterclaims, and cross-claims in the resolution of the issues being contested. Fed. R. Civ. P. 13 and 14 are intended to avoid circuity of action and to dispose of the entire subject matter arising from one set of facts in one action, thus administering complete and evenhanded justice expeditiously and economically. The intent of the Rules is that all issues be resolved in one action, with all parties before one court, complex though the action may be. However, if the district court should conclude that separate trials on one or more of the counterclaims, cross-claims, or issues would be conducive to expedition and economy, Rule 42(b) authorizes the judge to order separate trials on one or more of those claims. Reversed and remanded.

DISSENT: (McAllister, J.) The suit brought by LASA (P) was an action in contract, while Alexander's (D) cross-claim against Southern Builders and third-party complaint against the architect constituted actions in tort. The proofs required and the same issues of fact would not determine both the original action and Alexander's (D) cross-claims. Therefore, the judgments of the district should have been affirmed.

▶ **ANALYSIS**

Joinder of claims is generally permissive except under circumstances which make a counterclaim mandatory. Further, characterization and interpretation of the phrase "same transaction or occurrence" will determine a court's eventual ruling. Here, the majority interpreted the phrase broadly to include all actions related to the construction of the building involving both the contract and tort claims. The dissent, however, interpreted the phrase narrowly and looked to the basis for the claims, contract and tort, by which it characterized the transaction or occurrence.

■≡■

Quicknotes

CROSS-CLAIM A claim asserted by a plaintiff or defendant to an action against a co-plaintiff or co-defendant, and not against an opposing party, arising out of the same transaction or occurrence as the subject matter of the action.

■≡■

Ellis Canning Co. v. International Harvester Co.

Tractor owner (P) v. Tractor repair company (D)

Kan. Sup. Ct., 174 Kan. 357, 255 P.2d 658 (1953).

NATURE OF CASE: Action to recover damages for personal injuries.

FACT SUMMARY: Ellis Canning Co. (Ellis) (P) alleged that it had been damaged by a fire allegedly caused by International Harvester Co.'s (D) negligence. Ellis (P) recovered the full amount of its damages from its insurance company and brought this action to recover the amount for the use and benefit of the insurance company.

🏛 RULE OF LAW
An insured who has been fully paid for his loss is not the real party in interest and, hence, cannot maintain an action to recover the amount of such loss for the use and benefit of the insurer.

FACTS: Ellis Canning Co. (Ellis) (P) alleged that while servicing its tractor, International Harvester Co. (International) (D) negligently started a fire, thereby causing damage in the amount of $479.79. Ellis (P) was insured against the loss and was paid the full amount of its loss by its insurer. Ellis (P) commenced this action to recover $479.79 in its own name for the benefit and use of its insurance company. International (D) argued that since Ellis (P) was seeking to recover the amount paid by its insurer as full compensation for the damage to the tractor, the insurance company is the real party in interest, and Ellis (P) had no legal right to maintain this action.

ISSUE: Can an insured who has been fully paid for his loss maintain an action to recover the amount of such loss for the use and benefit of the insurer?

HOLDING AND DECISION: (Parker, J.) No. The controlling statute requires that every action must be prosecuted in the name of the real party in interest. Earlier decisions have allowed an insured to maintain an action in his name for the use and benefit of the insurer. However, the rule of those decisions has since been repudiated. The controlling rule now is that an insured who has been fully paid for his loss is not a real party in interest. Hence, he cannot maintain an action to recover the amount of such loss in his own name for the use and benefit of the insured. In such circumstances, the right of action against the alleged wrongdoer vests wholly in the insurer, and the insurer may, and indeed must, bring the action as the real and only party in interest. In this case, Ellis (P) may not bring this action against International (D) for the use and benefit of Ellis's (P) insurer. Affirmed.

▶ ANALYSIS

The real-party-in-interest rule is based on the theory that the party initiating a civil action should be the person who has the right to sue under the substantive law. Under the general rules of civil procedure, the following parties may sue on claims even though they have no beneficial interest therein: executor, administrator, guardian, bailee, or trustee of an express trust; a party with whom or in whose name a contract has been made for the benefit of another; and the U.S. government when expressly authorized by statute to maintain the action for the use or benefit of another. Care should be taken to distinguish the concepts of real party in interest, capacity to sue, and standing. A person may be the real party in interest but lack the capacity to sue due to age or mental incompetency. Or a person may have the capacity to sue but have assigned all interest in the claim before the action was instituted and, therefore, no longer be the real party in interest. When, for standing purposes, a plaintiff is required to show both that he has been adversely affected by the governmental conduct that is under attack and has suffered an injury to a legally protected right, standing may entail preliminary consideration of the merits of the case and, therefore, is quite different from the real party in interest.

Quicknotes

REAL PARTY IN INTEREST A party that will benefit from the successful litigation of an action, in contrast to a party with only a nominal interest in the subject matter of the action or who is legally entitled to enforce the particular claim.

SERIATIM In order; successively.

Ryder v. Jefferson Hotel Co.

Married hotel guests (P) v. Hotel (D)

S.C. Sup. Ct., 121 S.C. 72, 113 S.E. 474 (1922).

NATURE OF CASE: Joint action for personal injuries.

FACT SUMMARY: The Ryders (P) suffered personal losses as a result of insults from a Jefferson Hotel (D) servant.

RULE OF LAW
Where two or more persons suffer a tortious act arising out of the same occurrence or transaction, each person's cause of action must be severed and tried separately, if the torts are of a personal nature.

FACTS: While guests at the Jefferson Hotel (D), Charles and Edith Ryder (P), husband and wife, were roused from sleep by an employee of the hotel, Bickley. Bickley insulted Edith Ryder (P), and she and her husband were forced to leave the hotel. They filed suit against the Jefferson Hotel (D) for injuries to their reputations, credit card business, and for loss of custom, gains and profits to Charles Ryder (P). Both alleged a cause of action for breach of duty growing out of an innkeeper-guest relationship. Damages asked for were $10,000. Jefferson Hotel (D) demurred to the complaint on grounds that there was a misjoinder of causes of action as between the separate injuries of Charles and Edith Ryder (P). Demurrer was overruled and Jefferson Hotel (D) appealed.

ISSUE: Where a tort of a personal nature is committed against two or more persons in a common incident, must each person's right of action be severed and tried in separate actions?

HOLDING AND DECISION: (Marion, J.) Yes. Even though two plaintiffs might suffer similar injuries arising out of the same transaction, they cannot maintain a joint action and recover joint damages therefor. To maintain a joint action, there must be some prior bond of legal union between the persons injured so that the tortious conduct produces a wrong and consequent damage common to all. Thus, even though husband and wife have a close legal relationship, it is not one that is affected by a personal tort, such as slander, against them both. No joint cause of action arises. In the present case, the parties plaintiff are different, as are the potential elements of damage recoverable by each. Neither has the right to sue for the benefit of the other. Reversed.

DISSENT: (Fraser, J.) The offense was against husband and wife as co-partners, and the injury affected that marital relationship. Thus, it was a joint injury allowing joint recovery.

ANALYSIS

This type of restrictive procedure for joining causes of action meant more litigation, and in this modern era of congested court calendars, courts favor settling of various claims in one action, if possible. Thus, many states today have adopted the federal system that holds a plaintiff may join any cause of action, with or without any co-plaintiff, against any defendant. But no subject matter relationship is required among the causes of action joined.

Quicknotes

DEMURRER The assertion that the opposing party's pleadings are insufficient and that the demurring party should not be made to answer.

M.K. v. Tenet

Former CIA employees (P) v. CIA director et al. (D)

216 F.R.D. 133 (D.D.C. 2002).

NATURE OF CASE: Motion under Federal Rule 21 to drop some plaintiffs from a proposed amended complaint.

FACT SUMMARY: Former Central Intelligence Agency (CIA) employees (P) sought to amend their complaint against the CIA (D) by adding new plaintiffs, adding new defendants, and clarifying the original plaintiffs' claims. The CIA (D) moved to drop some plaintiffs from the proposed amended complaint.

> ## 🏛 RULE OF LAW
> An alleged pattern of obstruction of counsel justifies joinder of plaintiffs under Federal Rule 20(a).

FACTS: Six former Central Intelligence Agency (CIA) employees (P) submitted a proposed second amended complaint that named nine new plaintiffs, named thirty new defendants, and clarified the claims of the six original plaintiffs. The original complaint alleged that the CIA (D) had violated the CIA employees' (P) statutory privacy rights, as well as their constitutional rights, in an alleged pattern of obstructing plaintiffs' access to counsel. According to the proposed amended complaint, the CIA (D) repeatedly denied plaintiffs and their counsel access to files involving the CIA's (D) alleged employment-related retaliation, discrimination, and denial of promotions and overseas assignments. The CIA (D) moved to drop some plaintiffs from the proposed amended complaint, arguing that each plaintiff's claim arose in a different transaction or occurrence and would present unique questions of fact and law.

ISSUE: Does an alleged pattern of obstruction of counsel justify joinder of plaintiffs under Federal Rule 20(a)?

HOLDING AND DECISION: (Urbina, J.) Yes. An alleged pattern of obstruction of counsel justifies joinder of plaintiffs under Federal Rule 20(a) [renumbered as 20(a)(1)(A) and 20(a)(1)(B) in 2007]. Rule 20(a) permits joinder of all persons as plaintiffs whose claims arise out of "the same transaction, occurrence, or series of transactions or occurrences" if a question of law or fact common to all of them will "arise in the action." The CIA's (D) allegedly repeated efforts to thwart the efforts of plaintiffs and their attorneys to review plaintiffs' employment files is a "series of transactions or occurrences" within the meaning of Rule 20(a). Further, the alleged pattern of obstruction is also the common question of law or fact required by Rule 20(a). Additionally, all plaintiffs have alleged violations of the Privacy Act, and those allegations constitute a second question that is common to all plaintiffs. This ruling is further supported by the chief policy consideration that underlies Rule 20(a), the promotion of trial convenience, as stated in *United Mine Workers v. Gibbs*, 383 U.S. 715 (1966). Motion to amend granted and motion to sever denied.

▶ ANALYSIS

Like his ruling in denying the CIA's (D) motion to sever the plaintiffs' claims in this case (see *M.K. v. Tenet*, p. 112), Judge Urbina's ruling on the request to drop some plaintiffs from the proposed amended complaint here also requires little review beyond the plain language of Federal Rule 20(a)(1)(A)-(B) itself. A practice point worth noting is that the same consideration—such as the CIA's (D) alleged pattern of obstruction of counsel—can be used to satisfy more than one requirement under the Federal Rules.

■=■

Quicknotes

JOINDER The joining of claims or parties in one lawsuit.

■=■

Bank of California Nat. Assn. v. Superior Court

Estate executor (P) v. Court (D)

Cal. Sup. Ct., 16 Cal.2d 516, 106 P.2d 879 (1940).

NATURE OF CASE: Hearing on a petition for a writ of prohibition.

FACT SUMMARY: Smedley (P) brought an action to enforce a contract in which Boyd, decedent, promised to leave her entire estate to Smedley (P). She brought the action against Bank of California Nat. Assn. (D), executor of Boyd's will, and St. Luke's Hospital (D), the residuary legatee who was to recover the bulk of the estate. The will named many additional legatees, who Smedley (P) did not name as defendants.

⚖ RULE OF LAW
Necessary parties are those who are so interested in the controversy that they should normally be joined in order to enable the court to do complete justice, but whose interests are separable so they are not indispensable parties, that is, parties without whom the court cannot proceed.

FACTS: Boyd died intestate, leaving an estate valued at $225,000. Her will was admitted to probate and Bank of California (D) was appointed executor. The will left legacies and bequests amounting to $60,000 to a large number of legatees, many of whom lived outside the state and country. St. Luke's Hospital (St. Luke's) (D) received the bulk of the estate as residuary legatee. Smedley (P) brought an action to enforce an alleged contract in which Boyd agreed to leave Smedley (P) the entire estate. The complaint named Bank of California (D) and St. Luke's (D) as defendants. It prayed that Smedley (P) be adjudged owner of the entire estate. No other legatees were made defendants or served. None appeared. Bank of California (D) and St. Luke's (D) made a motion for an order to bring in the other defendants. The motion was denied, and they applied for a writ to restrain the court until the other defendants had been brought in.

ISSUE: Are legatees, named in a will, indispensable parties to an action brought against the executor and one legatee where it is alleged that the decedent has violated a contract by which he agreed to leave his entire estate to the plaintiff?

HOLDING AND DECISION: (Gibson, C.J.) No. Necessary parties are those who are so interested in the controversy that they should normally be made parties in order to enable the court to do complete justice but whose interests are separable, so the court may proceed to judgment without prejudicing their interests or the interests of the parties already before the court. Necessary parties may be affected by the decision or may be "necessary" parties to

a complete settlement of the entire controversy, but they are not indispensable to any valid judgment in the particular case. Although they should normally be joined, considerations of fairness, convenience and practicability are relevant, especially where it is impossible to find these other parties or impracticable to bring them in. Indispensable parties are those without whom the court cannot proceed. Many cases say that the court would have no jurisdiction to proceed without them. The objection is so fundamental that the court may, on its own motion, dismiss the proceedings or refuse to proceed until the indispensable parties are brought in. The question in this case is whether the other legatees were indispensable or necessary parties. In cases like this, the action is against the distributee personally. Each distributee is held individually as a constructive trustee solely of the property which came to her, and none is interested in the granting or denial of similar relief to others. Where there are a number of legatees, they would all be necessary parties since the main issue, the validity of the decedent's will, affects their property interests, and the entire matter, the disposition of all of the decedent's property, cannot be finally sealed without a binding adjudication for or against every legatee. But they are not indispensable parties. Unlike a case in which any judgment would affect the rights of absent persons, hence making them indispensable parties, the present case is one in which Smedley (P) may litigate her claim against Bank of California (D) and St. Luke's (D) alone and obtain a decree which binds them alone. The absent legatee-defendants, not being before the court, will not be bound by the judgment, and their property will not be affected. Alternative writ discharged and peremptory writ denied.

▎ANALYSIS

A party is deemed indispensable only if complete relief cannot be rendered unless he is joined, or he claims an interest in the subject of the action such that to proceed without him would impair his ability to protect his interest or expose the existing parties to the risk of double liability or inconsistent obligations. Following are examples of indispensable parties: in any action to determine ownership, title or right to possession, all co-tenants or joint tenants are indispensable parties; in a representative suit by a minority shareholder, the corporation is an indispensable party; courts are split on whether all joint obligees under a

Continued on next page.

note, lease, or other contractual obligation must be joined in an action to enforce the contract.

■■■

Quicknotes

INDISPENSABLE PARTY Parties whose joining in a lawsuit is essential for the adequate disposition of the action and without whom the action cannot proceed.

NECESSARY PARTIES Parties, whose joining in a lawsuit, is essential to the disposition of the action.

■■■

Provident Tradesmens Bank & Trust Co. v. Patterson

Estate administrator (P) v. Tortfeasor's estate (D)

390 U.S. 102 (1968).

NATURE OF CASE: Review of dismissal of a tort action for nonjoinder of an "indispensable" party.

FACT SUMMARY: In a multi-party action arising out of an auto accident, Provident Tradesmens Bank & Trust Co. (P) sought indemnification from other plaintiffs from Lumbermens Mutual Casualty Co. (D).

> **RULE OF LAW**
> In the absence of a party who cannot feasibly be joined, a court should not dismiss the action if, in "equity and good conscience," it could proceed without the party.

FACTS: An auto-truck collision killed Thomas Smith, the truck driver, and two of three auto occupants, Donald Cionci (driver) and John Lynch (passenger). A third auto passenger, John Harris, was injured. The owner of the auto, Edward Dutcher, had entrusted his car to Cionci. As a result of the accident, several tort actions were brought. Harris and Smith's estate sued Dutcher and the estates of Lynch and Cionci in a state court action. Lynch's administrator, Provident Tradesmens Bank & Trust Co. (Provident) (P), sued Cionci's estate and won a $50,000 settlement, which was uncollectible. Provident (P), facing liability to Harris and Smith's estate, looked elsewhere for a fund from which to satisfy that potential liability. Dutcher had a $100,000 liability insurance policy on his auto with Lumbermens Mutual Casualty Co. (Lumbermens) (D), covering liability of anyone driving with Dutcher's permission. But Lumbermens (D), upon notice, declined to defend Cionci's estate in the Provident-Cionci suit on ground that Cionci was not covered by Dutcher's policy; i.e., alleging Cionci had detoured from the expected use of the auto for which he had no permission. Provident (P) brought this diversity suit based on its $50,000 liquidated claim against Cionci's estate, asking for a declaration that Dutcher had given Cionci permission to use his car. Harris and Smith's estate was joined as plaintiffs. All plaintiffs were Pennsylvania residents. Dutcher, also a Pennsylvania resident, was not joined, and failure to join him at trial was not asserted by Lumbermens (D). The district court found for the plaintiffs, but the court of appeals reversed and dismissed the case on grounds that Dutcher was an "indispensable" party whose joinder would destroy diversity. Thus, the case was dismissed for lack of subject matter jurisdiction.

ISSUE: In the absence of a party who cannot feasibly be joined, should a court dismiss the action rather than proceed without the nonjoined party?

HOLDING AND DECISION: (Harlan, J.) No. Under Rule 19(b), a court must examine each case to determine whether, in equity and good conscience, it should proceed without a party who cannot feasibly be joined. There are four interests the court must look to. (1) The prejudicial effect a judgment would have on the absent party and parties to the action. In the present case, Provident (P) and the other plaintiffs were prejudiced by having a fully litigated judgment set aside. Lumbermens (D) was not prejudiced, since they failed to complain at trial of Dutcher's nonjoinder. And Dutcher was not harmed by his nonjoinder. If the plaintiffs sought damages against him personally, he could always assert the "permission" defense, as did Lumbermens (D), claiming any payments made by Lumbermens (D) on behalf of Cionci's estate should be credited to his, Dutcher's, liability. (2) Alternative measures the court might use to lessen any prejudice. Here, the court of appeals could have accepted a limitation of all claims to the amount of the insurance policy, thus precluding any subsequent suit against the nonjoined party, Dutcher. This would have effectively protected all parties' interests. (3) Whether the judgment rendered in the absence of a nonjoined party would be adequate. Again, the court should have considered modification of the judgment as an alternative to dismissal. This element refers to the public stake in having controversies settled in one litigation. (4) Will the plaintiff have any adequate remedy if the action is dismissed for nonjoinder? There was no reason for the court of appeals to throw away a valid judgment just because it did not settle the whole controversy as between Dutcher and the plaintiffs. Thus, efficiency considerations should have given way to the need to preserve a valid judgment for the plaintiffs so they would not be forced to relitigate. It was more efficient to preserve the judgment than to dismiss and force relitigation. Whether a party is indispensable causing a lawsuit to be dismissed in the absence of that party should be decided on a case-by-case basis. Here, the court of appeals adopted a too-rigid approach in applying joinder rules. Judgment vacated and case remanded.

▌ANALYSIS

Under the Federal Rules, a party is indispensable if complete relief is not possible among those already parties to an action unless he is joined, or to proceed without him would impair his ability to protect his interests or expose parties to the action to double liability. However, if an indispensable

Continued on next page.

party would destroy diversity of citizenship, then the case must be dismissed for lack of subject matter jurisdiction, i.e., the court can't proceed to a just conclusion without that party. Too strict an application of this rule results in misuse of joinder of parties as a post-trial tactic by the losing party. As in the present case, where a party loses at trial, that party may have the case dismissed by asserting that an indispensable party was not joined, and since his joinder would destroy the necessary diversity of citizenship, the case must be dismissed. Rule 19(b) is a "relief valve" for such tactics, allowing the court to apply equitable principles to achieve a more pragmatic solution.

■═■

Quicknotes

DIVERSITY OF CITIZENSHIP Parties are citizens of different states, or one party is an alien; a factor, along with a statutorily set dollar value of the matter in controversy, that allows a federal district court to exercise its authority to hear a lawsuit based on diversity jurisdiction.

INDEMNIFICATION Reimbursement for losses sustained or security against anticipated loss or damages.

■═■

Jeub v. B/G Foods, Inc.

Consumer (P) v. Restaurant (D)

2 F.R.D. 238 (D. Minn. 1942).

NATURE OF CASE: Motion to vacate an order joining a party as third-party defendant.

FACT SUMMARY: When Jeub (P) sued B/G Foods, Inc. (D) for serving spoiled ham, B/G Foods (D) sought indemnification by joining Swift & Co. as third-party defendants.

RULE OF LAW

In a federal action, impleader is permitted of a party who is or may be liable for indemnification to a party-defendant so long as the applicable state substantive law regarding indemnification is satisfied.

FACTS: Jeub (P) brought suit against B/G Foods, Inc. (D) alleging Jeub (P) suffered illness from eating ham served in one of B/G Foods' (D) restaurants. Prior to serving the answer, B/G Foods (D) obtained an ex parte order making Swift & Co., from whom B/G Foods (D) purchased the ham in a sealed container, a third-party defendant. In its third-party complaint, B/G Foods (D) disclaimed negligence for Jeub's (P) injuries, placing blame solely on Swift & Co. B/G Foods (D) asked that if Jeub (P) recovered against them, Swift & Co. should indemnify them for such recovery. Swift & Co. moved to vacate the ex parte order on several grounds, including the assertion that Rule 14 offered no substantive basis for joinder, and under Minnesota law, a right to indemnification existed only after the defendant suffered payment of any recovery.

ISSUE: May a party be impleaded in a federal action to determine that party's indemnification liability to a party-defendant where the applicable state law provides no right of indemnification exists until the defendant has been forced to pay damages?

HOLDING AND DECISION: (Nordbye, J.) Yes. Rule 14 [renumbered as 14(a)(1) in 2007] permits impleader of a party who is or "may be" liable. It is not limited to rights of indemnity which are presently enforceable. A party, such as B/G Foods (D), may invoke Rule 14 procedure to implead a party for the determination of possible liability of all parties concerned, even though B/G Foods (D) has no present action against Swift & Co. The purpose of Rule 14 is to determine the rights of all parties in one proceeding, avoiding subsequent independent actions for indemnification. As to Swift & Co.'s assertion that Rule 14 procedure violates applicable Minnesota law allowing indemnification only after a defendant has suffered some payment or loss in the action, any judgment against Swift & Co. may be stayed until B/G Foods (D) has paid or satisfied judgment against it. Swift & Co.'s motion to vacate is denied.

ANALYSIS

This case involves an *Erie* problem of conflicting state substantive law and federal procedural law. *Erie R. Co. v. Tompkins*, 304 U.S. 64 (1938). The existence of a right to indemnification, a prerequisite to impleader, is "substantive" for *Erie* purposes. Thus, the applicable state law of the forum governs, and if the state does not recognize a right of indemnification, then Rule 14 cannot create such a right.

Quicknotes

EX PARTE A proceeding commenced by one party without providing any opposing parties with notice or which is uncontested by an adverse party.

IMPLEADER Procedure by which a third party, who may be liable for all or part of liability, is joined to an action so that all issues may be resolved in a single suit.

INDEMNIFICATION Reimbursement for losses sustained or security against anticipated loss or damages.

Too, Inc. v. Kohl's Department Stores, Inc.

Intellectual property owner (P) v. Alleged infringers (D)

213 F.R.D. 138 (S.D.N.Y. 2003).

NATURE OF CASE: Motion under Federal Rule 14(a) for leave to file a third-party complaint against non-parties for contribution and indemnification.

FACT SUMMARY: Too, Inc. (P) sued multiple defendants, including Windstar Apparel, Inc. (Windstar) (D), for allegedly violating Too's (P) intellectual property rights and right to fair competition. Windstar (D) moved for permission to file a third-party complaint against two of its employees, Mia DeCaro and Paula Abraham, for their alleged liability in the underlying transactions.

RULE OF LAW
A trial court should permit a third-party complaint if the allegations involve the same core of facts as those stated in the original complaint, but not if the third-party allegations are facially without merit.

FACTS: Too, Inc. (P) sued Windstar Apparel, Inc. (Windstar) (D), among others, for allegedly infringing Too's (P) copyright and trademark rights, as well as for unfair competition, in transactions involving the marketing of designs of girls' sleepwear. Windstar (D) tried to implead two of its employees, DeCaro and Abraham, for their alleged liability in the alleged violations of Too's (P) rights in the sleepwear designs. Windstar (D) had hired DeCaro as a designer and Abraham as a salesperson for Windstar's (D) account with Kohl's Department Stores, Inc. (Kohl's) (D). DeCaro allegedly held out to Windstar (D) the designs at issue as her own, knowing that they would be sold to other retailers such as Kohl's (D). Windstar's (D) proposed third-party complaint alleged further that Abraham sold the designs to Kohl's (D) as DeCaro's own designs when she knew that Too (P) owned the rights to the designs.

ISSUE: Should a trial court permit a third-party complaint if the allegations involve the same core of facts as those stated in the original complaint, even if the third-party allegations are facially without merit?

HOLDING AND DECISION: (Marrero, J.) Yes and No. A trial court should permit a third-party complaint if the allegations involve the same core of facts as those stated in the original complaint, but not if the third-party allegations are facially without merit. A third-party complaint is appropriate where either the third-party defendant's liability to the third-party plaintiff depends on the resolution of the main claim or the third-party defendant contributed to the third-party plaintiff's liability. Here, DeCaro's and Abraham's liability indisputably would depend on Windstar's (D) own. DeCaro and Abraham are already material witnesses under the main complaint, and

permitting Windstar (D) to implead them thus clearly promotes judicial economy. Further, Windstar's (D) proposed third-party complaint states a claim upon which relief can be granted by alleging that DeCaro and Abraham both knew that they were infringing Too's (P) intellectual property rights. The proposed third-party claim against DeCaro and Abraham thus is not obviously unmeritorious. Also, neither proposed third-party defendant will be prejudiced by being impleaded; they would need to retain counsel later anyway, and impleading them will reduce the need for discovery. The proposed third-party claim for contribution, therefore, should be permitted. On the other hand, the proposed third-party claim for indemnification should not be permitted because New York law prohibits indemnification if the party seeking indemnification bore some fault for the alleged wrongdoing. Here, Windstar (D) almost certainly would bear at least part of the blame for any proven infringement of Too's (P) rights; the proposed third-party complaint itself does not allege that Windstar (D) is without blame. Accordingly, the third-party claim for indemnification is meritless and should not be permitted. Motion for leave to file third-party complaint granted in part and denied in part.

ANALYSIS

One lesson from *Too, Inc.* is that even proposed third-party claims must have merit. On that point Judge Marrero's analysis here, that the third-party claim for indemnification is "clearly without merit," at least raises an issue under Federal Rule 11. By signing the Rule 14(a) [renumbered as Rule 14(a)(1) in 2007] motion, Windstar's (D) counsel certified to the court that the claims in the proposed third-party complaint "are warranted by existing law," Federal Rule 11(b)(2), when the existing applicable law clearly did not warrant the claim for indemnification.

■=■

Quicknotes

CONTRIBUTION The right of a person or party who has compensated a victim for his injury to seek reimbursement from others who are equally responsible for the injury in proportional amounts.

INDEMNIFICATION Reimbursement for losses sustained or security against anticipated loss or damages.

■=■

Hancock Oil Co. v. Independent Distributing Co.

Corporate lessee (P) v. Purported landowner (D)

Cal. Sup. Ct., 24 Cal.2d 497, 150 P.2d 463 (1944).

NATURE OF CASE: Appeal of a motion granting a demurrer in an action to interplead two adverse claims.

FACT SUMMARY: Hancock Oil Co. (P) interpleaded Independent Distributing Co. (D) and Hopkins (D) in order to determine which party Hancock Oil Co. (P) owed the rental money to.

🏛 RULE OF LAW
If adverse claimants both claim the right to the same debt or property, the party owing the debt or holding the property can interplead both claimants and force them to litigate the issue of which claimant has the superior claim to the debt or property.

FACTS: Hopkins (D) leased property to Hancock Oil Co. (P) for which Hopkins (D) was to receive royalties at a specified rate. Independent Distributing Co. (D) filed an action against Hopkins (D) claiming that Hopkins (D) held the real property in trust for them but had leased it to Hancock Oil Co. (P). Independent Distributing Co. (D) sought an accounting of the rents of the land and claimed the rent and royalties were rightfully theirs. Hancock Oil Co. (P) then filed this action and interpleaded both Independent Distributing Co. (D) and Hopkins (D) in order to determine who Hancock Oil Co. (P) owed the rent money to. Independent Distributing Co. (D) filed an answer claiming to be the owner of the land and entitled to all of the rents and profits from it. Hopkins (D) filed a general demurrer and a special demurrer upon the ground of uncertainty. All the demurrers were sustained without leave to amend and Hancock Oil Co. (P) appealed that ruling. The trial judge appeared to base his decision on the grounds that a tenant may not question the title of his landlord at the date of the lease and, therefore, a tenant cannot interplead his landlord, as Hancock Oil Co. (P) had attempted to do.

ISSUE: Can a tenant interplead his landlord when there is another party also claiming a right to the rent money?

HOLDING AND DECISION: (Edmonds, J.) Yes. The common law bill of interpleader had four essential elements. First, the same thing, debt, or duty must be claimed by both or all the parties against whom the relief is demanded. In this case, both Independent Distributing Co. (D) and Hopkins (D) claimed the same rental money. Second, all of the adverse titles or claims must be dependent or be derived from a common source. Both claimants assert their right to the rental money derives from ownership of the land in question. Third, the one seeking the relief must not have or claim any interest in the subject matter. Hancock Oil Co. (P) did not have any interest in the rental money other than having to pay it and that doesn't qualify as a claim to the rental money. Fourth, the party seeking relief must have incurred no independent liability to either of the claimants. Hancock Oil Co. (P) was liable to Hopkins (D) for the rent. The last common law requirement has been relaxed by statute, however. If this were not so, very few parties would be able to use the bill of interpleader. This latter requirement did bar tenants from interpleading their landlords for a long time. Allowing the tenant to interplead his landlord also works to the advantage of the third-party claimant because he would be forced to establish his rights to the rental money in a separate action. The landlord may suffer some disadvantage in being forced to defend a suit in interpleader as, while the litigation continues, the rent is withheld from him without interest. The tenant is not allowed to maintain an interpleader without a showing that he actually faces double vexation in respect to liability. Hancock Oil Co. (P) did state a cause of action and the trial court was wrong in sustaining the demurrers. The judgment is reversed.

▶ ANALYSIS

The typical interpleader suit has two stages. In the first stage, it is determined if the interpleader is proper. If it is determined that it is proper, the party maintaining the interpleader deposits the money or property with the court and then retires from the case. The next stage is where the claimants determine who has the right to the property or money deposited with the court. Some common examples of interpleader are an escrow-holder interpleading funds deposited with him as to which several parties are making adverse claims, or a life insurance company interpleading the beneficiary of a life insurance policy and any other claimants of the insurance.

═▮

Quicknotes

DEMURRER The assertion that the opposing party's pleadings are insufficient and that the demurring party should not be made to answer.

IMPLEADER Procedure by which a third party, who may be liable for all or part of liability, is joined to an action so that all issues may be resolved in a single suit.

═▮

New York Life Insurance Co. v. Dunlevy

Insurer (D) v. Assignee of insurance policy (P)

241 U.S. 518 (1916).

NATURE OF CASE: Action to recover proceeds from a life insurance policy.

FACT SUMMARY: Dunlevy (P) instituted an action in California to obtain the proceeds of an insurance policy that had been awarded to Dunlevy's (P) father by a Pennsylvania court.

🏛 **RULE OF LAW**
Personal jurisdiction must be obtained over the individual in an interpleader action to have the judgment be binding on that individual.

FACTS: Dunlevy (P) filed this suit in a California court on January 14, 1910, against the New York Life Insurance Co. (D) and Gould (D), Mrs. Dunlevy's (P) father, to obtain the surrender value of a life insurance policy that Dunlevy (P) claimed had been assigned to her by her father. Dunlevy (P) was awarded $2,479.70, the amount of the surrender value, and the circuit court of appeals affirmed the decision. New York Life (D) claimed Dunlevy (P) was precluded by certain judicial proceedings in Pennsylvania where the proceeds from the insurance policy had been garnished and Gould (D) had been adjudged to be owner of the proceeds from the policy. In 1907, Boggs & Buhl recovered a valid personal judgment by default against Dunlevy (P) in a Pennsylvania court. In November 1909, Boggs & Buhl attempted to attach the proceeds from the insurance policy in order to satisfy the judgment awarded them against Dunlevy (P) in 1907. New York Life (D) and Gould (D) were summoned as garnishees. On February 5, 1910, after this suit had begun in California, New York Life (D) admitted that they owed the proceeds to someone and attempted to set up an interpleader action to determine who had the right to the money. New York Life (D) was allowed to pay the proceeds into the court. Notice was given to Dunlevy (P) in California in an attempt to have her present at the interpleader action. Dunlevy (P) did not appear at the trial held in Pennsylvania. The Pennsylvania court held that Gould (D) had not made an assignment of the proceeds of the insurance policy to Dunlevy (P) and so Gould (D) was awarded the money. Dunlevy (P) claimed that the interpleader action was not binding on her because the court did not have personal jurisdiction over her. New York Life (D) claimed that the Pennsylvania court had jurisdiction over Dunlevy (P) because the right to the insurance money was determined in a garnishment proceeding maintained to satisfy a judgment against Dunlevy (P). Because the Pennsylvania court had jurisdiction over Dunlevy (P) in the original action, they also had jurisdiction over Dunlevy

(P) in the action to satisfy the judgment against her. New York Life (D) appealed the California court decision to the United States Supreme Court.

ISSUE: Must a court have personal jurisdiction over parties in an interpleader action?

HOLDING AND DECISION: (McReynolds, J.) Yes. Because the Pennsylvania court had personal jurisdiction over Dunlevy (P), they would have continued to have jurisdiction over her through the garnishment proceedings. But the interpleader action was not really part of any garnishment proceeding. The issue of which party had the right to the insurance money was a totally different issue. The interpleader action was an attempt to bring about a final and conclusive adjudication of Dunlevy's (P) personal rights and not merely to discover property and apply it to her debts. The fact that the Pennsylvania court had jurisdiction over Dunlevy (P) in the one case does not give them jurisdiction over her in the interpleader action. The established general rule is that any personal judgment which a state court may render against one who did not voluntarily submit to its jurisdiction and who is not a citizen of the state is void because the court had no jurisdiction over his person. The Pennsylvania court ruling did not bar the action in California and, therefore, the judgment is affirmed.

▶ **ANALYSIS**

Shortly after the decision in this case was handed down, Congress passed the Federal Interpleader Act. This Act has been successively broadened several more times. It provides for nationwide service of process in order to reach all of the claimants. Also, venue is proper in any judicial district in which one or more of the claimants reside and the federal courts are granted jurisdiction in amounts as little as $500. The apparent intent of Congress was to avoid other decisions such as the one in this case.

Quicknotes

ATTACHMENT The seizing of the property of one party in anticipation of, or in order to satisfy, a favorable judgment obtained by another party.

GARNISHEE A party against whom a garnishment has been ordered; party holding the property of a judgment creditor who is directed to hold the property until a court determination of the proper disposition thereof.

Pan American Fire & Casualty Co. v. Revere

Insurance company (P) v. Accident claimants (D)

188 F. Supp. 474 (E.D. La. 1960).

NATURE OF CASE: Action to interplead all claimants of a liability insurance policy.

FACT SUMMARY: Pan American Fire & Casualty Co. (P) sought to interplead all parties to a multicar accident who were seeking to collect against the holder of the insurance policy.

RULE OF LAW
In the federal courts, an insurer can interplead all claimants to a particular policy if the claims would exceed the policy limit.

FACTS: On February 3, 1960, a large tractor and trailer collided head-on with a bus carrying schoolchildren. Four people on the bus were killed and 23 injured. Two cars also collided which were following the bus. Pan American Fire & Casualty Co. (Pan American) (P) alleged that three suits had already been filed against them and that numerous other claims had been made, as they were the liability insurer of the tractor-trailer. Pan American (P) sought to interplead all present and potential claimants, and asked that all parties be enjoined from initiating legal proceedings elsewhere or further prosecuting the actions already filed and that they be directed to assert their claims in the present suit. Pan American (P) deposited a bond in the full amount of its policy limits of $100,000, alleging that they had no further interest in the insurance proceeds and that they were a disinterested stakeholder. They also denied liability toward any and all claimants.

ISSUE: Can an insurer interplead all claimants to the proceeds of a liability insurance policy in the federal courts?

HOLDING AND DECISION: (Wright, J.) Yes. Pan American (P) can interplead all the claimants to the proceeds of the liability insurance policy. Fed. R. Civ. P. 22 and the Federal Interpleader Act have ended the necessity of distinguishing between a strict interpleader, where the plaintiff is a disinterested stakeholder, and a bill in the nature of interpleader where the plaintiff is himself a claimant by denying the validity of some or all of the other claims. At the common law, a bill of interpleader was considered an equitable remedy. A threat of multiple suits on the same obligation was sufficient to give the court of equity jurisdiction, but for the court of equity to have jurisdiction in an action in the nature of interpleader there needed to be other grounds for jurisdiction than the threat of multiple suits. The present law is that the only equitable ground necessary for interpleader, either strict or in the nature of interpleader, is exposure to double or multiple

suits on the same claim. Though the Interpleader Act makes no such requirement, Rule 22 apparently permits interpleader only if the claims are such that the plaintiff is or may be exposed to double or multiple liability. The requirement is not a strict one and there only need be a chance of double liability, no matter how improbable or remote. It is settled that an insurer with limited contractual liability who faces claims in excess of his policy limits is sufficient under Rule 22. There is an argument that tort claims do not justify interpleader, because it is too conjectural to assert that the claims will exceed the policy limits, that the liability is too remote, and that the right to a jury trial is lost because interpleader is an equitable action. At least in this case it is clear that the claims will exceed the policy limits and it is enough to be exposed to double liability to justify an interpleader. Each claimant can have a full opportunity to prove his case before a jury, reserving to the court of equity only the task of apportioning the funds between those who are successful if the aggregate of the verdicts exceeds the amount of the insurance proceeds. An injunction will be granted enjoining pending state court proceedings so that all parties will be required to bring their actions in this court. Because this wasn't a statutory interpleader, this court does not have nationwide service of process and will not be able to effect service of process on parties living outside the state. The Interpleader Act only provides for nationwide service of process throughout the United States in actions brought under a statutory interpleader. The prayer for interpleader is granted and the motion to dismiss is denied.

ANALYSIS

Interpleader in the federal courts can be brought under 28 U.S.C. § 1335, which is a statutory interpleader, or under Fed. R. Civ. P. 22. The requirement for the statutory interpleader is that two or more claimants are making adverse claims to the same debt, instrument, or property. Under Rule 22 interpleader, the plaintiff need only show that there are multiple claimants which may expose the plaintiff to multiple liability. Under Rule 22, jurisdiction must be established by complete diversity and by meeting the jurisdictional amount. Under the statutory interpleader, only minimal diversity is required and the jurisdictional amount is $500 instead of $10,000. Also, under the statutory interpleader, reach of process is nationwide.

Continued on next page.

Quicknotes

FED. R. CIV. P. 22 Permits interpleader if the claims are such that the plaintiff is or may be exposed to double or multiple liability.

INTERPLEADER An equitable proceeding whereby a person holding property which is subject to the claims of multiple parties may require such parties to resolve the matter through litigation.

State Farm Fire & Casualty Co. v. Tashire

Insurance company (P) v. Accident claimants (D)

386 U.S. 523 (1967).

NATURE OF CASE: Review of dismissal action in the nature of interpleader.

FACT SUMMARY: State Farm Fire & Casualty Co. (P) insured the driver of a truck involved in a collision involving a Greyhound bus and attempted to interplead all claimants.

🏛 RULE OF LAW
Insurance companies can invoke the federal interpleader before claims against them have been reduced to judgment. A party to a multiparty litigation can only interplead the claimants seeking the funds of that party.

FACTS: In September of 1964, a Greyhound bus collided with a pickup truck in northern California. Two of the passengers aboard the bus were killed; 33 others were injured, as were the bus driver and the driver of the truck and its passenger. Four of the injured passengers filed suit in California state courts seeking damages in excess of $1,000,000. Greyhound, the bus driver, the driver of the truck, and the owner of the truck, who was also the passenger in the truck, were named as defendants. Before these cases came to trial, State Farm Fire & Casualty Co. (State Farm) (P) brought this action in the nature of interpleader in the United States District Court for the District of Oregon. State Farm (P) had in force an insurance policy with respect to the driver of the truck providing for bodily injury liability up to $10,000 per person and $20,000 per occurrence. State Farm (P) asserted that claims already filed against it far exceeded their maximum amount of liability under the policy. They paid the $20,000 into the court and asked that the court require all claimants to establish their claims against the driver of the truck in this single proceeding and in no other. State Farm (P) named Greyhound, the bus driver, the driver of the truck, and owner of the truck, and each of the prospective claimants as defendants. Tashire (D) moved to have this action dismissed and in the alternative for a change of venue to the Northern District of California. The court refused to dismiss the action and granted the injunction that State Farm (P) had wanted, which provided that all suits against the driver of the pickup truck, State Farm (P), Greyhound, and the bus driver be prosecuted in the interpleader proceeding. On interlocutory appeal, the Ninth Circuit reversed the district court's decision. They ruled that an insurance company may not invoke federal interpleader until the claims against it have been reduced to judgment. The case was then appealed to the Supreme Court.

ISSUE: Can insurance companies invoke federal interpleader before the claims against them have been reduced to judgment?

HOLDING AND DECISION: (Fortas, J.) Yes. The 1948 revision of the Judicial Code made clear that insurance companies do not have to wait until claims against them have been reduced to judgment before making use of federal interpleader. Even though State Farm (P) had probably invoked federal interpleader jurisdiction, it was not entitled to an injunction enjoining prosecution of suits against it outside the confines of the interpleader proceeding and also extending the same protection to its insured, the alleged tortfeasor. Greyhound (D) was even less entitled to have the order expanded to require all actions against it and its driver to be brought in the interpleader proceeding. State Farm's (P) interest in this case is protected when the court restrains claimants from seeking to enforce against the insurance company any judgment obtained against its insured, except in the interpleader proceeding itself. State Farm (P) shouldn't be allowed to determine where dozens of tort plaintiffs must bring their claims. Interpleader was not made to force all the litigants in multiparty litigation to bring their actions in a particular court. Interpleader is to control the allocation of a fund among successful tort plaintiffs and not to control the underlying litigation against alleged tortfeasors. The decision of the court of appeals is reversed and the district court is to modify the injunction prohibiting the bringing of all other actions connected with the accident in any court except the interpleader proceedings. The injunction should only restrain claimants from seeking to enforce against State Farm (P) any judgment obtained against its insured, except in the interpleader proceeding itself. The judgment of the court of appeals is reversed.

DISSENT: (Douglas, J.) Under California and Oregon law, a claimant against the insured will only become a claimant against the insurance company only after a final legal judgment has been issued against the insured. To date, the insured party has not become legally obligated to pay any sum against any potential claimant. The majority's construction of the interpleader rule broadens its scope unnecessarily. Congress could establish a direct action statute allowing claims by victims against the insurance company. However, via the insurance policy and state law, the victims in this case are not claimants against the

Continued on next page.

insurance company until their claims against the insured have been reduced to a final judgment.

▶ *ANALYSIS*

This case points up the general nature of federal interpleader. Generally, the interpleader device allows a party to join all adverse claimants asserting several mutually exclusive claims (regarding the same property or debt) against him and require them to litigate to determine their own interests. Note that there are two types of federal interpleader. Rule 22 interpleader, limited by normal federal jurisdiction (e.g., federal question greater than $10,000, diversity, or citizenship), venue, and procedure requirements is available to any so-qualified parties who may be exposed to multiple liability if not permitted to interplead. 28 U.S.C. § 1335 interpleader (statutory) is more liberal as to jurisdiction than most federal rules and requires: (1) diversity of citizenship; (2) greater than only $500 be involved; (3) payment into the court of bond. Perhaps the greatest advantage of § 1335 interpleader, however, is "nationwide service of process."

Quicknotes

DIVERSITY OF CITIZENSHIP Parties are citizens of different states, or one party is an alien; a factor, along with a statutorily set dollar value of the matter in controversy, that allows a federal district court to exercise its authority to hear a lawsuit based on diversity jurisdiction.

INTERPLEADER An equitable proceeding whereby a person holding property which is subject to the claims of multiple parties may require such parties to resolve the matter through litigation.

Smuck v. Hobson

Board of education member (D) v. Schoolchildren (P)

408 F.2d 175 (D.C. Cir. 1969).

NATURE OF CASE: Motion to intervene in an action involving school racial discrimination.

FACT SUMMARY: Smuck (D) appealed and several other parties sought to intervene after the school board chose not to appeal a trial court ruling finding racial discrimination.

🏛 RULE OF LAW
The federal courts allow intervention when the party has an interest to be protected, denial of intervention would impair the party's ability to protect the interest, and the party is not adequately represented by others.

FACTS: In a prior case (*Hobson v. Hansen*, 269 F. Supp. 401 [D.D.C. 1967] in which Hansen (P)—a plaintiff here— was a defendant), a class action was brought on behalf of black and poor children against the Board of Education, alleging that their constitutional rights to equal educational opportunities were being violated because the schools were being operated in a racially and economically discriminatory manner. The court ruled in favor of the plaintiffs. The Board of Education decided not to appeal the case. At that point, Hansen, the Superintendent of Schools (who had resigned his position), and Smuck (D), also a defendant in that case and one of the dissenting Board members, filed notices of appeal. Hansen and 20 parents filed motions of intervention in the district court and in the court of appeals. The court of appeals delayed hearing on the appeal and remanded the motions of intervention for a hearing. The district court granted the motions to intervene, even though neither Hansen nor the parents had shown a substantial interest that could be protected only though intervention, in order to give the court of appeals an opportunity to pass on the intervening questions and the questions to be raised by the appeal on the merits. All the parties intervening in this case challenged the findings of the trial court that the Board of Education violated the Constitution in administering the District of Columbia schools.

ISSUE: Do federal courts allow intervention when the party has an interest to be protected, denial of intervention would impair the party's ability to protect the interest, and the party is not adequately represented by others?

HOLDING AND DECISION: (Bazelon, C.J.) Yes. Federal courts allow intervention when the party has an interest to be protected, denial of intervention would impair the party's ability to protect the interest, and the party is not adequately represented by others. To make this ruling, a balance must be reached so that trials do not

become so large and unmanageable because of intervention, while related issues can still be resolved in a single lawsuit. Interests do not have to be economic to be sufficient. The goal is to dispose of lawsuits in such a manner as to involve as many apparently concerned persons as is compatible with efficiency and due process. Because the motion to intervene wasn't made until after a judgment was reached, a strong showing is required to justify intervention. Hansen has resigned as Superintendent of Schools and is attempting to appeal in his former official capacity and as an individual. Whatever standing he may once have had, he lost when he resigned. The original decision was not a personal attack upon Hansen and it did not bind him personally once he left office. Hansen has no interest relating to the property or transaction that is the subject of the action sufficient to warrant intervention and so his motion for intervention and appeal are denied. Smuck is a member of the Board of Education and, while he was a named defendant in the action, the Board of Education was the principal figure. Smuck had an opportunity to defend the action in the decision not to appeal and, having done so, he lost his separate interest as an individual. Therefore, he will not be allowed to intervene. The parents, however, have an interest in the case because of their interest in the education of their children. The parents would be impaired in their ability to protect their interest if they were not allowed to intervene. Furthermore, the parents would not be adequately represented by others. The Board of Education has chosen not to appeal the case and the parents would be impaired in their ability to protect their interest if intervention were denied. Therefore, the parents will be permitted to intervene, but review is limited to the parts of the order that limit the discretion of the old or new board.

▶ ANALYSIS

When intervention is made as a matter of right under Fed. R. Civ. P. 24(a), no independent basis for jurisdiction is required. The intervenor's claim is considered as ancillary to the original action. This relieves the intervenor of the necessity meeting the diversity requirement and the jurisdictional amount requirement. When the intervention is made under 24(b), which is permissive intervention, the intervenor must meet the diversity of citizenship and the jurisdictional amount because the intervenor's claim is actually a new claim. If the intervenor could not meet the jurisdictional requirements, he would not be allowed to intervene.

Continued on next page.

Quicknotes

DIVERSITY OF CITIZENSHIP Parties are citizens of different states, or one party is an alien; a factor, along with a statutorily set dollar value of the matter in controversy, that allows a federal district court to exercise its authority to hear a lawsuit based on diversity jurisdiction.

INTERVENOR A party, not an initial party to the action, who is admitted to the action in order to assert an interest in the subject matter of a lawsuit.

INTERVENTION The method by which a party, not an initial party to the action, is admitted to the action in order to assert an interest in the subject matter of a lawsuit.

Class Actions

Quick Reference Rules of Law

Wal-Mart Stores, Inc. v. Dukes

Retail giant (D) v. Female employees (P)

131 S. Ct. 2541 (2011).

NATURE OF CASE: Class action based on gender discrimination.

FACT SUMMARY: A small group of women filed a gender discrimination claim against Wal-Mart Stores, Inc. (D). A class was certified, and the original small group of women who filed the claims wanted to represent the class. The class was the largest in history.

🏛 RULE OF LAW

(1) A class consisting of more than one million women employed by a single employer nationwide cannot be certified as a class if they do not meet the "commonality" threshold for class certification under Federal Rule of Civil Procedure 23(a)(2) because they cannot demonstrate all class members were subject to the same discriminatory employment policy.

(2) Claims for monetary relief may not be certified under Federal Rule of Civil Procedure 23(b)(2) where the monetary relief is not incidental to the injunctive or declaratory relief.

FACTS: Betty Dukes (P), a Wal-Mart Stores, Inc. (Wal-Mart) "greeter" at a Pittsburg, California, store, and five other women filed a class-action lawsuit in which they alleged that the company's nationwide policies resulted in lower pay for women than men in comparable positions and longer wait for management promotions than men. The U. S. District Court for the Northern District of California certified the class, finding Plaintiffs satisfied the requirements of Federal Rule of Civil Procedure 23(a)(2) and 23 (b)(2). The certified class was estimated to include more than 1.5 million women including all women employed by Wal-Mart nationwide at any time after December 26, 1998, making this the largest class action lawsuit in U.S. history. Wal-Mart (D) argued that the court should require employees to file on an individual basis, contending that class actions of this size—formed under Federal Rule of Civil Procedure 23(b) of the federal rules of civil procedure—are inherently unmanageable and unduly costly. The U.S. Court of Appeals for the Ninth Circuit upheld the class certification three times.

ISSUE:

(1) Can a class consisting of more than one million women employed by a single employer nationwide be certified as a class if they do not meet the "commonality" threshold for class certification under Federal Rule of Civil Procedure 23(a)(2) because they cannot demonstrate

all class members were subject to the same discriminatory employment policy?

(2) May claims for monetary relief be certified under Federal Rule of Civil Procedure 23(b)(2) where the monetary relief is not incidental to the injunctive or declaratory relief?

HOLDING AND DECISION: (Scalia, J.)

(1) No. A class consisting of more than one million women employed by a single employer nationwide cannot be certified as a class if they do not meet the "commonality" threshold for class certification under Federal Rule of Civil Procedure 23(a)(2) because they cannot demonstrate all class members were subject to the same discriminatory employment policy. The class action is "an exception to the usual rule that litigation is conducted by and on behalf of the individual named parties only." In order to justify a departure from that rule, "a class representative must be part of the class and 'possess the same interest and suffer the same injury' as the class members." Rule 23(a) ensures that the named plaintiffs are appropriate representatives of the class whose claims they wish to litigate. The Rule's four requirements: numerosity, commonality, typicality, and adequate representation—effectively "limit the class claims to those fairly encompassed by the named plaintiff's claims." The second of the Rule's four requirements, "proof of commonality," necessarily overlaps with the group's argument that Wal-Mart (D) engages in a pattern or practice of discrimination. Under Title VII, the central inquiry involves the reason for a particular employment decision, and the plaintiffs wish to sue for millions of employment decisions at once. Without something holding together the alleged reasons for those employment decisions, it would be impossible to say that examination of all the class members' claims will produce a common answer to the crucial discrimination question. The testimony of the plaintiffs' social science expert who claimed that Wal-Mart's (D) culture was susceptible to gender bias is unpersuasive. The testimony is useless to the question of whether the plaintiffs could prove a general policy of discrimination. Also rejected, is the use of aggregate statistical analyses and the mere existence of gender disparities in pay, promotion, or representation to meet the commonality burden. Instead, to show commonality, a plaintiff would at least need to demonstrate store-by-store disparities. Third, affidavits from 120 individuals, or one out of every 12,500 class members,

Continued on next page.

did not constitute "significant proof" that Wal-Mart (D) operates under a general policy of discrimination. The members of the plaintiffs' group held many different jobs, at different levels of Wal-Mart's (D) hierarchy, for variable lengths of time, in 3,400 stores, across 50 states, with many different supervisors (male and female), subject to a variety of regional policies that all differed. Some thrived while others did not. They have little in common but their sex and this lawsuit.

(2) No. Claims for monetary relief may not be certified under Federal Rule of Civil Procedure 23(b)(2) where the monetary relief is not incidental to the injunctive or declaratory relief. After satisfying the elements of Rule 23(a), the proposed class must satisfy at least one of the three requirements listed in Rule 23(b). The plaintiffs sought certification under Rule 23(b)(2), which applies when "the party opposing the class has acted or refused to act on grounds that apply generally to the class, so that final injunctive relief or corresponding declaratory relief is appropriate respecting the class as a whole." But Rule 23(b)(2) applies only when a single injunction or declaratory judgment would provide relief to each member of the class. It does not authorize class certification when each individual class member would be entitled to a *different* injunction or declaratory judgment against the defendant. Similarly, it does not authorize class certification when each class member would be entitled to an individualized award of monetary damages. The "predominance test" established by the Ninth Circuit, which permitted the certification of claims for monetary damages as long as claims for injunctive relief "predominated" over the claims for monetary damages, is rejected. Rather, the "incidental damages" test, which permits certification of claims for monetary relief as long as that relief "flow[s] directly from liability to the class as a whole," which "should not require additional hearings," is more appropriate. The adoption of a bright-line rule prohibiting all money damages from ever being certified under Rule 23(b)(2) is not considered here. Reversed.

CONCURRENCE AND DISSENT: (Ginsburg, J.) The class should not have been certified under Fed. R. Civ. P. 23(b)(2), because the plaintiffs, alleging discrimination in violation of Title VII, seek monetary relief that is not merely incidental to any injunctive or declaratory relief that might be available. But a class of this type may be certifiable under Rule 23(b)(3), if the plaintiffs show that common class questions "predominate" over issues affecting individuals, such as qualification for, and the amount of, back pay or compensatory damages, and that a class action is "superior" to other modes of adjudication. Whether the class the plaintiffs describe meets the specific requirements of Rule 23(b)(3) is not before the Court, and that matter should be reserved for consideration and decision on remand. But the majority disqualifies the class under 23(a)(2), holding that the plaintiffs cannot cross

the "commonality" line, and by doing so imports into the Rule 23(a) determination concerns properly addressed in a Rule 23(b)(3) assessment. The majority errs in importing a "dissimilarities" notion suited to Rule 23(b)(3) into the Rule 23(a) commonality inquiry.

ANALYSIS

This is a landmark case that was thoroughly analyzed in the media when it was released. Many criticized the decision as inappropriately and unfairly raising the bar for certification to the detriment of those with valid Title VII claims. District courts will now be required to scrutinize closely all alleged common questions of law and fact to determine if the proposed common questions generate common answers that are apt to drive resolution in each case. It will not be sufficient for plaintiffs to allege a "general policy" without proving the existence of the policy and its impact on each class member.

Quicknotes

CLASS ACTION A suit commenced by a representative on behalf of an ascertainable group that is too large to appear in court, who shares a commonality of interests and who will benefit from a successful result.

CLASS CERTIFICATION Certification by a court's granting of a motion to allow individual litigants to join as one plaintiff in a class action against the defendant.

Hansberry v. Lee

Black homebuyer (D) v. Neighbors (P)

311 U.S. 32 (1940).

NATURE OF CASE: A class action to enforce a racially restrictive covenant.

FACT SUMMARY: Lee (P) sought to enjoin a sale of land to Hansberry (D) on the grounds that the sale violated a racially restrictive covenant.

RULE OF LAW
There must be adequate representation of the members of a class action or the judgment is not binding on the parties not adequately represented.

FACTS: Hansberry (D), a black, purchased land from a party who had signed a restrictive covenant forbidding the sale of the land to blacks. Lee (P), one of the parties who signed the covenant, sought to have the sale enjoined because it breached the covenant, contending that the validity of the covenant was established in a prior case in which one of the parties was a class of landowners involved with the covenant. To be valid, 95 percent of the landowners had to sign the covenant, and the trial court in the prior case held that 95 percent of the landowners had signed the covenant. Hansberry (D) claimed that he and the party selling him the house were not bound by the res judicata effect of the prior decision, as they were not parties to the litigation. The lower court held that the first action would have to be challenged directly in order that it be set aside or reversed. Otherwise, its decision was still binding on all class members, including Hansberry (D). The case was appealed to the United States Supreme Court.

ISSUE: For a judgment in a class action to be binding, must all of the members of the class be adequately represented by parties with similar interests?

HOLDING AND DECISION: (Stone, J.) Yes. It is not necessary that all members of a class be present as parties to the litigation to be bound by the judgment if they are adequately represented by parties who are present. In regular cases, to be bound by the judgment the party must receive notice and an opportunity to be heard. If due process is not afforded the individual, then the judgment is not binding. The class action is an exception to the general rule. Because of the numbers involved in class actions, it is enough if the party is adequately represented by a member of the class with a similar interest. Hansberry (D) was not adequately represented by the class of landowners. Their interests were not similar enough to even be considered members of the same class. Lee (P) and the landowners were trying to restrict blacks from buying any of the land and Hansberry (D) was a black attempting to purchase land. When there is such a conflicting interest between

members of a class, there is most likely not adequate representation of one of the members of the class. There must be a similarity of interests before there can even be a class. Since there was no similarity of interests between Lee (P) and Hansberry (D), Hansberry (D) could not be considered a member of the class and so the prior judgment was not binding on Hansberry (D). Hansberry (D) was not afforded due process because of the lack of adequate representation. Reversed.

ANALYSIS

Rule 23(c)(3) requires that the court describe those whom the court finds to be members of the class. The court is to note those to whom notice was provided and also those who had not requested exclusion. These members are considered members of the class and are bound by the decision of the court whether it is in their favor or not. The Federal Rules allow a member of the class to request exclusion from the class and that party will not be bound by the decision of the court. Since a party must receive notice of the class action before he can request exclusion from the class, the court must determine if a party received sufficient notice of the action or if sufficient effort was made to notify him of the action. The rules state if the court finds that the party did have sufficient notice and was considered a member of the class, he is bound by the decision.

Quicknotes

CLASS ACTION A suit commenced by a representative on behalf of an ascertainable group that is too large to appear in court, who share a commonality of interests and who will benefit from a successful result.

RES JUDICATA The rule of law a final judgment by a court precludes subsequent litigation between the parties regarding the same cause of action.

Phillips Petroleum Co. v. Shutts

Oil land lessee (D) v. Royalty owners (P)

472 U.S. 797 (1985).

NATURE OF CASE: Appeal of award of damages in class action breach of contract lawsuit.

FACT SUMMARY: A state class action lawsuit involved a plaintiff class of which 97 percent had no contacts with the forum state.

🏛 RULE OF LAW
A state may exercise jurisdiction over a class action plaintiff even if the plaintiff's contacts with the state would not confer jurisdiction over a defendant.

FACTS: A class suit was filed in a Kansas court against Phillips Petroleum Co. (Phillips) (D) on behalf of about 33,000 royalty owners (P). The class was certified. Notice of the action was sent by first-class mail to each plaintiff, with an explanation that each plaintiff would be bound unless he "opted out" of the suit. At the end of the trial, damages were awarded against Phillips (D), and Phillips (D) sought certiorari to the Supreme Court, contending that the Due Process Clause prevented the Kansas courts from exercising jurisdiction over the plaintiffs having no contacts with Kansas, these being 97 percent of the plaintiffs.

ISSUE: May a state exercise jurisdiction over a class action plaintiff even if the plaintiff's contacts with the state would not confer jurisdiction over a defendant?

HOLDING AND DECISION: (Rehnquist, J.) Yes. A state may exercise jurisdiction over a class action plaintiff even if the plaintiff's contacts with the state would not confer jurisdiction over a defendant. The "minimum contacts" test of *International Shoe Co. v. Washington*, 326 U.S. 310 (1945), is a recognition that due process demands that a defendant should not be subjected to the expense and uncertainty of defending in an alien forum unless he has sufficient contact with the forum that would make it reasonable that he be expected to so defend. A class action plaintiff is in nowhere nearly as perilous a position as a civil defendant. The class action plaintiff need not travel, need not retain counsel, and, in fact, can sit back and do nothing. The court must certify the class, so the danger of improper inclusion in a class is minimal. Since the class action plaintiff is in nowhere near the danger of a civil defendant, he requires less protection under the Due Process Clause. Here, each plaintiff was notified and given the opportunity to "opt out" of the suit. This was all due process required. Affirmed in part, reversed in part, and remanded.

▶ ANALYSIS

The Court had to dispose of a threshold issue. It was contended that Phillips (D) did not have standing to raise the due process claims of the plaintiffs. The Court got past this argument by noting that the inclusion of the plaintiff class presented dangers to Phillips (D) independent of the rights of the plaintiffs, and, therefore, Phillips (D) had standing to complain of the plaintiff class.

Quicknotes

CLASS ACTION A suit commenced by a representative on behalf of an ascertainable group that is too large to appear in court, who share a commonality of interests and who will benefit from a successful result.

DUE PROCESS CLAUSE Clauses, found in the Fifth and Fourteenth Amendments to the United States Constitution, providing that no person shall be deprived of "life, liberty, or property, without due process of law."

Cooper v. Federal Reserve Bank of Richmond

Employees (P) v. Employer (D)

467 U.S. 867 (1984).

NATURE OF CASE: Review of order dismissing civil rights action.

FACT SUMMARY: Federal Reserve Bank of Richmond (D) contended that its successful defense of a class-action discrimination suit barred individual suits by members or potential members of the class.

🏛 RULE OF LAW
A successful defense of a class-action discrimination suit does not bar individual suits by members or potential members of the class.

FACTS: A class of former and current employees of Federal Reserve Bank of Richmond's (Bank) (D) Charlotte, North Carolina branch filed a class-action suit, alleging denial of equal promotional opportunity on account of their race. Several class members filed separate suits as well. At the trial of the class-action suit, the court found insufficient evidence of discriminatory patterns in promotions and entered judgment in favor of the Bank (D). The Bank (D) moved to dismiss the individual suits, contending that they were res judicata. The district court denied the motion but the Fourth Circuit Court of Appeals reversed. The United States Supreme Court granted review.

ISSUE: Does a successful defense of a class-action discrimination suit bar individual suits by members or potential members of the class?

HOLDING AND DECISION: (Stevens, J.) No. A successful defense of a class-action discrimination suit does not bar individual suits by members or potential members of the class. Res judicata and collateral estoppel work to bar relitigation of claims and issues already litigated. The issues litigated in a class-action discrimination suit and one of an individual nature are different: the former involves a pattern of discrimination, and the latter involves actual discrimination against a particular individual. One can exist without the other; a finding of an absence of a pattern does not preclude discrimination against an individual, and vice versa. Therefore, a successful defense of one type of suit does not bar litigation of the other. Reversed and remanded.

▶ ANALYSIS

Res judicata and collateral estoppel are judge-made rules, the purpose of both being judicial economy. The scope of the doctrines has never been clearly defined, and the rules regarding them tend to vary from jurisdiction to jurisdiction. The general trend over the last few years has been the expansion of their application.

■==■

Quicknotes

COLLATERAL ESTOPPEL A doctrine whereby issues litigated and determined in a prior proceeding are binding upon all subsequent litigation between the parties regarding that issue.

RES JUDICATA The rule of law that a final judgment by a court precludes subsequent litigation between the parties regarding the same cause of action.

■==■

Pretrial Devices for Obtaining Information: Depositions and Discovery

Quick Reference Rules of Law

In re Petition of Sheila Roberts Ford

[Parties not identified.]

170 F.R.D. 504 (M.D. Ala. 1997).

NATURE OF CASE: Petition under Federal Rule of Civil Procedure for pre-complaint deposition.

FACT SUMMARY: Sheila Roberts Ford, as personal representative of her slain father's estate, filed a Federal Rule of Civil Procedure 27 petition for permission to depose a sheriff who supervised the law-enforcement officers who shot and killed Ford's father. Her petition alleged, among other things, that she needed to depose the sheriff before filing a complaint, to perpetuate the sheriff's testimony.

🏛 RULE OF LAW
Federal Rule of Civil Procedure 27 does not permit a pre-complaint deposition without a showing that the deposition is necessary for perpetuating the witness's testimony.

FACTS: Law-enforcement officers in Elmore County, Alabama, shot and killed Ford's father, but she did not know which officers to sue for his death or even whether the shooting was justified. Rather than file suit, through counsel she filed a petition under Federal Rule 27 for permission to take the pre-complaint deposition of the county sheriff. Her petition alleged that she needed the deposition, before filing a complaint, in part to learn which officers to sue when she did file her anticipated complaint. Also, apparently to try to bring her petition squarely within the language of Rule 27, she alleged that she needed the deposition to ensure that the sheriff's testimony would remain accurate despite the possible effects of his fading memory or the influence of pretrial publicity.

ISSUE: Does Federal Rule of Civil Procedure 27 permit a pre-complaint deposition without a showing that the deposition is necessary for perpetuating the witness's testimony?

HOLDING AND DECISION: (Thompson, C.J.) No. Federal Rule of Civil Procedure does not permit a pre-complaint deposition without a showing that the deposition is necessary for perpetuating the witness's testimony. Rule 27 exists to enable perpetuation of testimony, not the normal discovery that follows the filing of a complaint. Against that proper purpose of Rule 27, Ford's argument that she needs the Rule 27 deposition to discharge her duties under Rule 11 [pre-2007 restyling of the Rules] has no merit. Although another federal trial judge has held otherwise [see *In the Matter of Alpha Industries*, 159 F.R.D. 456 (S.D.N.Y. 1995)] and although Rule 11 requires that Ford have some evidentiary basis before filing suit, she must solve her dilemma through another avenue besides a Rule 27 petition. Petition denied.

▶ ANALYSIS

As Judge Thompson strongly suggests, Ford's counsel had at least one ready alternative to a Rule 27 petition: File suit, naming only "unknown" defendants, and then conduct discovery under her complaint. See, e.g., *Bivens v. Six Unknown Federal Narcotics Agents*, 403 U.S. 388 (1971). Ford's counsel then could have discharged the obligations of the applicable Rules of Professional Conduct and of Federal Rule 11 by, for example, stipulating to a dismissal of the complaint [see Federal Rule 41(a)(1)(ii)] if the discovery demonstrated beyond reasonable question that the shooting of Ford's father was justified. On the other hand, if post-filing discovery enabled Ford to identify both the precise basis of her claims and the proper parties to sue, she also could have moved to amend her complaint under Federal Rule 15, naming the proper defendants and alleging more precise facts to support her claims.

Quicknotes

DEPOSITION A pretrial discovery procedure whereby oral or written questions are asked by one party of the opposing party or of a witness for the opposing party under oath in preparation for litigation.

Kelly v. Nationwide Mutual Insurance Co.

Damaged truck owner (P) v. Insurer (D)

Ohio Ct. C.P., 23 Ohio Op.2d 29, 188 N.E.2d 445 (1963).

NATURE OF CASE: Action to recover damages to personal property.

FACT SUMMARY: Kelly (P) sought to recover under an insurance policy. Nationwide Mutual Insurance Co. (Nationwide) (D) denied that the policy was in effect on the date of the damage. Nationwide (D) moved to require Kelly (P) to give more complete answers to Nationwide's (D) interrogatories.

🏛 RULE OF LAW
Interrogatories are proper that are relevant to an issue in the action, seek unprivileged information and information that would also be admissible as evidence, but do not seek discovery, the manner whereby the opponent's case is to be established, evidence that relates exclusively to his case, nor what his witnesses will testify.

FACTS: Kelly (P) sued to recover damages to a motor vehicle under the terms of a Nationwide Mutual Insurance Co. (Nationwide) (D) comprehensive insurance policy. He claimed that someone poured sugar into his fuel tank in April 1961. Nationwide (D) denied that such a policy was in effect in April 1961, and otherwise its answer amounted to a general denial. Attached to Nationwide's (D) answer was a list of 42 interrogatories directed to Kelly (P). Kelly (P) answered the interrogatories, but Nationwide (D) moved to require more complete answers by Kelly (P).

ISSUE: Does the plaintiff have to reveal to the defendant in advance of trial evidence what the plaintiff hopes to establish in support of his own case?

HOLDING AND DECISION: (Pontius, J.) No. The old rule was that the purpose of discovery was to aid a plaintiff in establishing his case or a defendant in establishing his defense and did not extend to aiding an adversary to destroy the opponent's case. However, recent cases have held interrogatories to be proper if they are designed to seek information pertinent to the action as distinguished from merely being pertinent to an issue raised by the pleading of the inquirer. This court chooses to follow the more modern rule. Interrogatories are proper that are relevant to an issue in the action, do not seek privileged information, and seek information which would also be admissible as evidence. However, this rule is limited by the further rule that interrogatories may not seek discovery of the manner whereby the opponent's case is to be established evidence which relates exclusively to his case, or to what his witnesses will testify. Many of Nationwide's (D) interrogatories in this case deal with matters arising at the time of or after Kelly's (P) alleged claim arose. They call for information as to the manner in which Kelly (P) may attempt to establish his cause of action and information not presumably within Kelly's (P) own personal knowledge. They call for information which Kelly (P) may or may not be able to produce through testimony of witnesses, and for the furnishing of information solely in support of Kelly's (P) cause of action. Hence, as to the interrogatories with the above-mentioned defects, Nationwide's (D) motion is partially overruled.

▶ ANALYSIS

The roots of discovery are found in early English equity practice, but the evolution of modern procedures did not begin until the merger of law and equity in the nineteenth century, and they progressed slowly until the adoption of the Federal Rules of Civil Procedure in 1938. Modern discovery has three major purposes: to preserve relevant information; to ascertain and isolate those issues that are actually in controversy; and to find out what testimony and other evidence is available on each of the disputed factual issues. There is a sharp division between those who favor broad discovery to obviate all traces of surprise and those who allege the need for privacy of investigation and development of evidence. It is argued that broad discovery will eliminate the advantage that a wealthy party enjoys over a poorer opponent. Others claim that such discovery will induce a lazy litigant to sit back while the opposing party investigates diligently and then, by simple use of discovery, to obtain all the fruits of that investigation. The basic limitation on discovery is that the material sought must be relevant to the subject matter involved in the action. Some courts, as the one in the above case, construe relevancy as encompassing only those matters which would be admissible at trial, but most courts construe it broadly to encompass information reasonably calculated to lead to the discovery of admissible evidence.

Quicknotes

DISCOVERY Pretrial procedure during which one party makes certain information available to the other.

Marrese v. American Academy of Orthopaedic Surgeons

Surgeon refused membership (P) v. Orthopaedic professional organization (D)

726 F.2d 1150 en banc (7th Cir. 1984), *rev'd on other grounds*, 470 U.S. 373 (1985).

NATURE OF CASE: Appeal from a contempt order.

FACT SUMMARY: In an antitrust action, the American Academy of Orthopaedic Surgeons (Academy) (D) refused to obey a discovery order of the district court.

🏛 RULE OF LAW
A motion to limit discovery under Rule 26(c) should not be granted where the party seeking discovery would incur hardship without the material sought, and the party against whom discovery is sought would suffer hardship if forced to produce the material sought, if the competing interests can be served with minimal damage to either.

FACTS: [Marrese (P) was denied membership in the American Academy of Orthopaedic Surgeons (the Academy) (D), a prestigious professional organization. Marrese (P) sued in state court and his complaint was dismissed. He then filed a federal antitrust action. As part of pretrial discovery, Marrese (P) sought to examine the Academy's (D) membership files, which contained much confidential information. This was ostensibly for the purpose of ascertaining whom to depose. The district court ordered the production of the files along with a protective order stating that Marrese (P) must keep the information confidential. The Academy (D) was held in contempt and fined. The Academy (D) appealed.]

ISSUE: Should a motion to limit discovery under Rule 26(c) be granted where the party seeking discovery would incur hardship without the material sought, and the party against whom discovery is sought would suffer hardship if forced to produce the material sought, if the competing interests can be served with minimal damage to either?

HOLDING AND DECISION: (Posner, J.) No. A motion to limit discovery under Rule 26(c) should not be granted where the party seeking discovery would incur hardship without the material sought, and the party against whom discovery is sought would suffer hardship if forced to produce the material sought, if the competing interests can be served with minimal damage to either. Rule 26(c) requires a district court judge to balance the interests of the two parties when considering a motion to limit discovery. If denied access to the discovery, the hardship to Marrese (P) is substantial, since without the records he seeks from the Academy (D), his antitrust suit will fail. But if forced to produce the records, the hardship to the Academy (D) is substantial, since its members have a right to privacy. The district court judge could have used various methods to

balance the interests: the judge could have conducted in camera review, or ordered the Academy (D) to supply redacted versions of the files, in which the names of members are blacked out, for example. The judge could have prevented Marrese's (P) abuse of the discovery process while still allowing him access to the information necessary to his case. The judge's powers under Rule 26 are broad. Reversed.

DISSENT: (Wood, J.) A discovery order should not be reversed unless an abuse of discretion is found. The district court framed its order after extensive review of the state court action and upon evidence and argument submitted by both parties. To say that the order as made was an abuse of discretion is to give insufficient deference to the trial court. The order should be affirmed.

▶ ANALYSIS

As litigation becomes ever more costly and sophisticated, so does discovery. Greater judicial involvement in the discovery process is inevitable, as was noted in the Advisory Committee Note, 97 F.R.D. 165, 218 (1983). Thus, overburdened courts will be faced with yet another time-consuming activity. One federal court, the Central District of California, has dealt with this problem by often assigning discovery disputes to magistrates rather than the presiding judge in an action.

Quicknotes

ANTITRUST Body of federal law prohibiting business conduct that constitutes a restraint on trade.

COMITY A rule pursuant to which courts in one state give deference to the statutes and judicial decisions of the court of another state.

DISCOVERY Pretrial procedure during which one party makes certain information available to the other.

Polycast Technology Corp. v. Uniroyal, Inc.

Buyer of company (P) v. Seller of company (D)

1990 WL 138968 (S.D.N.Y. 1990).

NATURE OF CASE: Non-party's motion for a protective order barring a deposition of one of its employees.

FACT SUMMARY: In litigation involving a contested sale of a wholly owned subsidiary, both parties conducted much non-party discovery with the firm that had provided auditing services for both parties. The auditing firm eventually moved for a protective order to bar a deposition of one of its management-level employees.

🏛 RULE OF LAW
A non-party witness should be ordered to be deposed if his testimony is relevant and not duplicative of other witnesses' testimony.

FACTS: Polycast Technology Corp. (Polycast) (P) sued Uniroyal, Inc. (D) for allegedly using misleading financial information to induce Polycast (P) to buy a Uniroyal (D) subsidiary, Uniroyal Plastics Company, Inc. (Plastics). Both Polycast (P) and Uniroyal (D) conducted substantial discovery from Deloitte & Touche (Deloitte), the firm that once provided auditing services for both parties. Deloitte objected to Uniroyal's (D) proposed deposition of the man who was the on-site manager during the audit of Plastics shortly after Polycast (P) bought the company. Deloitte argued that the manager's testimony was not relevant and that, to whatever extent it might be relevant, it merely duplicated information already produced by Deloitte.

ISSUE: Should a non-party witness be ordered to be deposed if his testimony is relevant and not duplicative of other witnesses' testimony?

HOLDING AND DECISION: (Francis, J.) Yes. A non-party witness should be ordered to be deposed if his testimony is relevant and not duplicative of other witnesses' testimony. Totally preventing depositions is disfavored, though non-party witnesses deserve more protection from questionably relevant discovery than do the parties themselves. The deposition of Deloitte's on-site manager here, though, should proceed because he oversaw Deloitte's audit of Plastics almost contemporaneously with the sale of Plastics to Polycast (P). Another witness's testimony about the audit does not relieve the need for deposing the on-site manager himself, especially when the prior witness could not recall key details about the pertinent information on the financial performance of Plastics at the time of the sale. Since Uniroyal (D) has already taken much discovery from Deloitte on this area, however, the on-site manager's deposition shall be limited to filling in the gaps left by earlier discovery responses, and the deposition shall be limited to one full day. Motion denied

as to barring the deposition, but granted to limit the scope of questioning and to limit the deposition to one full day.

▶ ANALYSIS

A trial judge's discretion in discovery matters is generally broad by the express terms of Federal Rule 26(c), which governs protective orders. Under Rule 26(c), the trial judge "may make any order which justice requires" on a request for a protective order. That discretion would have supported the order in *Polycast* to limit the scope of the questioning, and to limit the deposition to one full day, even if no party requested such an order.

Quicknotes

DISCOVERY Pretrial procedure during which one party makes certain information available to the other.

PROTECTIVE ORDER Court order protecting a party against potential abusive treatment through use of the legal process.

In re Auction Houses Antitrust Litigation

Auction house clients (P) v. Auction houses (D)

196 F.R.D. 444 (S.D.N.Y. 2000).

NATURE OF CASE: Motion to compel an international auction house based in the United Kingdom to answer interrogatories.

FACT SUMMARY: Christie's (D) resisted answering interrogatories on grounds that the person with knowledge of the requested information, the company's former chief executive officer (CEO), no longer worked for Christie's (D). Christie's (D), however, still had significant financial leverage over its former CEO through agreements the company had entered with him. Christie's (D) had not exhausted all possibility of encouraging its former CEO to provide the requested information.

🏛 **RULE OF LAW**
An international company should be compelled to answer interrogatories, despite its claims that the requested information is outside its control, if the company still has plausible avenues for acquiring the requested information and if other typical factors favoring compelling discovery from an international litigant are present.

FACTS: Plaintiffs filed a class suit against multiple auction houses and related officials for an alleged price-fixing conspiracy. A. Alfred Taubman (D), former chairman of Sotheby's (D), served written interrogatories upon Christie's (D) requesting detailed information about handwritten notes made by Christopher Davidge, the former chief executive officer (CEO) of Christie's (D). Christie's (D) objected to the interrogatories, asserting that it no longer had control of the requested information because Davidge no longer worked for Christie's (D). Taubman (D) moved for an order compelling answers from Christie's (D), including information known by Davidge. Christie's (D) still had significant, and relevant, financial leverage over Davidge: Christie's (D) owed Davidge at least £2 million under his termination agreement, but the payment was conditioned in part on Davidge providing information like that requested by Taubman's (D) interrogatories. After the litigation was under way, Christie's (D) also had entered a "defence agreement" with Davidge, in which the company agreed to indemnify Davidge, partly in exchange for his compliance with requests for information like those in Taubman's (D) interrogatories. Christie's (D) nonetheless objected to Taubman's (D) interrogatories. Taubman (D) filed a motion to compel the company's answers.

ISSUE: Should an international company be compelled to answer interrogatories, despite its claims that the requested information is outside its control, if the company still has plausible avenues for acquiring the requested information and if other typical factors favoring compelling discovery from an international litigant are present?

HOLDING AND DECISION: (Kaplan, J.) Yes. An international company should be compelled to answer interrogatories, despite its claims that the requested information is outside its control, if the company still has plausible avenues for acquiring the requested information and if other typical factors favoring compelling discovery from an international litigant are present. Federal Rule 33 requires a party to respond to interrogatories with information that is available to it. Here, Christie's (D) has done little more than ask Davidge to provide the requested information; the company has not forced the issue of his response by, for example, withholding payments under his termination contract because he is failing to perform on his part of the bargain by providing information such as that requested by Taubman (D). A further consideration in favor of compelling Christie's (D) to answer is that such an order complies with the typical factors for ordering discovery from international litigants: There is no particular governmental interest of the United Kingdom arguing against such an order; potential adverse consequences to Christie's (D) from such an order are minimal, since the company would have a strong defense in any contract action Davidge might bring if Christie's (D) would stop making payments to him under his termination agreement; the good faith of Christie's (D) in resisting the request is questionable, considering the lack of any substantial risk to Christie's (D) for pressuring Davidge to provide information; and the money Davidge stands to lose under his termination contract provides a reasonable incentive for him to provide the information, which means that an order compelling the answers has a reasonable chance of succeeding. Motion to compel answers to interrogatories is therefore granted.

▶ **ANALYSIS**

This case illustrates an often-overlooked feature of Rule 33. The rule states that "any party may serve upon any other party," not only any opposing party, "written interrogatories. ..." Here, Taubman's (D) service of interrogatories upon Christie's (D) complies with the letter and the spirit of that part of Rule 33.

◼▰◼

Continued on next page.

Quicknotes

DISCOVERY Pretrial procedure during which one party makes certain information available to the other.

INTERROGATORIES A method of pretrial discovery in which written questions are provided by one party to another who must respond in writing under oath.

■═■

Cable and Computer Technology, Inc. v. Lockheed Saunders, Inc.

Losing bidder (P) v. Winning bidder (D)

175 F.R.D. 646 (C.D. Cal. 1997).

NATURE OF CASE: Federal district court's consideration of defendant's motion to compel the plaintiff to answer specific interrogatories.

FACT SUMMARY: Cable and Computer Technology (P) brought suit against Lockheed Saunders, Inc. (D) after losing out on a radar simulator contract offered by the United States Air Force.

RULE OF LAW
An interrogatory is not objectionable simply because it calls for an opinion or contention that relates to a fact or the application of law to fact.

FACTS: After losing a contract to Lockheed Saunders, Inc. (Lockheed) (D), Cable and Computer Technology (P) brought suit against Lockheed (D) for breach of contract and fraud. During the litigation, Cable and Computer Technology (P) refused to answer several interrogatories propounded by Lockheed (D) on the grounds the interrogatories were improper "contention" interrogatories. Lockheed (D) filed a motion to compel Cable and Computer Technology (P) to answer the interrogatories.

ISSUE: Is an interrogatory objectionable simply because it calls for an opinion or contention that relates to a fact or the application of law to fact?

HOLDING AND DECISION: (Chapman, J.) No. An interrogatory is not objectionable simply because it calls for an opinion or contention that relates to a fact or the application of law to fact. Contention interrogatories come in many forms. Some ask a party to state all facts which support a particular contention stated in a complaint. Others ask a party to provide all evidence which supports various contentions in the complaint. Historically, interrogatories were used to elicit facts only. However, in the comments to the 1970 amendment to the Rules of Civil Procedure, it noted that past efforts to draw a line between facts and contentions were unsuccessful. Accordingly, a party answering an interrogatory may not object on the grounds the question calls for a contention or opinion. The burden is on the party opposing the motion to justify why it should not answer the interrogatory. A party is always at liberty to amend or supplement its answers later in discovery if different facts come to light. Accordingly, Cable and Computer Technology (P) should provide answers to the contention interrogatories at issue.

ANALYSIS

A typical contention interrogatory asks a party to provide all evidence supporting a specific claim made by the plaintiff in its complaint. Most courts today hold that such interrogatories are proper. Most civil cases are resolved prior to trial, so the efficient transfer of facts and evidence between the parties assists with the resolution process. Discovery disputes over interrogatories or requested documents are costly and some judges will require the parties to resolve the matter on their own to relieve the court from issuing an order.

Quicknotes

INTERROGATORIES A method of pretrial discovery in which written questions are provided by one party to another who must respond in writing under oath.

Schlagenhauf v. Holder

Bus driver (D) v. Passengers (P)

379 U.S. 104 (1964).

NATURE OF CASE: Action to recover damages for negligence.

FACT SUMMARY: Passengers injured in a bus collision sued Greyhound, Schlagenhauf (D), the bus driver, and the owners of the trailer with which the bus collided. The trailer owners claimed the accident was due to Schlagenhauf's (D) negligence and moved for a physical and mental examination of him.

🏛 RULE OF LAW

(1) Federal Rule of Civil Procedure 35, the rule that provides for physical and mental examinations of parties, is applicable to defendants as well as plaintiffs.

(2) Under Federal Rule of Civil Procedure 35, although the person to be examined under the rule must be a party to the action, he need not be an opposing party vis-à-vis the movant.

(3) Under Federal Rule of Civil Procedure 35, a person who moves for a mental or physical examination of a party who has not asserted his mental or physical condition either in support of or in defense of a claim, must affirmatively show that the condition sought to be examined is really in controversy and that good cause exists for the particular examination requested.

FACTS: A bus collided with a tractor-trailer. The injured passengers brought a negligence action against Greyhound, owner of the bus (D), Schlagenhauf (D), the bus driver, Contract Carriers (D), the owner of the tractor, and against the tractor driver and the trailer owner. Greyhound (D) cross-claimed against Contract (D) and the trailer owner. Contract (D) filed an answer to this cross-claim, stating that the collision was caused by Schlagenhauf's (D) negligence. Contract (D) petitioned for a mental and physical examination of Schlagenhauf (D) under Federal Rule of Civil Procedure 35. District Court Judge Holder granted the petition. Schlagenhauf (D) applied for a writ of mandamus to have Holder's order requiring his mental and physical examinations set aside.

ISSUE:

(1) Is Federal Rule of Civil Procedure 35, the rule that provides for physical and mental examinations of parties, applicable to defendants as well as plaintiffs?

(2) Under Federal Rule of Civil Procedure 35, must the party to be examined be an opposing party vis-à-vis the movant?

(3) Must a person, who moves for a mental or physical examination of a party (under Federal Rule of Civil Procedure 35), who has not asserted his mental or physical condition, either in support of or in defense of a claim, affirmatively show that the condition sought to be examined is really in controversy and that good cause exists for the particular examination requested?

HOLDING AND DECISION: (Goldberg, J.)

(1) Yes. Federal Rule of Civil Procedure, the rule that provides for physical and mental examinations of parties, is applicable to defendants as well as plaintiffs. Rule 35 applies to all parties to an action, and there is no basis for holding it applicable to plaintiffs and inapplicable to defendants. Issues cannot be resolved by a doctrine of favoring one class of litigants over another. In this case, the fact that Schlagenhauf (D) is a defendant does not make the rule inapplicable to him.

(2) No. Under Federal Rule of Civil Procedure, although the person to be examined under the rule must be a party to the action, he need not be an opposing party vis-à-vis the movant. Rule 35 only requires that the person to be examined is a party to the action. It does not require that he be an opposing party, vis-à-vis the movant. Insistence that the movant have filed a pleading against the persons to be examined would have the undesirable effect of an unnecessary proliferation of cross-claims and counterclaims and would not be in keeping with the aims of a liberal discovery policy. Here, Schlagenhauf (D) was a party to this action by virtue of the original complaint.

(3) Yes. Under Federal Rule of Civil Procedure, a person who moves for a mental or physical examination of a party who has not asserted his mental or physical condition either in support or in defense of a claim, must affirmatively show that the condition sought to be examined is really in controversy and that good cause exists for the particular examination requested. Rule 35 expressly requires that the condition sought to be examined must be in controversy, and there must be good cause for the examination. These requirements are not mere formalities and are not met by mere conclusory allegations of the pleadings, or by mere relevance to the case. They require an affirmative showing by the movant that each condition sought to be examined is really and genuinely in controversy and that good cause exists for each examination. Here, Schlagenhauf (D) did not assert his claim. Hence, Contract (D), a movant, must make an affirmative showing that Schlagenhauf's

Continued on next page.

(D) mental or physical condition was in controversy and that there was good cause for the examinations requested. Contract (D) requested examinations by an internist, an ophthalmologist, a neurologist, and a psychiatrist. Yet, the only allegations it made in respect to Schlagenhauf's (D) physical or mental condition were conclusory statements that he was not mentally or physically capable of driving a bus. The attorney's affidavit does have some additional statements about his vision and what an eyewitness saw. There is nothing in the pleading to support the examinations by the neurologist, internist, or psychiatrist. There was a specific allegation that Schlagenhauf's (D) vision was impaired. Were this the only exam requested, it would not be set aside. However, as the case must be remanded to the district court because of the other guidelines ordered, it would be appropriate for the district judge to reconsider this also in light of the guidelines set forth herein. Vacated and remanded.

CONCURRENCE AND DISSENT: (Black, J.) Plainly, the allegations of the other parties were relevant and put the question of Schlagenhauf's (D) health and vision in controversy.

DISSENT: (Douglas, J.) Neither the Court nor Congress up to today has determined that any person whose physical or mental condition is brought into question during some lawsuit must surrender his right to keep his person inviolate.

▶ *ANALYSIS*

Rule 35 provides that when the physical or mental condition of a party is at issue, the court, upon motion and for good cause, may order the party to submit to an examination by a physician. The party examined is, upon request, entitled to receive a copy of the written report of the examining physician. The rule provides that, by requesting and receiving a copy of the report, the party examined must, upon request, furnish copies of written reports made by his physicians.

Quicknotes

DAMAGES Monetary compensation that may be awarded by the court to a party who has sustained injury or loss to his person, property or rights due to another party's unlawful act, omission or negligence.

INVASION OF PRIVACY The violation of an individual's right to be protected against unwarranted interference in his personal affairs, falling into one of four categories: (1) appropriating the individual's likeness or name for commercial benefit; (2) intrusion into the individual's seclusion; (3) public disclosure of private facts regarding the individual; and (4) disclosure of facts placing the individual in a false light.

NEGLIGENCE Conduct falling below the standard of care that a reasonable person would demonstrate under similar conditions.

Tatman v. Collins

Injured vehicle operator (P) v. Truck driver (D)

938 F.2d 509 (4th Cir. 1991).

NATURE OF CASE: Plaintiff's appeal from lower court decision holding that plaintiff could not submit a deposition transcript of a treating physician at trial because it was only a discovery deposition.

FACT SUMMARY: During this personal injury action, Collins (D) took the deposition of Tatman's (P) treating physician. When the physician was unavailable for trial, Tatman (P) attempted to submit his deposition transcript at trial. The court denied the admission of the transcript on the grounds the deposition was only a discovery deposition and not proper for use at trial.

🏛 RULE OF LAW
When a witness's deposition is properly noticed and all parties had the opportunity to attend and cross-examine the witness, the deposition transcript may be later introduced at trial, subject to the rules of evidence, if the witness is unavailable at the time of trial.

FACTS: Collins (D), a truck driver, struck Tatman's (P) vehicle from behind, causing Tatman (P) to suffer injuries. A year later, Tatman (P) suffered a cerebral aneurysm and died. His treating physician, Dr. Joseph Amico, testified at his deposition that the aneurysm was caused by the injuries Tatman (P) suffered during the motor vehicle accident. At the time of trial, Dr. Amico was unavailable. Tatman (P) attempted to submit Dr. Amico's deposition testimony into evidence. The federal district court denied the evidence on the grounds the deposition was only a discovery deposition and it would be unfair to Collins (D) to allow such evidence at trial. Because Tatman's other expert's opinion relied upon Dr. Amico's deposition testimony, the court struck that opinion from evidence as well. The result was essentially fatal to Tatman's (P) case. The lower court also found that Dr. Amico lived within 100 miles of the local federal court district. Accordingly, Tatman (P) could not take advantage of the procedural rule excusing witnesses from having to testify if they live more than 100 miles from the courthouse. The jury found Collins (D) negligent but also found that Tatman's (P) later aneurysm was not causally related to the accident from a year earlier. Tatman (P) appealed to the Fourth Circuit Court of Appeals.

ISSUE: When a witness's deposition is properly noticed and all parties had the opportunity to attend and cross-examine the witness, may the deposition transcript be later introduced at trial, subject to the rules of evidence, if the witness is unavailable at the time of trial?

HOLDING AND DECISION: (Niemeyer, J.) Yes. When a witness's deposition is properly noticed and all parties had the opportunity to attend and cross-examine the witness, the deposition transcript may be later introduced at trial, subject to the rules of evidence, if the witness is unavailable at the time of trial. There is no longer any distinction under the Rules of Civil Procedure for depositions taken for discovery purposes or for later use at trial. In terms of admissibility at trial, the purpose of the deposition is irrelevant. As long as all parties were given proper notice, the deposition may be introduced at trial. Of course, the trial court judge has discretion to admit or deny the transcript on evidentiary grounds. Separately, the lower court incorrectly interpreted the rule allowing the introduction of a deposition transcript if the witness lives further than 100 miles from the district. The rule actually states the witness must live 100 miles from the courthouse. The lower court's interpretation meant that Dr. Amico did not live far enough away to be considered unavailable. However, using the proper interpretation, Dr. Amico was unavailable for trial because his office was more than 100 miles from the courthouse, as opposed to the district. Accordingly, the trial court could have allowed the introduction of the transcript, subject to the rules of evidence. Reversed and remanded.

DISSENT: (Hall, J.): The majority's opinion regarding the admissibility of the transcript under the Rules of Civil Procedure is correct. However, the testimony of the Tatman's (P) second expert should not have been allowed.

▶ ANALYSIS

The excerpted portion of this decision in the casebook deals only with the use of transcripts via the Rules of Civil Procedure. If a transcript complies with the Rules, the judge will still examine the testimony for admissibility under the applicable evidentiary standards. If a party knows a deposition witness may not be available for trial, the questioning of the witness at the deposition should be similar to a direct examination that would take place during the trial.

▬▬▬

Quicknotes

DEPOSITION A pretrial discovery procedure whereby oral or written questions are asked by one party of the opposing party or of a witness for the opposing party under oath in preparation for litigation.

▬▬▬

Hickman v. Taylor

Decedent's representative (P) v. Tug owner (D)

329 U.S. 495 (1947).

NATURE OF CASE: Action for damages for wrongful death.

FACT SUMMARY: Five crew members drowned when a tug sank. In anticipation of litigation, the attorney for Taylor (D), the tug owner, interviewed the survivors. Hickman (P), as representative of one of the deceased, brought this action and tried by means of discovery to obtain copies of the statements Taylor's (D) attorney obtained from the survivors.

> ## 🏛 RULE OF LAW
> Material obtained by counsel in preparation for litigation is the work product of the lawyer, and while such material is not protected by the attorney-client privilege, it is not discoverable on mere demand without a showing of necessity or justification.

FACTS: Five of the nine crew members drowned when a tug sank. A public hearing was held at which the four survivors were examined. Their testimony was recorded and was made available to all interested parties. A short time later, the attorney for Taylor (D), the tug owner, interviewed the survivors, in preparation for possible litigation. He also interviewed other persons believed to have information on the accident. Ultimately, claims were brought by representatives of all five of the deceased. Four were settled. Hickman (P), the fifth claimant, brought this action. He filed interrogatories asking for any statements taken from crew members as well as any oral or written statements, records, reports, or other memoranda made concerning any matter relative to the towing operation, the tug's sinking, the salvaging and repair of the tug, and the deaths of the deceased. Taylor (D) refused to summarize or set forth the material on the ground that it was protected by the attorney-client privilege.

ISSUE: Does a party seeking to discover material obtained by an adverse party's counsel in preparation for possible litigation have a burden to show a justification for such production?

HOLDING AND DECISION: (Murphy, J.) Yes. The discovery rules are to be accorded a broad and liberal treatment, since mutual knowledge of all the relevant facts gathered by both parties is essential to proper litigation. But discovery does have ultimate and necessary boundaries. Limitations arise upon a showing of bad faith or harassment or when the inquiry seeks material that is irrelevant or privileged. In this case, the material sought by Hickman (P) is not protected by the attorney-client privilege. However, such material as that sought here does constitute the work product of the lawyer. The general policy against invading the privacy of an attorney in performing his various duties is so well recognized and so essential to the orderly working of our legal system that the party seeking work-product material has a burden to show reasons to justify such production. Interviews, statements, memoranda, correspondence, briefs, mental impressions, etc., obtained in the course of preparation for possible or anticipated litigation fall within the work product. Such material is not free from discovery in all cases. Where relevant and nonprivileged facts remain hidden in an attorney's file and where production of those facts is essential to the preparation of one's case, discovery may be had. But there must be a showing of necessity and justification. In this case, Hickman (P) seeks discovery of oral and written statements of witnesses whose identity is well known and whose availability to Hickman (P) appears unimpaired. Here, no attempt was made to show why it was necessary that Taylor's (D) attorney produce the material. No reasons were given to justify this invasion of the attorney's privacy. Hickman's (P) counsel admitted that he wanted the statements only to help him prepare for trial. That is insufficient to warrant an exception to the policy of protecting the privacy of an attorney's professional activities. Affirmed.

CONCURRENCE: (Jackson, J.) Discovery was not intended to enable a learned profession to perform its functions without wits or on wits borrowed from the adversary.

▶ ANALYSIS

The *Hickman* decision left open a number of questions as to the scope of the work product doctrine and the showing needed to discover work product material. In 1970, Federal Rule of Civil Procedure 26(b)(3) was added to deal with the discovery of work product. It provides that documents are tangible things which were prepared in anticipation of litigation or for trial are discoverable only upon a showing that the party seeking such material has substantial need of them, and that he is unable without undue hardship to obtain the substantial equivalent of the materials by other means. The Rule states mental impressions, conclusions, opinions, or legal theories of an attorney or other representative of a party are to be protected against disclosure.

■=■

Continued on next page.

Quicknotes

WORK PRODUCT Work performed by an attorney in preparation of litigation that is not subject to discovery.

WORK PRODUCT RULE A doctrine excluding from discovery work performed by an attorney in preparation of litigation.

Upjohn Co. v. United States

Drug manufacturer (D) v. Internal Revenue Service (P)

449 U.S. 383 (1981).

NATURE OF CASE: Appeal from order compelling disclosure of internal memoranda.

FACT SUMMARY: Upjohn Co. (D) generated certain internal memoranda which the Government (P) wished to examine pursuant to a tax audit.

RULE OF LAW
(1) The attorney-client privilege extends to communications between a corporation's attorneys and nonmanagerial corporate employees.
(2) Federal Rule of Civil Procedure 26(b)(3) applies to, and especially protects, notes of oral statements by witnesses, and great need must be shown for their disclosure.

FACTS: Upjohn Co. (D), upon its discovery of possibly illegal payoffs, conducted an internal investigation wherein its attorneys or their investigators interviewed numerous employees. The Government (P) began a tax audit of Upjohn (D) to see what tax ramifications may have occurred. The Internal Revenue Service (IRS) (P) subpoenaed the memoranda of interviews. The attorneys for Upjohn (D) claimed that these were protected by the attorney-client privilege and the work product doctrine. The district court found they were not and ordered their disclosure. The Sixth Circuit affirmed, and this appeal followed.

ISSUE:
(1) Does the attorney-client privilege extend to communications between a corporation's attorneys and nonmanagerial employees?
(2) Does Federal Rule of Civil Procedure 26(b)(3) apply to, and especially protect, notes of oral statements from witnesses, and must great need be shown for their disclosure?

HOLDING AND DECISION: (Rehnquist, J.)
(1) Yes. The attorney-client privilege applies to communications between a corporation's attorney and nonmanagerial employees, and Federal Rule of Civil Procedure 26(b)(3) especially protects the notes made of interviews of witnesses. The attorney for a corporation will often gather information from nonmanagerial corporate employees, and not to shield these communications under the attorney-client privilege would undercut the important social policy behind the privilege, this being the need for open communications between individuals and their attorneys. The present action exemplifies this, since an indispensable part of the attorney's investigation required such communications.

(2) Yes. As to the notes of interviews, these generally contain evidence of an attorney's mental processes, and these processes are given the greatest of all protection under the work product doctrine, as codified by Federal Rule of Civil Procedure 26(b)(3). Very substantial need must be shown to justify the discovery of this, and this was not done here. Reversed and remanded.

ANALYSIS

The Court said that something greater than substantial need must be shown for materials containing an attorney's mental impression. The Court specifically declined to state that such materials could never be discovered. However, the language of 26(b)(3) seems to indicate this might be Congress's intent.

Quicknotes

ATTORNEY-CLIENT PRIVILEGE A doctrine precluding the admission into evidence of confidential communications between an attorney and his client made in the course of obtaining professional assistance.

WORK PRODUCT Work performed by an attorney in preparation of litigation that is not subject to discovery.

Cine Forty-Second Street Theatre Corp. v. Allied Artists Pictures Corp.

Movie theater operator (P) v. Neighboring theater owner (D)

602 F.2d 1062 (2d Cir. 1979).

NATURE OF CASE: Action seeking damages and injunctive relief for anticompetitive practices.

FACT SUMMARY: The magistrate concluded that Cine Forty-Second Street Theatre Corp. (P) had engaged in repeated and willful noncompliance with the court's orders regarding answering Allied Artists Pictures Corp.'s (D) interrogatories on the issue of damages, with the result that she precluded it from introducing evidence on that issue.

> 🏛 **RULE OF LAW**
> A grossly negligent failure to obey an order compelling discovery is sufficient to justify the severest disciplinary measures available under Federal Rule of Civil Procedure 37.

FACTS: Cine Forty-Second Street Theatre Corp. (Cine) (P) brought an action charging Allied Artists Pictures Corp. (Allied) (D) and others operating competing movie theatres with engaging in a conspiracy with motion picture distributors to cut off its access to first-run, quality films. It sought treble damages under the antitrust laws and injunctive relief. Allied (D) proposed interrogatories on the issue of damages, which Cine (P) repeatedly failed to answer adequately or on time, although given several extensions. Finally, the magistrate held that Cine (P) acted willfully in not complying with the court's orders concerning discovery as to the issue of damages and precluded Cine (P) from introducing evidence on that issue. This effectively amounted to a dismissal of the damage claim, leaving only the claim for injunctive relief. The district judge, to whom the order was submitted for approval, felt Cine (P) had been grossly negligent and no more and that this was insufficient to impose the severest sanctions of Federal Rule of Civil Procedure 37. Being unsure of the law, however, he certified an interlocutory appeal on his own motion.

ISSUE: Is gross negligence in failing to obey discovery orders sufficient to justify the severest disciplinary measures available under Federal Rule of Civil Procedure 37?

HOLDING AND DECISION: (Kaufman, C.J.) Yes. A grossly negligent failure to obey an order compelling discovery is sufficient to justify the severest disciplinary measures available under Federal Rule of Civil Procedure 37. Negligent, no less than intentional, wrongs are fit subjects for general deterrence. Gross professional incompetence no less than deliberate tactical intransigence may be responsible for the interminable delays and costs which plague modern complex lawsuits. In fact, Cine (P) has, by its gross negligence, frozen this litigation in the discovery

phase for nearly four years. There is simply no reason to avoid imposing harsh sanctions in such a situation. Reversed.

CONCURRENCE: (Oakes, J.) An unknowing client should not pay for the sins of his counsel.

▶ **ANALYSIS**

Under Federal Rule of Civil Procedure 37, a party who willfully disobeys a court order pertaining to discovery can be held in contempt and imprisoned or fined. On the other hand, the court may strike or dismiss any or all of that party's claim or defense, preclude the introduction of evidence in support of such, or hold certain facts to be established.

■=■

Quicknotes

DISCOVERY Pretrial procedure during which one party makes certain information available to the other.

GROSS NEGLIGENCE The intentional failure to perform a duty with reckless disregard of the consequences.

INTERROGATORIES A method of pretrial discovery in which written questions are provided by one party to another who must respond in writing under oath.

■=■

Case Management

Quick Reference Rules of Law

Velez v. Awning Windows, Inc.

Former employee (P) v. Former employer (D)

375 F.3d 35 (1st Cir. 2004).

NATURE OF CASE: Appeal from a $740,000 judgment for plaintiff in an employment-discrimination suit.

FACT SUMMARY: After Awning Windows, Inc.'s (AWI) (D) consistently dilatory approach to various pretrial deadlines, the trial court sanctioned AWI (D) by refusing to consider their late response on Velez's (P) motion for partial summary judgment on liability. The trial court thus treated Velez's (P) motion for partial summary judgment on liability as unopposed, and the court granted summary judgment for Velez (P) on liability. At a hearing limited to the issue of damages, a jury awarded plaintiff $740,000.

🏛 RULE OF LAW
A trial judge's case-management authority under Federal Rule 16 authorizes such drastic sanctions as entry of judgment and refusal to dismiss claims for repeated failures to comply with court-ordered pretrial filing deadlines.

FACTS: Velez (P) sued Awning Windows, Inc. (AWI) (D) and Ismael Nieves-Valle (Nieves) (D) for alleged employment discrimination in violation of 42 U.S.C. §§ 2000e et seq. and of several local discrimination laws. AWI (D) and Nieves (D) were dilatory in the litigation from its inception. They failed to answer Velez's (P) complaint, and the trial court eventually entered a default judgment against them. After the judge set aside the default judgment, following the death of Nieves (D) and the substitution of his estate (D) as the real party in interest, the parties conducted discovery. Velez (P) moved for partial summary judgment on the issue of liability, but the defendants failed to file a response to her motion. The trial court then held an omnibus scheduling conference, at which the court ordered the defendants to file several documents on or before specific dates; the written order also provided another extension of the deadline for filing a response to Velez's (P) summary-judgment motion. The court also explicitly ordered that a further failure to file a timely opposition to the summary-judgment motion would result in the court deeming that motion to be unopposed. In response, AWI (D) and Nieves's estate (D) only requested further extensions of the new and final deadline for opposing Velez's (P) motion for partial summary judgment. Without an ordered extension of the new deadline, the defendants filed their opposition on partial summary judgment as to liability almost one month late, along with a late memorandum on hearsay issues. The trial court kept its promise and deemed Velez's (P) motion as unopposed, and the court also sanctioned the defendants by denying their request to dismiss claims against Nieves (D) or his estate

(D). Having entered judgment for Velez (P) on liability, the court held a damages hearing that was tried to a jury, which returned a judgment for Velez (P) in the amount of $740,000. The defendants appeal, challenging the trial court's ruling on summary judgment, its sanctions by refusing to dismiss claims, and its refusal to consider the defendants' untimely memorandum on hearsay issues.

ISSUE: Does a trial judge's case-management authority under Federal Rule 16 authorize such drastic sanctions as entry of judgment and refusal to dismiss claims for repeated failures to comply with court-ordered pretrial filing deadlines?

HOLDING AND DECISION: (Selya, J.) Yes. A trial judge's case-management authority under Federal Rule 16 authorizes such drastic sanctions as entry of judgment and refusal to dismiss claims for repeated failures to comply with court-ordered pretrial filing deadlines. Here, the trial court clearly did not abuse its discretion by entering judgment for Velez (P) on liability; the defendants failed to make an adequate showing in the trial court to excuse their repeatedly tardy filing of their opposition on summary judgment, and they cannot be heard now, on appeal, to offer justifications that should have been presented to the trial judge. The defendants' failure to oppose summary judgment in a timely manner allowed Velez (P) to dictate the result on her request for judgment on liability, even on questions of fact, and the trial judge correctly so held. Additionally, despite the defendants' incorrect interpretation of one dismissal argument as going to a lack of subject matter jurisdiction, the trial court also correctly sanctioned the defendants by refusing their requests for dismissal. Finally, the refusal to entertain the defendants' untimely arguments on hearsay issues also falls squarely within the trial judge's sanctioning authority for failures to follow case-management orders. Affirmed.

▶ ANALYSIS

Sanctions can seem harsh, as they perhaps seem in *Velez*, but the sanctioning authority exists to ensure a fair, expeditious process for all litigants. As the trial judge in *Velez* wrote: "the judicial process depends heavily on the judge's credibility"—and part of that credibility comes from all parties knowing that a specifically ordered deadline will be enforced.

Continued on next page.

Quicknotes

DAMAGES Monetary compensation that may be awarded by the court to a party who has sustained injury or loss to his person, property or rights due to another party's unlawful act, omission or negligence.

DEFAULT JUDGMENT A judgment entered against a defendant due to his failure to appear in a court or defend himself against the allegations of the opposing party.

DISCOVERY Pretrial procedure during which one party makes certain information available to the other.

HEARSAY An out-of-court statement made by a person other than the witness testifying at trial that is offered in order to prove the truth of the matter asserted.

REAL PARTY IN INTEREST A party who will benefit from the successful litigation of an action, in contrast to a party with only a nominal interest in the subject matter of the action or who is legally entitled to enforce the particular claim.

SANCTIONS A penalty imposed in order to ensure compliance with a statute or regulation.

SUBJECT MATTER JURISDICTION The authority of the court to hear and decide actions involving a particular type of issue or subject.

SUMMARY JUDGMENT Judgment rendered by a court in response to a motion made by one of the parties, claiming that the lack of a question of material fact in respect to an issue warrants disposition of the issue without consideration by the jury.

In re Peterson

[Parties not identified.]

253 U.S. 300 (1920).

NATURE OF CASE: Petition for writ of mandamus and/or writ of prohibition.

FACT SUMMARY: [Parties not identified in casebook excerpt.] [A federal district court appointed an auditor to determine amounts due for the purchase and sale of coal and taxed the auditor's expenses as costs. The petitioner challenged the court's authority.]

🏛 RULE OF LAW
A court may appoint an auditor to define and simplify issues to help the court decide a case and include the auditor's expenses in taxable costs.

FACTS: [Parties not identified in casebook excerpt.] [A federal district court appointed an auditor to determine amounts due for the purchase and sale of coal. The court taxed the auditor's expenses as costs. The petitioner challenged the court's authority, and claimed that the appointment of the auditor violated his Seventh Amendment right to a jury trial.]

ISSUE: May a court appoint an auditor to define and simplify issues to help the court decide a case and include the auditor's expenses in taxable costs?

HOLDING AND DECISION: (Brandeis, J.) Yes. A court may appoint an auditor to define and simplify issues to help the court decide a case and include the auditor's expenses in taxable costs. The auditor's report, if accepted by the court, would be admitted at the trial before the jury as evidence of the facts and the conclusions of fact included in the report. The Seventh Amendment does not prohibit the introduction of such a method for determining what facts are actually in issue. The auditor's function is essentially the same as that of pleading: to focus the controversy on the questions that should control the result. There is also no federal legislation that forbids the court to provide for such a preliminary hearing and report, and courts have inherent power to provide themselves with help to perform their duties. As to the cost of the auditor, federal trial courts have in the past included in the taxable costs expenditures that are incidental but essential to trials by court or jury. Because courts have done so for a long time, and such practice has been confirmed by implication in many statutes, courts may continue to include in taxable costs such expenses. Petition denied.

▶ ANALYSIS

This decision is in line with Fed. R. Civ. P. 53(a)(1). The relevant part of the Rule provides: "[u]nless a statute provides otherwise, a court may appoint a master only to . . . (B) hold trial proceedings and make or recommend findings of fact on issues to be decided without a jury if appointment is warranted by . . . (ii) the need to perform an accounting or resolve a difficult computation of damages."

■━■

Quicknotes

FED. R. CIV. P. 53 Vests judges with discretionary power to refer a case to a master to aid in the performance of specific judicial duties.

■━■

Payne v. S.S. Nabob

Injured employee (P) v. Stevedore employer (D)

302 F.2d 803 (3d Cir. 1962).

NATURE OF CASE: Appeal of order excluding witnesses in personal injury admiralty action.

FACT SUMMARY: Payne (P) attempted to introduce two witnesses not listed in his pretrial report.

> 🏛 **RULE OF LAW**
> A court may exclude witnesses not listed in the pretrial report, even if no pretrial order is made.

FACTS: Pursuant to Fed. R. Civ. P. 16, the court, in an admiralty action by Payne (P), requested that the parties submit pretrial reports listing, among other things, anticipated witnesses. No pretrial order was issued. At trial, Payne (P) attempted to call two witnesses not included in the report. The court excluded them. Payne (P) appealed, contending that since no pretrial order was issued, he was not bound by his report.

ISSUE: May a court exclude witnesses not listed in the pretrial report, even if no pretrial order is made?

HOLDING AND DECISION: (McLaughlin, J.) Yes. A court may exclude witnesses not listed in the pretrial report, even if no pretrial order is made. The purpose of such reports is to frame the issues and the supporting evidence for the benefit of the court and the other parties. The duty to accurately make such reports is independent of whether the court issues a pretrial order. Here, the court elected not to issue a pretrial order. This, however, has no bearing on the court's right to insist on accurate pretrial reports, and the court was well within its discretion in excluding the witnesses. Affirmed.

▌ *ANALYSIS*

Prior to the enactment of Fed. R. Civ. P. 16, the issues of the trial were framed by the pleadings. This is still the rule in many state jurisdictions. With the advent of Fed. R. Civ. P. 16, however, this is no longer true in federal court. The pretrial order is considered to supersede the pleadings to frame the trial issues.

■=■

Quicknotes

ADMIRALTY That area of law pertaining to navigable waters.

LIBELLANT A party who files a libel action.

■=■

Nick v. Morgan's Foods, Inc.

Former employee (P) v. Former employer (D)

270 F.3d 590 (8th Cir. 2001).

NATURE OF CASE: Appeal from an order denying a motion to reconsider sanctions imposed against a party and its attorney for failing to participate in ordered pretrial mediation.

FACT SUMMARY: In an employment-discrimination suit, the trial court issued an order under Federal Rule 16 requiring pretrial mediation and listing several specific requirements for the parties for the mediation. Morgan's Foods, Inc. (D) failed to comply with the mediation order. The trial court imposed monetary sanctions against Morgan's Foods (D) for failing to follow the mediation order. The court imposed further monetary sanctions against Morgan's Foods (D) when the company filed a frivolous motion to reconsider the sanctions imposed for failing to follow the mediation order.

🏛 **RULE OF LAW**
Federal Rule 16(f) authorizes a trial judge to impose sanctions, including monetary fines, for failure to comply with orders on pretrial conferences.

FACTS: Nick (P) sued Morgan's Foods, Inc. (D) for alleged violations of Title VII of the Civil Rights Act, 42 U.S.C. §§ 2000e et seq. Morgan's Foods (D)was represented by both outside counsel, Robert Seibel, and in-house counsel, Barton Craig; only Craig had the authority to make business decisions for the company. After the parties agreed to pretrial mediation, the trial court issued its Order Referring the Case to Alternate Dispute Resolution (Referral Order). The Referral Order required compliance with the court's local rules. It also imposed several specific requirements on the parties for the mediation process, including supplying the mediator a memorandum of disputed facts and positions on liability at least seven days before the first mediation conference; ensuring that all persons with settlement authority attended all mediation conferences and participated in those conferences in good faith; and stating that any failure to meet any deadlines could justify an award of sanctions against a party or parties. Morgan's Foods (D) failed to supply the required memorandum to the mediator, and no representative of Morgan's Foods (D) with settlement authority beyond $500 attended the mediation conference. Craig did not attend the mediation conference, though he was available for consultation during the conference by telephone. Nick (P) made two settlement offers at the mediation conference, but Morgan's Foods (D) rejected them both without making a counteroffer. The court issued a show-cause order permitting Morgan's Foods (D) to show why it should not be sanctioned for failing to participate in the mediation. Morgan's Foods (D)

responded that the Referral Order was only a set of non-binding guidelines that the company had deliberately chosen not to follow because the order only would have wasted the company's time and money. Nick (P) filed a motion for sanctions against Morgan's Foods (D) for the company's failure to participate in mediation, requesting an award of the attorney's fees and costs she had incurred by participating in the mediation conference. After a hearing on the show-cause order and motion for sanctions, the court sanctioned Morgan's Foods (D) in the amount of $1,390.63 and the company's outside counsel, Seibel, in the amount of $1,390.62, for mediation fees and Nick's (P) attorney's fees. Morgan's Foods (D) also was ordered to pay a $1,500 fine to the Clerk of the Court for failing to comply with the Referral Order. Morgan's Foods (D) and Seibel were each ordered to pay an additional $30 to Nick (P) for her expenses incurred for attending the mediation conference. Nineteen days after the hearing, Morgan's Foods (D) filed a motion to reconsider the sanctions. The court denied that motion and imposed an additional fine of $1,250 each against Morgan's Foods (D) and Seibel, payable to the Clerk of the Court, for filing a frivolous motion to reconsider. Morgan's Foods (D) appealed, contesting only the sanctions requiring payment to the Clerk of the Court.

ISSUE: Does Federal Rule 16(f) authorize a trial judge to impose sanctions, including monetary fines, for failure to comply with orders on pretrial conferences?

HOLDING AND DECISION: (McMillian, J.) Yes. Federal Rule 16(f) authorizes a trial judge to impose sanctions, including monetary fines, for failure to comply with orders on pretrial conferences. The plain text of Rule 16(f) authorizes broad sanctioning authority to ensure compliance with orders on pretrial conferences; the authority expressly extends to "any other sanction" besides reasonable attorney's fees and expenses. That power clearly includes the authority to order fines payable to the Clerk of the Court. Although the outside counsel for Morgan's Foods (D) was the sole cause of the company's complete failure to participate in mediation, it is settled law a party may be held liable for its counsel's actions. The sanctions here were not unduly harsh anyway, but indeed were carefully tailored to reflect either the money that Morgan's Foods (D) saved or that Nick (P) lost because of the company's failure to participate in mediation. Affirmed.

Continued on next page.

▶ *ANALYSIS*

The operative word in the trial court's *Order Referring the Case to Alternate Dispute Resolution* is "order." An order does not state "nonbinding guidelines," as Morgan's Foods (D) incredibly argued in response to the show-cause order here. According to the sixth edition of *Black's Law Dictionary*, an order is "a mandate . . . command or direction authoritatively given." As such, an order is enforceable by the court's contempt authority or, as in *Nick*, by the sanctioning authority conferred by Federal Rule 16(f). Parties and their counsel are of course free to ignore court orders at their own peril. As *Nick* demonstrates, though, the peril is only too real.

■━■

Quicknotes

SANCTIONS A penalty imposed in order to ensure compliance with a statute or regulation.

■━■

CHAPTER 13

Adjudication Without Trial or by Special Proceeding

Quick Reference Rules of Law

Celotex Corp. v. Catrett

Asbestos manufacturer (P) v. Decedent's widow (P)

477 U.S. 317 (1986).

NATURE OF CASE: Appeal from reversal of grant of summary judgment.

FACT SUMMARY: The court of appeals reversed summary judgment in favor of Celotex Corp. (D) on the basis that Celotex (D) had not offered sufficient evidence rebutting Catrett's (P) allegations.

RULE OF LAW
Summary judgment must be entered against a party who fails to make a showing sufficient to establish the existence of an element essential to his case and on which he bears the burden of proof at trial.

FACTS: Catrett's (P) husband died, and she sued several asbestos manufacturers, claiming the death resulted from exposure to their products. Celotex Corp. (D), one of the manufacturers, moved for summary judgment on the basis that no evidence existed that the decedent had been exposed to Celotex's (D) products. The district court granted the motion, and the court of appeals reversed, holding that Celotex (D) had not offered sufficient evidence to rebut Catrett's (P) allegations. The United States Supreme Court granted certiorari.

ISSUE: Must summary judgment be entered against a party who fails to meet his burden of proof on any essential element of the cause of action?

HOLDING AND DECISION: (Rehnquist, J.) Yes. Summary judgment must be entered against a party who fails to make a showing sufficient to establish the existence of an element essential to his case and on which he has the burden of proof. Catrett (P) had the burden of showing that Celotex (D) had some level of culpability in order to go forward on her claim. She thus bore the burden of proof on this issue. Her failure to meet this burden and thus establish a genuine issue of material fact justified entry of summary judgment. Reversed and remanded.

CONCURRENCE: (White, J.) A moving defendant need not support his motion with sufficient rebuttal evidence in all cases.

DISSENT: (Brennan, J.) The nonmoving party may defeat a motion for summary judgment that asserts that the nonmoving party has no evidence by calling the court's attention to the supporting evidence in the record that was overlooked by the moving part.

▌ ANALYSIS

Summary judgment is a radical judicial tool which completely disposes of a case or issue prior to trial. The basis for the motion is the absence of a genuine issue of material fact. When such occurs, the only questions remaining are legal questions which are determined by the court. Because the result of a successful motion is the end of a case, the court exercises great restraint in granting them.

■■■

Quicknotes

BURDEN OF PROOF The duty of a party to introduce evidence to support a fact that is in dispute in an action.

ISSUE OF MATERIAL FACT A fact that is disputed between two or more parties to litigation that is essential to proving an element of the cause of action or a defense asserted, or which would otherwise affect the outcome of the proceeding.

SUMMARY JUDGMENT Judgment rendered by a court in response to a motion made by one of the parties, claiming that the lack of a question of material fact in respect to an issue warrants disposition of the issue without consideration by the jury.

■■■

Bias v. Advantage Intern., Inc.

Estate of basketball player (P) v. Business affairs representative (D)

905 F.2d 1558 (D.C. Cir.), *cert. denied*, 498 U.S. 958 (1990).

NATURE OF CASE: Appeal of the granting of a motion for summary judgment.

FACT SUMMARY: Basketball star Leonard Bias (P) died from a cocaine overdose. When his estate sued Bias's business manager, Advantage International, Inc. (D) for failure to procure insurance for Bias (P) as it had promised to do, Advantage International (D) argued that no insurer would have insured a cocaine user.

RULE OF LAW

Once a moving party has made a prima facie showing to support a motion for summary judgment, the motion will be granted unless the nonmoving party establishes specific facts showing a genuine issue for trial.

FACTS: The estate of basketball star Leonard Bias (P) brought suit against Advantage International, Inc. (Advantage) (D) which was Bias's (P) management company, for failing to secure life insurance for Bias (P) as it had promised to do. Bias (P) died from a cocaine overdose without the $1-million dollar life insurance policy that Advantage (D) had represented it had obtained. Advantage (D) moved for a summary judgment on the grounds that Bias's estate (P) did not suffer any damage from the failure of Advantage (D) to try to obtain life insurance for Bias (P) because even if they had attempted to obtain such a policy, they would not have been able to do so because of Bias's (P) known cocaine use. The district court agreed and granted the motion. Bias's estate (P) appealed.

ISSUE: Once a moving party has made a prima facie showing to support a motion for summary judgment, will the motion be granted unless the nonmoving party establishes specific facts showing a genuine issue for trial?

HOLDING AND DECISION: (Sentelle, J.) Yes. Once a moving party has made a prima facie showing to support a motion for summary judgment, the motion will be granted unless the nonmoving party establishes specific facts showing a genuine issue for trial. Here, Advantage (D) offered testimony of witnesses that clearly tended to show that Bias (P) was a cocaine user who would therefore have been uninsurable. Bias's estate (P) could have deposed these witnesses, or otherwise attempted to impeach their testimony, but failed to do so or even to try. Advantage (D) offered evidence that every insurance company inquires about prior drug use at some point in the application process. Bias's (P) evidence that some insurance companies existed in 1986 that did not inquire about prior drug use at certain particular stages in the application process does not

undermine Advantage's (D) claim that at some point every insurance company did inquire about drug use, particularly where a jumbo policy was involved. Bias's estate (P) failed to name a single particular company or provide other evidence that a single company existed that would have issued a jumbo policy in 1986 without inquiring about an applicant's drug use. Because Bias's estate (P) failed to do more than show that there was "some metaphysical doubt as to the material facts," the district court properly concluded there was no genuine issue of material fact as to the insurability of a drug user. Affirmed.

ANALYSIS

In *Bias*, the court noted that, rather than presenting any evidence or questioning any witnesses, to try to establish a case on non-cocaine use, Bias's estate (P) relied instead "on bare arguments and allegations" or on evidence that did not actually create a genuine issue for trial.

Quicknotes

MATERIAL FACT A fact without the existence of which a contract would not have been entered.

PRIMA FACIE An action, in which the plaintiff introduces sufficient evidence to submit an issue to the judge or jury for determination.

SUMMARY JUDGMENT Judgment rendered by a court in response to a motion by one of the parties, claiming that the lack of a question of material fact in respect to an issue warrants disposition of the issue without consideration by the jury.

Coulas v. Smith

Debtor (D) v. Creditor (P)

Ariz. Sup. Ct., 96 Ariz. 325, 395 P.2d 527 (1964).

NATURE OF CASE: Action to collect open account and promissory note.

FACT SUMMARY: Coulas (D) was cross-claimed against, filed an answer, but never showed up at the trial after a continuance had been granted.

> ## 🏛 RULE OF LAW
> A default judgment may not be entered against a defendant who has filed an answer.

FACTS: Smith (P) sued Bray on an open account and a promissory note. Bray cross-claimed against Coulas (D) on the grounds that Coulas (D) was really the party owing the debts. Coulas (D) filed an answer and a trial date was fixed. A continuance was granted when Bray and Smith (P) requested it. Coulas (D) never appeared at trial and the case was tried on its merits. Smith (P) obtained judgment against Coulas (D) on both counts and against Bray on the promissory note. Bray obtained a judgment against Coulas (D) on the note. Judgment was entered in 1958. In 1960, Coulas (D) filed a motion to set aside and vacate the judgment. He claimed that he had never received the statutory three-day notice prior to the granting of a default judgment.

ISSUE: Where an answer has been filed, can a default judgment be granted?

HOLDING AND DECISION: (Udall, C.J.) No. Once the defendant has answered, a default judgment may not be granted. If he does not appear at trial, the court must still examine the sufficiency of plaintiff's proofs and cause of action to determine their validity. If sufficient evidence exists, a judgment is granted. Since this was not a default judgment, the three-day statutory notice requirement is not applicable. Nor can Coulas (D) complain that he was not notified of the change in trial dates. There is a presumption that when a public officer is charged with a duty imposed upon him by law, that it has been carried out, unless the contrary can be shown. Finally, Coulas (D) should have been aware of the change in dates when he and his attorney showed up on the original trial date and found that they were not scheduled. Affirmed.

▌ ANALYSIS

In order to place this case in the proper perspective, it is necessary to distinguish between cases that are dismissed for default, versus those that are answered by the defendant, who then does not show at trial. Consider Federal Rule of Civil Procedure 55, which provides that in an action for recovery of money or damages, if the defendant has been served and has not answered or taken other action to indicate that the suit is being contested, then, after the expiration of the time allowed for filing the answer, the plaintiff may obtain a default judgment. Where the damages are liquidated, judgment is granted for the amount prayed for, plus costs and attorney fees (if allowed) and interest. If damages are not liquidated, then the court, at a hearing or through affidavits, will determine the merits and grant an award. Where an answer has been filed, by contrast, the default judgment may not be issued, and a trial must be held and the merits determined, even if the defendant doesn't appear. In that situation, the court will render judgment only after the plaintiff has proved each element of his case. Courts are far less likely to set aside this type of judgment, because there has been a trial, albeit a one-sided trial. In default proceedings, a simple showing of good cause will often allow the judgment to be set aside.

Quicknotes

CONTINUANCE The postponement of a case to a later date.

DEFAULT JUDGMENT A judgment entered against a defendant due to his failure to appear in a court or defend himself against the allegations of the opposing party.

PROMISSORY NOTE A written promise to tender a stated amount of money at a designated time and to a designated person.

Quick Reference Rules of Law

Beacon Theatres, Inc. v. Westover

Theatre owner (D) v. District court judge (D)

359 U.S. 500 (1959).

NATURE OF CASE: Petition for writ of mandamus to require a district judge to reverse his denial of request for a jury trial in a declaratory relief action.

FACT SUMMARY: Beacon Theatres, Inc. (Beacon) (D) threatened to bring an antitrust action against Fox (P) based on Fox's (P) contract granting it exclusive rights to show first-run movies. Fox (P) brought a declaratory relief action against Beacon (D). Beacon (D) counterclaimed, seeking treble damages and demanding a jury trial.

> ## 🏛 RULE OF LAW
> Only under the most imperative circumstances can the right to a jury trial of legal issues be lost through prior determination of equitable claims, and in view of the flexible procedures of the federal rules, the United States Supreme Court cannot now anticipate such circumstances.

FACTS: Fox (P) operated a movie theatre in San Bernardino. Its contracts with movie distributors granted it the exclusive right to show first-run movies in the San Bernardino competitive area and provided for "clearance," a period of time during which no other theatre could exhibit the same picture. Beacon Theatres, Inc. (Beacon) (D) built a theatre eleven miles away, and notified Fox (P) that it considered Fox's (P) contracts to be in violation of the antitrust laws. Fox (P) alleged that this notification together with threats of lawsuits gave rise to duress and coercion and deprived Fox (P) of its right to negotiate for first-run contracts. Fox (P) prayed for a declaration that the clearances were not in violation of the antitrust laws, and an injunction to prevent Beacon (D) from bringing an antitrust action against Fox (P). Beacon (D) filed a counterclaim asserting that there was no substantial competition between the two theatres and, hence, the clearances were unreasonable. It also alleged that a conspiracy existed between Fox (P) and its distributors to restrain trade and monopolize first-run movies in violation of the antitrust laws. Beacon (D) asked for treble damages. The district court found that Fox's (P) complaint for declaratory relief presented basically equitable issues. It directed that these issues be tried by the court without a jury before jury determination of the validity of Beacon's (D) charges of antitrust violations. Beacon (D) sought to vacate the order, but the appellate court refused. The United States Supreme Court granted review.

ISSUE: Where a complaint alleges circumstances that traditionally have justified equity to take jurisdiction, in light of the Declaratory Judgment Act and the Federal

Rules of Civil Procedure, would a court be justified in denying defendant a trial by jury on all legal issues?

HOLDING AND DECISION: (Black, J.) No. In this case, the reasonableness of the clearances granted Fox (P) was an issue common to Fox's (P) action for declaratory relief and to Beacon's (D) counterclaim. Hence, the effect of the district court's action could be to limit Beacon's (D) opportunity to try before a jury every issue which has a bearing on its treble damages suit. The determination of the issues of the clearances by the judge might operate by way of res judicata or collateral estoppel so as to conclude both parties with respect to those issues at the subsequent trial of the treble damage claim. Since the right to trial by jury applies to treble damages suits under the antitrust laws, the antitrust issues were essentially jury questions. Assuming that Fox's (P) complaint supports a request for an injunction, and further alleges the kind of harassment by a multiplicity of lawsuits which traditionally have justified equity to take jurisdiction, in light of the Declaratory Judgment Act and the Federal Rules of Civil Procedure, a court would not be justified in denying a defendant a jury trial on all the legal issues. Only under the most imperative circumstances can the right to a jury trial of legal issues be lost through prior determination of equitable claims. In view of the flexible procedures of the federal rules, the court cannot now anticipate such circumstances. Under the federal rules, the same court may try the legal and equitable claims in the same action. Hence, any defenses, equitable or legal, that Fox (P) may have to Beacon's (D) charges can be raised either in its declaratory relief suit or in its answer to Beacon's (D) counterclaim. Any permanent injunctive relief to which Fox (P) might be entitled could be given by the court after the jury renders its verdict. Reversed.

DISSENT: (Stewart, J.) The federal rules make possible the trial of legal and equitable claims in the same proceeding, but they expressly affirm the power of a trial judge to determine the order in which claims shall be heard. They did not expand the substantive law. In this case, Beacon's (D) counterclaim cannot be held to have transformed Fox's (P) original complaint into an action at law.

▌ *ANALYSIS*

The right to a jury trial depends not so much on the form of the action as on the kind of relief sought. Hence, so long as the ultimate remedy is legal in nature, the right is recognized, even though the plaintiff has invoked a

Continued on next page.

historically equitable procedural device, as demonstrated by this case. Here, the effect of the declaration of its rights sought by Fox (P) would be to defeat (or establish) Beacon's (D) claim for money damages. Hence, the issues must be tried before a jury.

■━■

Quicknotes

DECLARATORY JUDGMENT ACT Allows prospective defendants to sue to establish their nonliability.

■━■

Curtis v. Loether

Would-be tenant (P) v. Apartment owner (D)

415 U.S. 189 (1974).

NATURE OF CASE: On writ of certiorari in action for injunctive relief and damages for violation of fair housing provisions.

FACT SUMMARY: The Loethers (D), Caucasians, having been charged with racial discrimination in violation of the 1968 Civil Rights Act for failure to rent an apartment to Curtis (P), a black woman, sought a jury trial under the Seventh Amendment.

🏛 RULE OF LAW
The Seventh Amendment of the Constitution applies to actions enforcing statutory rights and requires a jury trial on demand if the statute creates legal rights and remedies enforceable in an action for damages in the ordinary courts of law.

FACTS: Curtis (P), a black woman, brought an action under § 812 of the 1968 Civil Rights Act, claiming that the Loethers (D), Caucasians, refused to rent an apartment to her because of her race, in violation of Title VIII of the fair housing provisions of the Act. Following the voluntary dissolution of a preliminary injunction, the case was tried on the issues of actual and punitive damages. The Loethers (D) made a timely request for a jury trial which the district court denied, holding that a jury trial was neither authorized by Title VIII nor by the Seventh Amendment. The district court then found that the Loethers (D) had, in fact, racially discriminated against Curtis (P). No actual damage was found but $250 in punitive damages was awarded. The court of appeals reversed on the issue of the right to jury trial, holding that it was guaranteed by the Seventh Amendment. Curtis (P) argued that the Seventh Amendment was inapplicable to new causes of action created by congressional enactment.

ISSUE: Are jury trials required under the Seventh Amendment in actions enforcing statutory rights, if the statute creates legal rights and remedies enforceable in an action for damages in the ordinary courts of law?

HOLDING AND DECISION: (Marshall, J.) Yes. Although, from a review of the legislative history to Title VIII, the question of whether jury trials were intended can be susceptible to arguments for and against, it is clear that the Seventh Amendment entitles either party to demand a jury trial in an action for damages in the federal courts under § 812 of the 1968 Civil Rights Act. It has long been settled that the Seventh Amendment right to jury trials extends beyond the common law actions existing when the Amendment was framed. As Justice Story pointed out in *Parsons v. Bedford*, 28 U.S. (3 Pet.) 433 (1830), the Amendment may be construed to cover all suits, of whatever form, dealing with legal rights as distinct from equity and admiralty jurisdiction. The applicability of the constitutional right to a jury trial in actions enforcing statutory rights has been regarded as a matter too obvious to be doubted. To dispel any further doubt, we now hold that the Seventh Amendment does apply to actions enforcing statutory rights and requires a jury trial upon demand, if the statute creates legal rights and remedies enforceable in an action for damages in the ordinary courts of law. Curtis (P) relied on *NLRB v. Jones and Laughlin Steel*, 301 U.S. 1 (1937), but that case merely stands for the proposition that the Seventh Amendment is inapplicable to administrative proceedings since jury trials would be incompatible with the concept of administrative adjudication. *Katchen v. Landry*, 382 U.S. 323 (1966), also relied on by Curtis (P), is also inapplicable since it dealt with a bankruptcy proceeding, which is regarded as a matter of equity. However, the instant action is a damages action, sounding in tort and enforcing legal rights; and when Congress provides for the civil enforcement of statutory rights involving rights and remedies of the sort typically enforced in actions at law, a jury trial must be available. Affirmed.

▶ ANALYSIS

If a legal claim is joined with an equitable claim, the right to jury trial on the legal claim, including all issues common to both claims, remains intact and the right cannot be abridged by characterizing the legal claim as "incidental to the equitable relief sought." The above case illustrates another instance in which the Seventh Amendment's guarantee of right to jury trial is applicable. Others include (1) declaratory actions presenting traditional common law issues; (2) actions for the recovery and possession of land; (3) proceedings in rem for the confiscation of goods on land; (4) stockholders' derivative actions for damages, and (5) civil rights actions to recover damages. Examples of cases in which the Seventh Amendment has been held applicable to statutory rights include (1) trademarks, (2) immigration cases, and (3) antitrust actions. Note, finally, that even if the preliminary injunction here had not been dissolved before trial, the fact that a damages action was involved would make the Seventh Amendment applicable.

■=■

Chauffeurs, Teamsters and Helpers Local 391 v. Terry

Union (D) v. Union members (P)

494 U.S. 558 (1990).

NATURE OF CASE: Review of denial of motion to strike jury demand in action for breach of the duty of fair representation.

FACT SUMMARY: The Teamsters Union (D), subject to a suit for breach of fair representation, contended that Terry et al. (P) were not entitled to a jury.

🏛 RULE OF LAW

A plaintiff in an action against a union for breach of duty of fair representation is entitled to a jury.

FACTS: Terry and other various members (Terry) (P) of the Teamsters Union, Local 391 (Union) (D), brought an action against the Union (D), contending that it did not represent them fairly in a grievance claim seeking back pay. Terry (P) requested a jury. The Union (D) moved to strike the jury demand. The district court denied the motion and the Fourth Circuit affirmed. The United States Supreme Court granted certiorari.

ISSUE: Is a plaintiff in an action against a union for breach of duty of fair representation entitled to a jury?

HOLDING AND DECISION: (Marshall, J.) Yes. A plaintiff in an action against a union for breach of representation is entitled to a jury. The Seventh Amendment guarantees a civil party a right to trial by jury in actions at law. Consequently, any decision as to whether a party is entitled to a jury depends on whether the issue being tried is legal or equitable, and whether the remedy sought is legal or equitable. Here, the action at issue is similar to an action for breach of fiduciary duty, an equitable action. At the same time, the action has elements of breach of contract, as the plaintiffs must show that their employer breached the collective bargaining agreement. Thus, the issue being tried is both legal and equitable. However, the remedy sought, damages, is wholly legal. This being so, the action is more legal than equitable, and the right to a jury therefore exists. Affirmed.

CONCURRENCE: (Brennan, J.) The right to a jury should be determined only with reference to the remedy sought.

CONCURRENCE: (Stevens, J.) This action is analogous to professional malpractice, a legal action.

DISSENT: (Kennedy, J.) The action is most analogous to breach of fiduciary duty, an equitable action.

▶ ANALYSIS

At common law, equity and law were separate. Their merger came after adoption of the Seventh Amendment. The radical transformation of forms of action since then has made Seventh Amendment jurisprudence an often confusing field.

■■■

Quicknotes

EQUITY Fairness; justice; the determination of a matter consistent with principles of fairness and not in strict compliance with rules of law.

■■■

Markman v. Westview Instruments, Inc.

Dry cleaning inventory system patent holder (P) v. Dry cleaner (D)

517 U.S. 370 (1996).

NATURE OF CASE: Review of directed verdict in favor of the defense in a patent infringement action.

FACT SUMMARY: Markman (P) contended that his Seventh Amendment right to a jury trial was infringed when the trial court ruled on the scope of Markman's (P) patent claim as a matter of law.

🏛 RULE OF LAW
Interpretation and construction of the scope of a patent claim is a matter of law and should be determined by the judge, not the jury.

FACTS: Markman (P) owned a patent for an Inventory Control and Reporting System for Drycleaning Stores. The patent described a system that could monitor and report the status and location of clothing within a dry cleaning store. Westview Instruments, Inc. (Westview) (D) began using a similar system in its dry cleaning establishments that could track invoices, but not the clothes themselves. Markman (P) filed a patent infringement suit. The dispute partially hinged on whether "inventory," as used in Markman's (P) patent, referred to cash or clothes. The jury ruled for Markman (P) but the trial court granted Westview's (D) motion for judgment as a matter of law. Markman (P) appealed, claiming that interpretation of the patent claim was the exclusive province of the jury under the Seventh Amendment. The appellate court affirmed and the United States Supreme Court granted Markman's (P) writ of certiorari.

ISSUE: Is interpretation and construction of the scope of a patent claim a matter of law?

HOLDING AND DECISION: (Souter, J.) Yes. Interpretation and construction of the scope of a patent claim is a matter of law and should be determined by the judge, not the jury. The Seventh Amendment provides for a right to trial by jury for legal actions. There is no question that patent infringement actions are legal in nature and must be tried to a jury. However, not every issue in a jury trial must be given to the jury for determination. Rather, it depends on whether the jury must decide the issue to preserve the substance of the right to a trial by jury. There is no direct historical antecedent to the issue of patent claim construction and interpretation. The best analogy is to the interpretation of terms of a land patent, which was historically performed by the judge rather than the jury. Additionally, the consideration of the interpretive skills of judges and juries is a proper consideration. Functionally, judges are better suited to construe terms of art since it is a technical exercise beyond most laypersons.

Furthermore, allowing judges to determine the issue would promote uniformity in the treatment of patent claims. Affirmed.

▶ ANALYSIS

The Court acknowledged Markman's (P) argument that courts would have to make credibility judgments about experts in order to decide what meaning to attach to disputed patent terms. Credibility is almost always a jury matter. However, the Court concluded that experience with document construction shows that there would be very few cases of this sort.

■━■

Quicknotes

DIRECTED VERDICT A verdict ordered by the court in a jury trial.

PATENT A limited monopoly conferred on the invention or discovery of any new or useful machine or process that is novel and nonobvious.

■━■

Flowers v. Flowers

Mother (P) v. Father (D)

Tex. Civ. App., 397 S.W.2d 121 (1965).

NATURE OF CASE: Child custody suit tried before a jury.

FACT SUMMARY: The jurors were told on voir dire examination that the evidence would show that Mrs. Flowers (P) drank socially and occasionally drank to excess. Schmidt, a prospective juror, stated that she was against drinking of any kind. However, in response to a leading question by the court, she said she would be able to decide the case on the facts submitted.

RULE OF LAW
Disqualification for bias or prejudice extends not only to the parties personally, but also to the subject matter of the litigation. But to disqualify, it must appear that the state of mind of the juror leads to the natural inference that she will not or did not act with impartiality.

FACTS: Mrs. Flowers (P) sued Mr. Flowers (D) for custody of their three little girls. The jurors were told on voir dire examination that the evidence would show that Mrs. Flowers (P) drank socially and on one or two occasions had drunk excessively. They were questioned as to whether that fact alone would prejudice them against her as a fit and proper person to have custody of the children. When examined as a prospective juror, Schmidt stated, "I am against drinking in any manner, any kind." The court then asked Schmidt a leading question to the effect that she would be able to decide the case on the evidence submitted. Schmidt replied affirmatively, and the court overruled Mrs. Flowers's (P) challenge of Schmidt for cause. A panelist who sat next to Schmidt stated by affidavit that Schmidt stated she felt sorry for Mr. Flowers (D) and that Mrs. Flowers (P) had run off and left Mr. Flowers (D) once before. The jury found in favor of Mr. Flowers (D), and Mrs. Flowers' (P) motion for a new trial was denied. She appealed.

ISSUE: Where it appears that the state of mind of a juror leads to the natural inference that she will not or did not act with impartiality, must she be disqualified?

HOLDING AND DECISION: (Chapman, J.) Yes. One of the disqualifications is if any person has a bias or prejudice in favor of or against either of the parties. This disqualification extends not only to the parties but also to the subject matter of the litigation. Bias is an inclination toward one side of the issue or another. However, to disqualify, it must appear that the state of mind of the juror leads to the natural inference that she will not or did not act with impartiality. Schmidt's statements indicate both prejudice and bias factually, and such a prejudgment of the case as to indicate she could not have acted with impartiality. Her affirmative answer to the court's leading question to the effect that she would be able to decide the case on the evidence submitted should be disregarded. The trial court abused its discretion in refusing to hold Schmidt disqualified. Reversed and remanded.

▶ ANALYSIS

Voir dire consists of the interrogation of those whose names are drawn as prospective jurors to see if there are any grounds for challenge. Challenges to jurors are either for cause or peremptory. Challenges for cause allow a prospective juror to be dismissed upon a showing of her actual or potential bias. Each side is also entitled to a certain number of peremptory challenges in order to remove a prospective juror without a showing of cause. Most jurisdictions give the trial judge discretion to determine how much of the voir dire she will conduct and how much will be left to counsel. Many federal judges ask all the questions of prospective jurors.

Quicknotes

VOIR DIRE Examination of potential jurors on a case.

Edmonson v. Leesville Concrete Company, Inc.

Injured (P) v. Construction company (D)

500 U.S. 614 (1991).

NATURE OF CASE: Appeal from finding of contributory negligence in personal injury action.

FACT SUMMARY: Civil litigant Edmonson (P) objected to Leesville Concrete Company, Inc.'s (D) use of two of its three peremptory challenges to remove black persons from the prospective jury.

🏛 RULE OF LAW
Race may not be used as a basis for peremptory challenges in a civil trial.

FACTS: Edmonson (P), a Black, sued Leesville Concrete Company, Inc. (Leesville) (D) for personal injury. Leesville (D) used its peremptory challenges to excuse two black potential jurors. The jury's award of total damages to Edmonson (P) was substantially reduced because the jury found him 80 percent at fault. Edmonson (P) appealed, contending that the use of the peremptory challenges violated the Fifth Amendment's Due Process Clause. The court of appeals affirmed. The United States Supreme Court granted review.

ISSUE: May race be used as a basis for peremptory challenges in civil trials?

HOLDING AND DECISION: (Kennedy, J.) No. Race may not be used as a basis for peremptory challenges in civil trials. This Court has already held, in the criminal context, that using race as a basis for peremptory challenges violates the equal protection rights of both litigants and potential jurors. The question becomes whether use of such peremptory challenges by a private litigant constitutes state action, because only state action implicates the Fifth and/or Fourteenth Amendments' equal rights guarantees. In those cases where the state is necessary to effect private discrimination, state action will be found. Peremptory challenges exist only in the context of litigation, which is a governmental function. Also, the jury pool is selected by governmental bodies. Therefore, the state is sufficiently involved in peremptory challenges to constitute state action. Therefore, race may not be used as a basis for peremptory challenges. Reversed and remanded.

DISSENT: (O'Connor, J.) The mere fact that it occurs in a courtroom does not make a peremptory challenge the result of state action. Without state action, peremptory challenges cannot and do not violate equal protection.

▶ ANALYSIS

The seminal case in the approach taken by the Court here was formulated in the case *Shelly v. Kraemer*, 334 U.S. 1

(1948). In that case, the Court held enforcement of a racially restrictive covenant to be unconstitutional. Judicial enforcement of such covenants, said the Court, constituted state action.

■=■

Quicknotes

CONTRIBUTORY NEGLIGENCE Behavior on the part of an injured plaintiff falling below the standard of ordinary care that contributes to the defendant's negligence, resulting in the plaintiff's injury.

DUE PROCESS CLAUSE Clauses, found in the Fifth and Fourteenth Amendments to the United States Constitution, providing that no person shall be deprived of "life, liberty, or property, without due process of law."

PEREMPTORY CHALLENGE The exclusion by a party to a lawsuit of a prospective juror without the need to specify a particular reason.

■=■

Denman v. Spain

Injured child (P) v. Deceased driver's estate administrator (D)

Miss. Sup. Ct., 242 Miss. 431, 135 So. 2d 195 (1961).

NATURE OF CASE: Action for damages for personal injuries caused by negligence.

FACT SUMMARY: Denman (P) was injured in an accident, which occurred when the car in which she was riding collided with a car driven by Ross. The jury found for Denman (P), but the judge granted Ross's motion for judgment non obstante verdicto (n.o.v.).

RULE OF LAW
If a jury verdict for plaintiff rests on conjecture rather than legally sufficient evidence, the defendant's motion for judgment n.o.v. will be granted.

FACTS: Denman (P) was injured when the car in which she was a passenger was involved in a head-on collision with a car driven by Ross. Since Ross was killed in the accident, Denman (P) sued the executrix of Ross's estate, Spain (D). The collision occurred on a rainy, foggy day. As evidence, Denman (P) introduced pictures of the position of the cars after the collision, but no skid marks or other evidence to show the point of impact between the two cars. Denman (P) also introduced testimony of a driver that three-quarters of a mile from the place of the accident he had been passed by Ross, who was then driving at a high rate of speed. Another driver testified that he had also been passed by Ross, who was then travelling at a high speed, 200 yards from the accident, but that Ross had returned to the correct side of the road after passing him; this driver also saw Ross's taillights until the accident. Denman's (P) case rested on the theory that the jury could find that Ross was operating his vehicle at a negligently excessive rate of speed for poor weather conditions, and that if Ross had been driving his car properly, the collision probably could have been avoided. The jury found for Denman (P), but the judge granted Spain's (D) motion for judgment n.o.v.

ISSUE: If evidence presented by one party is legally insufficient to sustain a jury verdict in his favor, may the judge overturn a jury verdict in that party's favor?

HOLDING AND DECISION: (Lee, J.) Yes. A jury verdict will be upheld only if the evidence presented is legally sufficient to sustain that verdict. If the evidence is legally insufficient to sustain the verdict, a motion for judgment n.o.v. will be entered, which causes judgment to be entered for the other party. Denman (P) had the burden of proving not only Ross's negligence but also that Ross's negligence proximately caused or contributed to the collision. The testimony of the first driver is inadmissible since his knowledge of Ross's speed was based on what he saw three-quarters of a mile from the accident. The evidence of the other driver of Ross's excessive speed from 200 yards before the accident to the point of impact is admissible. But that testimony only showed a negligent rate of speed, not that the Ross car was outside of its proper lane at the time of the accident. There was no eyewitness to the way the accident happened, and the pictures of the position of the cars after impact didn't reveal why it happened or who was responsible. Since the only evidence shows Ross's excessive of speed, but not that the speed was the cause of the accident, any conclusion that Ross was at fault must be based on speculation. Here, the jury verdict was based on a "possibility," and verdicts cannot be based on possibilities. Therefore, the evidence was legally insufficient to prove that Ross's negligence proximately caused the accident and the jury verdict in Denman's (P) favor will not be sustained. Affirmed.

ANALYSIS

The procedural device used in the *Denman* case is a motion for judgment non obstante verdicto, or judgment notwithstanding the verdict. The effect of granting such a motion is to nullify the verdict that has already been reached by the jury. This device is closely related to the directed verdict discussed in *Galloway*, 319 U.S. 372 (1943). The basic question raised in both devices is the same, whether the evidence submitted is legally sufficient, so the standard used for passing on the sufficiency of the evidence should be the same as ruling for a motion for a directed verdict. Since the same standard is used, the motion for judgment n.o.v. will result in overturning a jury verdict for one party when a directed verdict for the opposing party would also have been appropriate.

■=■

Quicknotes

DIRECTED VERDICT A verdict ordered by the court in a jury trial.

JUDGMENT N.O.V. A judgment entered by the trial judge reversing a jury verdict if the jury's determination has no basis in law or fact.

■=■

Reeves v. Sanderson Plumbing Products, Inc.

Employee (P) v. Employer (D)

530 U.S. 133 (2000).

NATURE OF CASE: Certiorari review of appeals court judgment.

FACT SUMMARY: [Parties not fully identified in casebook excerpt.] Reeves (P) brought an age discrimination claim against his employer, Sanderson Plumbing Products, Inc. (D). A jury returned a verdict in favor of the Reeves (P), but the U.S. Court of Appeals for the Fifth Circuit reversed, holding that the verdict was unsupported by the evidence.

🏛 RULE OF LAW
A prima facie case of discrimination, combined with sufficient evidence for the trier of fact to disbelieve an employer's legitimate, nondiscriminatory reason for its decision, may be sufficient as a matter of law to sustain a jury's finding of intentional discrimination.

FACTS: [Parties not fully identified in casebook excerpt.] Reeves (P) worked for his employer, Sanderson Plumbing Products, Inc. (Sanderson) (D), for forty years as an attendance monitor in the production department. He was fired when the company allegedly discovered that Reeves (P) failed to maintain accurate attendance records. Reeves (P), who was 57 years old when he was fired, filed suit against Sanderson (D) under the Age Discrimination in Employment Act of 1967, claiming that he was fired because of his age. At trial, Reeves (P) introduced evidence that he accurately recorded the attendance and hours of the employees under his supervision, and that his supervisor had shown age-based hostility in his dealings with the Reeves (P). Sanderson (D) explained that Reeves's (P) discharge was "shoddy record keeping," which was testified to by Reeves's (P) supervisor. Reeves (P) argued that Sanderson's (D) explanation was false and offered evidence that he properly maintained the records, and that discrepancies in the records were caused by the company's automated time clock, which often failed to scan employees' timecards. The supervisor acknowledged that the time clock sometimes malfunctioned. The jury found in favor of the Reeves (P). The U.S. Court of Appeals for the Fifth Circuit reversed, finding that while Reeves (P) may have offered enough evidence for a reasonable jury to find that Sanderson's (D) explanation for its decision to fire the Reeves (P) was pretextual, the ultimate issue was whether Reeves (P) presented sufficient evidence that his age motivated Sanderson's (D) decision, and Reeves (P) failed to do so.

ISSUE: May a prima facie case of discrimination, combined with sufficient evidence for the trier of fact to disbelieve an employer's legitimate, nondiscriminatory reason for its decision, be sufficient as a matter of law to sustain a jury's finding of intentional discrimination?

HOLDING AND DECISION: (O'Connor, J.) Yes. A prima facie case of discrimination, combined with sufficient evidence for the trier of fact to disbelieve an employer's legitimate, nondiscriminatory reason for its decision, may be sufficient as a matter of law to sustain a jury's finding of intentional discrimination. In age discrimination cases, generally, the plaintiff must establish a prima facie case of discrimination, and the burden of production then shifts to the defendant to show evidence supporting a legitimate, nondiscriminatory reason for the job action. In this case, Reeves (P) established a prima facie case of discrimination, Sanderson (D) provided its explanation, and Reeves (P) introduced evidence of pretext. In reversing, the Court of Appeals ignored the evidence supporting the prima facie case and challenging Sanderson's (D) explanation for its decision, incorrectly assuming that a prima facie case of discrimination, combined with sufficient evidence for the trier of fact to disbelieve Sanderson's (D) legitimate, nondiscriminatory reason for its decision, is insufficient as a matter of law to sustain a jury's finding of intentional discrimination. While a fact finder's rejection of the employer's legitimate, nondiscriminatory reason for its action does not compel judgment for the employee, judgment for the employee is permissible where the trier of fact infers that ultimate fact of discrimination from the falsity of the employer's explanation. In this case, because a prima facie case and evidence supporting a rejection Sanderson's (D) explanation may permit a finding of liability, the Court of Appeals erred in proceeding from the premise that Reeves (P) was required to introduce additional, independent evidence of discrimination. And apart from the Court of Appeals' misconception about Reeves's (P) burden, Sanderson (D) still was not entitled to judgment as a matter of law. In addition to establishing a prima facie case of discrimination and creating a jury issue as to the falsity of Sanderson's (D) explanation, Reeves (P) introduced evidence that the supervisor was motivated by age-based animus and was principally responsible for Reeves's (P) firing. That is all sufficient evidence for the jury to find that Sanderson (D) intentionally discriminated. Reversed.

▶ ANALYSIS

Prior to this decision, a circuit split existed concerning what evidence the reviewing court must consider in

Continued on next page.

deciding whether the evidence is sufficient to create a jury issue. The impact of that disparity affected litigants significantly, obviously, and the United States Supreme Court's decision in this case resolves the schism, at least to a degree, by holding that a plaintiff needs only to demonstrate a prima facie case of discrimination plus pretext— and no more—in order to defeat an employer's motion for summary judgment. The exact manner in which the case is applied by the various circuit courts has varied somewhat, however, and a crystal clear rule on the issue seems to be elusive.

■═■

Quicknotes

PRIMA FACIE CASE An action where the plaintiff introduces sufficient evidence to submit the issue to the judge or jury for determination.

■═■

Securities and Exchange Commission v. Koenig

Corrupt executive (D) v. SEC (P)

557 F.3d 736 (7th Cir. 2009).

NATURE OF CASE: Appeal of trial judgment.

FACT SUMMARY: During the trial of James Koenig (D), chief financial officer at Waste Management Inc., who was accused of fraudulent accounting practices by the Securities and Exchange Commission (P), the district court allowed the jury to ask questions. Koenig (D) appealed the district court's judgment against him.

🏛 RULE OF LAW
A judge may allow a jury to ask questions during a trial.

FACTS: During the twelve-week trial of James Koenig (D), chief financial officer at Waste Management, Inc., who was accused of fraudulent accounting practices by the Securities and Exchange Commission (P), the district court allowed the jury to ask questions. At the conclusion of the trial, the judge imposed a civil penalty of $2.1 million, and ordered Koenig (D) to disgorge certain bonuses he received. Koenig (D) appealed.

ISSUE: May a judge allow a jury to ask questions during a trial?

HOLDING AND DECISION: (Easterbrook, C.J.) Yes. A judge may allow a jury to ask questions during a trial. Research shows that 20 days is the longest trial any jury can fully understand, and the longer the trial goes, the more the jury forgets and the less accurate its decision becomes. The American Bar Association's American Jury Project recommends that judges allow jurors to ask questions of witnesses. Studies show that when jurors are allowed to ask questions, their attention improves, and the quality of the trial improves. In addition, no law prohibits jurors from asking questions of witnesses. Some judges have been occasionally skeptical, arguing that allowing jurors to ask questions will lead them to take positions too early in the trial, but judicial opposition has not amounted to more than that, and studies on the issue have concluded that the risks associated with taking sides early in the process are clearly outweighed by such benefits as keeping jurors alert and focused.

The judge in this case allowed jurors to submit questions to him, and he then decided which to ask and which to not ask, and that was the right thing to do. More censoring would have been unwarranted. It is not particularly worrisome that there were some glitches in the process, such as the judge forgetting to ask a few of the questions the jurors wanted asked, or that more than two-thirds of the 127 questions were asked by three jurors. Koenig's (D) argument that some of the questions indicat-ed jurors had made up their minds before the end of the trial is also without merit. Conclusions drawn inferentially from questions are unreliable, but to the extent that jurors' questions do provide information about their stance during trial, the lawyers and their clients are better served. Preventing jurors from asking questions won't prevent them from reacting to the evidence. It will only make it harder for lawyers to know how things are going. Affirmed and remanded.

▶ ANALYSIS

The practice of allowing jurors to ask questions of witnesses is not new, but it has recently undergone resurgence. The majority of state jurisdictions grant discretion to the trial court on the issue of whether or not jurors can ask questions. Some states have court rules or standard instructions for dealing with the issue and some judges are more eager to permit jurors to ask questions than others.

■═■

Nollenberger v. United Air Lines, Inc.

Decedent's representative (P) v. Airline (D)

216 F. Supp. 734 (S.D. Cal.), *vacated*, 335 F.2d 379 (9th Cir. 1963), *cert. dismissed*, 379 U.S. 951 (1964).

NATURE OF CASE: Wrongful death action.

FACT SUMMARY: The court submitted to the jury a request for both a general verdict and special interrogatories on the issue of the amount of damages to be awarded to Nollenberger (P).

🏛 RULE OF LAW
When the jury's answers to special interrogatories are consistent with one another but inconsistent with the general verdict, the answers to the special interrogatories will control.

FACTS: The jury was given 11 special interrogatories covering several factors relevant to the determination of damages such as life expectancy and probable earnings. The total computed on the basis of the answers to these interrogatories was greater than the amount of damages actually awarded under the general verdict.

ISSUE: If the answers to special interrogatories conflict with the general verdict, should the general verdict control?

HOLDING AND DECISION: (Hall, C.J.) No. The use of special interrogatories in the federal courts is authorized by Fed. R. Civ. P. 49. Under this rule, if the answers to special interrogatories cannot be harmonized with the general verdict, judgment may be entered in accordance with the answers to the interrogatories or both the verdict and interrogatories may be returned to the jury for reconsideration. If the answers to the interrogatories are consistent with one another and clearly reach a different result than the general verdict, the verdict will be entered based upon the interrogatories.

▶ ANALYSIS

This decision was reversed on appeal. The appellate court stated that the jury instructions included additional factors besides the 11 factors included in the interrogatories which could be considered in determining the amount of damages. Since the answers to the interrogatories and the general verdict could be reconciled by assuming that any difference resulted from these additional factors, and the judge has a duty to harmonize the answers and verdict if possible, the general verdict would stand. There are three types of verdicts which may be requested from a jury. A general verdict is just a finding in favor of one of the parties and entails a finding in favor of the prevailing party on every issue. The problem with a general verdict is, first, that there is no way of assuring that the jury correctly understood and applied the law and, second, if the instructions were erroneous on only one of the several issues present in the case, there must be a retrial of the entire case, since it cannot be determined from the verdict whether or not the verdict rested on the erroneously presented issue. The second type is the special verdict in which the jury answers certain specific factual questions submitted to it and the judge determines the prevailing party by applying the law to the answers. The advantage of this type of verdict is that the jury is involved in only purely factual issues and does not have to be instructed in the law, but there is a possible problem since the answers reached by the jury may be inconsistent with one another. A third type is the general verdict with special interrogatories as used in *Nollenberger* in which the jury answers specific factual questions and also decides the general verdict. The advantage of this method is that it can be determined if all the facts essential to the verdict were established by the evidence, but, as shown in *Nollenberger*, there is a real problem of possible inconsistencies. Special verdicts and special interrogatories are also criticized on the basis that they restrict the right to a jury trial by restricting the freedom of jury deliberations and eliminate the ability of the jury to temper any possible harshness resulting from the application of the law by the use of common sense.

■=■

Quicknotes

GENERAL VERDICT A verdict stating the prevailing party without specific factual findings.

SPECIAL INTERROGATORIES Written questions that are submitted to a jury for the determination of issues of fact necessary to a verdict.

SPECIAL VERDICT Determination by a jury of specific findings of fact in an action in which application of the law is left to the court.

■=■

Roberts v. Ross

Real estate agent (P) v. Property owner (D)

344 F.2d 747 (3d Cir. 1965).

NATURE OF CASE: Appeal of a decision dismissing an action for breach of contract.

FACT SUMMARY: Roberts (P) sought money that he alleged Ross (D) promised to pay him for producing a buyer for a house Ross (D) owned.

> 🏛 **RULE OF LAW**
> The trial court judge should prepare his own findings of fact and conclusions of law.

FACTS: Roberts (P) alleged that Ross (D) promised to pay him $3,087 for finding a buyer for a house that Ross (D) owned. Ross (D) claimed that he never made such a promise and raised the defense of the Statute of Frauds. On December 30, 1963, the trial judge entered an order stating that he had found for Ross (D) on the issues presented and directed Ross's (D) counsel to file proposed findings of fact and conclusions of law, and draft a judgment. Roberts's (P) counsel was allowed to file objections thereto, which he did. On January 14, 1964, the findings of fact, conclusions of law, and judgment prepared and filed by counsel were signed by the trial judge without change. The findings concluded as a matter of law that the plaintiff had failed to prove by a preponderance of the evidence that the sale of the property by Ross (D) was procured through the agency of Roberts (P) and that in any event the alleged promise, not being in writing, was within the Statute of Frauds. Roberts (P) appealed from the judgment entered thereon. The court dismissed Roberts's (P) complaint and he appealed that decision.

ISSUE: Should a trial court judge prepare his own findings of fact and conclusions of law in support of his decisions?

HOLDING AND DECISION: (Maris, J.) Yes. Ross (D) argued and set forth in the findings of fact that Roberts (P) had failed to prove the alleged agreement by a preponderance of the evidence and, therefore, the trial judge was justified in concluding that there was no enforceable agreement between the parties. There was nothing in the record that the trial judge filed with the decision that shows whether Ross (D) agreed to pay Roberts (P) a commission for producing a customer for the sale of the property. Also, there was no support in the record for the conclusion as a matter of law that Roberts (P) failed to prove by a preponderance of the evidence that the sale of the property by Ross (D) was procured through the agency of Roberts (P). The meaning of the word "agent" as used in the findings of facts is unclear. The entire findings and conclusions in this case did not provide a sufficient indica-tion as to how the trial judge reached his decision as is required by Fed. R. Civ. P. 52(a). Rule 52 requires the trial judge in all cases tried without a jury find the facts specially and state separately its conclusions of law thereon. The trial judge in this case had the counsel for Ross (D) prepare and submit findings of fact, conclusions of law, and a form of judgment. It is impossible for counsel to know the fact-finding and reasoning processes through which the judge has actually gone in reaching his decision and that is what is required. This rule is to help the judge formulate and articulate his findings of fact and conclusions of law in the course of his consideration and determination of the case and should be a part of his decision-making process. It is proper for the judge to invite counsel for both parties to submit to him proposed findings of fact and conclusions of law if he desires them to assist him in formulating his own findings and conclusions and reaching his decision. The district judges should, to comply with Rule 52, formulate their findings of fact and conclusions of law in the course of and as a part of their decision-making process and to articulate and file them at the time of announcing the decision, either in an opinion if filed at that time or in a separate document. These findings are necessary for the appellate court to properly review the findings of the lower court. In this case, it wasn't clear what those findings were. Reversed.

▶ **ANALYSIS**

In a Seventh Circuit opinion, the court ruled that in cases where the evidence is highly technical, the court may adopt the findings and conclusions of one of the counsels if the trial court's procedure is fair to both parties and they were not mechanically adopted. In *Leighton v. One William Street Fund, Inc.*, 343 F.2d 565, 567 (2d Cir. 1965), the court gave three purposes for Rule 52(a), which are: (1) to aid the appellate court by affording it a clear understanding of the ground of the basis of the decision of the trial court; (2) to make definite just what is decided by the case to enable the application of res judicata and estoppel principles to subsequent decisions; and (3) to evoke care on the part of the trial judge in ascertaining the facts.

━══▪

Quicknotes

STATUTE OF FRAUDS A statute that requires specified types of contracts to be in writing in order to be binding.

━══▪

Magnani v. Trogi

Decedent's widow (P) v. Tortfeasor (D)

Ill. App. Ct., 70 Ill. App. 2d 216, 218 N.E.2d 21 (1966).

NATURE OF CASE: Appeal of a decision granting a new trial in action brought under the Wrongful Death Act and the Family Expense Statute.

FACT SUMMARY: The court ordered a new trial because the jury didn't indicate how the damages were to be divided between the two different causes of action.

▥ RULE OF LAW
The trial judge in his discretion may grant a new trial when the verdict is not clear.

FACTS: Magnani (P) stated two separate causes of action in her complaint. In Count I she sought recovery of $30,000 as administratrix for the wrongful death of her decedent under the Wrongful Death Act. In Count II she sought reimbursement in her individual capacity for medical and funeral expenses she incurred as the result of the injury and death to her husband pursuant to the Family Expense Statute. The Wrongful Death Act provides that any recovery under that Act shall be distributed by the court to the widow and next of kin of the decedent in the proportion determined by the trial court. In this case, any award of the jury for a wrongful death would be apportioned by the trial court to the widow and minor son of the decedent. There would be no apportionment of any award made under the provisions of the Family Expense Statute. Even though there were two distinct causes of action in this case, neither party to this suit tendered separate forms of verdict for each of these counts. Rather, the court submitted a single form of verdict to the jury and neither party objected. The jury returned a verdict in favor of Magnani (P) and assessed the damages in the sum of $19,000. The jury returned its verdict on December 21, 1962, and on January 15, 1963, Trogi (D) objected to the verdict and made a motion for a judgment notwithstanding the verdict or for a new trial. The trial judge granted a new trial on both the issue of liability and damages on the grounds that it was impossible to tell how the damages were to be divided between the two different causes of action.

ISSUE: Can a trial judge in his discretion grant a new trial when he feels that the verdict is incomplete?

HOLDING AND DECISION: (Coryn, J.) Yes. The trial judge is allowed broad discretion in granting new trials. The reason for this is to allow the trial judge to correct errors that he or the jury might have made during the course of the trial. Courts of review have repeatedly stated that they will not disturb the decision of a trial court on a motion for a new trial unless clear abuse of discretion is affirmatively shown. Magnani (P) argued that

Trogi (D) waived his right to complain about the form of verdict because he raised the issue for the first time in his post-trial motion. Normally, this would be a valid argument, but in this case the jury's determination of liability and damages on each of the two causes of action was not made known. It appears that the jury found liability on the wrongful death action, but any conclusion about what the jury's verdict was regarding liability on the family expense action is pure conjecture. Also, the verdict gives no indication of the jury's determination as to what portion of the total verdict should be attributed to damages for the wrongful death and what portion, if any, to damages for medical and funeral expenses. It was clear in this case that the trial judge didn't abuse his discretion in granting a new trial. The order of the trial court granting a new trial is affirmed.

DISSENT: (Stouder, J.) Trogi (D) failed to object to the forms of verdict given to the jury at the trial and, therefore, waived his right to object. Trogi (D) also failed to show on appeal that he was prejudiced by the verdict.

▶ ANALYSIS

This case certainly indicates the majority view on the power of the judge to grant a new trial. Both state and federal courts do hold that it is abuse of discretion to grant a new trial when only harmless error is involved. Fed. R. Civ. P. 61 states that no error in either the admission or the exclusion of evidence, and no error or defect in any ruling or order, or in anything done or omitted by the court, or by any of the parties, are grounds for granting a new trial unless refusal to take such action appears to the court inconsistent with substantial justice. The court at every stage of the proceeding must disregard any error or defect in the proceeding which does not affect the substantial rights of the parties.

■=■

Quicknotes

FAMILY EXPENSE STATUTE Provides for recovery of medical and funeral expenses incurred as the result of injury and death of a family member.

WRONGFUL DEATH ACT Provides that any recovery shall be distributed to the widow and next of kin in proportion that the percentage of dependency of each such person upon the deceased bears to the sum of the percentages of dependency of all such persons.

■=■

Robb v. John C. Hickey, Inc.

Complainant (P) v. Corporate tortfeasor (D)

N.J. Cir. Ct., 19 N.J. Misc. 455, 20 A.2d 707 (1941).

NATURE OF CASE: Motions to clarify a verdict in an action for negligence.

FACT SUMMARY: The jury returned a verdict that was contradictory and unclear as to which party prevailed.

🏛 RULE OF LAW
Where the verdict is uncertain or ambiguous, the court will not substitute its verdict in place of it, and a new trial should be granted.

FACTS: The issues presented in this case were the negligence of John C. Hickey, Inc. (Hickey) (D) and the contributory negligence of Robb (P). The court instructed the jury that if they found that Hickey (D) was negligent and Robb (P) was contributorily negligent and that contributory negligence upon the part of Robb's (P) decedent had been established, the comparative degrees of the negligence of the parties was immaterial and Hickey (D) should be awarded the verdict. The jury returned a verdict in the absence of the judge and it was recorded at the clerk's desk as follows: "the jury finds that there was negligence on the part of both parties involved. We, therefore, recommend an award of $2,000." The jury found that both parties had been negligent but since they felt that Hickey (D) was more negligent than Robb (P), they recommended an award of $2,000 to Robb (P). Robb (P) moved to set aside the verdict on the ground that it is ambiguous, inconsistent, inadequate, and contrary to the charge of the court. Hickey (D) moved for a favorable verdict, contending that it was merely informal and the intent of the jury was to find for the defendants.

ISSUE: When the verdict is uncertain or ambiguous, can the court substitute its verdict in its place?

HOLDING AND DECISION: (Leyden, J.) No. A verdict must be responsive to the issues, and recommendations of the jury may be treated as surplusage and properly disregarded. For the verdict to be proper, it must be clear what the jury intended by their verdict. In this case, the jury found both parties were negligent, erroneously compared the degrees of their negligence, and recommended an award of $2,000 in favor of Robb (P). By finding both parties negligent, the verdict appears to be for the defendant because contributory negligence is an absolute defense, but what did the jury intend that the $2,000 award meant? The recommendation of an award to Robb (P) is pertinent to the issues because the liability of Hickey (D) to Robb (P) was in question. Therefore, it cannot be treated as surplusage and disregarded. Because the real

purpose of the jury was not clear, the verdict was defective in substance and in form. The court may mold an informal verdict to render it formal in order that it may coincide with the substance of the verdict as intended by the jury, but the intent of the jury must clearly and convincingly appear in the verdict. Because here the intent of the jury is not clear, the court should not substitute its verdict in its place. Reversed and remanded for a new trial.

▶ ANALYSIS

Most states are in accord with the decision in this case. However, if the jury has not been dismissed, they may be sent out again. Once the jury has been discharged, the court cannot correct or change the verdict. In such a circumstance, the party that is not satisfied with the verdict should make a motion for a new trial. If it is possible and both parties consent to it, the court may reassemble the jurors and ask them to explain their verdict or have them answer additional interrogatories. Fed. R. Civ. P. 49(b)(3) requires in the case of a general verdict with interrogatories that if answers to the interrogatories are inconsistent and some of the answers are also inconsistent with the general verdict, the court shall return the jury for further consideration of its answers and verdict or shall order a new trial.

Quicknotes

NEGLIGENCE Conduct falling below the standard of care that a reasonable person would demonstrate under similar conditions.

Duk v. MGM Grand Hotel, Inc.

Injured gambler (P) v. Casino (D)

320 F.3d 1052 (9th Cir. 2003).

NATURE OF CASE: Cross-appeals of jury verdict.

FACT SUMMARY: Fernando Duk (P) suffered a heart attack during detention by security guards at the MGM Grand Hotel, Inc. (MGM) (D), who held him after he became drunk and disruptive while gambling. Duk (P) sued MGM (D).

🏛 RULE OF LAW
Where a jury is still available, a court's decision to resubmit an inconsistent verdict for clarification is within its discretion.

FACTS: After a night of drinking and gambling at a casino owned by MGM Grand Hotel, Inc. (MGM) (D), Fernando Duk (P) got surly, and security guards asked him to leave. When he refused, the guards made a citizen's arrest and took Duk (P) to a detention room to await transport to a Las Vegas jail. Duk's (P) wife contacted security to inform them that Duk (P) is an insulin-dependent diabetic. After being in the detention room for 20 minutes, Duk (P) began having lung pain. The guards called for an ambulance and medics. Duk (P) claimed that he also complained of chest pain, but that MGM (D) failed to communicate that information to the medics. Two hours later, Duk (P) was taken to jail. He was released and went to a hospital, which determined he suffered a heart attack requiring a heart transplant. Duk (P) filed suit against MGM (D). Nevada's comparative negligence scheme awards damages only where the plaintiff is found to be 50 percent negligent or less, and the jury was instructed that if they found Duk (P) 50 percent negligent or less, they should determine damages. The jury found Duk (P) to be 65 percent negligent, but still awarded Duk (P) $3.3 million in damages. The district court resubmitted the verdict form to the jury and asked that it continue its deliberations to resolve the inconsistency. Twenty minutes later, the jury returned a new verdict apportioning 51 percent of the fault to MGM (D) and 49 percent to Duk (P), but leaving the award the same. The court then granted MGM's (D) motion for a new trial, and at the second trial, the jury returned a verdict for MGM (D).

ISSUE: Where a jury is still available, is a court's decision to resubmit an inconsistent verdict for clarification within its discretion?

HOLDING AND DECISION: (Hawkins, J.) Yes. Where a jury is still available, a court's decision to resubmit an inconsistent verdict for clarification is within its discretion. The district court relied on precedent holding that a new trial was necessary because the jury's deliberations appeared to be results-oriented, and there was, in the court's view, no rational reason to accept the second verdict over the first. But the amount of damages remained unchanged from the first verdict to the second, and it is therefore plausible that the jury changed the assignment of liability because it re-deliberated and changed its mind or clarified its thinking. But it can't be said here that the jury was clearly seeking a predetermined result, and since the trial court had a duty to reconcile the verdicts on any reasonable theory consistent with the evidence, its decision to disregard the second verdict and order a new trial was an abuse of its discretion. The trial court did not abuse its discretion by ordering resubmission of the first verdict, and the second verdict is therefore reinstated.

▶ ANALYSIS

This case illustrates that some circuit courts—in this case, the Ninth—will hold that the process of re-deliberation can explain an inconsistency between an original jury verdict and a second verdict that followed resubmission by the court. Because the inconsistency in this case could be reasonably explained, and the trial court is under a duty to reconcile verdicts on any reasonable theory consistent with the evidence, a new trial order was an abuse of discretion.

Aetna Casualty & Surety Co. v. Yeatts

Insurer (P) v. Abortionist (D)

122 F.2d 350 (4th Cir. 1941).

NATURE OF CASE: Appeal after denial of motion for judgment notwithstanding the verdict and for new trial.

FACT SUMMARY: Yeatts (D) and Aetna Casualty & Surety Co. (P) in a suit for indemnification on insurance policy.

🏛 RULE OF LAW
A federal trial judge may, in his sole discretion, set aside a jury verdict and grant a new trial where he finds the verdict is (1) contrary to the clear weight of the evidence, or (2) based on false evidence.

FACTS: Yeatts (D) sought indemnification from Aetna Casualty & Surety Co. (Aetna) (P) for liability incurred while he was allegedly committing a criminal act of abortion. Aetna (P) denied indemnification on grounds that the insurance policy excluded liability incurred while the insured was performing a criminal act. At trial, Yeatts (D) denied the criminal act. Aetna (P) failed to make a motion for directed verdict prior to the verdict. However, after the verdict, Aetna (P) moved for judgment notwithstanding the verdict and for a new trial on grounds the verdict was against the weight of credible evidence. The trial judge denied both motions and Aetna (P) appealed.

ISSUE: Can a federal trial judge set aside a jury's verdict and grant a new trial in his discretion?

HOLDING AND DECISION: (Parker, J.) Yes. The judge's power to set aside a verdict and grant a new trial is given him to prevent miscarriages of justice. He must examine the verdict and see if it was obtained falsely or was contrary to the clear weight of the evidence. This power to grant or refuse a new trial is in the trial judge's discretion and is not reviewable on appeal except on grounds of abuse of his discretion. In this case, the court of appeals held that while the trial judge possibly should have granted a new trial, there was no abuse of his discretion in denying Aetna's (P) motion for a new trial. Affirmed.

▶ ANALYSIS

This case is a good example of the improper use of procedural devices. First, Aetna (P) failed to make a motion for directed verdict prior to judgment. Although it may not have been granted, it was more likely to succeed than a motion for a new trial. To defeat a directed verdict, Yeatts (D) would have had to offer substantial evidence that he did not commit the alleged criminal act. Secondly, one of the prerequisites for a motion for judgment notwithstand-

ing the verdict (judgment non obstante verdicto) is that a motion for a directed verdict first be made. Here, Aetna (P) failed to make a motion for a directed verdict prior to non obstante verdicto motion, a clear procedural defect. Lastly, this left Aetna (P) with the one motion with which the trial judge had the broadest discretion—the motion for a new trial. In effect, the judge here could overturn the verdict solely if he disagreed with it. However, in dealing with a motion for a directed verdict, he is strictly limited to an examination of the evidence; his opinions are immaterial. This case thus points up the necessity to utilize the proper procedural devices to avoid limiting the available options before and after judgment is entered.

Quicknotes

DIRECTED VERDICT A verdict ordered by the court in a jury trial.

INDEMNIFICATION The payment by a corporation of expenses incurred by its officers or directors as a result of litigation involving the corporation.

JUDGMENT N.O.V. A judgment entered by the trial judge reversing a jury verdict if the jury's determination has no basis in law or fact.

Fisch v. Manger

Car accident victim (P) v. Tortfeasor (D)

N.J. Sup. Ct., 24 N.J. 66, 130 A.2d 815 (1957).

NATURE OF CASE: Appeal from denial of motion for a new trial in an action to recover damages for personal injuries.

FACT SUMMARY: Fisch (P) was awarded $3,000 in damages. His motion for a new trial was denied when Manger (D) agreed that the amount be increased to $7,500.

🏛 RULE OF LAW
It is within the discretion of a trial judge in state court to employ the practices of remittitur and additur, by which the denial of one party's motion for a new trial is conditioned upon the opposing party's consent to a reduction or increase in the amount of damages awarded.

FACTS: Fisch (P) suffered serious injuries in an automobile accident and received a jury award of $3,000. He moved for a new trial on the grounds of inadequacy because the award covered only his medical bills ($2,200) and lost wages ($620) but not his suffering and permanent injuries. Recognizing the gross inadequacy of the award, the trial judge wrote the parties advising that unless Manger (D) consented to an increase in the amount to $7,500, a new trial would be granted, limited to damages only. The judge stated that Fisch (P) was not entitled to a larger sum because he had a back condition before the accident. However, the evidence showed that his prior back condition had cleared up before the accident in dispute in this case. Manger (D) consented to the modification, and Fisch's (P) motion for a new trial was dismissed. Fisch (P) appealed.

ISSUE: Is it within the discretion of a trial judge in state court to employ the practices of remitter and additur, by which the denial of one party's motion for a new trial is conditioned upon the opposing party's consent to a reduction or increase in the amount of damages awarded?

HOLDING AND DECISION: (Jacobs, J.) Yes. It is within the discretion of a trial judge in state court to employ the practices of remittitur and additur, by which the denial of one party's motion for a new trial is conditioned upon the opposing party's consent to a reduction or increase in the amount of damages awarded. An order denying the defendant's application for a new trial on condition the plaintiff consent to a specified reduction in the jury's award is called a remittitur. An order denying the plaintiff's application for a new trial on condition the defendant consent to a specified increase in the jury's award is called an additur. Remittiturs have been recognized almost everywhere, whereas additurs are still outlawed in some states and in federal courts. However, the Seventh Amendment does not apply to proceedings in state courts. This court does not agree that there is a distinction between the two practices and holds that neither remittitur nor additur violate the state constitution. If fairly invoked, they serve the laudable purpose of avoiding a further trial where substantial justice may be attained on the basis of the original trial. However, in this particular case, it appears that the trial judge had a mistaken notion of the evidence, in that he stated that Fisch (P) was not entitled to a great sum due to his prior back condition. The evidence shows, however, that condition had cleared up before the accident in dispute here. Hence, justice will be best served by allowing a second jury to pass on the issue of damages. The case is reversed with direction for a new trial on the issue of damages.

CONCURRENCE: (Heher, J.) The additur practice sanctioned here contravenes the essence of the common-law right of trial by jury at the time of the adoption of the U.S. Constitution.

▶ *ANALYSIS*

The trial judge has a wide discretion in ruling on a motion for a new trial based on a claim that the damages are inadequate or excessive. This discretion may be exercised by granting or denying the motion outright, by granting a partial new trial, limited solely to the issue of damages, or by conditioning the grant of a new trial on remittitur or additur. As noted in this case, while federal courts allow remittitur, they do not allow additur. In *Dimick v. Schiedt*, 293 U.S. 474 (1935), the United States Supreme Court rejected additur as violative of plaintiff's right to a second jury trial on the issue of damages if the first award is inadequate. The Court also pointed out that the Seventh Amendment specifies that "no fact tried by a jury shall be reexamined otherwise than according to the rules of common law," and that additur was not allowed at common law. (Remittitur was so allowed.) That case has been severely criticized.

■■▬■

Quicknotes

ADDITUR Authority of a court to increase a jury's award of damages.

REMITTITUR The authority of the court to reduce the amount of damages awarded by the jury.

■■▬■

Doutre v. Niec

Injured beauty shop customer (P) v. Shop owner (D)

Mich. Ct. App., 2 Mich. App. 88, 138 N.W.2d 501 (1965).

NATURE OF CASE: Action to recover damages for personal injuries.

FACT SUMMARY: Doutre (P) received injuries as a result of a beauty treatment by Niec (D). At trial, Niec (D) was not allowed to testify as to the standard of care observed by beauty shops in their area. A new trial was granted, limited to the question of liability.

🏛 RULE OF LAW
The questions of liability and damages are so closely intertwined that they may not usually be separated, so that if a new trial is required on the issue of liability, the issue of damages must also be retried.

FACTS: Niec (D) operated a beauty shop in Flint. Doutre (P) suffered head and facial injuries as a result of a bleach and color treatment he was given by Niec (D). At trial, Niec (D) was not allowed to testify as to the standard of care observed by beauty shops in the Flint area when administering such treatments. Doutre (P) was awarded $10,000. Niec's (D) motion for a new trial was granted, but the new trial was limited to the question of liability. Doutre (P) appealed on the ground that the trial court's evidentiary ruling was correct, and Niec (D) appealed on the ground that it was error to limit the new trial to the issue of liability.

ISSUE: Can a new trial be ordered but limited to the issue of liability?

HOLDING AND DECISION: [Judge not stated in casebook excerpt.] No. First, it was error to exclude testimony as to the standard of care observed by beauty shops in the Flint area. Hence, a new trial is required, and such trial may not be limited to the issue of liability. It has long been recognized that the questions of liability and damages are so closely intertwined that they may not usually be separated. The only case that has been recognized so far is, where the liability is clear, a retrial of the issue of damages alone may be permitted. There is no compelling reason for extending this rule here, where the damages are not liquidated, and the liability was determined pursuant to a trial in which an admitted error touching on liability was permitted. Under these circumstances, the jury that determines the issue of liability should also have the responsibility of awarding damages. The order for a new trial is extended to all of the issues.

▶ ANALYSIS

In nonjury cases the court may in effect grant a partial new trial. It may order that the judgment be opened, that addi-

tional testimony be taken, and thereafter amend its findings of fact and conclusions of law; or it may make new findings and conclusions and direct the entry of a new judgment. In jury cases, however, the granting of a new trial has the effect of nullifying the judgment entirely, and the case must be tried all over again. A judge may, as noted above, grant a partial new trial, limited to the issue of damages.

■══■

Quicknotes

DAMAGES Monetary compensation that may be awarded by the court to a party who has sustained injury or loss to his person, property or rights due to another party's unlawful act, omission or negligence.

LIABILITY Any obligation or responsibility.

STANDARD OF CARE A uniform degree of behavior against which a person's conduct can be measured when determining liability in negligence cases.

■══■

CHAPTER 15

Securing and Enforcing Judgments

Quick Reference Rules of Law

Griggs v. Miller

Farm purchaser (P) v. Debtor's representative (D)

Mo. Sup. Ct., 374 S.W.2d 119 (1963).

NATURE OF CASE: Action in ejectment for possession of property and for damages for withholding possession.

FACT SUMMARY: Brookshire's (D) 322-acre farm, which was worth about $50,000, was sold at a public sale under general execution to satisfy judgments of $2,000 and $17,000.

RULE OF LAW
An execution is not leviable upon all the debtor's property, but only upon sufficient property owned by the debtor to satisfy the debt, interest, and costs, and failure to divide land and sell only enough to satisfy execution may be an abuse of discretion.

FACTS: On December 14, 1960, Sheriff Powell levied an execution on Brookshire's (D) farm to satisfy a judgment of $2,000 recovered against Brookshire (D). On January 11, 1961, he levied an execution on the 322-acre farm to satisfy a $17,000 judgment recovered against Brookshire (D). He sold the farm at a public sale on January 16, 1961, to Griggs (P) for $20,600. Powell did not advertise the farm for sale under the $17,000 judgment, and Brookshire (D) first knew of the levy under that judgment 30 minutes before the sale of the farm under the $2,000 judgment. The value of the farm was $50,000. On January 11, 1961, Brookshire (D) wrote Powell, saying he wanted only a portion of the farm to be sold. The farm could have been offered for sale in parcels. Also, Powell testified that he knew that Brookshire (D) owned corporate stocks and 200 head of cattle, worth at least $200 a head. Griggs (P) sued Brookshire (D) for possession of the farm. The court held that Griggs (P) was entitled to $2,483 in damages. Miller (D), as trustee of Brookshire's (D) estate following his incarceration, appealed.

ISSUE: Is it error for an officer levying an execution upon real property to sell the property for an amount much less than its market value without first attempting to satisfy the judgment debt by dividing the property and selling a portion of it?

HOLDING AND DECISION: (Per curiam, on Bohling, Sp. Commr's opinion) Yes. An execution is not leviable upon all the debtor's property, but only upon sufficient property owned by the debtor to satisfy the debt, interest, and costs. A sheriff conducting an execution sale is the agent of the property owner and the judgment creditor, and has the duty to protect the interests of both and to see that the property is not sacrificed. A sheriff must exercise care and discretion which a reasonably prudent person would exercise in such circumstances. A failure to divide land and sell only enough to satisfy execution has been considered an abuse of discretion. In this case, Brookshire's (D) 322-acre farm could have been divided, but it was not. The controlling statute provides that an officer shall divide the property if it is dividable and sell only as much as necessary to satisfy judgment. This was not done. It is not possible to justify the sale of $50,000 property for $20,000 to satisfy a $2,000 judgment and a $17,000 judgment which was not even properly advertised. If Brookshire (D) deposits $20,600 in the court within 30 days, the sale will be canceled; otherwise it will stand affirmed. Reversed and remanded.

ANALYSIS

For the most part, judgments for money or for possession of property are enforced by writs of execution, as at common law. Such a writ is not a command to the defendant, but an authorization to the proper officer (usually a sheriff or marshal) to do something. In the case of a money judgment, this will be to seize defendant's nonexempt property, sell it on execution sale, and apply the proceeds toward the satisfaction of the judgment. Many states also provide that a money judgment becomes a lien on the defendant's real property. If the judgment is for possession of property, the writ of execution authorizes the officer to take possession from the defendant and put the plaintiff into possession.

Quicknotes

LEVY The collection or assessment of a tax; the legal process pursuant to which property is seized and sold in order to satisfy a debt.

Reeves v. Crownshield

Creditor (P) v. Debtor (D)

N.Y. Ct. App., 274 N.Y. 74, 8 N.E.2d 283 (1937).

NATURE OF CASE: Appeal from being held in contempt.

FACT SUMMARY: A state statute allows a court to order a judgment debtor to make payment out of income. Refusal to pay after such an order is punishable as contempt. Crownshield (D) was held in contempt for his failure to pay after such an order.

RULE OF LAW
Imprisonment of a judgment debtor for failure to obey a court order to make payment out of income, where such order is made with due regard to the needs of the family, is not violative of the Due Process Clause.

FACTS: A state statute allows a court to order a judgment debtor to make payment out of income. Such orders must be made upon notice to the debtor and with due regard to the needs of the debtor and his family, as well as payments required by other creditors. Refusal to pay after such order is punishable as contempt. This procedure was invoked against Crownshield (D) in an attempt to collect a $400 judgment. He was employed by the federal government at a salary of $230 per month. He had no children and his wife's whereabouts were unknown. Aside from $48 a month paid as rent and living expenses, he had no financial obligations. The court ordered him to pay $20 per month until the judgment was satisfied. Upon his failure to pay he was held in contempt.

ISSUE: Is a statute which provides that a court may order a judgment debtor to make payment out of income and that refusal to pay after such an order is punishable as contempt, unconstitutional as in effect providing for imprisonment for debt?

HOLDING AND DECISION: (Finch, J.) No. Neither the state nor federal Constitutions contain provisions expressly prohibiting imprisonment for debt, and no cases are cited which hold that imprisonment for debt is barred by the Due Process Clause. However, whatever doubt may exist as to whether imprisonment for debt without regard to ability to pay may be treated as a deprivation of liberty without due process of law, there is no doubt that imprisonment for failure to obey an order which is made with due regard to the needs of the debtor and his family is not violative of the Due Process Clause. Without the right to punish as contempt, the court would have no power to enforce its order. To compel the judgment debtor to obey the order of the court is not imprisonment for the debt, but only imprisonment for disobedience of the order. Refusal to comply with the order is contumacious conduct, the same as a refusal to obey any lawful court order. In this case, Crownshield (D) does not contend that order to pay $20 per month is unjust, inequitable, or harsh. Nor does it violate due process. Further, the order is not unconstitutional as interfering with the operation of a federal instrumentality. It is true that a federal employee cannot be garnished, but a wage has been paid to him. A state is not prohibited from ordering that a portion of such wage be applied toward the payment of just debts. Affirmed.

ANALYSIS

Some judgments are largely self-executing, such as decrees of divorce or judgments quieting title. Others involve personal orders to a defendant and depend for their effectiveness on the contempt power. The personal order, as demonstrated here, is sometimes available for compelling the payment of money. This case also points out that such an order will not generally issue without a finding that the defendant has the ability to comply with it. In some states, the writ of execution authorizes the officer to take the defendant's body (i.e., jail him) under certain circumstances on certain kinds of money judgments. This body execution comes from the common law and is to be distinguished from the use of the contempt power, which is available only after a personal order to pay has been issued and disobeyed.

Quicknotes

CONTUMACIOUS Conduct in willful disobedience of the court giving rise to a finding of contempt.

DUE PROCESS CLAUSE Clauses, found in the Fifth and Fourteenth Amendments to the United States Constitution, providing that no person shall be deprived of "life, liberty, or property, without due process of law."

GARNISHEE A party holding the property of a debtor who is directed to hold the property until a court determination of the proper disposition thereof.

JUDGMENT DEBTOR A party against whom a judgment has been rendered and which has not been paid.

Appellate Review

Quick Reference Rules of Law

Liberty Mutual Insurance Co. v. Wetzel

Employer (D) v. Female employee (P)

424 U.S. 737 (1976).

NATURE OF CASE: Appeal from grant of partial summary judgment on issue of liability in civil rights action.

FACT SUMMARY: In a discrimination action, the district court granted the motion of Wetzel (P) for partial summary judgment as to liability only, and Liberty Mutual Insurance Co. (D) appealed.

RULE OF LAW

The granting of partial summary judgment as to liability only is not appealable under 28 U.S.C. § 1291.

FACTS: Certain employees brought suit against Liberty Mutual Insurance Co. (Liberty Mutual) (D), claiming violations of the Civil Rights Act of 1964. The district court granted the motion of Wetzel (P) for summary judgment as to liability only, but did not grant any requested relief. Liberty Mutual (D) appealed, and the court of appeals affirmed. Liberty Mutual (D) then appealed to the United States Supreme Court. Section 1291 by its terms only allows appeals of "final judgments," and the issue arose as to whether the partial summary judgment was an appealable final judgment.

ISSUE: Is the granting of partial summary judgment as to liability only appealable under 28 U.S.C. § 1291?

HOLDING AND DECISION: (Rehnquist, J.) No. The granting of partial summary judgment is not appealable under 28 U.S.C. § 1291. Section 1291 only allows appeals from "final judgments." A final judgment is just that—final. There is nothing more to do. Here, liability was established, but no relief was as yet given. The court's action was thus an interlocutory order, which would have to be appealed under 28 U.S.C. § 1292, for which the procedural requisites were not met here. Vacated and remanded.

ANALYSIS

In this action, the issue of jurisdiction to hear the appeal was apparently not brought up by either side. The Court brought it up on its own motion. Appellate jurisdiction is generally treated the same as subject matter jurisdiction. Unlike most defenses, the defense of lack of subject matter jurisdiction is never waived and can be brought up at any time by anyone involved. If the Court finds such an absence of subject matter jurisdiction, it is under a duty to dismiss, as the Court did here.

Quicknotes

LIABILITY Any obligation or responsibility.

SUMMARY JUDGMENT Judgment rendered by a court in response to a motion made by one of the parties, claiming that the lack of a question of material fact in respect to an issue warrants disposition of the issue without consideration by the jury.

Will v. Hallock

[Parties not identified.]

546 U.S. 345 (2006).

NATURE OF CASE: Appeal to the Supreme Court of U.S. Court of Appeals ruling on a motion.

FACT SUMMARY: Plaintiffs whose property was damaged by federal officers tried to bring a negligence claim against them after losing a Federal Tort Claims Act case against the government.

🏛 RULE OF LAW

If a claim under the Federal Tort Claims Act is dismissed on the grounds that it is covered by one of the Act's exceptions to the waiver of sovereign immunity, and a federal district court denies a motion of the individual federal agents to dismiss a subsequent suit brought against them, the federal appeals court does not have jurisdiction under the collateral order doctrine to hear an appeal of the district court's order.

FACTS: [U.S. Customs Service agents raided plaintiffs' residence and seized several computers. The plaintiffs were cleared of any guilt, and the computers were returned, but were damaged. They sued the government under the Federal Tort Claims Act (FTCA), and, while that action was pending, sued the agents separately for negligence. The district court dismissed FTCA case, and the agents then made a motion for dismissal of the negligence claims under a provision of the FTCA that bars suits where a judgment on the claim has already been entered. The district court denied the motion. Although the trial had not yet concluded, the Second Circuit Court of Appeals granted the agents' appeal of the district court's ruling on the motion and affirmed the district court, ruling that since the plaintiffs had not properly brought a claim in the original suit, no judgment had been entered.]

ISSUE: If a claim under the FTCA is dismissed on the grounds that it is covered by one of the Act's exceptions to the waiver of sovereign immunity, and a federal district court denies a motion of the individual federal agents to dismiss a subsequent suit brought against them, does the federal appeals court have jurisdiction under the collateral order doctrine to hear an appeal of the district court's order?

HOLDING AND DECISION: (Souter, J.) No. If a claim under the FTCA is dismissed on the grounds that it is covered by one of the Act's exceptions to the waiver of sovereign immunity, and a federal district court denies a motion of the individual federal agents to dismiss a subsequent suit brought against them, the federal appeals court does not have jurisdiction under the collateral order doc-

trine to hear an appeal of the district court's order. The scope of the collateral order doctrine is narrow. Only orders that cannot be effectively reviewed after a final judgment can be appealed before the close of the trial. The interest at stake is essential to this determination. In this case, the agents' interest in appealing the district court's order had no greater importance than the typical defense of claim preclusion and it therefore warranted no immediate appeal of right as a collateral order. Vacated and remanded.

▶ ANALYSIS

The casebook excerpt omits facts that might be helpful to understanding this case. The government seized the computers and business records of Susan Hallock because her husband was suspected of possessing child pornography. Her husband appeared to be the victim of identity theft, however, and no child pornography was found on Susan's computers, but the damage caused by the government forced her to shut down her software development business. She brought suit against the government under the FTCA, but it was dismissed for lack of subject matter jurisdiction, because it fell into one of the FTCA's categories of cases that still enjoyed sovereign immunity. But before the district court dismissed the case, Hallock filed the negligence case against the individual agents. The government argued that the plain language of the FTCA barred Hallock's second suit, which bars relitigation of FTCA claims that have been ruled upon. The government argued that the order dismissing her claims against the government qualified as a "judgment," even though the merits of her claim were not reached, and that the initial suit was brought "under" the FTCA even if Hallock could not recover on her claim.

■═■

Quicknotes

COLLATERAL ORDER Doctrine pursuant to which an appeal from an interlocutory order may be brought in order to hear and determine claims which are collateral to the merits of the case and which could not be granted adequate review on appeal.

SOVEREIGN IMMUNITY Immunity of government from suit without its consent.

■═■

La Buy v. Howes Leather Co.

District judge (P) v. Antitrust litigant (D)

352 U.S. 249 (1957).

NATURE OF CASE: Appeal from writ of mandamus ordering district judge to vacate reference to a master.

FACT SUMMARY: Judge La Buy (P) referred cases to a master, and Howes Leather Co. (D), one of the litigants, sought a writ of mandamus to vacate the reference.

🏛 RULE OF LAW
A court of appeals has the discretionary power, in exceptional cases, to review interlocutory orders of a lower federal court by writ of mandamus.

FACTS: District Court Judge La Buy (P), weighed down by the complexities of two antitrust cases, asked the parties to the actions to have a master hear the cases. When the parties did not respond, La Buy (P) entered an interlocutory order, sua sponte, referring the cases to a master on grounds that his court calendar was "congested," and that other exceptional conditions existed for the order. Howes Leather Co. (D), one of the parties to the actions, filed for a writ of mandamus, asking the court of appeals to compel La Buy (P) to vacate the reference to the master. The court of appeals issued the writ of mandamus under the All Writs Act (28 U.S.C. § 1651[a]) and La Buy (P) sought certiorari to the United States Supreme Court, attacking the writ of mandamus.

ISSUE: Does a court of appeals have the power to review, through a writ of mandamus, interlocutory orders of a lower federal court?

HOLDING AND DECISION: (Clark, J.) Yes. The power is granted under 28 U.S.C. § 1651(a), popularly called the All Writs Act. However, writs of mandamus should only be used in extreme cases. In the present case, La Buy (P) was well informed as to the antitrust suits before him. It is true that under Fed. R. Civ. P. 53(b) he had the authority to make reference to a master, but only if the cases proved too complicated for him to handle alone, or that some exceptional condition required reference. The Supreme Court found that La Buy's (P) judicial district had been warned for years by the court of appeals about its abuse of power in making excessive references to masters. As to La Buy's (P) reasons for reference, namely that his court was congested and antitrust suits were complex, the Supreme Court held (1) if references to masters were allowed to become excessive, this would result in an abdication of judicial function, depriving parties of a trial before a judge, and (2) since La Buy (P) was an experienced antitrust judge, the complexities of the antitrust litigation

before him entitled the parties to his expertise, not that of a less experienced master. Affirmed.

DISSENT: (Brennan, J.) The All Writs Act does not confer upon a court of appeals an independent appellate power to review interlocutory orders of a lower court.

▶ ANALYSIS

There is much conflict as to when a writ of mandamus should be used for review. Some authorities fear that mandamus is a threat to the rules against "piecemeal" litigation. See *Sears v. Mackey*, 351 U.S. 427 (1956). But writs of mandamus are not to be used as substitutes for appeal, even where hardship may occur due to delay or an unnecessary trial. The writ, although discretionary, is generally limited where there is an abuse of discretion by the trial court. The court having the power to issue the writ will consider such factors as irreparable harm, lack of speedy remedy, or undue hardship. But as a practical matter, appellate courts have used writs of mandamus as if they were appeals. Yet, the writ is rarely granted, especially where the interlocutory order of the lower court was within that court's discretion.

Quicknotes

ALL WRITS ACT Authorizes appellate review by way of extraordinary writ.

SUA SPONTE An action taken by the court by its own motion and without the suggestion of one of the parties.

WRIT OF MANDAMUS A court order issued commanding a public or private entity, or an official thereof, to perform a duty required by law.

Atlantic City Electric Co. v. General Electric Co.

Electricity supplier (P) v. Competitor (D)

337 F.2d 844 (2d Cir. 1964).

NATURE OF CASE: Pretrial appeal to set aside an interlocutory order.

FACT SUMMARY: The district court certified an order sustaining Atlantic City Electric Co.'s (P) objection to interrogatories for immediate appeal.

🏛 RULE OF LAW
Pretrial appeal should only be granted on interlocutory orders that are not otherwise appealable from an adverse trial judgment.

FACTS: Atlantic City Electric Co. (Atlantic) (P) alleged damages resulting from General Electric Co.'s (GE) (D) actions. GE (D) posed interrogatories to discover if Atlantic (P) had "passed on" the damages it allegedly suffered to its customers, thus precluding recovery to the extent they "passed on." The district court sustained Atlantic's (P) objections to the interrogatories, but certified the ruling for immediate appeal, under 28 U.S.C. § 1292(b), on grounds it involved a controlling question of law and substantial grounds for differing opinions.

ISSUE: Should an appellate court grant pretrial appeal on issues that are appealable from an adverse judgment at trial?

HOLDING AND DECISION: (Per curiam) No. Pretrial appeals pose problems as to the feasibility of deciding certain questions of law in advance of trial. Such appeals are within the discretion of the appellate court and are not automatically granted. They are viewed against the backdrop of the entire case. In the present case, the GE (D) request for pretrial discovery may extend the length of already extensive pretrial proceedings. In the event they lose, GE (D) will have an opportunity to correct the district court ruling on appeal. Meanwhile, it is not precluded from its "passing on" defense by denial of this pretrial appeal. Application denied.

▶ ANALYSIS

Courts of appeals do not favor interlocutory appeals under § 1292(b). Decisions to review interlocutory orders have emphasized that most of the pretrial appeals granted have been of exceptional nature. The rationale behind the appellate courts granting only a small number of applications for pretrial appeal is grounded on the desire for the resolution of issues at trial, and for the speedy determination of litigation.

Quicknotes

INTERLOCUTORY ORDER An order entered by the court determining an issue that does not resolve the disposition of the case, but is essential to a proper adjudication of the action.

Electrical Fittings Corp. v. Thomas & Betts Co.

Alleged infringer (D) v. Patent holder (P)

307 U.S. 241 (1939).

NATURE OF CASE: Action in equity for alleged infringement of a patent.

FACT SUMMARY: In a patent infringement case, Electrical Fittings Corp. (D) appealed a finding of the trial court, even though judgment was in its favor.

🏛 RULE OF LAW
A party may not appeal from judgment or decree in his favor for the purpose of obtaining a review of findings he deems erroneous which are not necessary to obtain the decree. However, where the finding is necessary to the decision, the defendant may appeal to have this portion of the decree eliminated.

FACTS: Thomas & Betts Co. (P) brought a suit in equity against Electrical Fittings Corp. (D) for alleged infringement of a patent. The district court held Claim 1 valid and then dismissed for failure to prove infringement. Thomas & Betts Co. (P) did not appeal, but instead filed in the Patent Office a disclaimer of Claim 2. Electrical Fittings Corp. (D) appealed that part of the decree which adjudicated Claim 1 valid. The circuit court of appeals, being of the opinion that the decree would not bind Electrical Fittings Corp. (D) in subsequent suits, if any, dismissed the appeal on the ground that the Electrical Fillings Corp. (D) had been awarded all the relief to which it was entitled.

ISSUE: May a party appeal a trial court's finding that was unnecessary to the decision even though judgment is in its favor?

HOLDING AND DECISION: (Roberts, J.) Yes. Since the decree itself purports to adjudge the validity of Claim 1, although the adjudication was immaterial to the disposition of the case, it stands as an adjudication of one of the issues litigated. Reversed and remanded.

▶ ANALYSIS

On the question of who has standing to appeal a decision, most courts have held that it is the one "aggrieved" by the judgment. Those not party to the suit who seek to appeal a decision are ordinarily not "aggrieved." Nor can one be aggrieved by a consent judgment. However, one who has moved for a new trial on all the issues, but instead, was limited to only a partial challenge, has been held to be sufficiently aggrieved.

Quicknotes

PATENT A limited monopoly conferred on the invention or discovery of any new or useful machine or process that is novel and nonobvious.

International Ore & Fertilizer Corp. v. SGS Control Services, Inc.

Seller of fertilizer (P) v. Cargo transporter (D)

38 F.3d 1279 (2d Cir. 1994).

NATURE OF CASE: Appeal from a judgment awarding damages for negligent misrepresentation.

FACT SUMMARY: A seller of fertilizer (P) sued its cargo transporter (D) for breach of contract and negligent misrepresentation. The trial judge denied relief for breach of contract but awarded the seller damages for the transporter's (D) negligent misrepresentation. The transporter (D) appealed, the seller (P) filed no cross-appeal, and the appellate court reversed the judgment on the negligent misrepresentation claim. The appeals court also considered whether it had the authority to reverse the trial court's order on the contract claim.

RULE OF LAW
A federal appeals court can decide an issue that an appellee fails to raise in a cross-appeal.

FACTS: International Ore & Fertilizer Corp. (International Ore) (P) entered a contract with SGS Control Services, Inc. (SGS) (D) to transport International Ore's (P) fertilizer to New Zealand. SGS (D) failed to clean its cargo ship, though, and International Ore's (P) fertilizer was contaminated before it reached New Zealand. The intended buyer in New Zealand refused the fertilizer, and International Ore (P) sued SGS (D) for breach of contract and for negligently misrepresenting the condition of the cargo ship. At trial, International Ore (P) lost on its potentially more valuable breach-of-contract claim but won a lesser award of damages on its negligent misrepresentation claim. SGS (D) appealed, but International Ore (P) did not file a cross-appeal. International Ore (P) did argue on appeal, however, in support of its evidence on the contract claim. The appellate court reversed the trial court's judgment on the negligent-misrepresentation count and considered reversing the trial court's order on the contract claim to instead enter judgment for International Ore (P) on that count of its complaint.

ISSUE: Can a federal appeals court decide an issue that an appellee fails to raise in a cross-appeal?

HOLDING AND DECISION: (Winter, J.) Yes. A federal appeals court can decide an issue that an appellee fails to raise in a cross-appeal. Generally, the party who prevailed in the trial court may not challenge a trial court's order on appeal if the party did not file a cross-appeal. This general rule means that an appellee cannot attack a trial court's order so as to enlarge his own rights under that order or to lessen the rights of his opponent. At the same time, an appellee may argue in support of a decree by using anything in the record, even if it contradicts the trial

judge's reasoning in some way. In this case, therefore, International Ore's (P) response to questions at oral argument properly brings the contract claim before the court, and the court therefore may rule on that claim. Accordingly, the judgment of the trial court is also reversed on the breach-of-contract count. Consistent with the rule against an appellee enlarging its rights when not filing a cross-appeal, however, International Ore's (P) recovery is limited to the damages awarded by the trial court for negligent misrepresentation.

ANALYSIS

Sometimes there's a fine line between, on the one hand, a court passively deciding the case that the parties put before it and, on the other hand, a court interpreting the case so aggressively that the court effectively raises issues sua sponte and decides a different case than the parties themselves elected to argue. At a minimum, *International Ore* shows a court that is testing the limits of that line.

Quicknotes

BREACH OF CONTRACT Unlawful failure by a party to perform its obligations pursuant to contract.

DAMAGES Monetary compensation that may be awarded by the court to a party who has sustained injury or loss to his person, property or rights due to another party's unlawful act, omission or negligence.

NEGLIGENT MISREPRESENTATION A misrepresentation that is made pursuant to a business relationship, in violation of an obligation owed, upon which the plaintiff relies to his detriment.

Corcoran v. City of Chicago

Injured citizen (P) v. Municipality (D)

Ill. Sup. Ct., 373 Ill. 567, 27 N.E.2d 451 (1940).

NATURE OF CASE: Action to recover damages for personal injuries arising out of negligence.

FACT SUMMARY: Corcoran (P) challenged, as unconstitutional, a state statutory provision which provided that appellate courts may review errors of fact where the judgment decreed is not sustained by the evidence or is against the weight of the evidence.

🏛 RULE OF LAW
Statutory authority that permits appellate courts to set aside verdicts on the grounds the findings of fact were not supported by the evidence is neither unconstitutional nor against the practice at common law.

FACTS: Corcoran (P) sued the City of Chicago (D) to recover damages for personal injuries allegedly arising out of carelessly and negligently maintained streets. Following a jury verdict in Corcoran's (P) favor, the City (D) moved for a new trial, which was denied. An appellate court found the verdict was against the manifest weight of the evidence and reversed the judgment for that reason. Statutory authority granted appellate courts power to review "error of fact, in that the judgment, decree or order appealed from is not sustained by the evidence or is against the weight of the evidence." Corcoran (P), in appealing to the state supreme court, sought to have the statute overturned as against the practice at common law and unconstitutional since it denied him the right to a trial by jury.

ISSUE: May an appellate court review errors of fact where the judgment decreed is, in the court's estimation, not sustained by the evidence or is against the weight of the evidence if statutory provisions permit it to do so?

HOLDING AND DECISION: (Murphy, J.) Yes. There are, admittedly, some cases which support the contention that at common law the power to award a new trial on the grounds the verdict was against the weight of the evidence rested solely in the trial court. This position is partially based on the theory that the trial judge saw and heard the witness testify and was for that reason in a better position to consider the evidence than the judges of a court of review who had not had such opportunity. Nevertheless, there was a practice at common law which permitted appellate courts to review errors of fact, allowing the judges to determine from the records and proceedings before them the credibility and weight of the evidence. Affirmed.

▶ ANALYSIS

A motion for a new trial is a request, in effect, that the trial judge exercise his discretion. He is allowed considerable latitude in ruling on the motion. On appeal, the appellate court determines not whether the jury's verdict was erroneously arrived at, but whether the trial judge, in denying the motion, abused his discretion. All doubts must be resolved in the trial judge's favor since he was actually present to gauge the witnesses' testimony and weigh the evidence.

Pullman-Standard v. Swint

Employer (D) v. Employee (P)

456 U.S. 273 (1982).

NATURE OF CASE: Review of appellate court's reversal of district court factual determination.

FACT SUMMARY: The court of appeals reversed a district court finding of lack of discriminatory intent in a civil rights action, and the Supreme Court granted review.

🏛 RULE OF LAW
A federal court of appeals is bound to follow a district court's factual determinations unless the determinations are clearly erroneous.

FACTS: Swint (P), among others, brought a civil rights action against Pullman-Standard (D), claiming that Pullman's (D) seniority system discriminated on the basis of race. The district court determined that no discriminatory intent, a condition for the establishment of liability, was present. The court of appeals found that there was such a motive and reversed. Fed. R. Civ. P. 52(a) provides that a district court's factual determinations are not to be disturbed unless clearly erroneous.

ISSUE: Is a federal court of appeals bound to follow a district court's factual determinations?

HOLDING AND DECISION: (White, J.) Yes. A federal appellate court must follow the factual findings of a district court unless they are clearly erroneous, as this is mandated in Fed. R. Civ. P. 52(a). It does not matter whether the fact is evidentiary or ultimate. Even ultimate factual determinations are not to be disturbed unless they are clearly erroneous. Here, the court of appeals did not apply the "clearly erroneous" standard, but rather simply disagreed with the district court and made its own factual determination as to motive. This is improper. Reversed and remanded.

▌ *ANALYSIS*

The rule stated here has an exception, and that is in the case of review of plaintiff verdicts in libel suits. The appellate courts in those cases are obligated to review not only legal conclusions, but factual ones as well. This was established by the United States Supreme Court as a safeguard for the protection of First Amendment rights. As yet, this rule has not been extended to review of actions involving many other Constitution-based rights.

Quicknotes

TITLE VII OF THE CIVIL RIGHTS ACT OF 1964 § 703(h) Requires that a seniority system be free of an intent to discriminate.

The Binding Effect of Prior Decisions: Res Judicata and Collateral Estoppel

Quick Reference Rules of Law

Rush v. City of Maple Heights

Accident victim (P) v. Municipality (D)

Ohio Sup. Ct., 167 Ohio St. 221, 147 N.E.2d 599; *cert. denied*, 358 U.S. 814 (1958).

NATURE OF CASE: Action to recover damages for personal injuries.

FACT SUMMARY: Rush (P) won in an action for damage to her personal property against the City of Maple Heights (D), and then commenced a second action against the City (D) for personal injuries, claiming that the first action was res judicata on the issue of negligence.

🏛 RULE OF LAW
Whether or not injuries to both person and property resulting from the same wrongful act are to be treated as injuries to separate rights or as separate items of damage, a plaintiff may maintain only one lawsuit to enforce his rights existing at the time such action is commenced.

FACTS: Rush (P) was injured in a fall from a motorcycle. In an action brought in municipal court for damage to her personal property, the court found that the City of Maple Heights (D) was negligent in maintaining its street and awarded Rush (P) $100 in damages. This judgment was appealed and affirmed. Rush (P) initiated a second action in another court for personal injuries she suffered in the same accident. She claimed that the issue of negligence was res judicata because of the judgment in the first action. In this second action, Rush (P) received an award of $12,000.

ISSUE: Where more than one cause of action arises from a single wrongful act, may the plaintiff raise all causes of action in one lawsuit in order to enforce his existing rights?

HOLDING AND DECISION: (Herbert, J.) Yes. Whether or not injuries to both person and property resulting from the same wrongful act are to be treated as injuries to separate rights or as separate items of damage, a plaintiff may maintain only one lawsuit to enforce his rights existing at the time such action is commenced. An earlier case, *Vasu v. Kohlers, Inc.*, 145 Ohio St. 321, 61 N.E.2d 707 (1945), must be distinguished. There, plaintiff's insurance company commenced an action against the defendant to recoup the money paid by it to cover the damage to plaintiff's automobile. Six months later, plaintiff commenced an action in the same court against the same defendant to recover for personal injuries he had suffered in the same collision. Meanwhile, in the insurance company's suit, judgment was rendered in favor of the defendant who then set it up as a bar to plaintiff's action. On appeal, this defense was denied. The *Vasu* case held: "(4) injuries to both person and property give rise to different rights and different causes of action; . . . (6) an indemnitor (i.e., insurance company) may prosecute a separate action to recover monies paid out to the insured; (7)

parties in privy are not bound unless made parties to the first action if their title or interest attached before the beginning of the action or the rendition of judgment; (8) a grantor or assignor (the insured) is not bound by any judgment against the grantee or assignee (the insurer) unless he is, in effect, made a party." In the instant case, (4) was not necessary to the decision in *Vasu* and, in fact, represented a minority rule. Following the majority rule, that in these days of code pleading, the prime concern should be to prevent multiplicity of suits, burdensome expense, delay to plaintiffs, and vexatious litigation against defendants. In those jurisdictions that follow the majority rule, separation of causes of action is recognized where an insurer has acquired the right to recover for money it has advanced to pay for property damages. Thus, Rush's (P) second action should not have been permitted to proceed. Reversed and judgment entered for the plaintiff.

CONCURRENCE: (Stewart, J.) The discussion in the *Vasu* case is not necessary to decide the issue presented in this case.

DISSENT: (Zimmerman, J.) Established law should remain undisturbed unless changing conditions mandate that prior decisions should be upset.

▶ ANALYSIS

There are three ways in which a prior adjudication, involving the same parties, and somehow related to the present action, can affect a case: (1) merger—plaintiff won in the first suit, his cause of action is merged in the court's judgment, and cannot be maintained again; (2) res judicata—plaintiff lost in the first suit, his cause of action is barred by judgment for the defendant and cannot be reasserted; (3) estoppel by judgment—where the second action does not involve the same cause of action as the earlier one, issues litigated in the first case are settled and cannot be re-argued in later proceedings.

▬▬■

Quicknotes

OBITER DICTA Statement by a judge in a legal opinion that is not necessary for the resolution of the action.

PARTIES IN PRIVY Parties who by virtue of some relationship other than contractual share a mutual interest.

RES JUDICATA The rule of law a final judgment by a court precludes subsequent litigation between the parties regarding the same cause of action.

▬▬■

Mathews v. New York Racing Association, Inc.

Ejected race track patron (P) v. Track operator (D)

193 F. Supp. 293 (S.D.N.Y. 1961).

NATURE OF CASE: Action for damages and injunction.

FACT SUMMARY: Mathews (P), having unsuccessfully sued employees of Thoroughbred Racing Protective Association (Thoroughbred) (D) in a prior action, brought a second suit on the same cause of action against Thoroughbred (D) and the latter's employer, the New York Racing Association, Inc. (D).

🏛 RULE OF LAW
The doctrine of res judicata operates as a bar to subsequent suits involving the same parties, or those in privity with them, based on a claim which has once reached a judgment on the merits.

FACTS: The New York Racing Association, Inc. (Association) (D) employed the Thoroughbred Racing Protective Association (Thoroughbred) (D), a private detective agency, for security purposes. Mathews (P) had brought a prior action against three employees of Thoroughbred (D), claiming that they had assaulted him at a race track operated by the Association (D). He claimed that the employees had made libelous statements against him, had him charged with disorderly conduct, and caused him to be convicted on that charge. In that action Mathews (P) had asked for money damages and an injunction restraining the employees from interfering with his attendance at race tracks, from publication of libelous statements, and from acting as peace officers. The court ruled against Mathews (P). Mathews (P) then brought this action against the Association (D) and Thoroughbred (D), both of whom moved for summary judgment on the ground of res judicata.

ISSUE: If a claim has previously been decided on its merits, will the doctrine of res judicata bar a subsequent suit brought on the same claim and involving the same parties or those in privity with them?

HOLDING AND DECISION: (MacMahon, J.) Yes. The doctrine of res judicata operates as a bar to subsequent suits involving the same parties, or those in privity with them, based on a claim which has once reached a judgment on its merits. The parties in this action are in privity with those in the earlier suit. This is true since a corporation acts only through its agents, and if the agents are not at fault, there is no basis for corporate liability. The Association (D) owned the race track and employed Thoroughbred (D) to act as its agent. The defendants in the first suit were employees of Thoroughbred (D). Therefore, the present corporate defendants are so identified in interest with their agents (the individual defendants in the earlier action) that they stand or fall with them. In addition, we have here the classic res judicata situation wherein the second claim between the parties is based on the same operative facts as the earlier one. The same facts are the basis of liability in each suit; the witnesses are the same, and the evidence is the same regardless of whether Mathews (P) is using it to prove the theory of libel or the theory of malicious prosecution. A plaintiff cannot splinter his claim into a multiplicity of suits and try them piecemeal at his convenience. Having alleged operative facts which state a cause of action, the plaintiff doesn't get yet another day in court by giving different reasons for the same invasion of rights than he gave in the first suit. Mathews (P) has had his day in court. The doctrine of res judicata must now take effect, putting an end to this litigation. The defendant's motion is granted.

▌ ANALYSIS

A judgment against an agent or employee may bind his principal or employer under the doctrine of respondeat superior; and a master or principal charged with liability under that doctrine may also avail himself of a judgment on the merits in favor to an agent or servant against the injured person in an action to which the principal or master was not a party. The judgment determines that the servant or agent was not culpable, and therefore his master or principal cannot be liable. And this is true whether the actions are separate or whether the employer and employee are joined. Substantial identity of the parties is all that is required. It is sufficient if the parties in the present action (in which the former judgment is being offered) were on opposite sides in the former case.

Quicknotes

PRIVITY Commonality of rights or interests between parties.

PRO SE An individual appearing on his own behalf.

RES JUDICATA The rule of law a final judgment by a court precludes subsequent litigation between the parties regarding the same cause of action.

SUMMARY JUDGMENT Judgment rendered by a court in response to a motion by one of the parties, claiming that the lack of a question of material fact in respect to an issue warrants disposition of the issue without consideration by the jury.

Jones v. Morris Plan Bank of Portsmouth

Car owner (P) v. Lender (D)

Va. Sup. Ct. App., 168 Va. 284, 191 S.E. 608 (1937).

NATURE OF CASE: Action to recover damages for conversion of automobile.

FACT SUMMARY: When Jones (P) failed for two months to meet installment payments under a conditional sales contract, the Morris Plan Bank of Portsmouth (D) obtained a judgment against him for the two payments, and later took possession of the automobile to satisfy a subsequent unpaid installment.

🏛 RULE OF LAW

If a transaction is represented by a single and indivisible contract and the breach gives rise to a single cause of action, it cannot be split into distinct parts and separate actions.

FACTS: Jones (P) purchased an automobile from Parker, a dealer. Jones (P) agreed to pay off the balance in twelve installment payments. This was evidenced by a note that contained an acceleration clause (in the event that any installment is not paid, the whole amount of the note becomes immediately due). Through a usual conditional sales contract, it was agreed that title to the car remained with the dealer until the entire purchase price was paid in full. Jones (P) failed to make payments for May and June when payable and the Morris Plan Bank of Portsmouth (Bank) (D) obtained judgment against him for the two payments. The judgment was satisfied by Jones (P). Later, when Jones (P) failed to meet the July installment payment, the Bank (D) instituted another court action, Jones (P) filed a plea of res judicata, and the Bank (D) took a nonsuit. The Bank (D) then took possession of the automobile without Jones's (P) consent, sold it, and applied the proceeds upon the note. Jones (P) sued the Bank (D) for conversion on the theory that the Bank (D), in obtaining a judgment for the May and June installments, had waived its right under the acceleration clause to sue for the balance. In addition, Jones (P) maintained that under the conditional sales contract, the sole purpose of which was to secure payment of the note, title to the automobile had passed to him. The Bank (D) countered by arguing that it was not bound, at the risk of waiving its right to claim the balance, to sue for all installments in one action.

ISSUE: If a transaction is represented by a single and indivisible contract and the breach gives rise to a single cause of action, can it be split into distinct parts and separate actions?

HOLDING AND DECISION: (Gregory, J.) No. If a transaction is represented by a single and indivisible contract and the breach gives rise to a single cause of

action, it cannot be split into distinct parts and separate actions. Here, it was essential that the Bank (D) institute an action for all of the installments due rather than institute its action for only two of the installments and later bring another action for others. The note and conditional sales contract constituted one single contract. The sole purpose of the conditional sales contract was to retain the title in the seller until the note was paid. When that condition was performed, the contract ended. One test to determine whether a demand is single or entire is to see if the same evidence will support both actions; if so, there is but one cause of action. Since all of the installments were due at the time of Jones's (P) default, the evidence needed to support the action on the two installments was the identical evidence necessary to maintain an action upon all of the installments. At the time the Bank (D) lost its right to bring any action for the remaining installments, title to the automobile passed to Jones (P). Reversed and remanded.

▶ ANALYSIS

According to the Restatement of Judgments § 62, Comment i (1942), if several interest coupons make up a bond, or if a series of notes secure a debt, an action on a single note or coupon will not bar later actions on other notes or coupons that are due. See *Nesbit v. Riverside Ind. District*, 144 U.S. 610 (1892).

■▬■

Quicknotes

CONDITIONAL SALES CONTRACT An agreement pursuant to which title to goods or land does not pass from seller to buyer until payment is tendered.

NONSUIT Judgment against a party who fails to make out a case.

RES JUDICATA The rule of law a final judgment by a court precludes subsequent litigation between the parties regarding the same cause of action.

■▬■

Mitchell v. Federal Intermediate Credit Bank

Debtor (P) v. Lender (D)

S.C. Sup. Ct., 165 S.C. 457, 164 S.E. 136 (1932).

NATURE OF CASE: Action for an accounting for proceeds of a crop.

FACT SUMMARY: Mitchell (P) pleaded the same facts, now the basis of an affirmative claim, in an earlier action where he appeared as a defendant although, at the time, he did not counterclaim or ask for relief.

RULE OF LAW
A defendant may not split his cause of action against a plaintiff using part of it as a defense to the first action and saving the remainder for a separate affirmative suit.

FACTS: In federal court, the Federal Intermediate Credit Bank (Bank) (D) had brought an action to recover on notes of Mitchell (P). Mitchell (P) defended by pleading that in order to obtain loans from the Bank (D) he had—at the behest of a bank agent—sold his crops through a grower's association and assigned his proceeds as security for the notes. This had been discounted with the Bank (D), but Mitchell (P) had never received any of it, the proceeds being received by the Bank (D). Mitchell (P), apart from his defense, did not counterclaim or ask for any relief. Judgment was for Mitchell (P) in that action. Later, Mitchell (P) sued for an accounting for the sum of the proceeds kept by the Bank (D), which was in excess of the notes. He did not seek to recover that part of the proceeds that satisfied his indebtedness on the notes, although he pled the same set of facts he raised as a defense in the earlier suit. The trial court ruled that Mitchell's (P) action was barred on the theory that his affirmative claim was merged in the earlier judgment.

ISSUE: May a defendant split his cause of action against a plaintiff using part of it as a defense to the first action and saving the remainder for a separate affirmative suit?

HOLDING AND DECISION: (Stabler, J.) No. A defendant may not split his cause of action against a plaintiff using part of it as a defense to the first action and saving the remainder for a separate affirmative suit. A party against whom an action is brought on a contract may allege specific breaches of the contract declared upon, and rely on them in defense. In the alternative, if he intends to claim, by way of damages for nonperformance of the contract, more than the amount for which he is sued, he must not rely on the contract in defense, but rather must bring a cross-action. He cannot use the same defense, first as a shield, and then as a sword. Since the transaction out of which Mitchell's (P) suit arises is the same transaction that

Mitchell (P) pleaded as a defense in the federal suit, he had the opportunity to have recovered in the federal action, upon the same allegations and proofs which he there made, the judgment which he now seeks. Thus Mitchell's (P) action against the Bank (D) is barred because he had the opportunity to counterclaim or ask for relief while defending the first suit, when both the defense and Mitchell's (P) action arose out of the same transaction. Affirmed.

ANALYSIS

Some state codes and the federal rules require that a defendant assert his counterclaim when it arises out of the same transaction involved in the plaintiff's case. Under Fed. R. Civ. P. 13(b), a counterclaim that does not arise out of the same occurrence is termed a permissive counterclaim and allows the defendant to choose, at his whim, whether or not to assert it. Nevertheless, the decision in this case still does not permit the defendant to divide his cause of action, using part as a defense in one action, and another part as a "sword" in a later one.

Quicknotes

COUNTERCLAIM An independent cause of action brought by a defendant to a lawsuit in order to oppose or deduct from the plaintiff's claim.

CROSS-ACTION A claim asserted by a defendant to an action against a plaintiff or co-defendant, arising out of the same transaction or occurrence as the subject matter of the original action.

Cromwell v. County of Sac

Bondholder (P) v. Bond issuer (D)

94 U.S. (4 Otto) 351 (1876).

NATURE OF CASE: Action to recover proceeds on four bonds.

FACT SUMMARY: Cromwell (P) attempted to demand payment on bonds issued by County of Sac (D) even though the issuance of the bonds had been declared fraudulent in a prior action.

🏛 RULE OF LAW
A judgment estops further action not only as to every ground of recovery or defense actually presented in an action, but also as to every ground that might have been presented when the subsequent action involves the same demand or claim in controversy, but where that subsequent action between the same parties is instituted upon a different claim or demand, the prior judgment operates as an estoppel only as to matters actually controverted, the determination of which were essential to the final verdict.

FACTS: County of Sac (County) (D) issued bonds in 1860 to a contractor for the erection of a court house. They were to be redeemed in 1868, 1869, 1870, and 1871. The court house was never built, however. Cromwell (P) then sued to force County (D) to redeem them. At trial, the trial court held that the bonds would only be redeemable if (1) Cromwell (P) had owned the bonds before the maturity date, and (2) he had actually given value to acquire them (since there was evidence of fraud in the original issuance). Cromwell (P) was estopped from proving the latter, however, because the court held that Cromwell's (P) participation in a previous attempt to redeem bonds, through a third party named Smith, which resulted in litigation. From judgment for County (D), Cromwell (P) appealed, contending that he was improperly estopped from proving his case because the claim in this case was essentially different from that in the Smith case.

ISSUE: Does the doctrine of collateral estoppel necessarily imply that a judgment between a set of parties on related issues precludes litigation of all other related issues between these parties?

HOLDING AND DECISION: (Field, J.) No. A judgment estops further action not only as to every ground of recovery or defense actually presented in an action but also as to every ground which might have been presented when the action involves the same demand or claim in controversy, but where that subsequent action between the same parties is instituted upon a different claim or demand, the prior judgment operates as an estoppel only

as to matters actually controverted, the determination of which were essential to the final verdict. There is a difference between the effect of a judgment as a bar or estoppel against the prosecution of a second action upon the same claim and its effect as an estoppel in another action between the same parties upon a different claim. In the former, final judgment for one party is the final determination of the rights involved. In the latter, only if an issue is actually raised, determined, and an essential part of the court's holding is the judgment final. Here, the determination of the Smith case that Smith was not a bona fide holder (i.e., had not given value for the bonds) and not entitled to redemption thereby, is not binding upon a separate claim made by Cromwell (P), even though he was found to be the beneficiary and real party in interest in the Smith case. Cromwell (P) is entitled to a separate determination of his rights in this different set of bonds. He should have been allowed to prove that he gave value for these bonds (i.e., as a new claim). Judgment reversed and case remanded.

▶ ANALYSIS

This case points up the general definition of collateral estoppel (and is cited for such). Essentially, where res judicata (merger, bar) is precluded because a case involves a new claim (cause of action), the first judgment will still operate as an estoppel to all matters (1) actually litigated in the prior action and (2) essential to its determination. Basically, collateral estoppel is parallel to the theory of res judicata. As res judicata is asserted to prevent double determinations of the same cause of action, collateral estoppel operates to prevent double determinations (must be essential to the holding) of the same issue. Note, however, that there is a split of authority as to whether default judgments and stipulated judgments operate as collateral estoppel.

▰▭▰

Quicknotes

COLLATERAL Secondary to the principal.

ESTOPPEL An equitable doctrine precluding a party from asserting a right to the detriment of another, who justifiably relied on the conduct.

▰▭▰

Russell v. Place

Patent holder (P) v. Alleged infringer (D)

94 U.S. (4 Otto) 606 (1876).

NATURE OF CASE: Action for patent infringement.

FACT SUMMARY: Russell (P) sued for damages for use of an invention of Russell's (P) by Place (D).

🏛 RULE OF LAW

It is well settled that a judgment of a court of competent jurisdiction upon a question directly involved in one suit is conclusive as to that question in another suit between the same parties, where it can be established that the precise question was raised and determined in the prior suit.

FACTS: Russell (P) sued Place (D) for patent infringement for the use of a patented process (by Russell [P]) for the treatment of leather with fat liquor. In his complaint, Russell (P) described his initial patent, its surrender for insufficient description of the invention, its reissue with amended specification, and a prior judgment against Place (D) for patent infringement. Place (D) set up as a defense "lack of novelty" of the leather treatment process. Russell (P) claimed that Place (D) was estopped from asserting this, however, by the prior judgment. From a judgment for Place (D), Russell (P) appealed.

ISSUE: Is a judgment in one suit between two parties controlling as to all questions arising in another suit between the same parties?

HOLDING AND DECISION: (Field, J.) No. It is well settled that a judgment of a court of competent jurisdiction upon a question directly involved in one suit is conclusive as to that question in another suit between the same parties, only where it can be established that the precise question was raised and determined in the prior suit. Further, these facts must either appear on the record or be shown by extrinsic evidence. If there is only uncertainty in the record as to whether the question was in fact determined or whether it was part of the court's holding, the question can freely be raised again in a subsequent suit (unless the uncertainty can be removed by extrinsic evidence). Here, there is no evidence that the question of novelty was ever raised in the first suit. Place (D) was correctly not estopped from asserting it, therefore. Affirmed.

▶ ANALYSIS

This case points up an essential corollary to the collateral estoppel rule. The question estopped must have been actually litigated and essential to the judgment (i.e., part of the holding or rationale supporting it), and this must be provable from the record or extrinsic evidence for the principle of collateral estoppel to apply. An "essential" question is one the determination of which played a necessary role in the outcome (holding, judgment) of the case. Note that the burden of proof is on the party seeking estoppel to prove that a question qualifies both as "actually litigated" and as an "essential question." This causes problems where general verdicts are involved to which many different determinations could have contributed.

■■■

Quicknotes

ESTOPPEL An equitable doctrine precluding a party from asserting a right to the detriment of another, who justifiably relied on the conduct.

INFRINGEMENT Conduct in violation of statute or that interferes with another's rights pursuant to law.

■■■

Rios v. Davis

Car accident victim (P) v. Other driver (D)

Tex. Civ. App., 373 S.W.2d 386 (1963).

NATURE OF CASE: Action to recover damages for personal injuries sustained in automobile collision.

FACT SUMMARY: The trial court, in an action where Davis (D) raised as a defense contributory negligence on the part of Rios (P), entered judgment in favor of Davis (D) on the grounds of res judicata because, in an earlier trial, the jury found Rios (P) to be negligent in the matter, although the first court's judgment only denied Davis (D) any recovery against Rios (P).

> ## 🏛 RULE OF LAW
> It is the judgment, and not the jury verdict or conclusions of fact, filed by a trial court which constitutes the collateral estoppel; and a finding of fact by a jury or a court which does not become the basis or one of the grounds of the judgment rendered is not conclusive against either party to the suit.

FACTS: In the first action, a third party (Popular Dry Goods Company), involved in a traffic collision, sued Davis (D). Davis (D) alleged contributory negligence on the third party's part, and joined Rios (P), who was also involved in the accident, as a defendant. Davis (D) sought to recover from Rios (P) the amount of damage to his automobile. The jury found the third party, Rios (P), and Davis (D) guilty of negligence proximately causing the collision. However, the judgment entered by the court denied the third party any recovery against Davis (D), and denied Davis (D) any recovery against Rios (P). Rios (P) then sued Davis (D) for negligence involved in the same accident. Davis (D) defended by claiming that Rios (P) was guilty of contributory negligence, and that the jury's findings in the first action were res judicata as to the second. On the latter basis, judgment was entered in favor of Davis (D).

ISSUE: Does the jury's findings in the first action operate as res judicata to the second even though the court's judgment in the first action ignored the findings?

HOLDING AND DECISION: (Collings, J.) No. The jury's findings in the first action were immaterial because the judgment entered in that case was in favor of Rios (P). The finding that Rios (P) was negligent was not essential or material to the judgment and the judgment was not based thereon. On the contrary, the finding that Rios (P) was negligent would, if it had been controlling, have led to a different result. Since the judgment was in favor of Rios (P), he had no right or opportunity to complain of or to appeal from the finding that he was guilty of such negligence, even if such finding had been without any support whatever in the evidence—the right of appeal is from a judgment and not a finding. Reversed and remanded.

▶ ANALYSIS

Where co-parties become adversaries in a subsequent suit, a judgment will not collaterally estop one party unless there is a claim for relief by one against the other. In the absence of an actual claim, it is immaterial their interests conflict and they come out on opposite sides of each issue.

Quicknotes

COLLATERAL ESTOPPEL A doctrine whereby issues litigated and determined in a prior proceeding are binding upon all subsequent litigation between the parties regarding that issue.

RES JUDICATA The rule of law a final judgment by a court precludes subsequent litigation between the parties regarding the same cause of action.

Commissioner of Internal Revenue v. Sunnen

I.R.S. (D) v. Taxpayer (P)

333 U.S. 591 (1948).

NATURE OF CASE: Action in tax court challenging deficiency assessment made by the Internal Revenue Service.

FACT SUMMARY: Taxpayer (P), having won a favorable determination in a prior year, sought to invoke the decision as res judicata to bar later challenges for other years where there was a complete identity of facts, issues, and parties.

🏛 RULE OF LAW
Where two cases involve taxes in different taxable years, collateral estoppel will be confined to situations where the matter raised in the second suit is identical in all respects with that decided in the first proceeding and where the controlling facts and applicable legal rules remain unchanged.

FACTS: In 1928, Sunnen (P) had licensed his corporation to use his patents in exchange for a royalty. In various years following, Sunnen (P) assigned his interest in these agreements to his wife who reported this income on her income tax returns. In 1935, Sunnen (P) prevailed in a tax court proceeding brought by the Commissioner of Internal Revenue (the Commissioner) (D), who had contended that the income was taxable to Sunnen (P) himself. Later, the exact same action was brought by the Commissioner (D) against Sunnen (P) on the same issue, except this time for royalties paid in 1937.

ISSUE: Where two cases involve taxes in different taxable years, will collateral estoppel be confined to situations where the matter raised in the second suit is identical in all respects with that decided in the first proceeding and where the controlling facts and applicable legal rules remain unchanged?

HOLDING AND DECISION: (Murphy, J.) Yes. Where two cases involve taxes in different taxable years, collateral estoppel will be confined to situations where the matter raised in the second suit is identical in all respects with that decided in the first proceeding and where the controlling facts and applicable legal rules remain unchanged. Collateral estoppel does apply in the income tax field but only insofar as it extends to any subsequent proceeding involving the same claim and the same tax year. Where a taxpayer secures a judicial determination of a particular tax matter which may recur without substantial variation for some years thereafter, a subsequent modification of the significant facts on a change or development in the controlling legal principles may make that determination obsolete, or erroneous, at least for future years.

Permitting a taxpayer to invoke his decision in a single year for a number of years is unfair to other taxpayers causing inequalities in the administration of taxes, discriminatory distinctions in tax liability, and a fertile basis for litigious confusion. Tax inequality can result as readily from neglecting legal modulations by the Supreme Court as from disregarding factual changes wrought by state courts. This reasoning is particularly apposite here since, if Sunnen (P) had not had the benefit of the earlier decision, his claim, in view of recent legal developments in the tax field, would have failed if brought now for the first time. Reversed.

▶ *ANALYSIS*

The Court's opinion here may be difficult to reconcile with its earlier decision in *Tait v. Western Maryland Ry.*, 289 U.S. 620, 624 (1933), where it was said: "The scheme of the Revenue Acts is an imposition of tax for annual periods, and the exaction for one year is distinct from that for any other. But it does not follow that Congress in adopting this system meant to deprive the government and the taxpayer of relief from redundant litigation of the identical question of the statute's application to the taxpayer's status. . . . Alteration of the law in this respect is a matter for the lawmaking body rather than the courts. . . . It cannot be supposed that Congress was oblivious of the scope of the doctrine (of res judicata), and in the absence of a clear declaration of such purpose, we will not infer from the annual nature of the exaction an intention to abolish the rule in this class of cases."

━━

Quicknotes

COLLATERAL ESTOPPEL A doctrine whereby issues litigated and determined in a prior proceeding are binding upon all subsequent litigation between the parties regarding that issue.

RES JUDICATA The rule of law a final judgment by a court precludes subsequent litigation between the parties regarding the same cause of action.

━━

Hanover Logansport, Inc. v. Robert C. Anderson, Inc.

Breaching lessor (D) v. Lessee (P)

Ind. Ct. App., 512 N.E.2d 465 (1987).

NATURE OF CASE: Appeal from denial of motion to dismiss consent decree for specific performance in action for breach of contract.

FACT SUMMARY: Robert C. Anderson, Inc. (P), in agreeing to a consent decree, unilaterally sought to reserve a cause of action for further litigation.

🏛 RULE OF LAW
A party who agrees to a consent decree may not unilaterally reserve a cause of action for further litigation.

FACTS: Robert C. Anderson, Inc. (Anderson) (P) leased premises from Hanover Logansport, Inc. (Hanover) (D). On the date occupancy was to begin, Hanover (D) did not surrender the premises. Anderson (P) sued for breach, seeking either lost profits or, in the alternative, specific performance. Hanover (D) later agreed to surrender the premises, and a consent decree of specific performance was agreed upon. In its agreement, Anderson (P) sought to reserve for litigation a cause of action for retrospective damages. Hanover (D) moved to dismiss, contending that the decree barred further litigation. The trial court denied the motion, and Hanover (D) appealed.

ISSUE: May a party who agrees to a consent decree unilaterally reserve a cause of action for further litigation?

HOLDING AND DECISION: (Staton, J.) No. A party who agrees to a consent decree may not unilaterally reserve a cause of action for further litigation. Consent decrees have both contract-like and judgment-like aspects. Some courts, in evaluating the preclusive effect of consent decrees, emphasize the contractual aspects and tend to look at the parties' intent. Other courts emphasize the judgment-like aspects and simply follow the generally applicable rules of res judicata and collateral estoppel. As the main purpose behind consent decrees is to encourage settlements, the contract approach is preferable. As a general rule, parties enter into consent decrees to end the litigation. While a party may reserve a cause of action, it must be clear from the decree that both parties accept this. Here, Hanover (D) did not assent to Anderson's (P) attempted reservation and, therefore, the attempted reservation was unassertable. Reversed and remanded.

▶ ANALYSIS

Most courts agree that consent decrees have res judicata effects. Collateral estoppel is much less accepted in this context. An element of collateral estoppel is actual litigation of an issue, and it is not at all clear that a consent decree actually embodies "litigation" of an issue.

■═■

Quicknotes

BREACH OF CONTRACT Unlawful failure by a party to perform its obligations pursuant to contract.

CONSENT DECREE A decree issued by a court of equity ratifying an agreement between the parties to a lawsuit; an agreement by a defendant to cease illegal activity.

■═■

Holmberg v. State, Division of Risk Management

Disabled employee (P) v. Employer (D)

Alaska Sup. Ct., 796 P.2d 823 (1990).

NATURE OF CASE: Appeal from denial of disability benefits in a workers' compensation action.

FACT SUMMARY: Holmberg (P) was denied permanent disability by the Alaska Workers' Compensation Board (D), but was later granted benefits by the Public Employees Retirement Board.

🏛 RULE OF LAW
Litigation conducted before one agency or official is generally binding on another agency or official of the same government because officers of the same government are in privity with each other.

FACTS: In February 1988, the Alaska Workers' Compensation Board (AWCB) (D) denied Holmberg (P) total disability for her back problems. Holmberg (P) appealed this decision. In April 1988, after the AWCB (D) decision, the Public Employees Retirement Board (PERB) awarded Holmberg (P) total disability as a result of accidents at work. PERB administered the Public Employees Retirement System (PERS), an independent retirement plan. Holmberg (P) supplemented her AWCB (D) appeal with the PERB decision and claimed that the PERB decision had a preclusive effect on AWCB (D). The superior court ruled for AWCB (D), and Holmberg (P) appealed.

ISSUE: Is litigation conducted before one agency or official binding on another agency or official of the same government because officers of the same government are in privity with each other?

HOLDING AND DECISION: (Moore, J.) Yes. Litigation conducted before one agency or official is generally binding on another agency or official of the same government because officers of the same government are in privity with each other. Here, however, preclusion may be defeated because there is an important difference in the function of the agencies and they are not in privity with one another. Privity does not exist because there is a difference in the authority of the respective agencies. PERS, the party against whom PERB ruled, is not a state agency, but an independent retirement plan, and therefore the interests of the state are not adequately defended when PERS is defending against a claim. AWCB (D) is a state agency and is therefore not in privity with PERS. Additionally, a final judgment retains all of its res judicata effects pending resolution on appeal. AWCB (D) made its decision first and, though it is on appeal, the later PERB determination that Holmberg (P) could not perform her duties cannot preclude AWCB's (D) earlier contrary determination. Affirmed.

▶ ANALYSIS

With respect to preclusion issues, the rights of the parties precluded must be given great attention. A judgment warranting preclusion must be valid, final, and on the merits. Oftentimes, the relationship of the parties will be one of the most important factors in assessing preclusion.

Quicknotes

PRIVITY Commonality of rights or interests between parties.

Bernhard v. Bank of America Nat. Trust & Savings Assn.

Estate administrator (P) v. Bank (D)

Cal. Sup. Ct., 19 Cal. 2d 807, 122 P.2d 892 (1942).

NATURE OF CASE: Appeal from defense verdict in action by administrator of estate to recover bank deposits allegedly misappropriated.

FACT SUMMARY: The Administrator (P) of Bernhard's estate had lost in an earlier probate action to recover funds drawn from bank account by a friend of Bernhard, and, failing to prevail against the friend, later sued the Bank (D), who sought to invoke collateral estoppel to prove, as a defense, that the withdrawals were undertaken with Bernhard's permission.

🏛 RULE OF LAW
In California and a minority of jurisdictions, a judgment in the first action may be asserted as a defense in a later action by one who was neither a privy with a party nor a party in the first suit, so long as the party against whom the judgment is raised was a party or privy with a party in the first suit.

FACTS: Before she died, Sather authorized Cook and Zeiler to draw upon her account so as to provide for her upkeep. Checks drawn were deposited by Cook and Zeiler in an account in Sather's name in the First National Bank of San Dimas. Cook later withdrew all of the balance from the Sather account and deposited it in a new account in his name in the San Dimas Bank. When Sather died, Cook became executor of the estate, and at the instance of the probate court filed an accounting, which made no mention of the money transferred by Sather to the San Dimas Bank. A probate hearing instigated by Bernhard (P), a beneficiary under Sather's will, was brought, but the probate court declared that Sather had made a gift to Cook of the account in the San Dimas Bank. Bernhard (P), who became administratrix of Sather's estate, then brought an action against the Bank of America (D), successor to the San Dimas Bank, seeking to recover the deposit on the ground the bank was indebted to the estate because Sather had never authorized the withdrawal of the account. The Bank (D) pleaded as a defense that this fact was res judicata by virtue of the finding of the probate court. The trial court found in favor of the Bank (D), and Bernhard (P) appealed.

ISSUE: In a minority of jurisdictions, may a judgment in a first action be asserted as a defense to a later action by one who was neither a privy with a party nor a party in the first suit, so long as the party against whom the judgment is raised was a party or a privy with a party in the first suit?

HOLDING AND DECISION: (Traynor, J.) Yes. Because of the mutuality requirement—one taking advantage of an earlier adjudication would have been bound by it, had it gone against him—most courts have held that only parties to the former judgment or their privies may take advantage of it. There is no compelling reason, however, for this. Many courts, and almost all commentators, have favored abandoning the "mutuality" requirement. Already, most courts have carved out an exception that the liability of the defendant asserting the plea of res judicata is dependent upon or derived from the liability of one who was exonerated in an earlier suit brought by the same plaintiff upon the same facts. This is based on the theory that it is unjust for one who has already had his day in court to reopen his case by merely switching adversaries. In determining the validity of a plea of res judicata, three questions are pertinent: (1) Was the issue decided in the prior adjudication identical with the one presented in the action in question? (Yes, here, the ownership of the money.); (2) Was there a final judgment on the merits? (Yes, the order of the probate court settling the executor's accounting.); (3) Was the party against whom the plea is asserted a party or in privity with a party to the prior adjudication? (Yes. Bernhard [P] represented all the legatees.) Thus, the Bank (D) may raise the earlier judgment as a "shield" in the second action brought by Bernhard (P), even though it was neither a party nor a privy with a party to the probate hearing. Affirmed.

▶ ANALYSIS

The broad scope of the *Bernhard* doctrine is not without its share of detractors. One major criticism has surfaced: The rule would work strange results in situations where multiple claims arise out of the same disaster. For instance, in airplane crashes, a judgment obtained by one passenger, or his estate, is conclusive against the airline even though all other previous actions were in favor of the airline. Following the adverse judgment, the *Bernhard* rule would hold the airline bound.

■═■

Quicknotes

PRIVY One who, after rendition of a judgment, has acquired an interest in the subject matter affected by the judgment through or under one of the parties.

■═■

Parklane Hosiery Co. v. Shore

Corporation (D) v. Stockholder (P)

439 U.S. 322 (1979).

NATURE OF CASE: Stockholders' derivative action for damages and rescission of merger.

FACT SUMMARY: In a prior Securities Exchange Commission suit, Parklane Hosiery Co. (Parklane) (D) was found to have issued a materially false and misleading proxy statement, and Shore (P) argued collateral estoppel precluded Parklane (D) from relitigating that issue in his stockholders' class action suit.

🏛 RULE OF LAW

A litigant who was not a party to a prior judgment is not per se precluded from using that judgment "offensively" to prevent a defendant from relitigating issues resolved in that earlier equitable proceeding.

FACTS: In an action brought by the Securities Exchange Commission (SEC), without any jury, Parklane Hosiery Co. (Parklane) (D) was found to have issued a materially false and misleading proxy statement. When Shore (P) and other shareholders later brought a class action suit for damages, rescission of a merger, and recovery of costs, it argued that collateral estoppel precluded Parklane (D) from relitigating the proxy statement issue. The district court held that imposition of collateral estoppel would deny Parklane (D) its constitutional right under the Seventh Amendment to a jury trial. The court of appeals reversed, holding collateral estoppel did apply. Parklane (D) appealed.

ISSUE: Can collateral estoppel be used "offensively" by a litigant who was not a party to a prior equitable proceeding to prevent a defendant from relitigating issues resolved therein?

HOLDING AND DECISION: (Stewart, J.) Yes. One who was not a party to a prior equitable proceeding is not per se precluded from using that judgment "offensively" to prevent a defendant from relitigating issues resolved therein. Although such "offensive" collateral estoppel does not promote judicial economy or operate as fairly as defensive collateral estoppel does in general, it should be left to the trial court's discretion to determine when it should be applied. It should not be allowed in cases where a plaintiff could easily have joined in the earlier action or where its application would be unfair to the defendant. Neither applies here. Shore (P) could not have intervened in the SEC suit and Parklane (D) had every reason to vigorously and thoroughly contest the SEC suit with anticipation that stockholder action on the same grounds might follow. Thus, collateral estoppel was properly allowed in this case. There was no violation of the

Seventh Amendment's guarantee of the right to a jury trial, for a litigant who has lost in an equity action is equally deprived of a jury trial whether he is estopped from relitigating the factual issues against the same party, as is always the case, or a new party. Affirmed.

DISSENT: (Rehnquist, J.) The development of non-mutual estoppel is a substantial departure from common law and its use in this case completely deprives Parklane (D) of its right to have a jury determine contested issues of fact. Even in the absence of the Seventh Amendment, there is a strong federal policy favoring jury trials and the strong possibility that a jury trial could lead to a different result from that obtained in the first action before the Court. This renders it unfair to estop Parklane (D) from relitigating the issues before a jury.

▶ ANALYSIS

Although it is now defunct, the mutuality rule with regard to collateral estoppel existed when the Seventh Amendment guaranteeing jury trial was adopted in 1791. It essentially provided one party to an action could invoke collateral estoppel only if he would himself be bound by the prior judgment he was attempting to impose on the other party.

■══■

Quicknotes

COLLATERAL ESTOPPEL A doctrine whereby issues litigated and determined in a prior proceeding are binding upon all subsequent litigation between the parties regarding that issue.

■══■

Martin v. Wilks

Municipality (D) v. White firefighters (P)

490 U.S. 755 (1989).

NATURE OF CASE: Review of order reinstating reverse discrimination action.

FACT SUMMARY: In a reverse discrimination action, it was contended that an earlier consent decree mandating certain affirmative action procedures barred a subsequent reverse discrimination action by parties not involved in the prior action.

RULE OF LAW

A consent decree mandating affirmative action does not have preclusive effect upon a subsequent challenge to those programs brought by persons not parties to the prior action.

FACTS: Several black firefighters brought a discrimination action against the City of Birmingham, Alabama (D). The suit was settled by way of a consent decree wherein certain affirmative action programs were mandated. Subsequently, several white firefighters (P) brought suit, contending that the affirmative action programs constituted reverse discrimination in violation of federal civil rights laws. The district court dismissed, holding that the prior judgment had preclusive effect as to the validity of the programs. The court of appeals reversed. The United States Supreme Court granted review.

ISSUE: Does a consent decree mandating affirmative action have preclusive effect upon a subsequent challenge to those programs brought by persons not parties to the prior action?

HOLDING AND DECISION: (Rehnquist, C.J.) No. A consent decree mandating affirmative action does not have preclusive effect upon a subsequent challenge to those programs brought by persons not parties to the prior action. It is a principle of general application in Anglo-American jurisprudence that one is not bound by a judgment in personam in which he was not a party. This rule is part of our deep-seated tradition that everyone should have his own day in court. However, the argument is made here that because the plaintiffs in this action had notice of the prior action and could have intervened, they cannot now complain of the prior judgment. This is incorrect. Fed. R. Civ. P. 24, which deals with intervention, is cast in permissive, not compulsory, terms. Rule 19, dealing with joinder, can be compulsory. Where Rule 19 is not invoked to join a nonconsenting party, as was not done here, a judgment cannot bind the nonparty. Affirmed.

DISSENT: (Stevens, J.) The Court has crafted a rule which, in essence, allows nonparties to appeal a final judgment an indeterminate time after it is entered.

ANALYSIS

This decision, and several others handed down the same year, provoked a reaction in the civil rights community. Congress eventually passed the Civil Rights Restoration Act, which was vetoed in 1990 but signed in 1991. The rule of this case was legislatively overruled.

Quicknotes

COLLATERAL ATTACK A proceeding initiated in order to challenge the integrity of a previous judgment.

Taylor v. Sturgell

Private citizen (P) v. Federal government (D)

553 U.S. 880 (2008).

NATURE OF CASE: Grant of certiorari.

FACT SUMMARY: [The Federal Aviation Administration's status as defendant was not expressly indicated in the casebook excerpt, but can be inferred. First names of other parties have been omitted by casebook excerpt.] After a federal appeals court determined that Taylor (P) could not pursue a suit in federal court because he had been "virtually represented" by an associate in a previous suit, Taylor (P) sought relief in the Supreme Court.

🏛 RULE OF LAW
The dismissal of a claim does not preclude a second individual, based on the concept of "virtual representation," from bringing a similar claim when both claims involve the same project and the parties to each suit are represented by the same attorney.

FACTS: [The Federal Aviation Administration's (FAA) status as defendant was not expressly indicated in the casebook excerpt, but can be inferred. First names of other parties have been omitted by casebook excerpt.] Herrick filed a Freedom of Information Act (FOIA) request seeking the plans and specifications for a rare aircraft from the Federal Aviation Administration (D). The FAA (D) refused to turn over the plans as "protected trade secrets," and Herrick filed suit against the FAA (D) to recover the plans. The district court found for the FAA (D), and the U.S. Court of Appeals for the Tenth Circuit affirmed. A month later, Taylor (P), represented by Herrick's attorney, filed another FOIA request seeking the plans. When the request was again denied, Taylor (P) filed suit in federal court in the District of Columbia. The district court determined that Taylor (P) had been "virtually represented" by Herrick in the first suit and therefore could not pursue the second suit in federal court. The U.S. Court of Appeals for the D.C. Circuit affirmed. Taylor (P) sought relief in the United States Supreme Court, arguing that the D.C. Circuit's finding that Taylor (P) and Herrick enjoyed a close enough relationship for virtual representation to apply conflicted with tests employed by several other circuits.

ISSUE: Does the dismissal of a claim preclude a second individual, based on the concept of "virtual representation," from bringing a similar claim when both claims involve the same project and the parties to each suit are represented by the same attorney?

HOLDING AND DECISION: (Ginsburg, J.) No. The dismissal of a claim does not preclude a second individual, based on the concept of "virtual representation," from bringing a similar claim when both claims involve the same project and the parties to each suit are represented by the

same attorney. "Nonparty preclusion" must be balanced against the historic tradition that everyone should have her own day in court. The general rule is against non-party preclusion, but the general rule has some exceptions that fall into six categories. First, a person who agrees to be bound by a judgment will be bound according to the terms of the agreement. Second, pre-existing substantive legal relationships between a non-party and party can bind a non-party to a judgment. Third, a non-party may be precluded from bringing his own claim, if he was adequately represented by someone with the same interests, and who was a party to a previous suit. Fourth, a non-party who assumes control over a case may be bound by the judgment in that case. Fifth, a party may not re-litigate an issue by using a proxy, such as an undisclosed agent. Sixth, special statutory schemes may prohibit repetitive litigation by non-parties if the scheme is consistent with due process. In this case, only the fifth category could apply. Thus, the case has to be remanded to determine whether Taylor (P) was Herrick's "undisclosed agent." If the courts below find that Taylor (P) is Herrick's agent, then nonparty claim preclusion will apply. Virtual representation should be applied rarely and under delineated exceptions to the general rule. The D.C. Circuit's decision is vacated and the case remanded.

▌ANALYSIS

By definition, the doctrine of virtual representation deprives litigants of their right to a day in court by binding them to judgments in cases in which they were not parties and in which they did not have the opportunity to defend their own interests. This decision sets forth the unanimous disapproval by the United States Supreme Court of the doctrine of virtual representation, and more clearly defines its previous decisions on non-party claim preclusion. As the Court indicated, virtual representation is in direct conflict with the "day-in-court" ideal, and because of this tension, virtual representation has always been the subject of controversy in lower courts.

Quicknotes

CERTIORARI A discretionary writ issued by a superior court to an inferior court in order to review the lower court's decisions; the Supreme Court's writ ordering such review.

Hart v. American Airlines, Inc.

Decedents' representatives (P) v. Airline (D)

N.Y. Sup. Ct., 61 Misc. 2d 41, 304 N.Y.S.2d 810 (1969).

NATURE OF CASE: Motion for joint trial and cross-motion for summary judgment in liability action brought against an airline.

FACT SUMMARY: Relatives (P) of victims of a plane crash filed suit against American Airlines, Inc. (D), seeking a judgment of liability and damages.

🏛 RULE OF LAW

Application of the doctrine of collateral estoppel requires: (1) an identity issue which has been decided in a prior action and is decisive of the present action; and (2) a full and fair opportunity to contest the decision now said to be controlling.

FACTS: An American Airlines, Inc. (American) (D) aircraft crashed in Kentucky on November 8, 1965, en route from New York to Kentucky, resulting in the death of fifty-eight of the sixty-two persons onboard. Multiple actions against American (D) were filed in New York state court, in other state courts, and in various U.S. district courts. The first case to be tried to conclusion was brought in the U.S. District Court, Northern District of Texas, and resulted in a liability judgment against American (D) that was subsequently affirmed on appeal. Landano (P) and Kirchstein (P) filed a similar action in New York, asserting that the doctrine of collateral estoppel should be conclusive on the issue of American's (D) liability. American (D) filed a motion for a joint trial, arguing that application of the doctrine of collateral estoppel was inapplicable. Landano (P) and Kirchstein (P) filed a cross-motion for summary judgment on the issue of liability.

ISSUE: Does application of the doctrine of collateral estoppel require: (1) an identity issue which has been decided in a prior action and is decisive of the present action; and (2) a full and fair opportunity to contest the decision now said to be controlling?

HOLDING AND DECISION: (Frank, J.) Yes. Application of the doctrine of collateral estoppel requires: (1) an identity issue which has been decided in a prior action and is decisive of the present action; and (2) a full and fair opportunity to contest the decision now said to be controlling. Both requirements have been amply met in this case. First, the issue of American's (D) liability for the crash is identical to the issue of liability litigated in the Texas action. Second, it is in no way disputed that American (D) had a full and fair opportunity to contest the issue of its liability during the course of the nineteen-day trial in the Texas action. American's (D) argument that it is entitled to a new trial in New York because Kentucky law was applied

in the Texas case is wholly without merit. Even if New York law would be more favorable to American (D), a New York court would also be obliged to apply substantive Kentucky law since that is where the crash occurred. Finally, American's (D) contention that the Texas verdict should not apply because the jury there did not realize that their verdict would determine American's (D) obligation to other plaintiffs is completely ludicrous. Landano's (P) and Kirchstein's (P) cross-motion for summary judgment is granted, and American's (D) motion for a joint trial is denied.

▶ ANALYSIS

The Restatement (Second) of Judgments provides for several exceptions to the doctrine of collateral estoppel, also known as issue preclusion. If the party against whom preclusion is sought had a significantly heavier burden of persuasion with respect to the issue in the first action than in the second, if the burden would be shifted to the party's adversary, or if the adversary would have a significantly different burden from one action to the next, then the doctrine of collateral estoppel will not operate. As the court pointed out in this case, however, the burden of proof would have been the same in any state court because Kentucky law would have to be applied.

Quicknotes

COLLATERAL ESTOPPEL A doctrine whereby issues litigated and determined in a prior proceeding are binding upon all subsequent litigation between the parties regarding that issue.

Thompson v. Thompson

Parent (P) v. Parent (D)

484 U.S. 174 (1988).

NATURE OF CASE: Review of dismissal of action seeking to vacate one child custody order and enforce another.

FACT SUMMARY: Thompson (P) filed a federal action under the Parental Kidnapping Prevention Act.

RULE OF LAW
The Federal Parental Kidnapping Prevention Act does not create a federal right of action.

FACTS: David Thompson (P) and Susan Clay (D) divorced, having had one child. Susan (D) took the child to Louisiana, and obtained an order giving her custody. David (P) remained in California, and obtained an order giving him custody. David (P) filed an action in federal court, contending that, under the federal Parental Kidnapping Prevention Act (P.K.P.A.), the California order was valid as against the Louisiana order. He sought an order so stating. The district court dismissed, holding the P.K.P.A. to not create a private federal right of action. The Ninth Circuit Court of Appeals affirmed, and the United States Supreme Court granted review.

ISSUE: Does the Federal Parental Kidnapping Prevention Act create a federal right of action?

HOLDING AND DECISION: (Marshall, J.) No. The Federal Parental Kidnapping Prevention Act does not create a federal right of action. The P.K.P.A. was enacted out of a perceived need by Congress to lend some uniformity throughout the nation regarding child custody orders. This being so, the Act is most naturally construed to furnish a rule of decision for courts to use in adjudicating custody disputes and not to create a new cause of action in federal courts. Reinforcing this conclusion is the fact that the Act was codified at 28 U.S.C § 1738A, right next to § 1738, which is the federal full faith and credit statute. It is thus clear that the Act was not designed to furnish a new right of action in federal courts. Affirmed.

ANALYSIS

The Full Faith and Credit Clause of the Constitution mandates states give enforcement to each other's adjudications. Custody and support orders have historically presented a problem, however. Jurisdiction in such cases is usually continuing as opposed to final adjudication being rendered. The clause has been held to apply to final orders only so many states have refused to apply the clause in matters of family law.

Allen v. McCurry

Police officer (D) v. Convicted felon (P)

449 U.S. 90 (1980).

NATURE OF CASE: Review of reversal of summary judgment for the defense in a 42 U.S.C. § 1983 civil rights action.

FACT SUMMARY: McCurry (P) sought to relitigate in federal court the constitutionality of a police search, which had already been held valid in a state court proceeding.

RULE OF LAW
The constitutionality of an official act may not be relitigated in a 42 U.S.C. § 1983 action after having been litigated in state court.

FACTS: McCurry (P), charged with illegal drug possession, unsuccessfully challenged the constitutionality of a police search and was convicted. He subsequently filed a civil rights action under 42 U.S.C. § 1983, alleging that the search was improper. The district court, holding that since the constitutionality of the search had already been litigated, it could not be litigated again, granted summary judgment dismissing the action. The court of appeals reversed, holding that collateral estoppel could not be applied in a § 1983 action. Allen (D) and other defendants sought review.

ISSUE: May the constitutionality of an official act be relitigated in a 42 U.S.C. § 1983 action after having been litigated in state court?

HOLDING AND DECISION: (Stewart, J.) No. The constitutionality of an official act may not be relitigated in a 42 U.S.C. § 1983 action after having been litigated in state court. The only limitation this Court has put on the application of collateral estoppel has been that it may not be applied against one not having had a fair opportunity to litigate the issue in the first instance. This is a constitutional limitation. Here, this is not the case, as McCurry (P) had such an opportunity. Another possible basis for non-application of collateral estoppel could be congressional intent. However, nothing in the language or legislative history of § 1983 indicates an intent of this nature. As there is no constitutional or statutory bar to applying collateral estoppel, it should be applicable in a § 1983 action. Reversed and remanded.

DISSENT: (Blackmun, J.) When 42 U.S.C. § 1983 was passed, collateral estoppel was not as widely used as today, and Congress could not have foreseen the need to address the issue. Moreover, the difference in burdens of proof between civil and criminal law makes the applicability of collateral estoppel in this instance improper.

ANALYSIS

Certain language in the opinion suggests that, in some cases, a plaintiff might be able to avoid the application of collateral estoppel. The Court noted that the party against whom it is invoked must have had a fair opportunity to litigate the issue. It is possible that if a plaintiff can show that the state proceedings were unfair or improper (by, for instance, a successful habeas corpus proceeding), the plaintiff can avoid preclusion.

Quicknotes

42 U.S.C. § 1983 Permits suit for damages arising out of civil rights violations.

COLLATERAL ESTOPPEL A doctrine whereby issues litigated and determined in a prior proceeding are binding upon all subsequent litigation between the parties regarding that issue.

SUMMARY JUDGMENT Judgment rendered by a court in response to a motion by one of the parties, claiming that the lack of a question of material fact in respect to an issue warrants disposition of the issue without consideration by the jury.

Semtek International Inc. v. Lockheed Martin Corporation

Injured (P) v. Alleged tortfeasor (D)

531 U.S. 497 (2001).

NATURE OF CASE: Review of dismissal of state action on res judicata grounds.

FACT SUMMARY: When Semtek International Inc.'s (Semtek) (P) breach of contract and tort claims were barred by California's two-year statute of limitations, Semtek (P) filed the same charges in Maryland, which had a three-year statute of limitations.

🏛 RULE OF LAW
Federal common law governs the claim-preclusive effect of a dismissal by a federal court sitting in diversity.

FACTS: Semtek International Inc. (Semtek) (P) sued Lockheed Martin Corporation (D) in California state court for breach of contract and tort. After removal to federal court in California, the action was dismissed because it was barred by the two-year statute of limitations. Semtek (P) filed the same claims in Maryland, which had a three-year statute of limitations. The Maryland court dismissed on res judicata grounds and Semtek (P) appealed. The Maryland Court of Special Appeals affirmed, and the United States Supreme Court granted certiorari.

ISSUE: Does federal common law govern the claim-preclusive effect of a dismissal by a federal court sitting in diversity?

HOLDING AND DECISION: (Scalia, J.) Yes. Federal common law governs the claim-preclusive effect of a dismissal by a federal court sitting in diversity. Since state, rather than federal law, is at issue here, there is no need for a uniform federal rule. The same claim-preclusive rule should apply, whether the dismissal was ordered by a federal or a state court. Here, there was no conflict between state law and federal interests. Reversed.

▌ *ANALYSIS*

The dismissal in this case simply barred refiling the same case in the same court. It did not bar refiling in other courts. This holding is in keeping with *Erie R. Co. v. Tompkins*, 304 U.S. 64 (1938).

Quicknotes

CERTIORARI A discretionary writ issued by a superior court to an inferior court in order to review the lower court's decisions; the Supreme Court's writ ordering such review.

REMOVAL Petition by a defendant to move the case to another court.

RES JUDICATA The rule of law a final judgment by a court precludes subsequent litigation between the parties regarding the same cause of action.

STATUTE OF LIMITATIONS A law prescribing the period in which a legal action may be commenced.

CHAPTER 18

Alternative Dispute Resolution

Quick Reference Rules of Law

In re African-American Slave Descendants' Litigation

Slave descendants (P) v. Corporations profiting from slavery (D)

272 F. Supp. 2d 755 (N.D. Ill. 2003).

NATURE OF CASE: Motion to appoint a mediator.

FACT SUMMARY: Persons alleging themselves to be both formerly enslaved African-Americans and descendants of such persons (slave descendants) (P) filed a motion to appoint a mediator for claims involving alleged past and present wrongs arising from the institution of slavery. With their motions to dismiss pending, all Corporations (D) vigorously objected to resolving the case through mediation.

🏛 RULE OF LAW
A federal court should not order mediation over a party's objection in the absence of positive law authorizing such an order.

FACTS: Persons alleging themselves to be both formerly enslaved African-Americans and descendants of such persons (slave descendants) (P) filed suit against multiple Corporations (D) which allegedly profited from the slave trade or from slave labor. Slave descendants (P) demanded, among other remedies, restitution for profits Corporations (D) allegedly unjustly gained by their participation in the institution of slavery. All Corporations (D) filed motions to dismiss. While those motions were pending, slave descendants (P) filed a motion to appoint a mediator to try to resolve the case without a ruling from the court. Corporations (D) opposed slave descendants' (P) efforts to resolve the case through mediation.

ISSUE: Should federal court order mediation over a party's objection in the absence of positive law authorizing such an order?

HOLDING AND DECISION: (Norgle, J.) No. A federal court should not order mediation over a party's objection in the absence of positive law authorizing such an order. In limited circumstances, courts may appoint a mediator even over one party's objection. Such power to order mediation can arise from four sources: local rules, statutes, the Federal Rules, and the inherent powers of the court. See *In re Atlantic Pipe Corp.*, 304 F.3d 135, 140 (1st Cir. 2002). Here, no local rule, statute, or Federal Rule authorizes mandatory mediation. Moreover, although the court does have the inherent power to order mediation, using it in this case would not help to end this litigation, especially in light of Corporations' (D) pending motions to dismiss. Slave descendants' (P) motion might be better taken if filed later, but it certainly is not well taken now. Motion denied.

▶ ANALYSIS

This order recognizes, among other things, the simple fact that courts can accomplish only so much. Just as a protective order provides no actual physical protection against a would-be aggressor, an order requiring mediation here would have caused no actual willingness in the defendants to try to settle the suit.

Quicknotes

MEDIATION A process of alternative dispute resolution engaged in before trial by the parties to a lawsuit either voluntarily of by court order in an attempt to resolve the case.

Glossary

Common Latin Words and Phrases Encountered in the Law

A FORTIORI: Because one fact exists or has been proven, therefore a second fact that is related to the first fact must also exist.

A PRIORI: From the cause to the effect. A term of logic used to denote that when one generally accepted truth is shown to be a cause, another particular effect must necessarily follow.

AB INITIO: From the beginning; a condition which has existed throughout, as in a marriage which was void ab initio.

ACTUS REUS: The wrongful act; in criminal law, such action sufficient to trigger criminal liability.

AD VALOREM: According to value; an ad valorem tax is imposed upon an item located within the taxing jurisdiction calculated by the value of such item.

AMICUS CURIAE: Friend of the court. Its most common usage takes the form of an amicus curiae brief, filed by a person who is not a party to an action but is nonetheless allowed to offer an argument supporting his legal interests.

ARGUENDO: In arguing. A statement, possibly hypothetical, made for the purpose of argument, is one made arguendo.

BILL QUIA TIMET: A bill to quiet title (establish ownership) to real property.

BONA FIDE: True, honest, or genuine. May refer to a person's legal position based on good faith or lacking notice of fraud (such as a bona fide purchaser for value) or to the authenticity of a particular document (such as a bona fide last will and testament).

CAUSA MORTIS: With approaching death in mind. A gift causa mortis is a gift given by a party who feels certain that death is imminent.

CAVEAT EMPTOR: Let the buyer beware. This maxim is reflected in the rule of law that a buyer purchases at his own risk because it is his responsibility to examine, judge, test, and otherwise inspect what he is buying.

CERTIORARI: A writ of review. Petitions for review of a case by the United States Supreme Court are most often done by means of a writ of certiorari.

CONTRA: On the other hand. Opposite. Contrary to.

CORAM NOBIS: Before us; writs of error directed to the court that originally rendered the judgment.

CORAM VOBIS: Before you; writs of error directed by an appellate court to a lower court to correct a factual error.

CORPUS DELICTI: The body of the crime; the requisite elements of a crime amounting to objective proof that a crime has been committed.

CUM TESTAMENTO ANNEXO, ADMINISTRATOR (ADMINISTRATOR C.T.A.): With will annexed; an administrator c.t.a. settles an estate pursuant to a will in which he is not appointed.

DE BONIS NON, ADMINISTRATOR (ADMINISTRATOR D.B.N.): Of goods not administered; an administrator d.b.n. settles a partially settled estate.

DE FACTO: In fact; in reality; actually. Existing in fact but not officially approved or engendered.

DE JURE: By right; lawful. Describes a condition that is legitimate "as a matter of law," in contrast to the term "de facto," which connotes something existing in fact but not legally sanctioned or authorized. For example, de facto segregation refers to segregation brought about by housing patterns, etc., whereas de jure segregation refers to segregation created by law.

DE MINIMIS: Of minimal importance; insignificant; a trifle; not worth bothering about.

DE NOVO: Anew; a second time; afresh. A trial de novo is a new trial held at the appellate level as if the case originated there and the trial at a lower level had not taken place.

DICTA: Generally used as an abbreviated form of obiter dicta, a term describing those portions of a judicial opinion incidental or not necessary to resolution of the specific question before the court. Such nonessential statements and remarks are not considered to be binding precedent.

DUCES TECUM: Refers to a particular type of writ or subpoena requesting a party or organization to produce certain documents in their possession.

EN BANC: Full bench. Where a court sits with all justices present rather than the usual quorum.

EX PARTE: For one side or one party only. An ex parte proceeding is one undertaken for the benefit of only one party, without notice to, or an appearance by, an adverse party.

EX POST FACTO: After the fact. An ex post facto law is a law that retroactively changes the consequences of a prior act.

EX REL.: Abbreviated form of the term "ex relatione," meaning upon relation or information. When the state brings an action in which it has no interest against an individual at the instigation of one who has a private interest in the matter.

FORUM NON CONVENIENS: Inconvenient forum. Although a court may have jurisdiction over the case, the action should be tried in a more conveniently located court, one to which parties and witnesses may more easily travel, for example.

GUARDIAN AD LITEM: A guardian of an infant as to litigation, appointed to represent the infant and pursue his/her rights.

HABEAS CORPUS: You have the body. The modern writ of habeas corpus is a writ directing that a person (body) being detained (such as a prisoner) be brought before the court so that the legality of his detention can be judicially ascertained.

IN CAMERA: In private, in chambers. When a hearing is held before a judge in his chambers or when all spectators are excluded from the courtroom.

IN FORMA PAUPERIS: In the manner of a pauper. A party who proceeds in forma pauperis because of his poverty is one who is allowed to bring suit without liability for costs.

INFRA: Below, under. A word referring the reader to a later part of a book. (The opposite of supra.)

IN LOCO PARENTIS: In the place of a parent.

IN PARI DELICTO: Equally wrong; a court of equity will not grant requested relief to an applicant who is in pari delicto, or as much at fault in the transactions giving rise to the controversy as is the opponent of the applicant.

IN PARI MATERIA: On like subject matter or upon the same matter. Statutes relating to the same person or things are said to be in pari materia. It is a general rule of statutory construction that such statutes should be construed together, i.e., looked at as if they together constituted one law.

IN PERSONAM: Against the person. Jurisdiction over the person of an individual.

IN RE: In the matter of. Used to designate a proceeding involving an estate or other property.

IN REM: A term that signifies an action against the res, or thing. An action in rem is basically one that is taken directly against property, as distinguished from an action in personam, i.e., against the person.

INTER ALIA: Among other things. Used to show that the whole of a statement, pleading, list, statute, etc., has not been set forth in its entirety.

INTER PARTES: Between the parties. May refer to contracts, conveyances or other transactions having legal significance.

INTER VIVOS: Between the living. An inter vivos gift is a gift made by a living grantor, as distinguished from bequests contained in a will, which pass upon the death of the testator.

IPSO FACTO: By the mere fact itself.

JUS: Law or the entire body of law.

LEX LOCI: The law of the place; the notion that the rights of parties to a legal proceeding are governed by the law of the place where those rights arose.

MALUM IN SE: Evil or wrong in and of itself; inherently wrong. This term describes an act that is wrong by its very nature, as opposed to one which would not be wrong but for the fact that there is a specific legal prohibition against it (malum prohibitum).

MALUM PROHIBITUM: Wrong because prohibited, but not inherently evil. Used to describe something that is wrong because it is expressly forbidden by law but that is not in and of itself evil, e.g., speeding.

MANDAMUS: We command. A writ directing an official to take a certain action.

MENS REA: A guilty mind; a criminal intent. A term used to signify the mental state that accompanies a crime or other prohibited act. Some crimes require only a general mens rea (general intent to do the prohibited act), but others, like assault with intent to murder, require the existence of a specific mens rea.

MODUS OPERANDI: Method of operating; generally refers to the manner or style of a criminal in committing crimes, admissible in appropriate cases as evidence of the identity of a defendant.

NEXUS: A connection to.

NISI PRIUS: A court of first impression. A nisi prius court is one where issues of fact are tried before a judge or jury.

N.O.V. (NON OBSTANTE VEREDICTO): Notwithstanding the verdict. A judgment n.o.v. is a judgment given in favor of one party despite the fact that a verdict was returned in favor of the other party, the justification being that the verdict either had no reasonable support in fact or was contrary to law.

NUNC PRO TUNC: Now for then. This phrase refers to actions that may be taken and will then have full retroactive effect.

PENDENTE LITE: Pending the suit; pending litigation under way.

PER CAPITA: By head; beneficiaries of an estate, if they take in equal shares, take per capita.

PER CURIAM: By the court; signifies an opinion ostensibly written "by the whole court" and with no identified author.

PER SE: By itself, in itself; inherently.

PER STIRPES: By representation. Used primarily in the law of wills to describe the method of distribution where a person, generally because of death, is unable to take that which is left to him by the will of another, and therefore his heirs divide such property between them rather than take under the will individually.

PRIMA FACIE: On its face, at first sight. A prima facie case is one that is sufficient on its face, meaning that the evidence supporting it is adequate to establish the case until contradicted or overcome by other evidence.

PRO TANTO: For so much; as far as it goes. Often used in eminent domain cases when a property owner receives partial payment for his land without prejudice to his right to bring suit for the full amount he claims his land to be worth.

QUANTUM MERUIT: As much as he deserves. Refers to recovery based on the doctrine of unjust enrichment in those cases in which a party has rendered valuable services or furnished materials that were accepted and enjoyed by another under circumstances that would reasonably notify the recipient that the rendering party expected to be paid. In essence, the law implies a contract to pay the reasonable value of the services or materials furnished.

QUASI: Almost like; as if; nearly. This term is essentially used to signify that one subject or thing is almost analogous to another but that material differences between them do exist. For example, a quasi-criminal proceeding is one that is not strictly criminal but shares enough of the same characteristics to require some of the same safeguards (e.g., procedural due process must be followed in a parole hearing).

QUID PRO QUO: Something for something. In contract law, the consideration, something of value, passed between the parties to render the contract binding.

RES GESTAE: Things done; in evidence law, this principle justifies the admission of a statement that would otherwise be hearsay when it is made so closely to the event in question as to be said to be a part of it, or with such spontaneity as not to have the possibility of falsehood.

RES IPSA LOQUITUR: The thing speaks for itself. This doctrine gives rise to a rebuttable presumption of negligence when the instrumentality causing the injury was within the exclusive control of the defendant, and the injury was one that does not normally occur unless a person has been negligent.

RES JUDICATA: A matter adjudged. Doctrine which provides that once a court of competent jurisdiction has rendered a final judgment or decree on the merits, that judgment or decree is conclusive upon the parties to the case and prevents them from engaging in any other litigation on the points and issues determined therein.

RESPONDEAT SUPERIOR: Let the master reply. This doctrine holds the master liable for the wrongful acts of his servant (or the principal for his agent) in those cases in which the servant (or agent) was acting within the scope of his authority at the time of the injury.

STARE DECISIS: To stand by or adhere to that which has been decided. The common law doctrine of stare decisis attempts to give security and certainty to the law by following the policy that once a principle of law as applicable to a certain set of facts has been set forth in a decision, it forms a precedent which will subsequently be followed, even though a different decision might be made were it the first time the question had arisen. Of course, stare decisis is not an inviolable principle and is departed from in instances where there is good cause (e.g., considerations of public policy led the Supreme Court to disregard prior decisions sanctioning segregation).

SUPRA: Above. A word referring a reader to an earlier part of a book.

ULTRA VIRES: Beyond the power. This phrase is most commonly used to refer to actions taken by a corporation that are beyond the power or legal authority of the corporation.

Addendum of French Derivatives

IN PAIS: Not pursuant to legal proceedings.

CHATTEL: Tangible personal property.

CY PRES: Doctrine permitting courts to apply trust funds to purposes not expressed in the trust but necessary to carry out the settlor's intent.

PER AUTRE VIE: For another's life; during another's life. In property law, an estate may be granted that will terminate upon the death of someone other than the grantee.

PROFIT A PRENDRE: A license to remove minerals or other produce from land.

VOIR DIRE: Process of questioning jurors as to their predispositions about the case or parties to a proceeding in order to identify those jurors displaying bias or prejudice.

Casenote® Legal Briefs